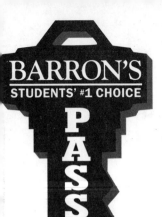

BARRON'S
STUDENTS' #1 CHOICE

PASS KEY

TO THE

GED

HIGH SCHOOL EQUIVALENCY EXAMINATION

Fourth Edition

Murray Rockowitz, Ph.D.
Former Chairman, Board of Examiners
New York City Board of Education
Former Principal,
John Philip Sousa Junior High School,
New York City
Former Chairman, English Department,
Charles Evans Hughes High School,
New York City

Samuel C. Brownstein
Former Chairman, Biology Department,
Wingate High School, Brooklyn, New York

Max Peters
Former Chairman, Mathematics Department,
Wingate High School, Brooklyn, New York

Ira K. Wolf, Ph.D.
Teacher of Mathematics,
Benjamin N. Cardozo High School,
Bayside, New York

Johanna M. Bolton
Instructor, Adult High School Program,
Daytona Beach Community College,
Daytona Beach, Florida

Robert Feinstein
GED Instructor for Adult Educational Services,
Northport-East Northport School District,
Northport, New York

Sally Ramsey
Former GED Instructor,
Southeastern Illinois College,
Harrisburg, Illinois

Louis Gotlib
Science Teacher,
Wissahickon Senior High School,
Ambler, Pennsylvania

BARRON'S EDUCATIONAL SERIES, INC.

All inquiries should be addressed to:
Barron's Educational Series, Inc.
250 Wireless Boulevard
Hauppauge, New York 11788
http://www.barronseduc.com

Library of Congress Catalog Card No. 00-041383

International Standard Book No. 0-7641-1372-0

Library of Congress Cataloging-in-Publication Data
Rockowitz, Murray.
  Barron's pass key to the GED high school equivalency exam /
Murray Rockowitz . . . [et al.]—4th ed.
       p.   cm.
   At head of title: Barron's
   ISBN 0-7641-1372-0 (alk. paper)
   1. General educational development tests—Study guides. 2. High
school equivalency examinations—Study guides. I. Title: Pass key to
the GED. II. Rockowitz, Murray.
LB3060.33.G45 R625   2001
373.126'2—dc21   00-041383
                                                      CIP

PRINTED IN THE UNITED STATES OF AMERICA
9 8 7 6 5 4 3 2 1

CONTENTS

PREFACE

Barron's PASS KEY TO THE GED is a shorter version of *Barron's How to Prepare for the High School Equivalency Examination,* which has helped over two million people like you obtain a high school equivalency diploma.

In today's tough job market, the key that opens the door to opportunity is a high school diploma. Without it, you can't get a good Civil Service position, a specialized course in the Armed Forces, admission to a good technical school, or a chance to become an apprentice in a good company.

This compact guide contains materials that will prepare you for the key areas of the test: correctness and effectiveness of expression (sentence structure, usage, punctuation, capitalization, and spelling); interpretation of reading materials in the social studies, natural sciences, literature and the arts; and general mathematical ability.

Keep this convenient book handy for study on the train as you go to work, or when you wait in the doctor's or dentist's office. Make every minute count. And, if after using this brief version, you feel you need more review and practice, turn to the complete edition of *Barron's How to Prepare for the High School Equivalency Examination,* the widely used, comprehensive guide with almost 800 pages of carefully prepared materials to help you achieve your two most important goals—a high school equivalency diploma and a good job.

ACKNOWLEDGMENTS

The authors gratefully acknowledge the kindness of all organizations concerned with the granting of permission to reprint passages, charts, graphs.

The copyright holders and publishers of quoted materials are listed below.

Pages 87–88, Passage from Arthur H. Doerr and J.L. Guernsey, *Principles of Geography—Physical and Cultural,* Second Edition Revised. Copyright © 1975 Barron's Educational Series, Inc.

Page 95, Pie Graph from *Annual Energy Review.* Copyright © 1995 *Energy Information Review.*

Page 97, Line Graph adapted from Klose and Lader, *College Review: United States History,* Vol. 2. Copyright © 1994 Barron's Educational Series, Inc.

Page 110, Photograph from Corbis-Bettmann Archive.

Pages 177–178, Article from *Investor's Business Daily,* December 1, 1997.

Page 381, Practice Examination, Cartoon for Questions 62–63: from *The Times Union,* July 1991.

Pages 408–409, Practice Examination, Passage for Questions 11–15: Excerpt from ALL GOD'S CHILDREN NEED TRAVELING SHOES by Maya Angelou, Copyright © 1986 by Maya Angelou. Reprinted by permission of Random House, Inc.

Pages 411–412, Practice Examination, Poem for Questions 21–25: from "Elegy for Jane" by Theodore Roethke, Copyright © 1950 by Theodore Roethke, in COLLECTED POEMS OF THEODORE ROETHKE, Reprinted by permission of Doubleday & Co., Inc.

1

THE GED HIGH SCHOOL EQUIVALENCY EXAMINATION

THE IMPORTANCE OF THE GED EXAMINATION

The General Education Development or GED Examination offers anyone who has not completed his or her high school diploma a way to earn a High School Equivalency Certificate. This is the equivalent of a high school diploma, and it is necessary for those who want to continue their educations in college or another career-oriented program. Having a high school diploma today is also very important if you want a good job.

EDUCATION PAYS

Median annual earnings of workers aged 25 to 64, in 1995 dollars.

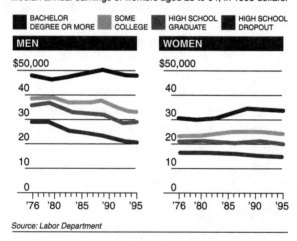

Source: Labor Department

Study these graphs briefly. Note that the black line indicates the average annual earnings of high school graduates aged 25 to 64. The bottom gray line represents the average annual earnings of high school dropouts of similar age. Compare the two lines for 1995. You see that high school graduates earned much more than high school dropouts. Men earned nearly $10,000 a year more; women earned over $5,000 a year more. Over the span of years from age 25 to age 64, a male high school graduate earns about $400,000 more than a high school dropout; the woman graduate earns over $200,000 more. It pays to have a high school diploma.

THE FIVE GED TEST AREAS

The GED Examination is divided into five tests:
1. Writing Skills
2. Social Studies
3. Science
4. Literature and the Arts
5. Mathematics

The five tests are designed to measure the knowledge and skills that a student should have acquired after four years in high school. One important thing about the tests is that, even though the questions may involve a specific area of study such as science, you don't have to memorize specific facts, details, dates, or even exact definitions. Much of this information is given to you in the test itself. You have to be able to read and understand the material that is presented and then to answer questions about it.

With the exception of the essay part of the Writing Skills test, all of the questions in the GED Examination are multiple-choice. You will be given a brief statement, short passage, map, table, or diagram, and then you will have to answer one or more multiple-choice questions about this material. This book will help you learn how to analyze and use information presented in these various ways.

COMMONLY ASKED QUESTIONS ABOUT THE GED TESTS

1. *Who can take the GED tests?* Adults who meet the eligibility requirements established by their state, territorial, or provincial departments of education can take the GED tests.
2. *Where are the GED tests given?* The address of your state, territorial, or provincial administrator can be obtained from your local high school. Write to that office for the location of the GED testing center nearest your home.

TIMETABLE OF A HIGH SCHOOL EQUIVALENCY EXAMINATION
Total: 7 hours, 35 minutes

	Section	Time Allowed*	Number of Test Items*	Description
Test 1	The Writing Skills Test Part I	75 min.	55	Sentence Structure (35%) Usage (35%) Mechanics (spelling, punctuation, capitalization) (30%)
	Part II	45 min.		Essay on a given topic
Test 2	The Social Studies Test	85 min.	64	History (30%) Economics (25%) Geography (20%) Political Science (25%)
Test 3	The Science Test	95 min.	66	Biology (50%) Earth Science ⎫ Chemistry ⎬ 50% Physics ⎭
Test 4	The Interpreting Literature and the Arts Test	65 min.	45	Current Literature (50%) Earlier Literature (25%) Commentary About Literature and the Arts (25%)
Test 5	The Mathematics Test	90 min.	56	Arithmetic (50%) Algebra (30%) Geometry (20%)

*****Note:** Format and timing are subject to change.

3. *What score is required to earn a High School Equivalency Diploma?* The standard score requirements vary for each state, territory, or province. You will find that in some states a candidate must earn a minimum score of 40 on each of the five test areas or a minimum average score of 45 for the five tests. The majority of states require a minimum average score of 45 and no individual test score below 35 or 40.

4. *What types of questions are on the GED tests?* Part II of the Writing Skills test requires a written essay. For the other test questions, you will be given information in the form of a written passage, graph, diagram, map, or table, and asked to answer one or more multiple-choice questions based on the information presented. Five answer choices are given for each question.

5. *How can experience outside the classroom help me pass the GED tests?* Many people worry about the difficulty of taking the GED Examination, especially if they've been out of school for a long time. What you should realize is that learning continues after you leave school. You read newspapers and follow political events; you travel and talk to many different people; you listen to the radio, watch television, and go to the movies. All of these experiences are forms of learning and add to your educational background.

6. *Why are maturity and motivation strong assets?* More mature students have experiences that will help them visualize or understand situations that may be involved in a problem on the GED Examination. Also, older students understand the need for good study habits and have the self-discipline to work regularly in this book. With the mature decision to study for the GED tests, half the battle is over. Many educators know that motivation, the desire to learn, is the first step toward success.

7. *When are you ready to take the GED Examination?* After reviewing and doing the practice exercises, take the practice test in Chapter VIII, and score your results. If your scores are in the category Good or Excellent, you are probably ready to walk into the examination room with confidence. If, however, you did not attain such scores, do not apply for the GED Examination until you have studied further. Concentrate on the areas in which you are weak.

ORGANIZING YOUR PLAN OF STUDY

SOME STUDY HINTS

Educators agree that, for learning to be efficient, certain steps must be followed. As a mature person, you will probably appreciate the value of carefully following these ten tips for successful study.

1. **Physical conditions.** Find a quiet place. Tolerate no distraction—noise or music. Do not work in an overheated room.

2. **Timing.** You will learn faster and remember longer if you study in several short sessions rather than in one long session. Do not attempt to study for an entire weekend. Fatigue will set in after a few hours. It is wiser to spend some time each day rather than to "cram" your work into one or two days.

3. **Schedule for study.** A study schedule must be workable, realistic, practical, and, above all, suited to you and your other obligations. Decide which days and hours you can spare for study. Make a schedule, and stick to it.

4. **Using odd moments.** Put spare time and wasted moments to work. Riding on the bus or train may be a good time to memorize troublesome spelling words and to study rules of grammar or definitions of unfamiliar terms.

5. **Efficiency.** Most people find that learning occurs faster in the early part of the day. Perhaps you can work into your schedule some time for study before your day's work begins or on weekend mornings. Certainly you should not schedule study in the later hours of the evening.

6. **Review periods.** On certain days, plan to review. Take stock of yourself in these study periods. This review will serve at least two purposes. It will definitely reinforce the learning, and the gratification of knowing that you have acquired new material will stimulate you to learn more.

7. **Writing while you learn.** Wherever possible, write what you are studying. Spelling can best be learned by writing. Get into the habit of writing down key ideas of the passages you read. This writing will focus attention on your learning, will help you avoid distractions that may cause your mind to wander, and will provide an opportunity to check up on yourself. Also, educators believe that the more senses employed while studying, the more effective the learning will be.

8. **Reading.** The best way to improve reading comprehension is by practicing reading. You will find that a great part of the test involves the interpretation of reading material. Read your newspaper very carefully. Make it a habit to read the editorials. If possible, engage a member of your family or a friend in frequent discussions of the ideas presented in your newspaper. Of course, this book has specific

reading exercises on the various phases of the test. But remember: there is no substitute for general reading.

9. **The dictionary.** The most important single book, in addition to this one, that can help you prepare for the High School Equivalency Examination is the dictionary. It is important to have one nearby as you study. A suggested inexpensive dictionary is the pocket-size paperback edition of *Webster's New World Dictionary of the American Language*.

10. **S Q 3R.** A popular way to remember the five important steps needed to study effectively is the S Q 3R method.

- S stands for survey. You examine the material to be learned to get a general idea of the content.
- Q stands for question. You turn the topic, the title of the section you are studying, into a question or questions. For example, if the title of the section is "Drawing Conclusions," you turn it into a challenging question: "How do I draw conclusions from what I read?"
- The first of the three R's stands for read. You use the reading skills that are taught in this book, such as locating the main idea, finding details, reading critically, detecting propaganda, determining cause and effect, and comparing and contrasting ideas.
- The second R stands for recite. You close the book and speak aloud from memory. Include especially the main ideas you have located and any name, word, or fact you find difficult to remember.
- The third R stands for review, which literally means to "view" or see again. You look over your notes, the lines you have highlighted, or the outline you have made. Do this again until you are sure you have mastered the material, for example, spelling words that trouble you or a rule of punctuation you find hard to remember.

This is a summary of the S Q 3R method of study:

<u>S</u> urvey
<u>Q</u> uestion
<u>R</u> ead
<u>R</u> ecite
<u>R</u> eview

BEFORE THE TEST DATE

1. **Practice reading and writing.** Besides using the material in this book, spend more time reading. Read the local newspaper and some magazines. Also practice writing. Write letters to friends and relatives. Instead of using the telephone, use your pen.

2. **Don't rush to take the tests.** Don't be in too big a hurry to apply for the GED Examination. First be sure that you are prepared by taking the exercises and tests in this book. Even though most states will let you retake the tests after a waiting period, a notice that you failed the first time is unpleasant and may even discourage you from trying again. Instead of rushing into the examination and trusting to good fortune for a passing grade, it's better to wait until you know that you're ready. Also, don't procrastinate and cram all your study into the last few days. This rarely works. It's much better to set a realistic study schedule that gives you enough time to prepare.

3. **Know what to expect.** By the time you finish the preparation material in this book, you will be familiar with all the kinds of questions you will encounter on the GED tests. The exercises and practice test questions in this book are very similar to the actual test questions. Knowing what to expect will relieve some of your anxiety about taking the exam.

4. **Be relaxed.** It's a good idea to relax the evening before you take the GED Examination. A good night's sleep will help you to think logically; you'll be well rested and alert. Also, do not eat a heavy meal, which will make you feel dull and sleepy, before you take the test.

TACTICS AND STRATEGIES IN THE EXAMINATION ROOM

1. **Allow plenty of time to get to the test site.** Taking a test is pressure enough. You don't need the extra tension that comes from worrying about whether you will get there on time.

2. **Read all directions and questions carefully.** Answer the question given, not one you expected. Look for key words, such as *except*, *exactly*, and *not*. Carefully examine tables, graphs, and diagrams so you don't miss important information.

3. **Don't expect trick questions.** A straightforward presentation is used in all test sections.

4. **When you have difficulty finding an answer, eliminate choices that are definitely wrong.** Then consider the remaining choices.

5. **Don't let one or two challenging questions upset you.** Some questions are definitely harder than others. Remember you do not have to get 100 percent on this examination. No one does.

6. **Don't get bogged down on any one question.** If a question is taking too much time, circle it and make a guess. Then, if you have time at the end of the examination, go back and review the circled questions.

7. **Change answers only if you have a good reason for doing so.** Don't change your answer on a hunch or a whim. Most often the first judgment that you make is correct.

8. **Check answer order frequently.** Make sure you are putting your answers in the right spaces.

9. **Use your time wisely.** After taking the practice tests in this book, you will be familiar with the proper pace needed to complete each test.

10. **Be careful not to make stray pencil marks on the answer sheet.** These may interfere with the rating of your performance. If you wish to change an answer, be sure to erase your first mark completely. The rating machine will automatically mark an answer wrong if more than one choice is made. Also, do not fold or crease the answer sheet.

11. **Answer all questions, even if you have to guess.** Your score will be determined by the number of correct answers; no points are deducted for wrong answers. For this reason it is better to guess at an answer than to not respond at all. Of course, wherever possible, eliminate as many wrong answers as you can before guessing. Every answer you eliminate improves your chance of guessing correctly.

12. **Remain as calm as possible.** If you consider yourself a person who "goes to pieces" on tests, cheer up! Psychologists claim that more than 90 percent of us think we don't perform well on tests *of any kind*. Nobody likes tests. But more than 80 percent of the people who have taken the High School Equivalency tests in the New York area, for example, have passed them. They must be doing something right. And so can you—with the right attitude and careful preparation.

2
WRITING SKILLS, PART I

SENTENCE STRUCTURE

A sentence is the basic means of communicating an idea.

A sentence may be defined as a group of words having a subject and a predicate and expressing a complete thought. Each sentence should be separated from the one that follows it by some form of end punctuation such as a period, a question mark, or an exclamation point.

RUN-ON SENTENCES

In one important group of errors, you may fail to separate two or more sentences by using the proper punctuation. Instead, you may either use no punctuation at all or incorrectly use a comma. The general term for this group of errors is the *run-on sentence* or, if a comma is incorrectly used, the *comma splice*.

This type sentence can result from an incorrectly used or omitted conjunction or adverb.

EXAMPLE
Wrong:
Joe was elected class president *x* he is very popular.

Correct:
Joe was elected class president *because* he is very popular.

SENTENCE FRAGMENTS

In another important group of errors, you may fail to complete the sentence. (You will remember that a sentence is defined as a group of words having a subject and a predicate and expressing a complete thought.) In the kind of error called a *sentence fragment*, either the subject is left out, so that a predicate is left standing by itself (e.g., "Wish you were here.") or a part of the predicate is broken off from the sentence and made to stand by itself (e.g., "Walking down the street.").

9

EXAMPLE

Wrong:
Am having a wonderful time. Wish you were here.

Correct:
I am having a wonderful time. *I* wish you were here.

In each case, without the subject it is impossible to know *who* is doing the action indicated in the predicate.

PARALLEL STRUCTURE

A major error in structure is failure to keep parts of the sentence that perform the *same purpose* in the *same form*. This is called an error in parallel structure.

Here is an example of such an error.

Wrong:
Joe likes *swimming, fishing,* and, if he has the time, *to take* a long walk.

The sentence tells us three things Joe likes. They are related to us by words that are the objects of the verb *likes*, and they serve the same purpose. But are their forms alike? Let us line them up vertically.

Joe likes   swimming
             fishing
             to take a long walk

No, they are not. *Swimming* and *fishing* are verbs used, in the *-ing* form, as nouns. *To take*, however, is an infinitive. Words having the same function should have the same form. Then, the sentence has parallel structure. The sentence should read:

Joe likes   swimming
             fishing
             taking a long walk

Correct: Joe likes *swimming*, *fishing*, and, if he has the time, *taking a long walk.*

MISPLACED MODIFIERS

A modifier is a word or a group of words that help describe another word or group of words by giving a more exact meaning. The modifier may be an adjective (a *big* house) or an adverb (walk *slowly*), an adjective clause (the man who came to *dinner*) or an adjective phrase (Jeanie *with the light brown hair*), an adverbial clause (he arrived *when the clock struck twelve*) or an adverbial phrase (he arrived *on time*). Very often, confusion in meaning takes place when a modifier is used incorrectly.

A modifier that is misplaced in a sentence may cause confusion in meaning.

EXAMPLE
Wrong:
Fred cut himself while shaving *badly.*

The word *badly* is a misplaced modifier. It is an adverb that modifies the meaning of the verb *cut* and, therefore, should be placed where there is no doubt about what it modifies. (It certainly isn't intended to modify *shaving.*)

Correct:
Fred cut himself *badly* while shaving.

The meaning is completely changed by the placement of the modifier. Now the sentence means what the writer intended to say.

Dangling Modifiers

In the case of the *dangling modifier*, the problem is that there is no word or words to which the modifier clearly refers.

EXAMPLE
Wrong:
Standing on the corner, *the car* passed me by.

It is important to note that merely turning the incorrect sentence around will not keep the modifier from dangling.

Wrong:
The car passed me by, *standing* on the corner.

The sentence has to be rewritten to read:

Correct:
While I was *standing* on the corner, the car passed me by.

Standing is now part of the verb and is no longer dangling.

USAGE

AGREEMENT

Subject and Verb

A common error is failure to provide agreement between subject and verb. The basic rule is:

> THE VERB MUST AGREE WITH ITS SUBJECT
> IN *NUMBER* AND IN *PERSON.*

EXAMPLE   *Joe*, despite the fact that he was a newcomer, *was* elected president.
[*Joe* is still the subject—singular.]

EXAMPLE   *Joe*, together with all his friends, *was* welcomed warmly.
[*Joe* is still the subject—singular.]

EXAMPLE   A *box* of chocolates *is* on the table.
[*Box*, the subject, is singular.]

Most of the time, *pronouns* will be involved in this type of error. Some pronouns that can cause confusion are:

Singular Pronouns		Singular or Plural Pronouns
anybody	neither	any
anyone	nobody	all
each	no one	more
either	one	most
everybody	somebody	none
everyone	someone	some

However, *compound subjects* may also be involved. When a subject has more than one part and the parts are connected by *and* or by a word or groups of words similar in meaning to *and*, it is considered a *compound subject* and is plural.

EXAMPLES

Joe *and* his friend *are* here.

To study hard, to play hard, to enjoy life are desirable aims.

Her outstanding contribution to school athletics, her service as class officer, and her excellent scholastic record qualify her for the position of president.

EXCEPTION

A compound subject that consists of two singular subjects connected by *either...or*, or *neither...nor* is considered a singular subject.

EXAMPLE

Neither Joe nor his friend *is* here.

> **Note:** Agreement is always with the number of the part of the subject nearest the verb.
>   **EXAMPLE**   Neither Joe nor I *am* voting for Frank.

Sometimes the subject comes after the verb. It is still the subject and may be singular or plural.

EXAMPLE

Pasted in the upper right-hand corner of the envelope were two ten-cent stamps.
[*Stamps* is the subject, even though it is the last word in the sentence. The verb is plural because the subject, *stamps*, is plural.]

EXAMPLE

There are many ways to show you care.

Pronoun and Antecedent

Another common error is failure to provide agreement between a pronoun and the noun it is replacing, its *antecedent*. The basic rule is:

A Pronoun must agree with its Antecedent in *number, gender,* and *person.*

Number
If the antecedent is singular, the pronoun replacing it is singular.

> **EXAMPLE**   Joe does *his* homework.
> [The pronoun *his* takes the place of Joe. *Joe* is singular (one person); therefore, the pronoun is singular]

Gender
If the antecedent is masculine, the pronoun replacing it is masculine. If the antecedent is feminine, the pronoun replacing it is feminine.

> **EXAMPLE**   Susan does *her* homework.

Person
Note above that both *Joe* and *Susan* are in the third person. Therefore, the pronouns replacing each must be in the third person—*his, her.*

> **EXAMPLE**   *Joe and* his *friend* brought *their* books.

> **EXAMPLE**   *Either* Kathy *or* the boys should explain *their* reasons.

Some Special Problems
1. PRONOUNS THAT APPEAR TO BE PLURAL BUT ARE, IN FACT, SINGULAR
Some pronouns appear to refer to more than one person, but they never refer to more than one person *at a time*. Others may be either singular or plural.

Singular Pronouns		Singular or Plural Pronouns
anybody	neither	any
anyone	nobody	all
each	no one	more
either	one	most
everybody	somebody	none
everyone	someone	some

The following sentence may sound a little strange to you, but it is correct.

EXAMPLE

Every student must do *his* homework every day.

2. PRONOUNS THAT REFER TO NOUNS THAT APPEAR TO BE PLURAL BUT ARE SINGULAR IN FORM

These pronouns require a verb in the singular.

EXAMPLE

The team continued *its* winning streak.

3. PRONOUNS WITH INDEFINITE ANTECEDENTS

The antecedent must be clear or the sentence rephrased.

EXAMPLE

Wrong:

Frank told Joe to take *his* books to school.

[To whom does *his* refer—to Frank or to Joe? The sentence must be rewritten to clear up this confusion.]

Correct:

Frank told Joe to take Frank's books to school for him.

or better

Frank said to Joe: "Take my books to school for me."

Practice

1. Will everyone who has the right answer raise their hands?
2. Every participant must do his best.
3. The mother told her daughter to take her laundry to the laundromat.
4. One of my friends who went to school with me lost his mother.
5. Either the workers or the foreman are expected to attend.

Answers

1. Will everyone who has the right answer raise his hand?
2. Correct.
3. The mother told her daughter, "Take my laundry to the laundromat."
4. Correct.
5. Either the workers or the foreman is expected to attend.

Practice in Agreement

In each sentence, five parts are underlined and numbered. Where there is an error in agreement, choose the number of the underlined part that contains the error. If there is no error, choose answer 5. <u>No sentence contains more than one error.</u> These are included in the sentence correction type of multiple-choice item.

1. Luis, accompanied by <u>his</u> friend <u>are</u> waiting to see whether you
                        (1)   (2)

   and <u>I</u> <u>are</u> joining them. <u>No error</u>
      (3)(4)   (5)

2. <u>There</u>, Mr. Chairman, <u>is</u> all the reports that the committee prepared
     (1)   (2)

   in <u>its</u> work as well as the notes <u>that</u> were taken. <u>No error</u>
     (3)   (4)   (5)

3. <u>There's</u> several ways for the city to solve <u>its</u> fiscal problems, but <u>one</u>
     (1)   (2)   (3)

   of them is not to lose <u>its</u> integrity. <u>No error</u>
                     (4)   (5)

4. News from abroad <u>is</u> that each country is supporting <u>its</u> own
                    (1)   (2)

   policies despite the fact that <u>ours</u> <u>are</u> superior to theirs. <u>No error</u>
                              (3) (4)   (5)

5. Let everyone who <u>agrees</u> raise <u>his</u> hand so that neither George
                    (1)   (2)

   nor I <u>am</u> in doubt about what the majority opinion <u>is.</u> <u>No error</u>
        (3)   (4)   (5)

6. Margaret asked Rosa to take <u>her</u> clothes to the cleaners and to make
                             (1)

   certain that <u>none</u> of <u>them</u> <u>were</u> in need of repair. <u>No error</u>
              (2)   (3)   (4)   (5)

7. Watching <u>our</u> game <u>were</u> Fred and his father and his mother, together
            (1)   (2)

   with <u>their</u> other children and <u>their</u> neighbors. <u>No error</u>
       (3)   (4)   (5)

8. <u>Each</u> American must ask <u>himself</u>: "<u>Don't</u> it matter if we pollute
     (1)   (2)   (3)

   <u>our</u> environment?" <u>No error</u>
     (4)   (5)

9. "Neither I nor they are attending the game," we said to its promoter.
      (1)   (2) (3)   (4)
   No error
      (5)

10. Everyone gave her opinion that a blue and white suit was the best
      (1)   (2)   (3)
    choice for Liz to wear although there were exceptions. No error
                                              (4)   (5)

Answer Key

1. **2**	3. **1**	5. **5**	7. **5**	9. **5**
2. **2**	4. **5**	6. **1**	8. **3**	10. **5**

What's Your Score?

_____right,   _____wrong

Excellent	9–10
Good	8
Fair	7

If you scored lower, restudy this section, concentrating on the rules and examples.

Answer Analysis

1. **2**   Luis, the subject of the sentence, is singular, so the verb should be singular: *is* instead of *are*.

2. **2**   The subject of the sentence, *reports*, follows the verb. Since the subject is plural, the verb should be plural: *are*, not *is*.

3. **1**   The subject is *ways*, which follows the verb. The verb must be plural to agree with the plural subject. *There's* should be *There are*.

4. **5**   No error.

5. **5**   No error.

6. **1**   The antecedent of *her* is not clear. Is it Margaret or Rosa? Depending on the answer, *her* should be changed to *Margaret's* or *Rosa's*.

7. **5**   No error.

8. **3**   The correct form of the third person singular of the verb *do* is *does*. Doesn't it...is correct.

9. **5**   No error.

10. **5**   No error.

CASE OF NOUNS AND PRONOUNS

Nouns

Only in the *possessive case* do the forms of most nouns change.

Nominative Case

EXAMPLE   *Frank* hit Joe.
[*Frank* is the subject.]

Objective Case

EXAMPLES   Joe hit *Frank*.
[*Frank* is the object.]

Ellen ate the *salad*.
[*Salad* is the object.]

Possessive Case

EXAMPLE   Cesar's friend went away.
[A noun requires an apostrophe to indicate possession.]

Pronouns

Nearly all pronouns have different forms in the nominative, objective, and possessive cases. Only the pronoun forms *you* and *it* do NOT change when the case changes from *nominative* to *objective* or vice versa.

BASIC RULES FOR THE CASE OF PRONOUNS
Nominative

1.   The subject of a verb (a noun or a pronoun) is in the nominative case. This is true whether the subject is singular or compound.

EXAMPLE   *Wrong:*   Me and Frank are good friends.
Correct: Frank and I are good friends.

2.   A predicate pronoun, whether singular or plural, is in the nominative case.

EXAMPLES
They thought that the visitor was *he*.
Frank and Joe knocked on the door. "It is *they*," Sue said.

---

3. Pronouns in apposition with nouns in the nominative case are also in the nominative case.

   EXAMPLE

   The two *contestants*, *she* and *I*, were tied for first place.

Objective

4. The object of a verb (a noun or pronoun) is in the objective case. This is true whether the object is singular or compound.

   EXAMPLES

   They applauded *him* and *her*.
   Did they face Frank and *us* in the contest?

5. The object of a proposition is in the objective case. This is true whether the object is singular or compound.

   EXAMPLES

   Everyone but *her* did the homework.
   Between *you* and *me*, Sue is my best friend.

6. Pronouns in apposition with nouns in the objective case are also in the objective case.

   EXAMPLES

   They gave the prizes to the *winners*, *her* and *me*.
   For *us amateurs*, it is fun to watch professionals perform.

7. The subject of an infinitive is in the objective case; the same is true for the object of an infinitive.

   EXAMPLES

   We asked *him* to go.
   We wanted him to ask *them* to come along.

Possessive

8. Pronouns in the possessive case, unlike nouns in the possessive case, never have an apostrophe.

   EXAMPLES

   The dog wagged *its* tail.
   We have met the enemy and they are *ours*.
   She has *hers*; they have *theirs*.

VERBS

The *verb*, the part of the sentence that indicates the action carried out by the subject, *also indicates* when the action was carried out. It does so by its tense.

Tense

Verb: to live	
Present tense:	live
Past tense:	lived
Future tense:	shall live
Present perfect tense:	has, have lived

Examples of the use of tense:

Note the way in which the rest of each sentence is affected.

Present tense:	I *live* in New York *now.*
Past tense:	I *lived* in New York *last year.*
Future tense:	I *shall live* in New York *next year.*
Present perfect tense:	I *have lived* in New York for *five years.*

Verb Forms

The principal parts of *to live, to see, to do,* and *to lie* are:

Verb	Past	Past Participle
live	lived	lived
see	saw	seen
do	did	done
lie	lay	lain

Many of the difficulties you have with verbs involve the *irregular verbs.* These change form in either the past or the past participle or in both. The most frequent error is the use of the wrong part of the verb, most often the past participle for the simple past.

EXAMPLES	*Wrong:*	*Wrong:*
	I seen him do it.	I done it.
	Correct:	*Correct:*
	I *saw* him do it.	I *did* it.

Frequently Used Irregular Verbs

Verb	Past Tense	Present Perfect Tense
be	I was	I have been
bring	I brought	I have brought
drink	I drank	I have drunk
eat	I ate	I have eaten
get	I got	I have got *or* gotten
go	I went	I have gone
have	I had	I have had
lay	I laid (place)	I have laid
lie	I lay (recline)	I have lain
run	I ran	I have run
speak	I spoke	I have spoken
swim	I swam	I have swum
take	I took	I have taken
throw	I threw	I have thrown
write	I wrote	I have written

What is the proper sequence of tenses for verbs in the main and dependent clauses of a complex sentence?

This can vary, but some common sequences follow.

VERB SEQUENCES	
Main Clause	**Dependent Clause**
Present tense:	**Present tense:**
I *gain* weight	when I *eat* too much.
Present tense:	**Past tense:**
I *believe*	that he *studied* for the examination.
Past tense:	**Past tense:**
The audience *applauded*	when the soloist *finished*.
Past tense:	**Past perfect tense:**
I *played* my first concert	after *I had studied* piano for three years.
Note: The action of the dependent clause (the studying) took place *before* the action in the main clause.	
Future tense:	**Present tense:**
I *shall leave*	when he *comes*.

ADJECTIVES AND ADVERBS

An **adjective** is used to describe a noun or pronoun.

EXAMPLE
He wore a *dark* hat.

An **adverb** is used to modify a verb, an adjective, or another adverb.

EXAMPLE
He played *very poorly*.
[*Poorly* modifies *played*; *very* modifies *poorly*.]

USE OF A VERB THAT DESCRIBES A CONDITION, NOT AN ACTION

If the verb is not used as an action verb, or if the verb describes a condition, then an *adjective rather than an adverb* must follow it.

EXAMPLES
He looks *sick*.
[*Sick* describes *he*.]

I feel *good*.
[*Good* describes *I*.]

Some Special Problems
ADJECTIVES INDICATE THE DEGREE TO WHICH THEY DESCRIBE NOUNS

Degree is indicated in one of two ways:

- the adverb *more* or *most* is placed before the adjective;
- The suffix *-er* or *-est* is added to the adjective.

EXAMPLES
He was *more quiet* than she.
He was *quieter* than she.
He was the *most friendly* person there.
He was the *friendliest* person there.

**Never use a negative adverb
and a negative adjective in the same sentence**

EXAMPLE
Wrong:
He doesn't do *no* work.
[A negative adverb—*n't [not]* and a negative adjective—*no*]

Correct:
He doesn't do *any* work.

CAPITALIZATION

BASIC RULES OF CAPITALIZATION

1. Capitalize the first word of a sentence.

   ### EXAMPLE
   We went to the theater.

2. Capitalize the first word of a direct quotation.

   ### EXAMPLE
   He said, "Don't give up."

3. Capitalize the first word of a line of poetry.

   ### EXAMPLE
   "Poems are made by fools like me . . ."

4. Capitalize proper nouns (names of specific persons, places, or things).

   ### EXAMPLES
   Winston Churchill; Mr. James Jones; New York City; Main Street; City Hall

5. Capitalize proper adjectives (adjectives formed from proper nouns).

   ### EXAMPLES
   American; Shakespearean

6. Capitalize names of specific organizations or institutions.

   EXAMPLES
   Sousa Junior High School; Columbia University; American Red Cross; Federal Bureau of Investigation

7. Capitalize days of the week, months of the year, and holidays. (*Note:* Do not capitalize seasons, e.g., winter.)

   EXAMPLES
   Sunday; June; Thanksgiving

8. Capitalize languages. (Note: These are the *only* school subjects that are capitalized.)

   EXAMPLES
   French; Hebrew
   I study English, Spanish, biology, mathematics, and social studies.

9. Capitalize races and religions.

   EXAMPLES
   Hindu; Christian

10. Capitalize references to the Deity and to the titles of holy books.

    EXAMPLES
    the Almighty; the Old Testament; the Koran

11. Capitalize titles of people when they are followed by a name, being careful to capitalize both the title and the name. (*Note:* If a specific person is meant, the name may, at times, be omitted.)

    EXAMPLES
    President George W. Bush; Dr. Schweitzer; Her Majesty the Queen

12. Capitalize titles of works of literature, art, and music.

    EXAMPLES
    War and Peace (note that articles, short prepositions, and conjunctions such as *and* are not capitalized in titles); *American Gothic*; *Beethoven's Fifth Symphony*

13. The pronoun *I* is capitalized at all times.

    EXAMPLES
    I walked one mile south to the school.

14. Sections of the country are capitalized, but directions are not.

> **EXAMPLES**
> I lived in the South for five years.
> We traveled south.

15. Capitalize specific places and addresses, but do not capitalize the second half of a hyphenated number.

> **EXAMPLE**
> Times Square; 25 Main Street; 65 West Thirty-third Street.

PUNCTUATION

BASIC RULES OF PUNCTUATION
The Period is used after
1. a sentence that makes a statement;

> **EXAMPLE**
> He arrived on time.

2. a sentence that gives a command;

> **EXAMPLE**
> Sit up straight.

3. some abbreviations and contractions.

> **EXAMPLES**
> Mr., lb., a.m., etc.

The Question Mark is used after a sentence that asks a question.

> **EXAMPLE**
> Did you like the game?

The Exclamation Point is used after a sentence that emphasizes a command or that conveys strong feeling.

> **EXAMPLES**
> Stop writing immediately!
> What a pleasant surprise!

The Comma is

1. used to separate a word or words that indicate the person to whom a remark is addressed;

   EXAMPLES

   John, please come here.
   You may come, little friend, if you like.

2. used to separate a word or words that are in apposition with a noun; that is, add information about the noun;

   EXAMPLE

   Nancy, my secretary and receptionist, is very efficient.

3. used to set off expressions or phrases that are inserted in the sentence and that interrupt the normal word order;

   EXAMPLES

   Notre Dame, in my opinion, will win the championship.
   Joan, on the other hand, disagrees with us;

   Note: The next two rules (4 and 5) do not apply to short introductory phrases and clauses and short independent clauses.

4. used after introductory phrases and clauses, particularly when they are long or when the meaning may be temporarily confused if the comma is omitted;

   EXAMPLES

   When the dog jumped up, Darryl's parents became frightened.
   After a long but exciting trip through the Alps, Amy returned tired but happy.
   Springing into action, the police caught the bandit.

5. used to separate independent clauses of a compound sentence joined by a conjunction such as *and, but, for, nor, or, so,* or *yet;*

   EXAMPLE

   Joe decided to attend the game, but I remained at home.
   but
   Joe returned but I remained.

6. used to separate items in a series;

   EXAMPLES
   The box contained books, toys, games, and tools.
   Jason, Meghan, and Sarah are going to the office today.
   [If the comma is omitted after "Meghan," it might seem that Jason was being told that Meghan and Sarah were going to the office.]
   For breakfast he had juice, ham and eggs, and coffee.

7. used before the text of a quotation; in a divided quotation, commas are used to set off the speaker;

   EXAMPLES
   The teacher said, "Return to your seats."
   "Return to your seats," said the teacher, "so we may continue the lesson."

8. used to set off clauses and phrases that are not essential to the meaning of the sentence *(No commas are needed if the clause or phrase is essential to the meaning intended by the speaker or writer.)*;

   EXAMPLE
   Jan, who was seated beside me, left early.
   [Note that the clause "who was seated beside me" is not essential to the sentence, which, without it, would read, "Jan left early."]
   but
   The students who studied hard passed the test.
   [The clause "who studied hard" is essential since only the students who studied hard passed. Without this clause the meaning intended by the writer—that students who did not study hard failed—would not be clear to the reader.]

   The comma also has a number of uses that are the result of custom:

9. after the salutation in a friendly letter;

   EXAMPLE
   Dear Dad,

10. after the complimentary close in all letters;

   EXAMPLE
   Very truly yours,

11. between the day of the month and the year in writing a date;

   EXAMPLE
   May 24, 1919

12. between the city and the state in writing an address;

   EXAMPLE
   Brooklyn, New York 11201
   Note: **Do NOT** use a comma
   —between a subject and its verb when the verb immediately follows the subject;

   EXAMPLE
   The boys on the team celebrated their victory.
   —to separate parts of a compound predicate.

   EXAMPLE
   They enjoyed a good dinner and saw a play.

The Semicolon is used to

1. separate independent clauses in a sentence; either a semicolon or a comma may be used when the clauses are short;

   EXAMPLE
   I came; I saw; I conquered. (*or* I came, I saw, I conquered.)

2. separate items in a series when these items contain commas;

   EXAMPLE
   The guests included William H. Rehnquist, Chief Justice of the United States; Colin Powell, Secretary of State; and Richard Cheney, the Vice President.

The Colon is used

1. to introduce a series or a list of items;

   EXAMPLE
   These items were included on the shopping list: fruit, vegetables, meat, fish, and ice cream.

2. before a restatement, an illustration, or an explanation of the main idea of the sentence;

EXAMPLE

I have but one rule of conduct: do unto others as you would be done by.

3. after the salutation of a business letter;

EXAMPLE

Dear Sir:

The Apostrophe is used to

1. indicate possession;

    a. In general, to make a singular noun possessive, add an apostrophe and *s ('s)* to words not ending in *s.*

EXAMPLE

boy's hat

    b. To make a plural noun possessive, add an apostrophe if the noun ends in *s.* If it does not end in *s,* add an apostrophe and *s.*

EXAMPLES

ladies' hats
men's coats

2. indicate that one or more letters have been omitted in a contraction;

EXAMPLE

He didn't come.

3. indicate the plural of letters or numbers;

EXAMPLE

There are 4 *s*'s in Mississippi

Note: Before adding the apostrophe to make the possessive, first form the plural of the noun;

EXAMPLE

child—children—children's

—Do *not* break up a word by using the apostrophe. The apostrophe can be added only at the end of a word.

EXAMPLE   *Wrong:* ladie's hats   *Correct:* ladies' hats

Parentheses are used to enclose any words that explain or add to an idea or ideas contained in a sentence. Parentheses are always used in pairs (that is, one opens and the other closes the included word or words).

EXAMPLE
Frank Jones (author of *Ideas that Work*) has written many best sellers.

Quotation Marks are used to

1. indicate the titles of works that are *part* of a book; (*Note:* The title of a whole book is underlined to indicate that the title should be italicized in print.)

EXAMPLES
I particularly enjoyed Chapter 3, "Your Pet as a Companion."
"Trees" is a poem by Joyce Kilmer.

2. set off a direct quotation of the speaker or the writer. (*Note:* Only the speaker's or writer's exact wording may be used.) Indirect quotations, quotations that do not use the exact words of the speaker or writer, do *not* require quotation marks.

EXAMPLES
Nathan Hale said: "I regret that I have but one life to give for my country."
The boy said that he would be late.
    but
The boy said, "I will be late."
Note: In almost every case, the comma and the period are enclosed within the quotation marks.

SPELLING

Modern educational research has made the job of becoming a good speller a lot easier than it used to be. We now know which words are used most frequently in print. In fact, thorough mastery of the words on the following lists will enable you to spell correctly approximately *two thirds* of the words you use in writing.

The Basic 100

The first list contains 100 basic words that you should know thoroughly.

ache	done	making	there
again	don't	many	they
always	early	meant	though
among	easy	minute	through
answer	enough	much	tired
any	every	none	tonight
been	February	often	too
beginning	forty	once	trouble
believe	friend	piece	truly
blue	grammar	raise	Tuesday
break	guess	read	two
built	half	ready	used
business	having	said	very
busy	hear	Saturday	wear
buy	heard	says	Wednesday
can't	here	seems	week
choose	hoarse	separate	where
color	hour	shoes	whether
coming	instead	since	which
cough	just	some	whole
could	knew	straight	women
country	know	sugar	won't
dear	laid	sure	would
doctor	loose	tear	write
does	lose	their	writing

How do you go about studying this list?

One way involves the following steps.

1. Fold a sheet of paper into three parts, holding the paper sideways.
2. Fold the left third of the paper over so that it covers the center part.
3. Look at the word, noticing the difficult spot or spots. Say it aloud carefully.

4. Look at the word again, spelling it aloud by syllables. We'll help you with the problem of dividing words into syllables later on.
5. Spell the word aloud by syllables again, without looking at it this time.
6. Look at the word a third time, copying the letters on the folded part of the paper while you say them aloud by syllables.
7. Turn the fold back, this time writing the letters on the right-hand third of the paper while you again say them aloud by syllables.
8. Fold the left third of the paper over again so that you can compare the word you originally copied with the word you wrote from memory. If it is spelled correctly, turn the fold back and write the word twice more on the central third of the paper, being careful to spell the word aloud by syllables each time. If you made an error, the word will require more study, particularly of the letter or syllable you misspelled.
9. Master this list before turning to the next list. This second word list contains 200 words that are somewhat more difficult than the basic 100, but that are still rated "Easy" by those who test spelling ability. The letters or parts of the words that cause difficulty are underlined.

200 Often Used Easy Words

absence	aroused	changing	crowd
accept	arrival	chief	curtain
accident	article	children	customer
address	asked	choice	
adjourn	athletic	chosen	decided
advice	attacked	climbed	delivery
advise	attention	cloth	destroy
airplane	author	clothes	determine
allowed		cloud	device
almost		coarse	dictator
already	because	collar	didn't
altogether	before	common	different
American	brakes	conceal	dining
amount	breathe	confident	discussed
annual		conquer	divided
anxious	careful	corner	doesn't
around	carrying	course	dropped
	certain		

due
dying

earliest
easily
effect
eighth
eliminate
English
entirely
envelope
etc.
everybody
evidently
excellent
expense
experience
extremely

fatigue
formerly
forth
forward
fourteen
fourth
future

generally
genius
gentlemen
good-bye
guard

handful
handle
handsome
hasn't
height
hoping

hundred
hungry
hurrying

interesting
invitation
its
it's

jealous

ladies
later
latter
led
library
losing
lying

magazine
merely
minutes
movable

neither
nevertheless
nickel
niece
ninety
ninth

o'clock
officer
operate
owing

paid
partner
passed

past
perform
perhaps
permanent
planning
politics
possible
presence
probably
prominent
promptly
proved
purpose

quarter
quiet
quite
quizzes

realize
really
receipt
received
recognize
reference

safety
salary
sandwich
scarcely
secretary
sentence
shining
shriek
speech
stopped
stories
strength
stretched

strictly
striking
studying
succeed
success
summer
surely
surround

terrible
than
they're
thorough
those
threw
together
toward
tries
twelfth

until
unusual
useful

varied

wasn't
weather
weird
welfare
whose
wonderful
wouldn't
written

you're
yours

Most Frequently Made Errors

Over sixty percent of all spelling errors are caused by either <u>leaving out a letter</u> that belongs in a word or <u>substituting one letter for another</u> (usually because of incorrect pronunciation of the word).

An example of a word misspelled because of a letter left out is *recognize*. Many students mispronounce the word by leaving out the "g"; they also, therefore, leave out the "g" when they spell the word.

An example of a word misspelled because one letter is substituted for another is *congratulations*. Many students mispronounce the word by substituting the voiced "d" sound for the unvoiced "t" sound; they also, therefore, substitute a "d" for the "t" when they spell the word.

Other words that are misspelled because of the omission or substitution of letters are:

accidentally	environment	library	surprise
arctic	escape	partner	temperature
candidate	February	postpone	tragedy
chocolate	government	prejudice	tremendous
diphtheria	laboratory	probably	usually

Over twenty percent of all errors are caused by either <u>adding letters to a word</u> or <u>reversing two letters within the word.</u>

An example of a word to which a letter is added is *equipment*. Some people incorrectly pronounce the word with a *t* after the *p*. As a result, they add a *t* to the word when they spell it.

An example of a reversal of letters within the word is the simple word *doesn't*. Very often, the letters *e* and *s* are reversed and the student spells the word incorrectly—"dosen't."

Other words that are misspelled because of the addition or reversal of letters are:

asparagus	*(not* "gras"*)*
athletics	*(no e after the th)*
barbarous	*(no i after the second bar)*
chimney	*(no i after the m)*
disastrous	*(no e after the t)*
hundred	*(not* "derd"*)*

int<u>ro</u>duce	*(not* "ter"*)*
lightning	*(no e after the t)*
mischievous	*(no i after the v)*
mo<u>dern</u>	*(not* "dren"*)*
<u>per</u>cent	*(not* "pre"*)*
<u>per</u>formance	*(not* "pre"*)*
<u>per</u>spire	*(not* "pre"*)*
<u>pro</u>duce	*(not* "per"*)*
<u>pro</u>fession	*(not* "per"*)*
<u>pro</u>nounce	*(not* "per"*)*
<u>pro</u>tect	*(not* "per"*)*
remembrance	*(no e after the b)*
sec<u>re</u>tary	*(not* "er"*)*
umbrella	*(no e after the b)*

The next most common error is the confusion of two words having the <u>same pronunciation</u> but <u>different spellings and meanings</u>. These are called *homonyms.* In this humorous sentence—"A doctor must have lots of patients (patience)"—there is no way of our knowing which word the speaker means if the sentence is spoken. Therefore, we don't know how to spell the word. The words *patients* and *patience* are homonyms.

Forty of the most frequently used groups of homonyms follow. Be certain to check the meaning of each word in each group so that you can figure out the spelling from the meaning of the word as it is used in a sentence.

air; ere; heir	hole; whole	sew; so; sow
ate; eight	hour; our	stationary;
blew; blue	knew; new	stationery
bough; bow	know; no	steal; steel
brake; break	lead; led	straight; strait
buy; by	mail; male	some; sum
cent; scent; sent	meat; meet	son; sun
coarse; course	pail; pale	their; there; they're
for; four	pair; pare; pear	threw; through
forth; fourth	peace; piece	to; too; two
grate; great	principal; principle	way; weigh
groan; grown	read; red	wood; would
hear; here	right; write	your; you're
him; hymn	road; rode	

How to Become a Good Speller

There are three things you can do to help eliminate the frequently made errors and to equip yourself with the skills you will need to become a good speller.

Learn how to syllabicate. Knowing how to syllabicate—divide a word into syllables—will help you avoid many kinds of errors. This skill is particularly helpful with words of more than average length. Here are some simple rules that will help you to syllabicate properly.

RULES ON HOW TO SYLLABICATE

1. When a word has more than one vowel sound, it is broken into parts or syllables.

EXAMPLES

strength	*strength*	[one syllable]
metal	*me/tal*	[two syllables]

2. Every syllable contains a sounded vowel or a pair of vowels sounded as one vowel (digraph).

EXAMPLES

going	*go/ing*	[sounded vowel in each syllable]
breakout	*break/out*	[pairs of vowels sounded as one vowel in each syllable]

3. Sometimes a sounded vowel forms a syllable by itself.

EXAMPLE

again   *a/gain*

4. Double consonants usually are separated.

EXAMPLES

mitten	*mit/ten*
possesses	*pos/ses/ses*

5. A consonant between two vowels usually is joined to the vowel that follows it.

EXAMPLES

local   *lo/cal*   **final**   *fi/nal*

---

6. When the suffix "ed" is added to a word ending in "d" or "t," it forms a separate syllable.

EXAMPLE
added   *add/ed*

Applying these rules to the words listed earlier will help you avoid many of the common types of errors, particularly in the omission and addition of letters.

EXAMPLES
ath / le / tics
chim / ney
um / brel / la
ac / ci / den / tal / ly

Learn the correct pronunciation of the word you must spell. Mispronunciation is known to be one of the most common causes of misspelling. Your best ally in learning the pronunciation of a word is the dictionary. Knowing the correct pronunciation will help you attack successfully such words as:

EXAMPLES
Feb / ru / a / ry
[The first *r* is often not pronounced.]

gov / ern / ment
[The first *n* is often not pronounced.]

choc / o / late
[The second *o* is often not pronounced.]

Learn the most helpful spelling rules, and know how to apply them.

BASIC RULES OF SPELLING
 1. Plurals of most nouns are formed by adding *s* to the singulars.

EXAMPLE
house, hous*es*

 2. When the noun ends in *s*, *x*, *ch*, or *sh*, the plural generally is formed by adding "*es*."

EXAMPLES
gas, gas*es*
box, box*es*
witch, witch*es*
dish, dish*es*

3. a. The plural of a noun ending in *y* preceded by a consonant is formed by changing *y* to *i* and adding *es*.

EXAMPLE
lady, lad*ies*

b. The plural of a noun ending in *y* preceded by a vowel does not change *y* to *i* EXCEPT for words ending in *quy*.

EXAMPLES
toy, toy*s*
but
soliloquy, soliloqu*ies*

4. a. A word that ends in *y* preceded by a consonant usually changes *y* to *i* before a suffix unless the suffix begins with *i*.

EXAMPLE
beauty, beaut*iful*

b. A word that ends in *y* preceded by a vowel usually keeps the *y* when a suffix is added.

EXAMPLE
coy, coy*er*

5. a. A word that ends in silent *e* generally keeps the *e* when a suffix beginning with a consonant is added.

EXAMPLE
care, care*ful*

b. A word that ends in silent *e* generally drops the *e* when a suffix beginning with a vowel is added.

EXAMPLES
believe, believ*able*
move, mov*ing*

6. **Exceptions to Rule 5.**
   Words ending in *ce* and *ge* keep the letter *e* before *able* and *ous*.

   EXAMPLES
   notice, notic*eable*
   change, chang*eable*
   courage, courag*eous*

7. A one-syllable word that ends in one consonant following a short vowel generally doubles the consonant before a suffix that begins with a vowel.

   EXAMPLES
   big, big*gest*
   thin, thin*ner*

8. A word of more than one syllable that ends in one consonant following one short vowel generally doubles the final consonant before a suffix beginning with a vowel *if* the accent is on the last syllable.

   EXAMPLES
   omít, omit $\boxed{t}$*ed*
   regrét, regret $\boxed{t}$*ing*
   allót, allot $\boxed{t}$*ed*

9. The letter "i" is generally used before "e" except after "c."

   EXAMPLES
   bel*ie*ve, rec*ei*ve
   There are many exceptions, as:
   either
   neither
   neighborhood
   weigh
   leisure

10. An apostrophe is used to show that a letter has been omitted in a contraction.

    EXAMPLES
    it is, it's
    they are, they're

11. An abbreviation is always followed by a period.

EXAMPLE
etc.

12. Nouns of Latin origin ending
—in *us* become *i* in the plural,

EXAMPLE
rad*ius*, rad*ii*
—in *a* become *ae* in the plural,

EXAMPLE
formul*a*, formul*ae*
—in *um* become *a* in the plural,

EXAMPLE
medi*um*, medi*a*
—in *is* become *es* in the plural,

EXAMPLE
ax*is*, ax*es*

13. The suffix *ful* is spelled with a single *l*.

EXAMPLES
help*ful*
tablespoon*ful*

(*Note:* The word *full* itself is the only exception.)

Practice with Spelling

In each set of words, find the misspelled word if there is one. <u>No set has more than one misspelled word</u>. If there is no misspelled word, choose answer 5. This kind of error is included in the sentence correction type of multiple-choice item.

1. (1) rein
   (2) conceited
   (3) cheif
   (4) shield
   (5) no error

2. (1) greif
   (2) wield
   (3) relieve
   (4) besiege
   (5) no error

3. (1) proceed
   (2) succeed
   (3) preceed
   (4) exceed
   (5) no error

4. (1) illegal
   (2) illegible
   (3) unatural
   (4) uncivilized
   (5) no error

5. (1) prespective
   (2) present
   (3) proceed
   (4) proposal
   (5) no error

6. (1) combustible
   (2) intelligible
   (3) perceptable
   (4) taxable
   (5) no error

7. (1) tangible
   (2) lamentible
   (3) considerable
   (4) separable
   (5) no error

8. (1) logically
   (2) typically
   (3) verbally
   (4) globally
   (5) no error

9. (1) practically
   (2) exceptionally
   (3) significantly
   (4) intelligently
   (5) no error

10. (1) advantagous
   (2) perilous
   (3) desirous
   (4) adventurous
   (5) no error

11. (1) mischievious
    (2) previous
    (3) poisonous
    (4) mountainous
    (5) no error

12. (1) murderous
    (2) slanderous
    (3) grievous
    (4) beauteous
    (5) no error

13. (1) momentous
    (2) marvelous
    (3) outragous
    (4) hazardous
    (5) no error

14. (1) channal
    (2) acquittal
    (3) flannel
    (4) kernel
    (5) no error

15. (1) sparkle
    (2) disciple
    (3) thimbal
    (4) clerical
    (5) no error

16. (1) corpuscle
    (2) muscle
    (3) proposal
    (4) morsel
    (5) no error

17. (1) nickle
    (2) pickle
    (3) logical
    (4) neutral
    (5) no error

18. (1) signal
    (2) medical
    (3) swivel
    (4) shuttel
    (5) no error

19. (1) senator
    (2) investigator
    (3) inventer
    (4) stenographer
    (5) no error

20. (1) actor
    (2) ancestor
    (3) purchaser
    (4) elevater
    (5) no error

21. (1) begger
    (2) bookkeeper
    (3) regular
    (4) singular
    (5) no error

22. (1) calender
    (2) passenger
    (3) collar
    (4) hangar
    (5) no error

23. (1) spectator
  (2) educator
  (3) dollar
  (4) receiver
  (5) no error

24. (1) pendant
  (2) brilliant
  (3) superintendent
  (4) permanent
  (5) no error

25. (1) descendant
  (2) repentant
  (3) defendent
  (4) president
  (5) no error

Answer Key

1. **3**	6. **3**	11. **1**	16. **5**	21. **1**
2. **1**	7. **2**	12. **5**	17. **1**	22. **1**
3. **3**	8. **5**	13. **3**	18. **4**	23. **5**
4. **3**	9. **5**	14. **1**	19. **3**	24. **5**
5. **1**	10. **1**	15. **3**	20. **4**	25. **3**

Answer Analysis

1. **3**	chief	14. **1**	channel
2. **1**	grief	15. **3**	thimble
3. **3**	precede	16. **5**	no error
4. **3**	unnatural	17. **1**	nickel
5. **1**	perspective	18. **4**	shuttle
6. **3**	perceptible	19. **3**	inventor
7. **2**	lamentable	20. **4**	elevator
8. **5**	no error	21. **1**	beggar
9. **5**	no error	22. **1**	calendar
10. **1**	advantageous	23. **5**	no error
11. **1**	mischievous	24. **5**	no error
12. **5**	no error	25. **3**	defendant
13. **3**	outrageous		

ADDITIONAL WRITING SKILLS

CORRECT USE OF WORDS

Here are thirty pairs of words that are frequently confused and misused. Study the distinctions between the words in each pair.

Accept, Except   Hanged, Hung
Aggravate, Irritate   Imply, Infer
Already, All Ready   In, Into
Altogether, All Together   Latest, Last
Among, Between   Learn, Teach
Amount, Number   Myself, Me
Around, About   Pour, Spill
As, Like   Precede, Proceed
Beat, Bet   Principal, Principle
Beside, Besides   Quite, Quiet
Borrow, Lend   Raise, Rise
Both, Each   Rob, Steal
Bring, Take   Set, Sit
Can, May   Stand, Stay
Fewer, Less   Stationary, Stationery

FREQUENT ERRORS IN WORD USE

1. **DON'T USE** the expression *being that*. Instead, use a conjunction such as *because* or *since*.

   Wrong: Being that he was first, he won the prize.
   Correct: *Since* he was first, he won the prize.

2. **DON'T USE** the expression *could of*, *should of*, or *would of*. Instead, use the correct expression (with *have*) for which any of these spoken distortions is an incorrect substitute.

   Wrong: He could of been the winner if he had tried.
   Correct: He *could have* been the winner if he had tried.

3. **DON'T USE** the expression *different than*. Instead, use *different from*.

    Wrong: Playing baseball is different than playing softball.
    Correct: Playing baseball is *different from* playing softball.

4. **DON'T USE** incorrect prepositions.

    Wrong: May I borrow a dollar off you?
    Correct: May I borrow a dollar *from* you?

    Wrong: Come over our house for a party.
    Correct: Come *to* our house for a party.

5. **DON'T USE** *don't* in the third person singular. Use *doesn't*, which is the contraction of *does not*.

    Wrong: He don't belong here.
    Correct: He *doesn't* belong here.

6. **DON'T USE** any article after the expression *kind of* or *sort of*.

    Wrong: He's not the kind of a person I like.
    Correct: He's not the *kind of* person I like.

7. **DON'T USE** the expression *the reason is because*. Use *the reason is that* since the words *reason* and *because* have similar meanings; a *reason* is indeed a cause.

    Wrong: The *reason* he left is because he did not get a raise.
    Correct: The *reason* he left *is that* he did not get a raise.

8. **DON'T USE** *who's* when you mean *whose*. *Whose* should be used to show possession. *Who's* is a contraction of *who is*.

    Wrong: I know who's book this is.
    Correct: I know *whose* book this is.

3

WRITING SKILLS, PART II

THE ESSAY TEST

The essential skills in writing are:
1. Writing effective, interesting, and varied sentences;
2. Writing effective paragraphs;
3. Putting these together in planning, writing, and revising your essay;
4. Managing time.

To write effectIve sentences:
1. Use personal pronouns (I, you, we, your) where possible;
2. Prefer using active verbs to passive verbs, not "The examination was passed by me," but "I passed the examination."
3. Use conversation when appropriate. In a 200-word essay, you may be able to use a single exchange of words.

To write varied sentences:
1. Vary the types of sentences (simple, compound, complex);
2. Vary the purpose of the sentences (ask a question, give a command, use an exclamation point where appropriate);
3. Vary sentence length. Use a short one for emphasis.

To write effective paragraphs:
1. Have a clearly stated topic sentence;
2. Develop it by details, by illustration and example, by defining or explaining an idea, by comparison (likes) or contrast (differences), or by reasons and proof;
3. Vary the sentences in the paragraph. Vary the purpose and length of sentences;
4. Vary paragraph length. A one-sentence paragraph can emphasize an important point.
5. Organize the paragraph to emphasize the important idea, at the beginning and then developing it, or at the end leading up to it.

To allot your time properly:

1. Read the instructions completely and make sure you understand what you are going to write about—three to five minutes.
2. Make an outline—five to ten minutes.
3. Write a 200-word essay—twenty to twenty-five minutes.
4. Revise and edit the essay—five minutes.

TYPES OF ESSAYS

What are the different types of essays?

Basically there are three different types of essays. They are persuasive, expository, and narrative. Depending on the topic that will be given to you on your GED test, you will be able to pick out what type of essay you need to write and set it up with ease. Expository and persuasive essays are set up in five paragraphs while narratives can be set up in three or four. In this section we will go through the three different types of essays and what makes each unique.

The Persuasive Essay

This type of essay requires you to take a stand on an issue and develop an argument explaining why you have made this particular choice. You will need to use personal experiences in your explanations or information that you know. This essay is set up in five paragraphs.

EXAMPLE

Prompt

Many states have enacted laws throughout the years to help people stay safe. One such law that has been passed in many states is the seat belt law.

Discussion Question

Do you feel that states have the right to tell people they must wear a seat belt in an automobile?

Sample Persuasive Essay

Seat belt laws have been enacted in many states. I feel that they are very important for the safety of all Americans. This law saves countless lives each year, makes sure our children are safe, and gives me a sense of security when I get behind the wheel of a car. I believe that seat belt laws are very important and should be enforced in every state.

There are many people alive today because of the enforced seat belt laws. This law makes sure that people who ordinarily don't wear seat belts in automobiles are restrained in case of an accident. I know personally that the seat belt laws work because I, who was once a non-seat belt wearer, was in an accident. I only wore the seat belt because of this law. I was lucky. It saved my life when my car rolled over one night on a rain-slick road. Instead of being thrown out of the car and possibly killed or injured, I was safe.

Children are also safer because of this law. It is required by law that all children be restrained in a car safety seat or seat belt. This keeps the child safe in case of an accident. It also gives the adult driving the comfort of knowing the child is not moving around the automobile where he or she could be injured by opening a door and falling out.

When I get behind the wheel of a car and snap on my seat belt, I feel comfortable knowing that I have a better survival rate should I be in an accident. I want to make sure that I am here to enjoy life for a long time, and by wearing a seat belt in the car I know that I am increasing my odds of surviving an accident.

Seat belt laws are important to me and should be to everyone! They help save lives, keep our children safe, and give me security in the automobile. I would recommend that every state have seat belt laws.

The Expository Essay

This essay requires you to explain, describe, or interpret a particular situation, experience, or idea by again using personal experiences or information. This essay is set up in five paragraphs.

EXAMPLE

Prompt

There have been many great books written through the years. Think of three books that you have read that have affected your life in some way. They may have affected you in a small way or a profound way.

Discussion Question

What are three books that you have read that have affected you in some way?

Sample Expository Essay

Books have always been a big part of my life. I have read many books through the years but three of my favorite books are, *The King, the Mouse, and the Cheese, Little Women,* and *Silas Marner.* I have read these many times and each time I do, they add joy to my life.

The King, the Mouse, and the Cheese was the first book I remember reading. When I was in second grade we were required to do a book report. This book was my choice. I remember my mother reading the book with me and helping me decide what I would say about the book. On the day of the report I stood at the front of the room and quickly reported on the story. The class loved it and everyone wanted to check the book out of the library. This book gave me the joy of reading and made me want to continue.

When I was a teenager, *Little Women* quickly became a favorite of mine. It was a story of four sisters and how they grew from girls into young women. This story discussed friendship, love, and war. It gave me a sense of family and an appreciation for my own.

The last book on my favorite list is, *Silas Marner.* This is a story written by George Eliot. It is about a man who loved gold and came to realize that a little girl was more important that all the gold in the world. It gave me a wonderful message that there are more important things than material possessions.

Books can be a wonderful asset to anyone's life. These marvelous stories can bring fulfillment, appreciation, and values.

The Narrative Essay

This type of essay requires you to recount a personal experience by using sequencing skills, details, or descriptions. It is basically recounting a story of what has happened to you. This essay is set up in three or four paragraphs.

EXAMPLE

Prompt
Everyone seems to have a memorable event that took place in his or her life. Think of an event that seems to stand out in your memory.

Discussion Question
What made this event different from all of the others? Was it a time of great happiness or sadness? Was it funny?

Sample Narrative Essay

The event that is most memorable to me was a Mother's Day in 1978. This was the day that my brother and I decided to take our Mom out for a wonderful day at the museum and dinner. What started out as good intentions ended up costing us more than we anticipated.

The day started out fine as we left our home in my brother's big old black car and traveled two hours into the city to the museum. As soon as we arrived at the museum, we noticed that the day was already getting warm. We went quickly inside the air-conditioned museum and spent several hours wandering around looking at the entire collection of paintings, statues, and even automobiles. After we looked at everything in the museum, we decided we were getting hungry and were eager to go to eat dinner. We left the building and found the car. As my brother turned the key, all we heard was a terrible grinding noise that told us we weren't going anywhere. Stuck! My brother went inside and called a tow truck to take the car in for repairs. My mother gave my brother money to fix the car and then she and I waited at the museum for his return. This was a time before cell phones were being used and we had no idea how long it was going to take. In the meantime, it was getting hotter and we were getting hungrier. We went back into the museum and looked around for several more hours until closing time. We then had no choice but to go outside and sit in the stifling heat. We were miserable! Finally, the familiar big old black car came into view and we gladly jumped in. The first place we went was a place to eat.

What started out as a nice trip ended up being a day of misery. Mother's Day, 1978, will be one I will never forget. I'm sure my mother and brother feel the same way.

SETTING UP AN ESSAY

When you take your GED Writing Skills, Part II test, you will be given a prompt and/or a discussion question. You will write your essay on this question.

The prompt on the Writing Skills, Part II test will be a subject that will be familiar to you. You will not be graded on how much you know about the material but how well you can relate your ideas.

In this segment we will go through the three types of essays (expository, persuasive, and narrative) from beginning to end. There will be explanations for each paragraph included in the essay along with the essay in its entirety. You will be able to see and understand the process of a three-, four-, or five-paragraph essay.

What must be included in an essay?

An essay must have a clear *focus* that states the *main idea*. *Details* are needed to support that focus. The essay must be set up in a format that makes sense and allows the essay to be read easily and understood by the reader.

Essays have three main parts:

1. The first is an *introduction*. This is the main idea of the essay. The introduction is the first paragraph of the essay. Without an introduction the essay has no focus and would be hard to understand.

2. The second part of the essay is the *body*. The body is the meat of the essay. This is where the supporting details are added. The body of the essays we will write will have one, two, or three paragraphs.

3. The last part of an essay is the *conclusion*. This is the final paragraph of the essay. Not only is it important to have a focus and supporting details but it is equally important to make sure you summarize your essay by tying all the ideas together at the end.

Setting Up an Expository Essay

Expository Prompt
Throughout the year there are many holidays that people in the United States celebrate. Some are religious holidays such as Christmas and Easter, while other holidays celebrate the lives of famous Americans such as George Washington and Abraham Lincoln.

Discussion Question
Think of some holidays that are important to you. Why are these holidays important to you?

How to Set Up an Expository Essay
Focus: What is the main idea of the essay?

Think: Is it about Christmas, Easter, George Washington, and Abraham Lincoln or is it about you? This essay is about you and particular holidays that you relate to your personal life.

First Step: Decide on *three* specific ideas to explain, describe, or interpret in your essay.

Think: What are three holidays that you enjoy? Let's say that you enjoy Veteran's Day, Independence Day, and Christmas. These three holidays will become your second, third, and fourth paragraph in your five-paragraph essay once a main idea and details are established. The first paragraph in your essay will be an introduction and the last a summary.

Main Idea: What is the main idea of the essay going to be? Look again at the prompt and see what the discussion question is asking: "Why are these holidays important to you?" You cannot use this statement as your main idea for the essay, but you can reword it to make it into a main idea: "Holidays are important to me." Now you have your main idea.

First Paragraph: The first paragraph begins with the main idea of the essay and includes the three ideas you want to discuss.

Think: What is the main idea of the essay? What are the three ideas you wanted to explain?

EXAMPLE

Holidays are important to me. There are many holidays I enjoy, but the three I enjoy most are Veteran's Day, Independence Day, and Christmas.

This paragraph now includes the main idea of your essay and the three ideas (holidays, in this case) that will be discussed. You may note that this paragraph is made up of only two sentences, yet it relays perfectly the main idea of the essay and the three ideas you are going to discuss. You may, however, add an extra sentence to help express the main idea.

EXAMPLE

Holidays are important to me. There are many holidays I enjoy, but the three I enjoy most are Veteran's Day, Independence Day, and Christmas. These holidays all have a special meaning to my family and me.

Second Paragraph: You are now ready to set up your second paragraph. In this paragraph you will take your first idea (Veteran's Day) and create a topic sentence (main idea) for the paragraph and then create detail sentences that support the idea.

Think: What would be a good main idea for your second paragraph if the idea you are writing about is Veteran's Day? Mentally take notes of details about why Veteran's Day is important to you. Is it because you have veterans in your family? Is it because you have lost loved ones in a war? Is it because you get a day off from work to be with your family? Whatever the reason, think of a main idea for this paragraph. When you write your main idea for the paragraph make sure it is broad enough to cover several sentences of discussion; for example, "Veteran's Day is an honorable holiday." This is a broad statement that allows you to add sentences that explain why it is important to you. If your main idea was "Veteran's Day is important to me because my father was in the Vietnam War," your detail sentences would be limited to a discussion of your father in the Vietnam War.

EXAMPLE

Veteran's Day is an honorable holiday. It is a day when I think about the men and women serving our country in the military. Veteran's Day is a day on which I think about the men and women who gave their life for me so that I might have freedom. On this day I take my children to the Veteran's Day services so that they will learn to appreciate and respect the veterans of the past and present in our country.

Third Paragraph: The third paragraph relates to the second idea (holiday) from your introductory paragraph. In this case it is Independence Day. The third paragraph is set up in the same way as the second.

Think: Create a main idea or topic sentence. Think of detail sentences that you want to include. Again, try to think of a broad main idea. It will be easier to think of details to go along with it.

EXAMPLE

Independence Day is a great summer holiday. On Independence Day my family gathers together for our annual family reunion. The kids have a great time lighting sparklers and playing traditional games outdoors. We top off the day by watching the great display of fireworks.

This paragraph has a broad main idea and all details are focused on it. It also includes personal supporting details.

Fourth Paragraph: The fourth paragraph uses your final or third idea (holiday) from your introductory paragraph. This idea is Christmas. Again, this paragraph is set up just as paragraphs two and three.

Think: Create a main idea for your third idea (holiday). This will be about Christmas. What can you write that would be broad enough to include supporting details? If you wrote, "I receive many gifts for Christmas," your detail sentences would be limited only to those gifts you received. If you wrote, "Of all the holidays, Christmas is my favorite," you have a much broader approach to adding details.

EXAMPLE

Of all the holidays, Christmas is my favorite. Christmas is a time of joy and generosity in my family. It is a time when all my family gathers together in front of the fireplace to sing Christmas carols. I love to watch the little children in my family open their gifts on Christmas morning. It seems to be almost magical.

Fifth Paragraph: This is the last paragraph and its purpose is to summarize the entire essay. As with the other four paragraphs, this paragraph also needs a main idea. This paragraph may also need special phrases to show closure such as: "In summary," "In conclusion," "In short."

Think: Create a main idea that summarizes the entire essay. This paragraph does not need as many detail sentences as the other paragraphs but one or two would help support the summary. What was the entire essay about? What do you need to include in your summary of the entire essay? Make sure to put in the three ideas you have been explaining.

EXAMPLE

In summary, there are many holidays that are important to my family and me. Three of these holidays are Veteran's Day, Independence Day, and Christmas.

The word count for the entire essay is 256 words. You can clearly see that each paragraph is focused, contains main ideas and details, has structure, and yet is simple. Take a look at what the entire essay looks like put together. Notice how it flows easily from one paragraph to the next.

Holidays are important to me. There are many holidays I enjoy, but the three I enjoy most are Veteran's Day, Independence Day, and Christmas. These holidays all have a special meaning to my family and me.

Veteran's Day is an honorable holiday. It is a day when I think about the men and women serving our country in the military. Veteran's Day is a day on which I think about the men and women who gave their life for me so that I might have freedom. On this day I take my children to the Veteran's Day services so that they will learn to appreciate and respect the veterans of the past and present in our country.

Independence Day is a great summer holiday. On Independence Day my family gathers together for our annual family reunion. The kids have a great time lighting sparklers and playing traditional games outdoors. We top off the day by watching the great display of fireworks.

Of all the holidays, Christmas is my favorite. Christmas is a time of joy and generosity in my family. It is a time when all of my family gathers together in front of the fireplace to sing Christmas carols. I love to watch the little children in my family open their gifts on Christmas morning. It seems to be almost magical.

In summary, there are many holidays that are important to my family and me. Three of these holidays are Veteran's Day, Independence Day, and Christmas.

Setting Up a Persuasive Essay

Persuasive Prompt

At any given evening, with most any family relaxing at home, there will be the familiar ringing of the telephone. Usually it's neighbors, friends, or family, but every so often it is a telemarketer trying to get us to purchase numerous items ranging from new tires, credit cards, or siding, to insurance. Sometimes we decide to purchase these items, and sometimes we become annoyed at the constant calling.

Discussion Question

How do you feel about telemarketers calling your home? Do you feel they are a vital part of our economy by providing a service to people or do you feel they are interrupting your personal time with your family?

How to Set Up a Persuasive Essay

Focus: What is the main idea of the essay going to be? It is about telemarketers calling your home. The main question is, how do you feel about this? You are required to take a stand on this issue. Do you feel that these calls are important or are they an invasion of your privacy?

First Step: Decide what your stand is on the issue. Next, think of *three* specific reasons why you feel the way you do.

Think: What are the three reasons that you do or do not like telemarketers calling your home. Let's say your stand is that you do not like them calling your home. Here are your three possible reasons:

1. The first reason you do not like their calling is that you do not want to spend your time at home being pressured by salespeople.

2. Your second reason may be that you do not trust people selling items over the phone.

3. Your third reason may be that you don't need or want the product that is being offered.

Main Idea: Take a look at the essay prompt and question. What is the main idea of the essay going to be? Remember to make your first statement or main idea broad enough that you will be able to write a lot about it. You will begin your first paragraph with the main idea of the essay and include your three reasons. Remember, in a persuasive essay you are required to take a stand so this essay is written in the first person, "I." Your main idea may be stated something like this: "There are many reasons why I don't like telemarketers calling my home."

First Paragraph: The first paragraph is the introduction. It will begin with your main idea and have one or two more sentences that support the main idea. Remember to include in your introduction your three reasons why you feel the way you do. This will be the focus of the body of the essay.

Think: What was your main idea? What were your three reasons?

EXAMPLE

There are many reasons why I don't like telemarketers calling my home. Three of these reasons are that they interrupt my family time, I don't trust giving out financial information to them over the phone, and I don't always need or want the products they offer.

This paragraph now includes your main idea of the essay and three reasons why you don't like telemarketers calling your home. Notice that the paragraph is made up of only two sentences. You may want to add a third sentence to help support the main idea.

EXAMPLE

There are many reasons why I don't like telemarketers calling my home. Three of these reasons are that they interrupt my family time, I don't trust giving out financial information over the phone, and I don't always need or want the products they offer. I know telemarketers have a job to do, but I just don't like the interruptions they cause.

Second Paragraph: You are now ready for your second paragraph. This is the body of the essay. In this paragraph you will take the first reason from your introduction and create a main idea. Then you will create supporting details for the main idea.

Think: What will be the main idea for your second paragraph? Your first reason in your introduction states: "They interrupt my family time." You will need to use these words to create your main idea. You may write, "When telemarketers call my home, I feel that they interrupt my family time." Now you need to think of at least three more sentences that would support how you feel about this particular reason.

EXAMPLE

When telemarketers call my home I feel that they interrupt my family time. It seems that every time my family and I sit down to dinner, the phone rings. Instead of spending time with my children, I end up listening to several minutes of chatter. I hate to be rude and hang up the phone, but I admit that is what I sometimes have to do to get back to my family.

Third Paragraph: The third paragraph relates to your second reason in your introduction. The second reason you don't like telemarketers calling is, "I don't feel comfortable giving out financial information over the phone." The third paragraph is still the body of the essay and it is set up just as the second paragraph with a main idea and details.

Think: Create a main idea using your second reason. It may be, "I don't feel comfortable giving out financial information over the phone to a telemarketer." After you have your main idea, you need to think of about three sentences that support the main idea of your third paragraph.

EXAMPLE

I don't feel comfortable giving out financial information over the phone. I don't know the person on the other end and it could be someone dishonest. I realize that not all telemarketers are dishonest. It's just that it makes me nervous to give out credit card information when anyone could be listening.

Fourth Paragraph: This paragraph is set up like the second and third paragraphs and is also part of the body of the essay. The main idea of the fourth paragraph relates to your third reason in your introduction. Your third reason is, "I don't always need or want the products they are selling."

Think: What is a good main idea using your last reason? Think of about three sentences that will support your main idea for the fourth paragraph. Your last main idea may be, "Telemarketers don't usually offer any products that I would be interested in purchasing."

EXAMPLE

Telemarketers don't usually offer any products that I would be interesting in purchasing. It seems that most telemarketers who call my home try to send me information on acquiring credit cards. Some try to sell expensive encyclopedias or even light bulbs. One telemarketer even offered to sell me siding for my brick home!

Fifth Paragraph: This is the last paragraph in your five-paragraph persuasive essay. It is also called the conclusion. It is important that you summarize your entire essay and draw a conclusion in this paragraph.

Think: Create a main idea that summarizes the entire essay. What was the essay about? What was your stand on the issue? Make sure that you put in your conclusion the three reasons you explained.

EXAMPLE

I don't like telemarketers calling my home. There are many reasons for this. Some of these reasons are that they interrupt my family time, I don't feel comfortable giving out financial information over the phone, and I don't usually need or want any of the products they are selling.

You have now completed your persuasive essay. Let's take a look at how the entire essay looks when it is put together. The word count for this essay is 280 words. It doesn't take very many sentences to make up the 200 words you need to write in your essay. The persuasive essay we just wrote has only three or four sentences in each paragraph.

There are many reasons why I don't like telemarketers calling my home. Three of these reasons are that they interrupt my family time, I don't trust giving out financial information over the phone, and I don't always need or want the products they offer. I know telemarketers have a job to do, but I just don't like the interruptions they cause.

When telemarketers call my home, I feel that they interrupt my family time. It seems that every time my family and I sit down to dinner, the phone rings. Instead of spending time with my children, I end up listening to several minutes of chatter. I hate to be rude and hang up the phone, but I admit that is what I sometimes have to do to get back to my family.

I don't feel comfortable giving out financial information over the phone. I don't know the person on the other end and it could be someone dishonest. I realize that not all telemarketers are dishonest. It's just that it makes me nervous to give out credit card information when anyone could be listening.

Telemarketers don't usually offer any products that I would be interesting in purchasing. It seems that most telemarketers who call my home try to send me information on acquiring credit cards. Some try to sell expensive encyclopedias or even light bulbs. One telemarketer even offered to sell me siding for my brick home!

In summary, I don't like telemarketers calling my home. There are many reasons for this. Some of these reasons are that they interrupt my family time, I don't feel comfortable giving out financial information over the phone, and I don't usually need or want any of the products they are selling.

Setting Up a Narrative Essay

The narrative essay is set up differently from the expository or persuasive essays. It can have three, four, or even five paragraphs. It is usually easier to set it up in three or four. In the following example we will set it up into three paragraphs. It still has the same three basic parts: the introduction, body, and conclusion. In the narrative essay each paragraph will represent one of the basic parts. Remember that the narrative essay is written in the first person and discusses a personal issue.

Narrative Prompt

Do you remember when you got your first real job? It may have been one when you were still in high school. Maybe it was at the service station across town or being a waiter or waitress. How did you feel about this job? Try to recall how you felt about your first job.

Discussion Questions

Think about your first job. How did you feel about it? How did you get this job? What made it so special?

How to Set Up a Narrative Essay

Focus: What is the main idea of your essay going to be? It is about your first job and why it was important to you.

First Step: Decide what you want your main idea sentence to say.

Think: Your first sentence or main idea needs to state what type of job you are going to discuss in your essay.

Main Idea: Suppose that your first job was as a waitress or waiter in a restaurant. Your first sentence may be, "I will never forget my first job as a waitress in a small-town café."

First Paragraph: In your first paragraph you will need to include your main idea sentence and at least one or two other sentences to help support the main idea. Remember that the first paragraph is the focus for the entire essay.

EXAMPLE

I will never forget my first job as a waitress in a small-town café. I was only sixteen years old and felt so excited. This was the beginning of my independence.

This simple paragraph focuses on the first job and its importance to the writer.

Second Paragraph: The second paragraph in the narrative essay is the body of the essay. Since the essay is written in the first person and tells about an experience of the writer, it is important to put in time order the words that show sequencing of details. Begin the body of the essay with the first event you want to share. Then continue in order. Put in thoughts and feelings as you write your sentences.

EXAMPLE

The summer after I turned sixteen my mother thought it was time for me to find a summer job. She had heard that there was an opening for a waitress in a small local café. I wasn't too happy about giving up my life of leisure for the summer, but I decided to give it a try. The pay for the job was a dollar an hour, which I thought was a lot of money. I started my job on the first day washing dishes. I washed and washed. After a few days, I was promoted to pouring coffee at the snack bar. I thought this was great compared to the dishwashing and even managed to make a tip now and then. Later on, I was given the job of waiting on the customers. It wasn't as easy as it looked and I made my share of mistakes. Finally, by the end of the summer, I had made a little money, but what was most important was the experience I gained.

Make sure that your detail sentences refer to the main idea of the essay. Keep your sentences in sequence. Notice that the writer above uses time order words such as *after a few days, later on,* and *finally.* This allows the reader to understand exactly what order the actions in the paragraph are taking place.

Third Paragraph: The final paragraph in the narrative essay is the conclusion. This paragraph sums up the entire essay.

EXAMPLE

My first job was a great experience for me. It helped me to gain my first taste of independence while also gaining some great experience.

The word count for the entire narrative essay is 227 words. Let's take a look at how it would read when put together.

I will never forget my first job as a waitress in a small-town café. I was only sixteen years old and felt so excited. This was the beginning of my independence.

The summer after I turned sixteen my mother thought it was time for me to find a summer job. She had heard that there was an opening for a waitress in a small local café. I wasn't too happy about giving up my life of leisure for the summer, but I decided to give it a try. The pay for the job was a dollar an hour, which I thought was a lot of money. I started my job on the first day washing dishes. I washed and washed. After a few days, I was promoted to pouring coffee at the snack bar. I thought this was great compared to the dishwashing and even managed to make a tip now and then. Later on, I was given the job of waiting on the customers. It wasn't as easy as it looked and I made my share of mistakes. Finally, by the end of the summer, I had made a little money, but what was most important was the experience I gained.

My first job was a great experience for me. It helped me to gain my first taste of independence while also gaining some great experience.

CREATING QUICK OUTLINES FOR ESSAYS

Creating a quick outline before you write your essay will save you some time in writing. It will help to keep your essay in focus. Below we will go through three outlines for the previous essays. When you create an outline, you will need to jot down your ideas on scrap paper and not include this outline in your actual essay, but only use it as a reference.

The Expository Outline

The expository essay is written in a five-paragraph form. Therefore, you will need to number your outline into five sections and write your main idea for each paragraph beside each number. Remember when writing your outline that your first paragraph is the introduction and contains your three main points. Paragraphs two, three, and four will be about the three main points. Typically, outlines are written in Roman numerals.

EXAMPLE

I.   Holidays are important to me.
II. Veteran's Day is an honorable holiday.
III. Independence Day is a great summer holiday.
IV. Of all the holidays, Christmas is my favorite.
V.   In summary, there are many holidays that are important to my family and me.

Once you have your five main paragraph sentences, you can insert your detail sentence ideas under each main idea.

Important Holidays to Me

I.   Holidays are important to me.
  A. Holidays I enjoy are Veteran's Day, Independence Day and Christmas.
  B. Holidays have special meaning.

II. Veteran's Day is an honorable holiday.
  A. Men and women in the service
  B. Take children to services

III. Independence Day is a great summer holiday.
  A. Family reunion
  B. Kids play games
  C. Watch fireworks

IV. Of all the holidays, Christmas is my favorite.
  A. Generosity
  B. Family gathers together
  C. Opening gifts

V.   In summary, there are many holidays that are important to my family and me.
  A. Veteran's Day, Independence Day, and Christmas

Do not spend a great deal of time jotting down your outline. The outline is meant to save you time. Your detail sentences do not necessarily have to be written out completely in your outline. They can be fragments that you can add to when you write your complete essay. From the above outline you can use the ideas to create your sentences for your five-paragraph essay.

The Persuasive Outline

The persuasive essay is also written in five-paragraph form. To begin the persuasive outline, number your five paragraphs with Roman numerals and write a main idea for each paragraph. The first sentence in your outline is going to state your stand on the issue you will be writing about. This is the focus of the essay. The next three sentences in your outline will be about your three points explaining why you made this stand. Your final sentence is the main idea for your conclusion.

EXAMPLE

    I.   I don't like telemarketers calling my home.
   II.   Telemarketers interrupt my family time.
  III.   I don't like giving out financial information.
  IV.   I don't like the products from telemarketers.
   V.   There are many reasons I don't like telemarketers calling.

After writing your main ideas for each paragraph, continue with adding your details to each paragraph. For each detail sentence assign a letter of A, B, C, etc.

Why I Don't Like Telemarketers Calling My Home

    I.   I don't like telemarketers calling my home.
      A.   Interrupt family time, financial information, and don't need or want products

   II.   Telemarketers interrupt family time.
      A.   Phone rings during family time
      B.   Hanging up on callers

  III.   I don't feel comfortable giving out financial information.
      A.   I don't know person calling
      B.   Credit card information

  IV.   Telemarketers don't offer products I need or want.
      A.   Offer products such as credit cards
      B.   Offer products such as encyclopedias or light bulbs

   V.   I don't like telemarketers calling my home.
      A.   Interrupt family time, financial information, and products

---

The Narrative Outline

The narrative outline is written in a three-paragraph form. Number your three main idea sentences with Roman numerals and then write the main idea for each paragraph. Remember, in a narrative essay, the first paragraph is the introduction, the second is the body, and the third is the conclusion.

EXAMPLE

   I.   I will never forget my first job as a waitress.

  II.   My mother thought it was time for me to get a job.

 III.   My first job was a great experience.

After you have decided what you want your main ideas to be in your narrative essay, continue with detail sentences for each paragraph.

My First Job

   I.   I will never forget my first job as a waitress.
- A. Felt excited
- B. New experience

  II.   My mother thought it was time for me to get a job.
- A. Heard about an opening
- B. Gave up summer vacation
- C. Was paid a dollar an hour
- D. Washed dishes
- E. Promoted to pouring coffee
- F. Waited on customers
- G. Made some mistakes
- H. Made money and gained experience

 III.   My first job was a great experience.
- A. Helped me gain independence and experience

ESSAY PRACTICE

Below is a prompt for a practice essay. On a separate sheet of paper write a quick outline and then begin your essay. Remember that the outline is for your own benefit and is not to be turned in with the essay. Time yourself as you write.

Prompt

American people have become more health conscious in the past few years. More people seem to be exercising regularly and watching what they eat.

Discussion Question

What are some ways that you can help yourself to become healthier or maintain your own good health?

Write an essay of about 200 words in which you explain or present your reasons for this topic. Give supporting details and examples in your essay. You have 45 minutes to write on this topic.

Sample Answer

After you finish writing your essay, compare it to the sample essay below. You may have come up with similar ideas. Everyone will not choose the same three points to write about in their essay. As long as you can provide clear, focused main ideas and details to back them up, you should be on the road to success!

Since the above prompt was an expository theme, you should have written five paragraphs. Look now at the sample outline.

Sample Outline

I.   There are many ways in which I stay healthy.
   A.   eat right
   B.   exercise daily
   C.   try not to worry

II.   I always try to eat the right types of food each day.
   A.   eat from the four main food groups
   B.   drink plenty of water

III.   Before I begin each day I make sure I exercise at least ten minutes.
   A.   start out with stretching exercises
   B.   work up to more strenuous exercise

IV.   Worry has a big effect on my health.
   A.   simple things don't bother me
   B.   relaxing

V.   There are many ways to stay healthy but I choose to eat right, exercise, and not worry.

Sample Essay from Outline

Maintaining Good Health

There are many ways in which I can stay healthy. I try to eat right, exercise daily, and try not to worry. If I do all of these things, I feel better emotionally and physically.

I always try to eat the right types of food every day. Eating from the four basic food groups always helps. By doing this I make sure I get all the vitamins and minerals that I need each day. I also drink plenty of water instead of soft drinks with added sweeteners. I feel that this is better for me.

Before I begin each day, I make sure I exercise at least ten minutes. I begin with stretching exercises. Later, I work up to more strenuous exercises that really get my heart rate up.

Worry has a big effect on my health. I don't let simple things bother me. I usually take a few minutes each day to relax.

There are many ways to stay healthy, but I choose to eat right, exercise, and not worry. With the combination of these three things, how can I go wrong?

REVISING THE ESSAY

Remember to reread your essay once you have completed it. If you have allotted your time well, you should have five minutes to complete this very important part of essay writing.

Below is a set of guidelines to follow when revising your essay.

Check Yourself

1. Check for the main idea in the first paragraph of all three types of essays.
2. Check for your three points in your first paragraph of a persuasive or expository essay.
3. Check to make sure in the persuasive and expository essays that the second, third, and fourth paragraphs include a topic sentence related to the three points in your first paragraph.

4.   Check to make sure in your narrative essay that you include sequencing and time order words.
5.   Do your detail sentences in each paragraph stick to the topic? Keep the focus of the essay.
6.   Check for run-on sentences, correct punctuation, capitalization, subject/verb agreement, and spelling.
7.   Check for a summary at the end of the essay. Do you have a clear ending for your essay?
8.   Do you have a clear and focused introduction, body, and conclusion?
9.   Do you have about 200 words in your essay?

For practice, revise the essay that you wrote in the previous segment.

Only after you have read and revised your essay should you feel that you have completed the Writing Skills, Part II Test. Don't hesitate to make changes or corrections to your paper. As long as your writing is legible, neatness is not a consideration.

4

SOCIAL STUDIES

READING AND INTERPRETING SOCIAL STUDIES MATERIALS

HOW TO READ POLITICAL SCIENCE, HISTORY, ECONOMICS, AND GEOGRAPHY

Reading in the social studies requires a number of skills that are common to all reading materials. When you read in any subject, you want to identify the *main ideas* of the writer. So, too, in social studies you need to get at the key thoughts being expressed.

Locating the Main Idea

If you read too slowly, you may miss the main point because you have gotten too involved in details. It is important, therefore, that you first read the selection through to the end rather quickly *before* you turn to the questions.

Where do you look for the main idea? Most often you will find it in the topic sentence, usually the first sentence in the passage. Sometimes, however, the writer will withhold the main idea until the last sentence, building up to it throughout the entire selection. At other times, the writer will include both a main idea and an important secondary (or subordinate) idea.

To train yourself in **locating the main idea,** ask yourself the same questions that will be asked of you on the examination.

1. What is the main idea of the passage?
2. What is the best title for the passage?
3. If I were choosing a suitable headline for the article in a newspaper, what headline would I choose?
4. What is the *topic sentence* of this paragraph or paragraphs; that is, the sentence that includes the ideas contained in all the other sentences?

Finding Details

After you have determined the main idea, the next step is to *locate the facts supporting the main idea or details* that flow from the main idea. If, for example, the main idea of a passage is that democracy is the best form of government, the author will undoubtedly provide facts or reasons to support this statement or include facts that show the superiority of democracy to other forms of government. If the main idea is a general conclusion that many persons with physical disabilities have overcome them and become famous, details would probably include such examples as Helen Keller and Franklin D. Roosevelt.

How do you locate a detail? You go back to the selection a second or third time to dig it out of the passage. It most frequently will come in the middle or toward the end of the selection. Sometimes clues in the passage steer you to the detail or fact in question. Clues for locating details may read:

An example is...
One reason is...
An argument in support of (or against)...is...
A reason for...is...

To train yourself in **locating details,** ask yourself these questions:
1. What examples are given to illustrate the main point?
2. What reasons are offered to support the author's position?
3. What arguments for or against a proposal does the author present?
4. When, where, and how did something happen?
5. What did someone do?
6. Why did he or she do it?

To find the proper detail, it will be necessary for you to *learn how to skim,* that is, to read rapidly to locate the piece of information you are seeking. You can do this only if you know specifically what you need to find in a given selection and limit your reading to finding only that fact.

Determining Organization

Note the manner in which the writer organizes his or her material. This will help you to follow the author's thoughts effectively. The writer may organize his or her material chronologically, that is, in the order in which a series of events happened. Alternatively, the writer may organize the material logically by presenting the arguments *for* a position in one paragraph and the arguments *against* in another. Or the writer may present his or her ideas in the order of their importance, with the most important ideas first. This, in fact, is the way a newspaper article is written—"from the top down"—in case the reader doesn't have time to finish it all.

If you can determine the organization of a passage, you can zero in on the relationship between the main parts of a passage.

Clues to Finding the Relationship between the Main Parts of a Passage

Sequence of ideas is indicated by such words as:

first	next	finally
second	further	

Additional ideas are indicated by such words as:

and	furthermore	likewise
besides	also	in addition

Opposing or contrasting ideas are indicated by such words as:

on the other hand	but	yet
however	still	although

Drawing Conclusions

Another step involves *drawing conclusions from the material presented.* Conclusions are often indicated by such words as:

thus	accordingly	consequently
therefore	so	as a result

Sometimes, however, the author does not draw the conclusion, but leaves it to you, the reader, to do so. You infer the conclusion from the materials presented; you draw the inference as a result of details you have noted and the relationships you have determined (time sequence, logical order, cause-and-effect, among others). Thus, if an author indicates that a given president vetoed many bills, you might infer that the president and the Congress differed in their thinking about legislation, perhaps because the Congress was controlled by a political party different from that of the president.

> To train yourself to **make inferences** properly in order to draw a conclusion, ask yourself these questions:
> 1. What do I think will happen next? (inference or prediction as to the outcome)
> 2. Putting these arguments together, what conclusion can I reach?
> 3. If one result was caused by something, will a similar effect take place in another situation where the same cause is operating?
> 4. What is the writer suggesting, rather than saying outright?

Reading Critically

In addition to drawing conclusions and making inferences, it is essential in social sciences that you react to what you have read. Often you must judge the material you are reading, not merely understand it. Historians, political scientists, economists, sociologists, and anthropologists often present one side of the story, their side, but there is almost always another side. In other words, they may "slant" the material to suit their bias by including only facts and arguments favorable to their own view and omitting everything else. It is essential for you to *read critically.* Do *not* accept everything that is written just because it appears in print.

You must develop the habit of challenging the author by raising questions, judging the completeness and truth of the information presented, and distinguishing fact from opinion.

A *statement of fact* is one that can be proved true by consulting a reliable source of information such as an encyclopedia, an almanac, or an official government document. Here is an example.

EXAMPLE

The federal government spends billions of dollars each year helping states with aid to needy persons: needy through unemployment, disability, or family problems.

This statement can be verified by consulting the official federal budget.

A *statement of opinion or belief* is one that expresses the feelings, thoughts, or beliefs of a person or persons, and that cannot be proved to be true by reference to any reliable source at the present time.

EXAMPLE

It is believed that by the year 2002, population will have outstripped food production and starvation will be widespread.

This is a prediction in the form of a statement or belief attributed to an unidentified source ("It is believed...") that cannot be proved until the year 2002. It is possible that others may have their own beliefs. In any case, the statement is definitely not a fact.

Note that certain words are clues to statements of opinion.

Words That Are Clues to Statements of Opinion

claim	probably
believe	possibly
think	might
consider	should (have)
will be	could (have)
likely	ought

Words That Probably Reflect Opinion Rather Than Fact

better	undesirable
worse	necessary
desirable	unnecessary

REMEMBER: Always apply the test, "Can this statement be proved by reference to a reliable source?"

It is important to distinguish fact from opinion in the printed word when writers unconsciously allow their opinions or biases to enter into their writing. It is even more important to do so when a writer slants his or her material deliberately.

You can read critically if you ask yourself the following questions:

1. Why is the author writing this selection?
2. What is the author trying to get me, the reader, to believe?
3. Is the author presenting a balanced or one-sided view of the situation?
4. Is the author omitting essential information?
5. Is the author appealing to my mind or to my emotions and prejudices?
6. Does the author have some hidden reason for writing what he or she writes?
7. Is the author accurate? Or does he or she deal in half-truths?
8. Does the author use words with specific agreed-upon meanings, or does he or she use words that are "loaded" because they have special meanings?

Detecting Propaganda and Propaganda Techniques

When writers deliberately spread ideas or opinions to benefit themselves or institutions to which they belong or to damage opponents or opposing institutions, they are engaging in propaganda. A propagandist tries to influence your thinking or behavior and to turn your opinions and actions in a certain direction. He or she uses words that appeal to your emotions—your fears, your loves, your hates—rather than to your reason, to your ability to think clearly, in order, ultimately, to make you do things in a way you never ordinarily would do.

Six common techniques in propaganda are:

1. *Name-calling.* The writer tries to influence you by attaching a bad name to an individual, group, nation, race, policy, practice, or belief.

   EXAMPLE

   It would be wise to pay no attention to that loony liberal (or retarded reactionary, depending upon the writer's point of view).

   Certain names are loaded with emotional overtones: Fascist, Red, Nazi, Commie. You must note carefully in what way and for what purpose these terms are used. Name-calling is a common propaganda technique.

2. *Glittering generalities.* The writer attaches "good" names to people and policies, in the hope that you will accept them without really looking into the facts.

    EXAMPLE

    > The writer appeals to our emotions by using such "good" terms as *forward-looking, peace-loving, straight-shooting,* and *idealistic.*

    > We all love progress, peace, honesty, and idealism so we tend to accept rather than challenge. Always ask the questions "why" and "how" when "good" terms are applied to people and policies.

3. *Transfer.* The writer tries to use the approval and prestige of something or some institution we respect to get us to accept something else in which he or she is interested.

    EXAMPLE

    > Most Americans are law-abiding and respect their police officers. One who writes on behalf of an athletic league supported by the local police will try to get you to transfer your approval of the police to the athletic league he or she is sponsoring.

    > Always examine the person or institution receiving the transfer on its own merits rather than on the merits of the original institution you love and respect.

4. *Testimonial.* Advertisements on television and radio make wide use of testimonials. A top athlete endorses a breakfast cereal. A beautiful actress recommends a cosmetic cream. An ex-senator testifies to the value of a credit card. A testimonial is a recommendation made by someone on behalf of a person, a product, or an institution.

    But is the athlete an expert on nutrition? Is the actress an expert on skin care? Is the politician an expert on personal money management? REMEMBER: these people are being paid to make these testimonials. You must ask yourself whether the person making the testimonial is expert enough to do so before you believe what you read or hear.

    More subtle is newspaper reporting that is based on *indirect* testimonials.

EXAMPLES

> Official circles report...; It was learned from a senior government official...; A reliable source stated...

> Always ask *which* circles, *which* official, *which* source. Be careful of any information that comes from a high *unidentified* source.

5. ***Card-stacking.*** The writer attempts to get you to see only one side of a particular issue. To do so, he or she will use half-truths and omit the other side of the argument. Examples occur frequently in "authorized" biographies that present a person's life in glowing terms, including all the good qualities while omitting or toning down the poor ones. When reading about an issue, always note whether both sides have been discussed or whether the cards have been stacked by the writer on one side of the issue only.

6. ***Bandwagon.*** The writer tries to make you go along with the crowd. Since most people like to follow the trend, they will respond favorably to such statements as "Nine out of ten Americans prefer..." or "...sells more... than all other companies put together." In politics, the bandwagon technique is often seen in action in national political conventions. "Join the swing to...."

   The bandwagon-approach writer does not want you to think clearly for yourself. You should always ask *why* you should join the others, and not do so because your emotions have gotten the better of you.

REMEMBER:

A critical reader

- does not believe everything he or she reads simply because it is in print;
- accepts as true only statements that can be proved or that are made by reliable authorities;
- separates fact from opinion, recognizes emotional language and bias, and is aware of slanting by omission.

Determining Cause and Effect

A reading skill frequently used in social studies involves determining the relationship between events. Events rarely occur in isolation. They are generally the result of other events that happened earlier.

EXAMPLE

>The Japanese bombed Pearl Harbor on December 7, 1941. The United States then declared war on Japan.

>The bombing of Pearl Harbor was the cause; the declaration of war was the result or effect of the bombing. Always try, when reading of an event, to determine its cause or causes. *Here is a question involving cause and effect:*

Question

1. President Franklin D. Roosevelt's New Deal policy led to numerous government agencies, created in an effort to combat the effects of the Great Depression. One major result of this policy was to
   (1) weaken the power of the chief executive
   (2) strengthen the policy of laissez-faire
   (3) increase the power of the federal government
   (4) expand the importance of states' rights
   (5) lessen the need for judicial review

Answer and Analysis

The question asks for a result of President Franklin D. Roosevelt's New Deal policy. The opposite results occurred from those listed as Choices 1, 4, and 5; that is, the New Deal strengthened the power of the chief executive; weakened the importance of states' rights, and increased the need for judicial review. Choice 2, the policy of laissez-faire, provides for little or no interference by government in the affairs of business, clearly an incorrect response. Only Choice 3 is correct because the New Deal program called for executive action to advance economic recovery and social welfare.

Comparing and Contrasting Ideas and Organizations

Another frequently needed skill in social studies reading involves the ability to compare and contrast institutions and events. You may be asked to compare American democracy with French democracy, contrast democracy with communism, compare the platforms of the Republicans and Democrats, or contrast the role of women in the eighteenth century with their role in the twentieth.

Question

1. The careers of Theodore Roosevelt and Franklin D. Roosevelt were similar because each man

    (1) was an outstanding military leader before becoming president

    (2) led the cause for international peace, but involved the United States in a war

    (3) succeeded to the presidency upon the death of the preceding president

    (4) believed in a strong presidency and acted accordingly

    (5) represented the same political party

Answer and Analysis

You are asked to compare the careers of two American presidents. Franklin D. Roosevelt was not an outstanding military leader before becoming president. Theodore Roosevelt did not involve the United States in a war. Franklin D. Roosevelt did not succeed to the presidency upon the death of the preceding president. Theodore Roosevelt was a Republican; Franklin D. Roosevelt, a Democrat. Thus Choices 1, 2, 3, and 5 are incorrect. Choice 4 is correct because both Roosevelts were strong presidents: Theodore Roosevelt was a trust buster, had a Square Deal policy, and pursued an expansionist foreign policy; Franklin D. Roosevelt carried out New Deal policies and a Good Neighbor policy with Latin America, and he led the nation for most of World War II.

Learning Social Studies Vocabulary and Deriving Meaning from Context

In social studies as in science, vocabulary is of critical importance. Words found in social studies may

- represent complicated ideas, such as *nationalism, referendum, mercantilism;*
- imply a whole set of ideas, such as *feudalism, militarism, bimetallism;*
- have meanings specific to the social studies although they have other meanings as well, such as *Axis, act, shop;*
- come from foreign languages, such as *apartheid, junta, laissez-faire;*
- have meanings that go beyond the usual ones, such as *dove, plank, scab.*

Try to derive the correct meaning from the *context*—the words with which the term appears in a sentence.

You can **check your understanding of the meaning of the vocabulary** in a given selection by asking yourself:

1. What is the key word in the sentence (paragraph, selection)?
2. What is the meaning of the word in *this* sentence (context)?
3. What is the exact meaning (denotation) of the word in this selection?
4. What is the extended meaning (connotation) of the word in this selection? (What does it *suggest* as well as say?)
5. What is the effect of a given word on me?
6. What is the special meaning of this word in social studies?

Political Science

There are the following four key committees at a political convention.

- The *Credentials Committee.* This group decides who is an official delegate entitled to vote.
- The permanent *Organization Committee,* which picks the convention's officers, including the chairperson. This official decides who can speak at the convention and who cannot.
- The *Rules Committee,* which makes the rules by which the convention and the party organization are run.
- The *Resolutions and Platform Committee,* which writes the party platform. Usually, a convention lasts about four days. Typically, a temporary convention chairperson opens the convention with a *keynote address,* which is meant to set the tone of the convention— and quite frequently does. The real business of the day, however, goes on behind the podium, where the Credentials Committee settles disputes over *delegate credentials.*

On the second day the *party platform* is read, debated, and usually voted upon. A *permanent chairperson* is installed, and the convention is asked to approve the reports of its major committees.

On the third day actual *nominations* for presidential candidates are taken. States are called alphabetically at the Republican Convention, by lottery at the Democratic. Each state may nominate one candidate, second a nomination already made, yield (surrender the floor to another state), or pass. After each nomination there is usually a loud demonstration for the nominee.

Balloting begins only after nominations have been closed. A *simple majority*—one more than half the votes—is all that is needed to win. Every Republican presidential candidate since 1948 and every Democratic one since 1952 has won on the first ballot. If no one wins a simple majority on the first ballot, the vote is taken again until a candidate is picked.

By the fourth day a *presidential nominee* has usually emerged. He, in turn, addresses party leaders and tells them whom he prefers for *vice president.* Usually he gets his way.

Finally, the two candidates make their *acceptance speeches,* go through a few ceremonial events, and the *convention ends.*

1. The main idea of the above selection is
    (1) choosing a president and vice president
    (2) four key committees
    (3) how Republican and Democratic conventions differ
    (4) conventions: American political dramas
    (5) how conventions are organized and run
2. The vice-presidential candidate is chosen by the
    (1) party leaders
    (2) roll-call vote
    (3) Rules Committee
    (4) permanent convention chairman
    (5) presidential nominee
3. In the next convention, it is most likely that the party candidates will be nominated by
    (1) simple majority on the second ballot
    (2) plurality on the second ballot
    (3) two-thirds vote on the first ballot
    (4) simple majority on the first ballot
    (5) plurality on the first ballot
4. The INCORRECTLY paired group below is
    (1) Organization Committee—convention chairperson
    (2) permanent chairperson—keynote address
    (3) nominees—acceptance speeches
    (4) states—nominations
    (5) simple majority—choice of nominee

5. One difference between Republican and Democratic conventions is the way in which
   (1) committees are organized
   (2) convention chairpersons are chosen
   (3) nominations for presidential candidates are made
   (4) balloting takes place
   (5) party platforms are decided

6. The writer of this selection has organized the passage
   (1) logically
   (2) psychologically
   (3) chronologically
   (4) argumentatively
   (5) critically

Answer Key

1. **5**   2. **5**   3. **4**   4. **2**   5. **3**   6. **3**

History

The United States is often considered a young nation, but in fact it is next to the oldest continuous government in the world. The reason is that its people have always been willing to accommodate themselves to change. We have been dedicated to equality, but have been willing to realize it by flexible means. In the European sense of the term, America's political parties are not parties at all, because they do not divide over basic beliefs. Neither wishes to overturn or replace the existing political and economic order; they merely desire to alter it at slower or faster rates of speed.

One of our proudest achievements has been the creation of a system of controlled capitalism that yields the highest living standards on earth, and has made possible a society as nearly classless as man has ever known. The profit system as it has developed in America shares its benefits with all parts of society: capital, labor, and the consuming masses. Yet even this was the result of trial and error. Unprincipled businessmen had first to be restrained by government, and by the growing power of organized labor, before they came to learn that they must serve the general good in pursuing their own economic interests. Now labor is feeling the restraint.

Even our creed of democracy is not fixed and unchangeable. Thus the statesmen of the early republic, though they strongly believed in private enterprise, chose to make the post office a government monopoly and to give the schools to public ownership. Since then, government has broadened its activities in many ways. Americans hold with Lincoln that "the legitimate object of government is to do for a community of people whatever they need to have done but cannot do at all, or cannot do so well for themselves, in their separate and individual capacities."

1. The main quality of the United States stressed in this passage is its
    (1) youth
    (2) equality
    (3) high living standards
    (4) profit system
    (5) flexibility
2. The widely held belief about the United States with which the passage mentions disagreement concerns American
    (1) political parties
    (2) capitalism
    (3) private enterprise
    (4) labor
    (5) public ownership
3. All of the following are characteristic of the United States, according to the passage, EXCEPT a
    (1) dedication to equality
    (2) classless society
    (3) belief in democracy
    (4) profit system
    (5) controlled capitalism
4. An agency that performs a function of which Lincoln, according to his quoted words, would most approve is the
    (1) U.S. Office of Education
    (2) U.S. Chamber of Commerce
    (3) National Guard
    (4) Public Service Commission
    (5) Federal Aviation Administration

5. The creation of the U.S. government post office monopoly is cited as an example of a
(1) replacement of the existing economic order
(2) restraint of unprincipled businesspersons
(3) control of organized labor
(4) flexible view of private enterprise
(5) system of shared profits

6. According to the passage, which of the following statements is true?
(1) Our political parties agree on goals but not on methods.
(2) Business has a larger share of profits than labor.
(3) Government has tended to restrict its role in American life.
(4) Americans are conservative where change is required.
(5) Americans have kept their democratic beliefs intact.

7. The author's view of change in America is
(1) critical
(2) cautious
(3) favorable
(4) qualified
(5) unclear

Answer Key

1. **5**   2. **1**   3. **2**   4. **5**   5. **4**   6. **1**   7. **3**

Economics

Could the United States fall into the depths of another Great Depression?

Economists can't say for sure. Most feel, however, that past depressions have taught us how to avoid economic disaster.

We've learned, for example, of the need for

- *Government regulation of the stock market.* The Securities Act of 1933 made stock dealings less of a shell game by bringing them out into the open. The Securities Exchange Act of 1934 set up the Securities and Exchange Commission (S.E.C.), which acts as a sort of official consumer watchdog group. One of its jobs is to warn the investing public against the sort of crazy speculating that preceded the 1929 crash.

- *A permanent Council of Economic Advisers to take the economy's pulse for the government.* The Employment Act of 1946 created the Council of Economic Advisers. Its recommendations in 1949, 1958, 1969, and 1985, observers feel, helped keep the recessions of these years from becoming depressions.

- *A Federal Deposit Insurance Corporation (F.D.I.C.) to promise government backing of bank deposits.* The F.D.I.C. insures certain bank deposits. Such insurance has so far prevented the type of bank runs—panic withdrawals—that forced thousands of banks to close their doors in the early 1930s.

- *A federal relief system for jobless people.* State and local governments struggled to provide relief for the poor in the early years of the Great Depression. For the most part, they failed. They, too, ran out of money.

The New Deal introduced Social Security, a government pension plan. Government insurance followed for workers who are laid off or can't work because of injuries. Veterans' benefits and public assistance (welfare) are two other forms of government help in which Washington became involved during the 1930s.

These *transfer funds,* as they are called, don't merely help the recipients. In the long run, they help the whole economy by giving people buying power. This buying power helps keep up the demand for bonds. Thus, it helps keep factories open and factory workers employed.

For these and other reasons, many economists believe that we are now in better control of the U.S. economy, which, in the 1990s, is one of the strongest in the world.

1. The selection emphasizes
   (1) the effects of the Great Depression
   (2) the contributions of the New Deal
   (3) the strength of the U.S. economy
   (4) ways to avoid economic disaster
   (5) the role of people's buying power
2. All of the following are associated with the New Deal EXCEPT
   (1) Social Security
   (2) Council of Economic Advisers
   (3) veterans' benefits
   (4) welfare
   (5) unemployment insurance

3. All of the following were characteristics of the Great Depression that economists sought to correct EXCEPT
(1) stock market speculation
(2) bank failures
(3) unemployment
(4) soaring inflation
(5) poverty

4. The federal government stepped in where state and local governments failed in
(1) regulating the stock market
(2) backing bank deposits
(3) providing relief for the jobless
(4) providing veterans' benefits
(5) introducing Social Security

5. Which of the following statements is NOT true?
(1) The United States avoided depressions in each decade following the Great Depression.
(2) Bank panics have been avoided since the Great Depression.
(3) The Securities and Exchange Commission alerts investors to the kind of stock market activity that preceded the Great Depression.
(4) Transfer funds help the unemployed.
(5) We have learned how to prevent another Great Depression.

6. We can conclude from the author's presentation that he sees another Great Depression as
(1) inevitable
(2) likely
(3) unlikely
(4) impossible
(5) predictable

Answer Key
1. **4**   2. **2**   3. **4**   4. **3**   5. **5**   6. **3**

Geography

Geography may be subdivided into several areas of study.

Physical Geography In the study of physical (natural) geography, stress is laid upon the natural elements of man's environment. These include topography, soils, earth materials, earth-sun relationships, surface and underground water, weather and climate, and native plant and animal life. Physical geography must also include the impact of man on his physical environment as well as those influences omnipresent in nature.

Cultural Geography In cultural geography emphasis is placed upon the study of observable features resulting from man's occupation of the earth. These features include population distribution and settlement, cities, buildings, roads, airfields, factories, railroads, farm and field patterns, communication facilities, and many other examples of man's work. Cultural geography is one of the very significant fields of geographic inquiry.

Economic Geography In economic geography, the relationship between man's efforts to gain a living and the earth's surface on which they are conducted are correlated. In order to study how man makes a living, the distribution of materials, production, institutions, and human traits and customs are analyzed.

Regional Geography In regional geography the basic concern is with the salient characteristics of areas. Emphasis is placed upon patterns and elements of the natural environment and their relationships to human activities. By using the regional technique in studying geographic phenomena, what otherwise might be a bewildering array of facts is brought into focus as an organized, cohesive pattern.

Systematic Geography It is also feasible to study the geography of a small area or the entire surface of the earth in systematic fashion. Settlement, climates, soils, landforms, minerals, water, or crops, among others, may be observed, described, analyzed, and explained. Research in systematic geography has proved to be very valuable.

1. This passage describes geography's
   (1) growth
   (2) scope
   (3) importance
   (4) role in the social sciences
   (5) principles
2. The difference among the five areas of geography described is one of
   (1) method
   (2) importance
   (3) emphasis

(4) recency

(5) objectivity

3. A student interested in the influence of a geographical feature of a region on available jobs would study

   (1) physical geography

   (2) cultural geography

   (3) economic geography

   (4) regional geography

   (5) systematic geography

4. A meteorologist would likely be most interested in

   (1) physical geography

   (2) cultural geography

   (3) economic geography

   (4) regional geography

   (5) systematic geography

5. An urban sociologist would probably study

   (1) physical geography

   (2) cultural geography

   (3) economic geography

   (4) regional geography

   (5) systematic geography

6. A person studying the problems of the Middle East will use the approach found in

   (1) physical geography

   (2) cultural geography

   (3) economic geography

   (4) regional geography

   (5) systematic geography

7. A conservationist studying the effects of such human activities as strip mining and land erosion would turn to

   (1) physical geography

   (2) cultural geography

   (3) economic geography

   (4) regional geography

   (5) systematic geography

8. That aspect of geography that seeks to study in a planned and orderly way the geography of a small area is
  (1) physical geography
  (2) cultural geography
  (3) economic geography
  (4) regional geography
  (5) systematic geography

Answer Key
1. **2**   2. **3**   3. **3**   4. **1**   5. **2**   6. **4**   7. **1**   8. **5**

PRACTICE WITH INTERPRETING TABLES, GRAPHS, AND MAPS

Since study of the social sciences involves the gathering and interpretation of facts, you will frequently encounter various methods for presenting the facts you need. Most often, these facts will be presented in the form of tables, charts, or maps. Let us deal with each of these methods in turn.

Tables

The ability to read tables is an important skill because tables are the most common means of presenting data in the social studies.

What is a table? It is an arrangement of figures, usually in one or more columns, which is intended to show some relationship between the figures. In political science, a table may show the growth of the number of eligible voters in national elections. In economics, a table may show the annual incomes of various groups within the population of a country. A table may also show the relationship between two factors, for example, between the amounts of education of various groups as related to their annual incomes.

First note the title of the table on the next page: Sizes, Populations, and Densities of the World's Largest Nations and Regions.

Now, look at the headings of the columns in the table. Six headings are given: Country, Size, Population 1968, Population 1990, People per Square Mile 1968, People per Square Mile 1990.

Next, locate the columns to which each heading is related. In the first column, the different countries or areas of the world are listed. The next column gives their sizes in square miles. The next two columns list population figures for 1968 and 1990, and the last two give the numbers of people per square mile for the same two dates.

Having identified the title, the column headings, and the columns to which they relate, you are now in a position to *locate facts*.

**SIZES, POPULATIONS, AND DENSITIES
OF THE WORLD'S LARGEST NATIONS AND REGIONS**

1	2	3	4	5	6
		Population (U.N. Estimate)		People per Square Mile	
Country	Size (sq. mi.)	1968	1990	1968	1990
USSR*	8,600,000	238,000,000	290,122,000	28	33.5
Canada	3,850,000	21,000,000	26,620,000	5	7.5
China	3,700,000	730,000,000	1,133,000,000	197	306.7
United States	3,600,000	200,000,000	251,394,000	57	68.3
Brazil	3,300,000	88,000,000	150,368,000	27	45.8
India	1,200,000	534,000,000	853,373,000	437	698.0
Other Areas					
Japan	143,000	101,000,000	123,692,000	706	848.0
Southeast Asia	1,692,000	270,000,000	447,000,000	159	262.9
Middle East	3,784,000	261,000,000	306,400,000	69	81.0
Africa— south of the Sahara	8,600,000	254,000,000	500,000,000	30	62.2

Note the great increase of population in the 22 years that separate the two sets of figures. Scientists estimate that the earth's present population will double in the next 50 years.

*Note that "USSR" refers to all the former republics of the former Soviet Union.

Questions

1. What is the size of the United States?
2. What was the population of India in 1968? What is the U.N. estimate of the population of India in 1990?
3. What was the number of people per square mile in Japan in 1990?
4. What country's population grew to over 1 billion between 1968 and 1990?

Answers

1. **3,600,000 square miles**   3. **848.0**
2. **534,000,000   853,373,000**   4. **China**

Answer Analysis

1. The second column from the left lists sizes. Put your finger at the top of that column, and move it down until you locate the figure on a line with United States—3,600,000.
2. Locate the column for population in 1968. Put your finger at the top of the column, and move it down to the figure on a line with India—534,000,000. Do the same for 1990.
3. Locate the column for people per square mile in 1990. Find the number on a line with Japan—848.0.
4. To answer this question, you have to locate two populations, one in 1968 and one in 1990. You also must locate a figure that is over 1 billion. Scan both columns of population figures. Only one is over 1 billion, that of China in 1990. In the column to the immediate left for 1968, the figure for China's population is 730,000,000, so that figure grew to 1,133,000 in 1990.

Now you are ready to *find relationships between facts.* This type of question requires you to locate one figure and then relate it to at least one other figure.

Questions

1. What is the basic trend of the world's population?
2. What is the basic trend in the number of people per square mile?
3. From 1968 to 1990, what country or area had the smallest increase in population?
4. In what country or area did the number of people per square mile double?

Answers and Analysis

1. Compare column 4 (pop. 1990) with column 3 (pop. 1968). In every instance, the population in 1990 is greater. The conclusion can be reached that population is increasing all over the world.
2. Compare column 6 (people per square mile—1990) with column 5 (people per square mile—1968). The conclusion can be reached that the number of people per square mile is increasing all over the world.

3. Subtracting the figures in column 3 (pop. 1968) from those in column 4 (pop. 1990), it is apparent that Canada had the smallest increase, 5,620,000, in population.

4. Comparing the figures in columns 5 and 6 for people per square mile in 1968 and 1990, it is clear that in Africa—south of the Sahara the number of people per square mile more than doubled, from 30 to 62.2.

Now you can proceed to the most difficult skill of all—*inferring conclusions from the facts presented.* Sometimes you can draw a conclusion from the table alone. Other times, you must add facts from your general knowledge.

Questions

1. What conclusion can you draw from Japan's population figures?
2. What conclusion can you draw about the population in Africa—south of the Sahara?
3. What major problem may exist for Canada's population?
4. What common problems may China, India, and Japan experience?

Answers and Analysis

1. Japan has the most crowded population in the world, with attendant problems of housing, health, and transportation among others.
2. The half-billion population of Africa—south of the Sahara is spread over 8,600,000 square miles. This fact will result in problems of distribution of goods and services to the countries of the area.
3. A similar problem exists for Canada, with the added possibility that adequate manpower may not be available.
4. The high population density in each country suggests potential difficulty in providing food, shelter, and other essential services to the inhabitants.

Summary of How to Read a Table
1. Note the title.
2. Look at the column headings.
3. Locate the column to which the other columns are related.
4. Locate facts.
5. Find relationships between facts.
6. Infer conclusions from the facts presented.

Graphs

The Circle (Pie) Graph

Tables, as you have just seen, are composed of columns of figures selected to show the relationship between facts that the social studies writer considers important. Very often, the author will present these same facts in another way so that you can visualize them more readily and draw conclusions more easily. The writer does this by means of a graph.

Let us look at the following set of facts arranged in a table. They concern the principal religions of the world in the year 1991.

Principal Religions of the World, 1991			
Buddhist	6%	No religion	21%
Christian	33%	Other	1%
Hindu	13%	Para-religions	8%
Islam	18%		

Looking at these facts in table form, you find it hard to draw any ready conclusions. But when you see them in the form of a circle (pie) graph, you are able to immediately visualize the relationships that exist between them.

PRINCIPAL RELIGIONS OF THE WORLD, 1991

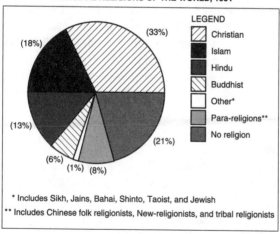

* Includes Sikh, Jains, Bahai, Shinto, Taoist, and Jewish
** Includes Chinese folk religionists, New-religionists, and tribal religionists

Now use this graph to answer the following questions.

Questions

1. Which religion has the most followers?
2. Which of the individually named religions has the fewest followers?
3. Which two religions account for more than half of the world's population?
4. Which proportion of the world's people do not practice a religion?

Answers

1. **Christian**
2. **Buddhist**
3. **Islam and Christianity**
4. **21%**

Answer Analysis

The answers almost leap up at you from the circle graph. The Christian religion has by far the largest slice of the circle; all of the religions combined under "Other" are hardly visible. By visually combining the various slices of the pie, you can see that the Christian and Islamic religions account for just over half of the total pie. By referring to the legend and then back to the pie, you can see that a large slice of the pie represents people who practice no religion. Just by inspection, you can estimate the number at around one-fifth or 20% of the total. The actual figure (21%) is provided.

The circle graph can also help you to compare visually two sets of facts. Here are a circle graph and a graph of another type (the bar graph).

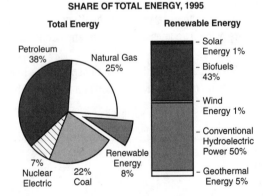

SHARE OF TOTAL ENERGY, 1995

Note the title—Share of Total Energy, 1995
Note the unit used—percent of 100
Note the date—1995

Note the major categories—petroleum, natural gas, renewable energy, coal, nuclear electric

Study both graphs carefully and answer the following questions.

Questions

1. What are the most important sources of energy?
2. To reduce our dependence on oil imports, the use of which sources would have to be increased?
3. What percent of total energy does conventional hydroelectric power contribute?

Answers and Analysis

1. **Three sources—petroleum, natural gas, and coal—amount to 70% of total energy.**
2. **The percents of the other sources—natural gas, coal, renewable energy, and nuclear electric—would have to be increased from their current total of 62%.**
3. **The circle graph tells you that renewable energy contributes 8% of the total energy consumed. Now look at the bar graph. Conventional hydroelectric power contributes half of renewal energy, or 4% of total energy.**

The Line Graph

This common type of graph shows relationships between facts by plotting points on a coordinate plane (two lines are involved) and connecting them with straight lines.

As an example, let us construct a line graph based on the following data about world population growth between 1650 and 2000 (estimated).

Year	World Population in Millions
1650	550
1750	725
1850	1175
1900	1600
1950	2490
1993	5554
2000 (est.)	6500

To construct the graph, draw a horizontal line and, perpendicular to it, a vertical line. Let:

- the horizontal line (technically known as the *abscissa*) represents the period of years from 1650 to 2000 (est.);
- the vertical line (technically known as the *ordinate*) represents world population.

To plot the line graph, start with the first line of data—year 1650, world population 550 million. Go up the ordinate 550, and place a dot there. Then find the next date, 1750, on the abscissa and go up the ordinate and place a dot opposite 725. Next find the date 1850 on the horizontal line and go up to a point opposite 1175. Place a dot there. Continue to do the same thing for each year on the table. Then draw a straight line from dot to dot to complete the graph.

What can you tell or visualize from this line graph?

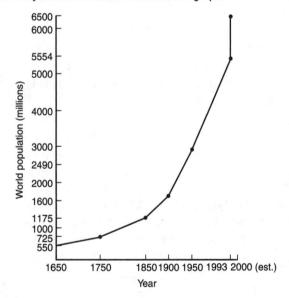

Questions

1. What is the trend of the world population?
2. What was the world population in 1900?
3. In what 50-year period was the increase the greatest?
4. In the period covered by the graph, approximately how many times did the population grow?

Answers
1. **The trend is sharply upward.**
2. **1600 million**
3. **1950–2000 (est.)**
4. **About 12 times, from 550 million to 6500 million**

Answer Analysis
1. The plotted line always trends upward, with the slant becoming steeper in recent decades to indicate accelerating population growth.
2. First find the year 1900 on the abscissa. Then move your finger straight up to the point in line with the ordinate indicating the population. The number is 1600 million.
3. The growth is greatest where the line is steepest—between 1950 and 2000 (est.).
4. The population grew from 550 million to 6500 million, or about 12 times.

The Bar Graph
A bar graph is very much like the line graph we just studied. There is the same visual presentation of one set of facts in relation to another set. There is the same horizontal line (abscissa) representing one set of facts. The same vertical line (ordinate) represents the other set.

For a bar graph, however, you do not put a dot at the point that represents one fact in relation to another, nor do you connect those points by lines. Instead, you make bars of equal width and of heights that indicate the relationship. Thus, you could change the line graph you just studied to a bar graph by making a bar for each point identified.

The bar graph below is entitled "Aging Societies." It gives the percentages of population 65 and over for five countries at four different times, two past and two projected. It also indicates by small pie graphs the

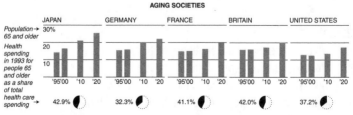

AGING SOCIETIES

Source: Organization of Economic Cooperation and Development

percentages of health spending in 1993, in each country, for people 65 and over as a share of total health care spending.

Use these graphs to answer the following practice questions.

Questions

1. In what country will the government have to spend the most in the year 2020 for health care for the aging?
    (1) Japan
    (2) Germany
    (3) France
    (4) Britain
    (5) United States

2. Which country will have the greatest population under 65 in 2020?
    (1) Japan
    (2) Germany
    (3) France
    (4) Britain
    (5) United States

3. Which countries have the most similar aging characteristics?
    (1) Japan and Germany
    (2) Germany and France
    (3) France and Britain
    (4) Britain and the United States
    (5) Japan and the United States

4. Which country will have the least stable growth of population over 65 for the rest of this century?
    (1) Japan
    (2) Germany
    (3) France
    (4) Britain
    (5) United States

5. What country was the least responsive to the health-care needs of its aging population in 1993?
    (1) Japan
    (2) Germany
    (3) France
    (4) Britain
    (5) United States

Answer Key
1. **1**   2. **5**   3. **3**   4. **1**   5. **2**

Answer Analysis

1. **1** In 2020, 25% of the population of Japan will be 65 or older, at least 4% more than any other country in the graph.
2. **5** In 2020, the United States will be the only country with an over-65 population below 20%.
3. **3** For France and Britain, percents are nearly identical for 1995, 2000, and 2010. The two countries will have the identical percent of population 65 or older in 2020, and in 1995 differed by less than 1% in percent of health care spending for the elderly as a share of total health-care spending.
4. **1** Japan will have an increase in population over 65. The other countries will remain at the same level.
5. **2** The pie graphs show that Germany spent least, approximately 9 to 10% less than France and Britain, for similar numbers of elderly.

Maps

A map is a visual representation of all or part of the surface of the earth. A map may or may not include a number of aids to help you visualize the surface it is depicting. It will always include a *title*. If the map uses symbols, it will always include a *legend* (or key) to give the meaning of those symbols. It may also include:

- latitude and longitude to indicate direction and help you to find a specific location;
- a scale of miles to indicate what distance on the map equals a specific distance in miles on land;
- a grid, or square, usually identified by a set of letters on one axis (vertical or horizontal) and a set of numbers on the other, so that a place can be found in, for example, a grid identified as F 3 or H 7;

Important aids that you must learn to use in order to read a map are its *title* and its *legend* (or key). Since ancient times, maps have played a unique role in presenting information about the world, and maps are extremely useful in locating places and distances in any part of the world.

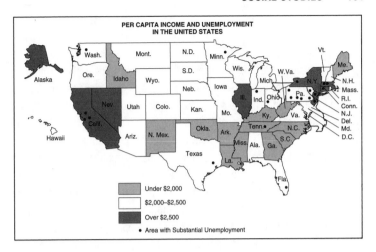

In the 1500s Gerardus Mercator, a Dutch mapmaker, coined the word *atlas* to describe a collection of maps. The atlas is unique because only it, with its maps, actually shows *where* things are located in the world. Only on a map can the countries, cities, roads, rivers, and lakes covering a vast area be seen all at once in their relative locations. Routes between places can be traced, trips planned, boundaries of neighboring countries examined, distances between places measured, and the paths of rivers and the sizes of lakes visualized.

Places can be found by looking up the place name in the index at the back of the atlas. There is usually a letter-number key next to the name of the place, **A3**, for example. This will help you find the place on a grid or square on the map. The letters are usually located to the left or right of the map, the numbers to the top or bottom of the map.

	1	2	3
A			•
B			

Sometimes, if the place is big enough, you can find it on the map visually.

Distances between places can be figured by using the scale of miles, usually on the bottom of the page.

Place a ruler over the scale to find how many miles a given ruling is, then place the ruler between two places on the map to find the length. For example, if a distance on the scale is 20 miles to one inch and the distance on the map is 1¹/₂ inches, the distance is 1¹/₂ times 20, or 30 miles between the two points on the map. Determining directions can be done by using a series of lines drawn across the map—the lines of latitude and longitude. Lines of latitude are drawn east and west, from left to right. Lines of longitude are drawn north and south, from top to bottom. The lines of latitude appear as curved lines; the lines of longitude are straight lines that come together toward the top of the map.

Lines of latitude and longitude not only help you find direction, they help you locate places. Parallels of latitude are numbered in degrees north and south of the equator. Lines of longitude are numbered in degrees east and west of an imaginary line running through Greenwich, England, near London. Any place on earth can be located by the latitude and longitude lines running through it. For example, Chicago, Illinois, is located at 41° 53' N (north of the equator), and 87° 40' W (west of the Greenwich prime meridian—the line of 0° 0' longitude).

Maps usually use symbols, points, dots, or stars (for cities, capital cities, or points of interest), or lines (roads, rivers, railroads). Help in understanding the symbols is provided by a legend or key found in an atlas near the map. The map on the previous page is in many respects typical of the maps you will encounter. The following questions will sharpen your skills in map reading.

Questions

1. What is the *title* of the map?
2. What three indications make up the *legend*?
3. What does • mean?
4. What is the average per capita income of the population of the state of New York?
5. What is the average per capita income of the population of the state of New Mexico?
6. What is the average per capita income of the population of the state of Iowa?
7. Which state has a larger per capita income, Alaska or Hawaii?

Answers and Analysis

1. The title of the map is "Per Capita Income and Unemployment in the United States." See the heading above the map.
2. The dark gray areas indicate per capita income over $2,500; the white areas indicate per capita income between $2,000 and $2,500; the light gray areas indicate per capita income under $2,000.
3. The • indicates an area with substantial unemployment.
4. Since New York is a dark gray area, its per capita income is over $2,500.
5. Since New Mexico is a light gray area, its per capita income is under $2,000.
6. Since Iowa is a white area, its per capita income is between $2,000 and $2,500.
7. Since Alaska is a dark gray area (per capita income over $2,500) and Hawaii is a white area (per capita income between $2,000 and $2,500), Alaska has a larger per capita income than Hawaii.

This map introduces a complication, the idea of substantial unemployment, a feature that is not typical of most maps. That idea is the topic of questions 3–7 that follow.

Additional Questions

1. Per capita income in Maine is most nearly equal to per capita income in
   (1) Washington
   (2) Idaho
   (3) Utah
   (4) Nevada
   (5) Missouri
2. Which generalization is best supported by the map?
   (1) All New England states have per capita incomes of over $2,000.
   (2) All states along the Atlantic seaboard have a high per capita income.
   (3) All southern states have incomes below $2,000.
   (4) All states along the Pacific coast have per capita incomes of $2,000 or over.
   (5) Most states have per capita incomes over $2,500.

3. According to the map, in which state is unemployment a major problem?
   (1) Pennsylvania
   (2) Florida
   (3) Alabama
   (4) Texas
   (5) Washington

4. Which state has both a per capita income of between $2,000 and $2,500, and an area with substantial unemployment?
   (1) Kansas
   (2) Ohio
   (3) Kentucky
   (4) Mississippi
   (5) California

5. Which state has a high per capita income and substantial unemployment?
   (1) Florida
   (2) Louisiana
   (3) Minnesota
   (4) California
   (5) Nevada

6. Unemployment is less of a problem in Indiana than in
   (1) Massachusetts
   (2) Tennessee
   (3) Mississippi
   (4) Louisiana
   (5) Arizona

7. Which conclusion concerning the state of Tennessee is supported by the map?
   (1) It is larger than Montana and richer than Mississippi.
   (2) It has more unemployment than Georgia and was richer than Kentucky.
   (3) It is as rich as Arkansas and poorer than Nevada.
   (4) It had less unemployment than Oklahoma and more unemployment than Georgia.
   (5) It is smaller than Minnesota and richer than Illinois.

Answer Key

1. **2**   2. **4**   3. **1**   4. **2**   5. **4**   6. **1**   7. **3**

Answer Analysis

1. **2**   The answer is Choice 2 since both states are light gray areas, with per capita incomes under $2,000.

2. **4**   Choice 4 is correct. California had a per capita income of over $2,500; Washington and Oregon had incomes between $2,000 and $2,500; all have incomes of $2,000 or over per capita. Choice 1 is incorrect since Maine has an income of less than $2,000. Choice 2 is wrong since three states—North Carolina, South Carolina, and Georgia—have incomes lower than $2,000. Choice 3 is incorrect since Texas, Florida, and Virginia have incomes above $2,000. Choice 5 is incorrect; only 10 states have per capita incomes over $2,500.

3. **1**   On the map, Pennsylvania has six dotted areas with substantial unemployment; Florida, Washington, and Texas have one each and Alabama has none. Choice 1 is correct.

4. **2**   You have to find a white area with a dot. Only Ohio, Choice 2, fits these criteria.

5. **4**   You have to find a dark gray area with several dots. Only California, Choice 4, fits this description.

6. **1**   You need to locate a state with more than one dot since Indiana has one such dot. The correct answer is Choice 1, Massachusetts, which has two dots.

7. **3**   The map compares Tennessee with other states with regard to per capita income *and* unemployment. Choice 1 is wrong since Montana is larger. Choice 2 is wrong since Tennessee is not richer than Kentucky but the same. Choice 4 is wrong since Tennessee has more unemployment than both Oklahoma and Georgia. Choice 5 is incorrect since Tennessee is poorer than Illinois. Choice 3 is correct; both Tennessee and Arkansas have per capita incomes of less than $2,000, while Nevada has a per capita income of over $2,500.

BASICS IN INTERPRETING POLITICAL CARTOONS

Political cartoons, as a distinct art form, first became important in the second half of the nineteenth century.

1.   Most cartoons deal with a single important issue, usually an election campaign issue, questions of peace or war, or corruption in government.

2. The cartoonist frequently uses an exaggerated likeness, or caricature, of some well-known person or institution, for example, Uncle Sam, as the main focus of attention. Or he or she may use or create a familiar symbol to represent an important idea; a dove for peace, a tiger for Tammany Hall.

3. Reading is kept to a minimum so that the appeal is largely visual. A few words at most are used to drive home an idea, so the visual appeal of the political cartoon is universal. Boss Tweed pointed out that, even if his followers could not read, they could "look at the d——n pictures." Thus, the cartoonist presents an issue in simplified form, stripped of all relatively unimportant details, in a way that his readers can understand.

4. The cartoonist graphically presents his or her own point of view or that of a newspaper or magazine. The cartoonist is usually openly anticorruption or antiwar, and portrays the object of his or her criticism in the ugliest manner possible.

Because of the visually appealing use of a caricature and/or a symbol focusing critically on a single important issue, the political cartoon is a powerful means of shaping public opinion. Its appeal to the emotions is difficult to equal, and its influence continues to the present day.

How, then, do you interpret a political cartoon when you encounter it on the High School Equivalency Examination?

Here are a few suggestions:

Step 1. *Identify the caricatures or symbols used in the cartoon.* For historical cartoons, you may need some social studies background. In contemporary cartoons, the caricatures and symbols are easier to identify.

Step 2. *Identify the issue being exposed or criticized by the cartoonist.*

Step 3. *Determine the point of view being expressed by the cartoonist.*

Now look at the following cartoon, study it, and try to answer the questions based on it.

Questions

1. What issue is the subject of this cartoon?
2. What do the elephant and the donkey represent?
3. What is each trying to do?
4. What point of view is the cartoonist expressing?

Answers and Analysis

1. The issue is campaign-funding abuse, as indicated on the cookie jar.
2. The elephant is the traditional symbol of the Republican party; the donkey, of the Democratic party.
3. Each has a hand in the cookie jar and is trying to extract money for the campaign.
4. The cartoonist finds both parties at fault even though he portrays the equally guilty Republicans expressing disapproval of the Democrats.

PRACTICE WITH INTERPRETING POLITICAL CARTOONS

1. The main purpose of the preceding cartoon is to
   (1) portray the conflict between Republicans and Democrats
   (2) show the superiority of the Republicans over the Democrats
   (3) show the superiority of the Democrats over the Republicans
   (4) show that Republicans and Democrats are both at fault in campaign fund-raising
   (5) show that Democrats do not feel guilty about their campaign fund-raising
2. The cartoonist achieves his purpose by
   (1) exaggerating the conduct of both parties
   (2) arousing our sympathy for both parties
   (3) portraying the humor of the conduct of both parties
   (4) favoring Republicans over Democrats
   (5) showing the irony of the Republicans' conduct

Answer Key

1. **4**   2. **5**

Answer Analysis

1. **4**   Choice 4 is correct because the cartoonist indicates that both parties have their hands in the cookie jar and are guilty of campaign fund-raising abuses. Neither party is superior to the other, nor does either feel guilty.
2. **5**   The irony arises from the fact that each party has a hand in the jar, yet the Republican elephant is faulting the Democratic donkey for an abuse of which both are equally guilty.

PRACTICE WITH INTERPRETING HISTORICAL DOCUMENTS

The Declaration of Independence

When in the Course of human events it becomes necessary for one people to dissolve the political bonds which have connected them with another, and to assume among the powers of the earth, the separate and equal station to which the Laws of Nature and of Nature's God entitle them, a decent respect to the opinions of mankind requires that they should declare the causes which impel them to the separation.

We hold these truths to be self-evident, that all men are created equal, that they are endowed by their Creator with certain unalienable Rights, that among these are Life, Liberty and the pursuit of Happiness. That to secure these rights, Governments are instituted among Men, deriving their just powers from the consent of the governed. That whenever any Form of Government becomes destructive of these ends, it is the Right of the People to alter or to abolish it, and to institute new Government, laying its foundation on such principles and organizing its powers in such form, as to them shall seem most likely to effect their Safety and Happiness.

Questions

1. The main purpose of the Declaration of Independence is to
   (1) justify separation from another government
   (2) obey the laws of nature
   (3) earn a decent respect for others' opinions
   (4) influence the course of human events
   (5) join the powers of the earth
2. All of the following rights are included EXCEPT
   (1) life
   (2) liberty
   (3) pursuit of happiness
   (4) equal opportunity
   (5) safety
3. The Declaration states that governments derive their powers from
   (1) the powers of the earth
   (2) the Laws of Nature
   (3) the Laws of Nature's God
   (4) the opinions of mankind
   (5) the governed

Answer Key

1. **1**   2. **4**   3. **5**

Answer Analysis

1. **1**   The Declaration states that "a decent respect to the opinions of mankind requires that (a people) should declare the causes which impel them to the separation."

2. **4** All the rights are mentioned except equal opportunity, although that might be interpreted as being included in the pursuit of happiness.

3. **5** It is stated that governments derive "their just powers from the consent of the governed."

PRACTICE WITH INTERPRETING PHOTOGRAPHS

Question

1. The purpose of this photograph is to depict
    (1) the illegal use of child labor
    (2) factory conditions
    (3) a strict foreman
    (4) ill-clothed children
    (5) oyster shucking

Answer Analysis

3. **1** Young children were illegally used in a sweatshop to make clothing.

PRACTICE WITH INTERPRETING PRACTICAL DOCUMENTS

Internal Revenue Service Publication 529
Job Search Expenses

You can deduct certain expenses in looking for a new job in your present occupation, even if you do not get a new job. You cannot deduct these expenses if:

(1) You are looking for a job in a new occupation, or

(2) There was a substantial break between the ending of your last job and your looking for a new one.

You cannot deduct your expenses if you are seeking employment for the first time.

Employment and outplacement agency fees. You can deduct employment and outplacement agency fees you pay in looking for a new job in your present occupation.

Résumé. You can deduct amounts you spend for typing, printing, and mailing copies of a résumé to prospective employers if you are looking for a new job in your present occupation.

Travel and transportation expenses. If you travel to an area and, while there, you look for a new job in your present occupation, you may be able to deduct travel expenses to and from the area. You can deduct the travel expenses if the trip is primarily to look for a new job.

Questions

1. You can deduct expenses if you are a mechanic
   (1) looking for a new job as a computer programmer
   (2) returning to work after many years
   (3) looking for your first job
   (4) looking for a job in another garage
   (5) going back to school

2. Expenses that can be deducted include all of the following EXCEPT
   (1) cost of distributing your résumé
   (2) travel time primarily for personal activity
   (3) travel looking for a new job in a new area as a mechanic
   (4) travel looking for a new job as a mechanic in your present area
   (5) certain travel and transportation expenses

3. The main purpose of this regulation is to
    (1) get more tax money from job seekers
    (2) ease the burden of job seekers
    (3) catch violators of Internal Revenue Service regulations
    (4) list allowable deductions
    (5) list expenses that are not deductible

Answer Key

1. **4**   2. **2**   3. **2**

Answer Analysis

1. **4**   It is specifically stated that you can deduct expenses if you are looking for a job in your present occupation. The mechanic, in this case, will still be a mechanic in another garage.
2. **2**   The expenses for a trip on personal business cannot be deducted.
3. **2**   The instructions of the Internal Revenue Service help job seekers by allowing them to deduct legitimate expenses.

HANDLING SOCIAL STUDIES SKILLS QUESTIONS

The Social Studies test no longer tests your ability to recall information such as dates, isolated facts, or events. It now emphasizes higher level skills. It does so by testing your ability to understand the written word or graphics, to analyze and apply the given information and ideas, and to evaluate the accuracy of the information and the conclusions based on it.

COMPREHENSION ITEMS

Twenty percent of the test, or about 13 items, require you to understand the meaning and purpose of written material, passages or quotations, and information contained in maps, graphs, tables, and political cartoons. These items test your ability to restate information, summarize ideas, and identify incorrectly stated ideas. The question will usually include a quotation and be followed by the words "This most nearly means" or "The best explanation of this statement is" or "The author believes or suggests."

EXAMPLE

A CODE

Never DO, BE, or SUFFER anything in soul or body, less or more, but what tends to the glory of God.

Resolved, never to lose one moment of time; but improve it the most profitable way I possibly can.

Resolved, to think much, on all occasions, of my own dying, and of the common circumstances which attend death.

Resolved, to maintain the strictest temperance in eating and drinking.

Question

1. The author of the code believes that people should be mainly concerned with
   (1) monetary issues
   (2) luxuries
   (3) patriotism
   (4) spiritual matters
   (5) politics

Answer and Analysis

The passage reflects the ideas of Puritanism, a code that stresses spiritual concerns.

You can answer this question correctly if you read the passage carefully and decide what is being emphasized. Then, look for the answer that identifies that emphasis. In this question, the emphasis is on living for the glory of God, concern for one's manner of dying, and discipline in such material concerns as eating and drinking. The spiritual is stressed. Indeed, you can answer the question even if you do not know it is the Puritan Code that is being quoted. The correct choice is 4.

APPLICATION ITEMS

Thirty percent of the test, or about 19 items, require you to use information and ideas in a situation other than that indicated to you in the question. Applying information and ideas is a high-level skill because you must not only understand the general content, but also be able to transfer it to the context of a particular situation. In other words, you must go from the general information you are given to a specific case.

EXAMPLE

The principle of judicial review provides for the judiciary to determine the constitutionality of both state and federal laws.

Question

1. Which action best illustrates the principle of judicial review?
   (1) Congress enacts civil rights legislation.
   (2) The Senate approves appointment of federal judges.
   (3) An act of Congress is struck down by the Supreme Court.
   (4) The states refuse to cooperate with the federal authorities in crime control.
   (5) Congress overrides a presidential veto.

Answer and Analysis

The principle of judicial review means the power of the U.S. Supreme Court to rule on the constitutionality of acts of Congress, state legislatures, executive officers, and lower courts. The only choice that involves a court action is Choice 3, a specific application of this principle to an act of Congress. You must apply the principle of judicial or court reexamination to an act of Congress.

The purpose of another form of question or item on the High School Equivalency Examination Social Studies Test is to test your ability to apply given information that defines ideas in historical documents, divisions of subject matter in the social studies, systems of government, economics, psychology, and groups of basic concepts in the four areas of the social studies. You will have to:

1. understand information that is presented in defined categories, usually five in number;
2. relate a situation, action, or event to those categories;
3. arrive at an application of the information in the categories to the given situation, action, or event.

An illustration will make this clear. In this example, the information presented in defined categories is the central idea of each of five articles of the Bill of Rights, the first ten amendments to the Constitution.

EXAMPLE

The first ten amendments to the Constitution make up the Bill of Rights ratified by Congress in 1791. Parts of five of the amendments read as follows:

(A) Article 1—Congress shall make no law...abridging the freedom of speech or of the press.

(B) Article 2—The right of the people to keep and bear arms shall not be infringed.

(C) Article 5—No person...shall be compelled in any criminal case to be a witness against himself, nor be deprived of life, liberty, or property, without due process of law.

(D) Article 7—The right to trial by jury shall be preserved.

(E) Article 8—Excessive bail shall not be required...nor cruel and unusual punishments inflicted.

The questions that follow deal with three ways in which the given information can be used by three individuals in three different situations.

Questions
Indicate the amendment (article) most likely to be cited in support of his or her position by

1. an opponent of capital punishment
    (1) Article 1
    (2) Article 2
    (3) Article 5
    (4) Article 7
    (5) Article 8
2. a member of the National Rifle Association
    (1) Article 1
    (2) Article 2
    (3) Article 5
    (4) Article 7
    (5) Article 8

3. a person accused of a criminal act who is testifying at his or her trial
   (1) Article 1
   (2) Article 2
   (3) Article 5
   (4) Article 7
   (5) Article 8

Answers and Analysis

You must apply the categorized information to each situation.

The correct answer to question 1 is Choice 5. An opponent of capital punishment will cite Article 8's prohibition against cruel and unusual punishment.

The correct answer to question 2 is Choice 2. A member of the National Rifle Association will cite Article 2, "The right of the people to keep and bear arms shall not be infringed."

The correct answer to question 3 is Choice 3. The person on trial might "take the Fifth," citing the provision of Article 5 that "no person...shall be compelled in any criminal case to be a witness against himself."

Try another item set in this format.

EXAMPLE

Psychology is the science of behavior and of human thought processes. There are a number of closely interrelated branches of human psychology.

(A) Social psychology investigates the effect of the group on the behavior of the individual.

(B) Applied psychology puts to practical use the discoveries and theories of psychology as in industrial psychology.

(C) Clinical psychology diagnoses and treats mental disorders and mental illnesses.

(D) Comparative psychology deals with different behavioral organizations of animals including human beings.

(E) Physiological psychology attempts to understand the effects of body functions on human behavior.

Questions

Each of the following describes a proposed study. Indicate which branch of psychology is most clearly involved.

1. A company wants to study the effects of music piped into a factory where workers are on an assembly line.
   (1) Social psychology
   (2) Applied psychology
   (3) Clinical psychology
   (4) Comparative psychology
   (5) Physiological psychology

2. A drug rehabilitation center wants to study the role of peer pressure on a teenager in a drug prevention program.
   (1) Social psychology
   (2) Applied psychology
   (3) Clinical psychology
   (4) Comparative psychology
   (5) Physiological psychology

3. A grant is available for a study of schizophrenia, a disorder characterized by hallucinations and delusions.
   (1) Social psychology
   (2) Applied psychology
   (3) Clinical psychology
   (4) Comparative psychology
   (5) Physiological psychology

Answers and Analysis

The correct answer to question 1 is Choice 2. Applied psychology puts the findings of industrial psychologists to practical use, in this case for people who work on an assembly line.

The correct answer to question 2 is Choice 1. Social psychologists are concerned with the effects of groups, in this case teenagers, who put pressure on their peers to use drugs.

The correct answer to question 3 is Choice 3. Clinical psychologists would apply for the grant because of their interest in schizophrenia, a mental disorder.

ANALYSIS ITEMS

Thirty percent of the test, or about 19 items, requires you to break down information into its parts to determine their interrelationships. These items involve the ability to identify cause-and-effect relationships, separate fact from opinion, separate conclusions from supporting statements, and show that you can recognize assumptions on which conclusions are based.

Question

1. Democracy may be defined as government by the people directly or through representatives chosen in free elections. Which quotation from the Declaration of Independence best describes the fundamental principle of democracy in the United States?

    (1) "imposing taxes on us without our consent"
    (2) "governments long established should not be changed for light and transient causes"
    (3) "depriving us, in many cases, of the benefits of trial by jury"
    (4) "deriving their just powers from the consent of the governed"
    (5) "quartering large bodies of armed troops among us"

Answer and Analysis

Not only must you understand the meaning of each possible answer, but you must analyze it to determine which is a *fundamental* principle of government in the United States. First you must understand; then you must analyze.

You have to go through all of the following steps:

Choice 1: imposing taxes without consent—meaning taxation without representation

Choice 2: governments long established should not be changed for light causes—meaning change in government must be for good reason

Choice 3: benefits of trial by jury—meaning the right to trial by jury

Choice 4: deriving powers from consent of the governed—meaning the government gets its power from those it governs, the people

Choice 5: quartering armed troops—meaning compulsion to keep soldiers in homes

Now the test of a *fundamental* principle of government in the United States must be applied to each.

Choice 1 is not fundamental; it is a grievance.

Choice 2 refers not to the government of the United States, but to changing governments in general.

Choice 3, trial by jury, is an important right, but it is not as fundamental as Choice 4, which states that the U.S. government is a democracy in which the people rule through their elected representatives. This is an absolutely fundamental principle.

Choice 4 is the only correct interpretation that can be made.

Choice 5 refers to unauthorized quartering of soldiers—important, but not fundamental.

EVALUATION ITEMS

Twenty percent of the test (about 13 items) is the most difficult. You must make judgments about the soundness or accuracy of information. These questions test your ability to determine whether facts are adequately documented or proved, whether they are appropriately used to support conclusions, and whether they are used correctly or incorrectly in the presentation of opinions or arguments.

Question
1. Which statement is an opinion rather than a fact?
    (1) France was involved in the Vietnam conflict before the United States entered it.
    (2) There are tensions between mainland China and Taiwan.
    (3) Peace will be achieved by regional agreements throughout the world.
    (4) Great Britain has become a full member of the European Common Market.
    (5) The United States is a member of the North Atlantic Treaty Organization.

Answer and Analysis
Five statements are presented. Four are facts that can be proved or verified by evidence—that France was involved in Vietnam; that mainland China and Taiwan have tensions; that Great Britain is a member of the

European Common Market; that the United States is a member of the North Atlantic Treaty Organization. Choice 3, peace will be achieved by regional agreements throughout the world, is an opinion or a hypothesis—not a fact—and it remains to be proved.

PRACTICE WITH SOCIAL STUDIES SKILLS QUESTIONS

Comprehension

1. During the last 150 years, immigrants were attracted to the United States because manpower needs increased. This occurred when the United States was experiencing periods of
    (1) economic expansion
    (2) economic depression
    (3) war
    (4) political change
    (5) stability

2. "The privilege to be involved and to conduct a business in any manner that one pleases is not guaranteed by the Constitution. The right to engage in certain businesses may be subject to various conditions. Laws regulating businesses have been found to be valid. We find no justification to reject the state law under question."

    Which is best illustrated by the passage?
    (1) residual powers
    (2) legislative consent
    (3) judicial review
    (4) executive order
    (5) executive privilege

3. Which is a basic assumption of the graduated income tax?
    (1) The ability to pay increases as wealth increases.
    (2) Each wage earner should contribute to the government the same percentage of his or her income.
    (3) The middle class should bear the burden of financing the government.
    (4) Citizens should pay the costs of government services in proportion to their use of such services.
    (5) Taxes on the wealthy should not be too great.

4. "In a sense the people of the Third World were forced to help pay for the Industrial Revolution in the West."

Which statement most clearly supports this viewpoint?
(1) The colonizing powers encouraged industries in their colonies.
(2) Western nations depended upon raw materials from their colonies.
(3) Financial centers of the world blocked investments in these new nations.
(4) The Third World is now experiencing an Industrial Revolution.
(5) The Third World supplied most of the manpower needed by the West.

5. "Public opinion is of major significance in social control."

The author of this statement most probably means that
(1) the influence of public opinion on government leaders is very limited
(2) problem solving is simplified when public opinion is not known
(3) public opinion may be predicted accurately, especially in the time of national crisis
(4) government officials must pay attention to public opinion in the formulation of policies
(5) polls provide little help to lawmakers

Analysis

THE BUSINESS CYCLE

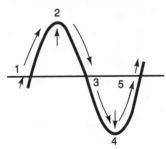

6. If economic indicators place the economy at a point on the cycle between 1 and 2, then the Council of Economic Advisers would most likely suggest which action to the president?
(1) planned deficit spending
(2) increasing income tax rates

   (3) lowering interest rates

   (4) increasing government expenditures

   (5) encouraging higher wages

7. "The showpieces are, with rare exceptions, the industries dominated by a handful of large firms. The foreign visitor, brought to the United States...visits the same firms as do the attorneys of the Department of Justice in their search for monopolies."

The best explanation of this seemingly contradictory behavior is that

   (1) only the largest corporations will allow foreign visitors to inspect their factories

   (2) both State and Justice Department officials oppose the development of monopolies

   (3) the developing countries of the world are interested only in large corporations

   (4) the largest corporations often pioneer in research and production methods

   (5) small firms do not welcome foreign investment

8. "Why, by interweaving our destiny with that of any part of Europe, entangle our peace and prosperity in the toils of European ambition, rivalship, interest, humor, or caprice?"

Which action by the United States best reflects the philosophy expressed in this quotation?

   (1) passage of legislation restricting immigration

   (2) rejection of the Treaty of Versailles

   (3) enactment of the Lend-Lease Act

   (4) approval of the United Nations Charter

   (5) membership in the North Atlantic Treaty Organization

9. "If a nation expects to be ignorant and free, in a state of civilization, it expects what never was and never will be."

Which idea is most strongly supported by this statement?

   (1) the government's right to tax

   (2) universal suffrage

   (3) a strong central government

   (4) compulsory education

   (5) abolition of slavery

10. "Ours is a country where people...can attain to the most elevated positions or acquire a large amount of wealth...according to their talents, prudence, and personal exertions."

This quotation most clearly supports the idea that
(1) upward social mobility and the work ethic are closely related
(2) economic collectivism is part of American life
(3) regulated capitalism reflects private initiative
(4) the United States has a centrally controlled economic system
(5) the U.S. economic system favors the wealthy

Application

11. Which is the most valid statement concerning the problem of balancing human wants with limited resources?
(1) It exists only in societies with a free enterprise economy.
(2) It has been solved in nations with strong governmental controls over economic activity.
(3) It has become less of a problem with the advancements in technology.
(4) It exists in all societies, no matter what the economic system.
(5) It will be solved by the year 2000.

12. A "strict constructionist," one who would permit the federal government to exercise only those powers specifically granted by the U.S. Constitution, would favor which of the following actions?
(1) the institution of programs for social reform
(2) annexation of territory by the United States
(3) bypassing constitutional restraints
(4) limiting the power of the federal government
(5) increasing the power of the states

A basic principle of the U.S. Constitution is the division of governmental power in the executive, the legislative, and the judicial branches. Legislative powers are vested in Congress; judicial powers, in the Supreme Court and federal court system; executive powers, in the president and his governmental machinery. Thus, a system of checks and balances exists among the three branches of government.

Each of the following is an example of the system of checks and balances in operation. Identify the one branch that is checking the other by choosing the appropriate response.

13. Congress overrides a presidential veto.
    (1) the executive checks the legislative
    (2) the executive balances the judicial
    (3) the judicial balances the legislative
    (4) the legislative checks the executive
    (5) the legislative checks the judicial

14. The Senate refuses to confirm a presidential nominee for an ambassadorship.
    (1) the executive checks the legislative
    (2) the executive balances the judicial
    (3) the judicial balances the legislative
    (4) the legislative checks the executive
    (5) the legislative checks the judicial

15. The president nominates a Supreme Court justice.
    (1) the executive checks the legislative
    (2) the executive balances the judicial
    (3) the judicial balances the legislative
    (4) the legislative checks the executive
    (5) the legislative checks the judicial

Evaluation

16. Which statement would be most *difficult* to prove?
    (1) Japan's emperors have reigned but have seldom ruled.
    (2) The workers of the United States are better workers than those of Japan.
    (3) In the post-World War II period, the United States was the source of much cultural borrowing by the Japanese.
    (4) Japanese technology in the 1970s was more advanced than it was in the 1940s.
    (5) The cost of living in Japan has been rising ever since World War II.

17. Which statement would be most *difficult* to prove?
    (1) Popular ideas of third parties in the United States tend to be adopted by the major political parties.
    (2) The Articles of Confederation rendered more authority to the state government than to the federal government.
    (3) The Sherman Antitrust Act was used to reduce the effectiveness of labor unions.
    (4) World War II was necessary in order to end the Great Depression.
    (5) The right to vote has been extended in the twentieth century.

18. Which information about country *X* would be most useful to the head of a government establishing a foreign policy toward country *X*?
   (1) an analysis of the national resources and goals of country *X*
   (2) a file containing the major public statements made by the leaders of country *X* concerning their nation's foreign policies
   (3) an analysis by religious leaders of the major religious groups and beliefs of the people of country *X*
   (4) a newspaper report summarizing the treaties and international agreements of country *X*
   (5) knowledge of the party to which leaders of country *X* belong

19. Which statement expresses an opinion rather than a fact?
   (1) The United States did not join the League of Nations.
   (2) At one time, the United States was on the gold standard.
   (3) President Franklin D. Roosevelt made unnecessary concessions to the Russians at Yalta.
   (4) The Oregon Dispute was settled by extending the 49th parallel to the Pacific Ocean.
   (5) The United States is a member of NATO.

20. "The privilege to be involved and to conduct a business in any manner that one pleases is not guaranteed by the Constitution. The right to engage in certain businesses may be subject to various conditions. Laws regulating businesses have been found to be valid. We find no justification to reject the state law under question."

Which concept would most likely be REJECTED by the author of this passage?
   (1) laissez-faire
   (2) welfare
   (3) competition
   (4) profit motive
   (5) antitrust legislation

Answer Key

1. **1**	4. **2**	7. **4**	10. **1**	13. **4**	16. **2**	19. **3**
2. **3**	5. **4**	8. **2**	11. **4**	14. **4**	17. **4**	20. **1**
3. **1**	6. **2**	9. **4**	12. **4**	15. **2**	18. **1**	

5

SCIENCE

READING AND INTERPRETING SCIENCE QUESTIONS

There are several types of questions on the Science test, and each calls for a specific plan of attack.

SINGLE-ITEM QUESTIONS

In this type, a short paragraph of one or two sentences is followed by a single question. Your first task in dealing with this kind of question is to identify the main idea or ideas presented, and the best way to do this is to start by reading the paragraph and the question quickly, without stopping to be sure you understand every point. This will give you some sense of the content of the question and of the kind of information you will need to answer it. Fix in your mind the main idea of the paragraph.

Next, reread the question carefully. You may be able to select the correct answer at once. If you have any doubt, go back to the paragraph and reread it carefully, searching for the answer to the question.

Practice this technique on the following question:

Question

Growing plants will not develop their green color, caused by the chlorophyll in their leaves, unless they have both sunlight and the necessary genetic system.

If a seedling growing in dim light turns out to be colorless, what could be done to find out why?

1. Give it a new set of genes.
2. Add chlorophyll to the soil.
3. Graft it onto a green plant.
4. Move it into the sunlight.
5. Add fertilizer to the soil.

Answer and Analysis

A quick reading tells you that the main idea deals with the factors involved in the development of a plant's green color. Now go back to the paragraph and read it again. After rereading, you know that the crucial factors are sunlight and genes. This narrows the answer possibilities to Choices 1 and 4. Since there is no way to give the plant a new set of genes, the answer is Choice 4.

MULTIPLE-ITEM QUESTIONS BASED ON READINGS

Some questions require you to read a passage consisting of several paragraphs and then to answer a number of questions about the material. In this case, you need to study the passage carefully *before* you look at the questions. As you read, note two or three main ideas.

To find the main ideas in the passage, look for key words. These are words such as *aorta* and *nucleus* and *ecosystem* that are normally used in a scientific context. Once you have found these words, they should lead you to one of the main ideas in the passage.

EXAMPLE

The annual migration of birds is a complex process that is only partly understood. Some birds that hatch in the Arctic fly thousands of miles to South America each winter, and then return to the place where they were born. The adults make these trips separately from their offspring. The young birds, however, find their way to the correct wintering grounds even though no adult bird shows them the way. No one knows how they are able to do this.

Biologists do understand, however, that in temperate zones the urge to migrate is prompted by a change in the length of daylight. As days grow shorter in the fall, certain physical changes occur in the birds, such as degeneration of the ovaries or testes. These changes are accompanied by restlessness and the urge to fly south.

There is some evidence that birds navigate using many clues, including the earth's magnetic field, the position of the sun in the sky, visible land forms, and even the pattern of the stars at night. How they know the route, however, is a complete mystery. It can be called instinct, but that is simply a word that explains little.

As you read this passage through for the first time, you should identify several key words, such as *migration, degeneration, ovaries, testes, navigate, magnetic field*. Now use these words to locate the main ideas in the passage. They will probably lead you to three main ideas: (1) the changing length of daylight is the signal that prompts migration; (2) birds use a number of clues to navigate; and (3) how they know the route is completely unknown.

Once you have these main ideas firmly fixed in your mind, you are ready to read the questions. Refer to the passage as needed to find the answers.

Question
What is the most probable factor that prompts birds to migrate north in the spring?
1. depletion of the food supply during the winter
2. the disappearance of snow from the ground
3. the coming of warmer weather
4. the increase in the amount of daylight
5. the instinct to fly north

Answer and Analysis
One of the main ideas tells you that, in the fall, migration is prompted by the decreasing length of daylight. It is surely reasonable to suppose that the reverse is true in the spring, so the answer is Choice 4.

Question
What has the study of migration revealed about how birds know what route to follow?
1. Young birds learn by following their parents.
2. Birds are born with an instinct that tells them the route.
3. Birds use several different means of navigation.
4. The changing length of daylight gives birds the necessary clues.
5. So far, investigation has not given any answers to the question.

Answer and Analysis
One of the main ideas, already extracted from the passage, is Choice 5—the answer. The passage says that Choice 1 is not true, and Choice 2 offers a word, *instinct*, but not an explanation. Choices 3 and 4 are true, but irrelevant to this particular question.

QUESTIONS BASED ON GRAPHS, DIAGRAMS, AND DATA TABLES

Line Graphs

A line graph is a common way to show how something changes or to show the relationship between two or more things. This kind of graph uses two scales, one going up the left side of the graph, called the vertical axis, and another along the bottom of the graph, called the horizontal axis.

If you are given a line graph on the GED test, read it carefully. Note the title, the labels on the vertical and horizontal axes, and the legend or key if there is one. Take your time, and pay attention to all of the printed material as well as the lines and the scales. Only then will you be ready to answer questions based on the line graph.

Here is a sample for you to work on:

EXAMPLE
The graph below represents the temperatures of a white sidewalk and a black asphalt driveway on a sunny day. The surfaces are side by side, and the measurements were made during a 24-hour period.

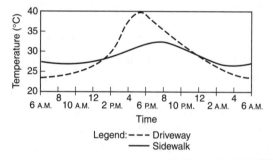

Legend: --- Driveway
——— Sidewalk

What are the features of this graph? The vertical axis represents temperatures between 20 and 40 degrees Celsius. It does not matter whether you are familiar with the Celsius scale of temperature or not. All you need to be able to do is recognize the changes and the intervals from one temperature to another.

The horizontal axis represents the time of day. It is divided into 4-hour intervals for a 12-hour period.

According to the legend, the solid line on the graph represents the temperature of the sidewalk and the dashed line represents the temperature of the driveway. Note that both temperatures increase during daylight hours and start to decrease in the late afternoon or early evening.

Now you are ready for the questions.

Question

At noon, what was the temperature of the driveway?

1. 22°C
2. 26°C
3. 28°C
4. 30°C
5. 32°C

Answer and Analysis

Noon is halfway between 10 A.M. and 2 P.M., so start by placing the point of your pencil halfway between these two points on the horizontal scale. Move it straight up until it meets the dashed line, which represents the driveway. Now move the pencil point to the left; it meets the temperature scale at 26°. The answer is Choice 2.

Question

What is the difference in the times when the two surfaces reach their maximum temperatures?

1. The driveway reaches its maximum about 4 hours before the sidewalk.
2. The sidewalk reaches its maximum about 4 hours before the driveway.
3. The driveway reaches its maximum about 2 hours before the sidewalk.
4. The sidewalk reaches its maximum about 2 hours before the driveway.
5. Both surfaces reach their maximums at the same time.

Answer and Analysis

The dashed line (driveway) peaks at about 4 P.M., halfway between 2 P.M. and 6 P.M. The solid line (sidewalk) peaks a little before 8 P.M. The difference is fairly close to 4 hours, so the answer is Choice 1.

Bar Graphs

Whereas a line graph is used to show how something changes, a bar graph is used to compare several quantities. Like a line graph, a bar graph has a vertical axis marked off as a kind of scale. The horizontal axis is used to indicate the different quantities that are being compared.

Look at a bar graph the same way you would a line graph. Read the title and the legend (if any). Then note the information given on the horizontal axis and on the vertical axis.

EXAMPLE

The following graph represents the counts of three kinds of leukocytes (white blood cells) in an animal that was administered a standard dose of a drug starting on day 4.

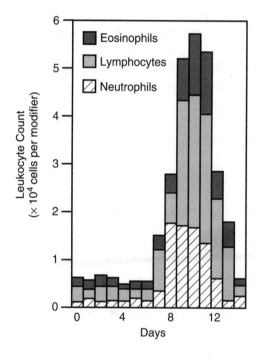

Note that the numbers of the three different kinds of leukocytes are indicated by using different patterns in the bars. Note also that the effect is short lived.

Question

How long did the medication take to produce its maximum effect?

1. 4 days
2. 6 days
3. 8 days
4. 10 days
5. 12 days

Answer and Analysis

Remember that the drug was started on day 4. The peak of leukocyte production was reached on day 10. Day 10 – Day 4 equals 6 days from the time the drug was administered to peak effect, Choice 2.

Question

In regard to amount of increase, how did the three different kinds of leukocytes react to the medication?

1. All three increased in roughly the same proportion.
2. The neutrophils increased proportionally more than the others.
3. The eosinophils increased proportionally more than the others.
4. There was proportionally less increase in the eosinophils.
5. There was proportionally less increase in the lymphocytes.

Answer and Analysis

At the peak, the ratios were about 1/4 neutrophils and 1/5 eosinophils, which were not much different from the starting ratios. The answer is Choice 1.

Pie Charts

A pie chart is a circular graph in which the circle is divided into sections. Pie charts are useful when a particular item of information is a part, that is, a fraction or percentage, of a whole.

The first thing to notice on a pie chart is the labels, which tell you what the various segments represent. Each label is usually accompanied by a number that indicates what part of the whole this segment represents. Next you should note the sizes of the segments to get some idea of which are largest and which are smallest.

EXAMPLE

The pie chart below indicates the average numbers of macroscopic (large) organisms in one area.

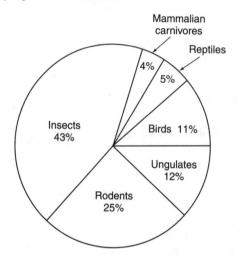

Note that insects, although physically the smallest of the animals represented, are the largest group—43%. Hoofed animals (ungulates) make up 12%.

Question

Which statement is supported by the chart?

1. Birds eat either insects or seeds.
2. Most reptiles are carnivores.
3. Eighty percent of the ecosystem consists of herbivores.
4. The ecosystem in this study was a savannah.
5. Insects are important because they are plant pollinators.

Answer and Analysis

Although Choices 1 and 2 are true statements, nothing on the chart indicates what birds or reptiles eat. Choice 4 is an excellent assumption, but nothing on the chart proves this statement conclusively. Choice 5 is partly true, but again is not supported by the chart. The best answer is Choice 3. If you know that a great many insects, ungulates (hoofed animals), and rodents eat plants, and if you add up the number represented by their portions of the chart, the total is 80%.

Diagrams

Diagrams, sometimes called graphics, show the relationships among the various parts of an object. Some parts may be inside others, be connected to others, or even be completely separate. When you see a diagram, the first things to look for are the connections between parts. Be sure to read all of the labels.

EXAMPLE

The following diagram represents the human ear. Empty spaces are shown in black.

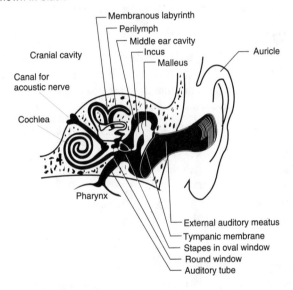

You should see at once that the external auditory meatus is an empty space separated from the middle ear cavity by the tympanic membrane. The middle ear cavity contains three bones.

Question

The incus is inside the

1. malleus
2. middle ear cavity
3. tympanic membrane
4. round window
5. auditory tube

Answer and Analysis

The label "Incus" points to something white, a bone. The label "Middle ear cavity" indicates a black area, a cavity. The answer is Choice 2.

Data Tables

When a series of objects or situations, each having a certain value, is under consideration, a data table is used to make comparison easy. The table is in columns, each column headed by a label that tells what the column contains. If there are numerical data, the column head will also indicate the unit of measure, usually in parentheses. There are no special precautions in reading a data table; just be sure you know what the headings mean.

EXAMPLE

The following table gives the symbols, atomic numbers, and average atomic weights of the most common elements in the Earth's crust. The atomic number is the number of protons in the atom.

Element	Symbol	Atomic Number	Average Atomic Weight (daltons)
Aluminum	Al	13	27.0
Calcium	Ca	20	40.1
Carbon	C	6	12.0
Iron	Fe	26	55.8
Magnesium	Ma	12	24.3
Oxygen	O	8	16.0
Potassium	K	13	39.1
Silicon	Si	14	28.1
Sodium	Na	11	23.0

Question

How many protons are there in a molecule of magnesium oxide (MgO)?

1. 4
2. 8
3. 12
4. 16
5. 20

Answer and Analysis

Just add the 12 in magnesium to the 8 in oxygen; the answer is Choice 5.

HANDLING SCIENCE SKILLS QUESTIONS

The makers of the GED Examination try to test you for a wide range of skills. You can be asked to do something as simple as restating an idea from the passage, or something as complex as evaluating the scientific validity of an experiment. The questions are generally grouped into four levels of skill.

THE FOUR SKILLS

It is not worth your while to try to determine to which of the four levels any one question belongs, or to develop special strategies for each of the four levels. In taking the test, this sort of approach would consume valuable time and require you to use a part of your thinking ability that is best reserved for answering questions. Nevertheless, it is a good idea to become familiar with the four levels of skill that are investigated in the test.

Comprehension

Comprehension is the simplest level. What it comes down to is this: Do you understand the passage, graph, or diagram? Can you rephrase some of the information in it? Can you summarize it? Can you identify a simple implication of the information given?

Here are some examples of the simple comprehension type of question:

Question
Elements can be either mixed mechanically to form a mixture, or combined chemically to form a compound. In a mixture, the properties of each of the elements present are recognizable. A mixture is rather like a stew in which the carrots, potatoes, and tomatoes are all identifiable. In a compound, however, the original elements are no longer recognizable as themselves, and another form of matter with its own characteristics has been produced.

Which of the following is NOT a mixture?

1. iron filings in sawdust
2. sugar water
3. vegetable soup
4. rust
5. soda water

Answer and Analysis

If you understood the passage, you know that the components of a mixture remain separate and identifiable, while the components of a compound are changed into a new form of matter. The only answer in which the elements have been completely altered is Choice 4, rust, the chemical combination of iron and oxygen. All of the other substances can be separated into their original parts.

Question

The scientific name of an animal is printed in italic type and has two parts. The first word (capitalized) is the name of the genus to which the animal belongs. The second word (lower case) is the name of its species within the genus. Here are the English and scientific names of five birds:

A. American robin, *Turdus migratorius*
B. European robin, *Erithacus rubecula*
C. European blackbird, *Turdus merula*
D. Military macaw, *Ara militaris*
E. Red-breasted blackbird, *Sturnella militaris*

Of the following pairs, which belong to the same genus?

1. A and B only
2. D and E only
3. B and C only
4. A and C only
5. C and E only

Answer and Analysis

Since the passage deals only with scientific names, you can ignore the English names. The first word of the scientific name is the same for two birds in the same genus, so the answer is Choice 4.

Question

When you place a solution in a test tube and then spin the test tube very rapidly in a machine called a centrifuge, the materials in the solution will separate, with the densest ones on the bottom and the least dense ones on top.

The following diagram represents the result of spinning a suspension of broken cells in a centrifuge. Which is the correct conclusion?

1. Ribosomes are more dense than mitochondria.
2. Nuclei are more dense than mitochondria.
3. Mitochondria and ribosomes are equal in density.
4. The cell consists of only solid components.
5. Nuclei are less dense than mitochondria.

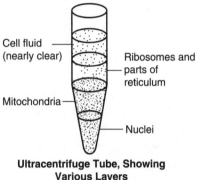

**Ultracentrifuge Tube, Showing
Various Layers**

Answer and Analysis
The correct choice is 2 because the most dense particles settle at the bottom after spinning.

Question
The soft body feathers of a bird are useful as insulation, while the stiff feathers of the wings and tail form airfoil surfaces, like those of an airplane wing. If a new species of bird is found that has no stiff feathers, it is safe to assume that it

1. cannot fly
2. lives in a tropical country
3. migrates south in winter
4. lives mainly in the water
5. is able to run rapidly

Answer and Analysis
This question calls for you to make a simple deduction. If the stiff feathers are used in flight, a bird without them cannot fly, so the answer is Choice 1.

Question

The table below gives the densities of four kinds of materials found in the Earth:

Substance	Density (g/cm³)
Water	1.00
Petroleum	0.86
Wood chips	0.75
Sand	2.10

If a mixture of all four materials is placed in a cylinder, shaken, and allowed to stand, the materials will settle out with the most dense on the bottom. What will the cylinder look like?

1. The sand and wood chips will be mixed together on the bottom, and the water will be on top of the petroleum.
2. The sand will be on the bottom; above will be the water with the wood chips in the layer between the petroleum and the water.
3. The wood chips will form a layer above the sand on the bottom, and the water will form a layer over the petroleum.
4. The sand will be on the bottom; the petroleum will form a layer over the water, with the wood chips floating on top.
5. The water will be on the bottom, with the wood chips floating on it; the petroleum and sand will be mixed above the water.

Answer and Analysis

The materials, top to bottom, must be in the sequence of increasing density—wood chips, petroleum, water, sand—so the answer is Choice 4.

Application

If you have thoroughly understood the information provided in the passage, graph, diagram, or table, you should be able to apply what you have learned. The application questions ask you to use the general principle contained in the information, but to apply that principle to a different situation.

Here are some examples:

Question

Study the graph below, which shows the percentage distributions of the Earth's surface elevation above, and depth below, sea level.

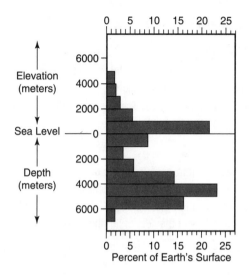

Approximately what total percentage of the Earth's surface is below sea level?

1. 30%
2. 50%
3. 70%
4. 80%
5. 90%

Answer and Analysis

There are more shaded bars below than above sea level on the graph. Adding up the lengths of all the shaded bars below sea level yields a total of about 70%. This represents the total percentage of the Earth's surface below sea level. The correct answer is Choice 3.

Question

High-energy sound waves are known to produce long-term damage to the ears, resulting in loss of ability to hear high frequencies. Which of the following individuals is most likely to have good high-frequency hearing after many years of work?

1. a rock musician
2. an aircraft mechanic
3. a riveter
4. an accountant
5. a sawmill operator

Answer and Analysis

Again, you cannot get the answer just by looking back at the information. You have to look at the list of choices to figure out who is least likely to have been exposed to loud noise. The answer is Choice 4. All the other occupations involve continuous, loud noises.

Question

A 20-watt fluorescent lamp produces as much light as a 100-watt incandescent bulb. The lighting in a factory is redesigned to provide the same amount of light when half of the incandescent lamps are replaced with fluorescents. What fraction of the cost of lighting is saved?

1. 10%
2. 20%
3. 30%
4. 40%
5. 80%

Answer and Analysis

A complete change to fluorescents would save 80 of every 100 watts. Since only half of the lamps are changed, the saving is half this, 40%; the answer is Choice 4.

Question

When an animal eats another that contains PCB pollutants, the PCB concentrates in the predator's liver. The following food relationships exist in a certain ecosystem:

> Big fish eat little fish.
> Little fish eat plankton.
> Wolves eat otters.
> Otters eat big fish.

If the water of a pond contains PCB, which of the following will have the greatest concentration of PCB?

1. otters
2. wolves
3. big fish
4. plankton
5. little fish

Answer and Analysis
The concentration of PCB must increase in the sequence plankton, little fish, big fish, otters, wolves, so the answer is Choice 2.

Question
Many foods, such as bread, potatoes, and spaghetti, contain a great deal of starch. An enzyme in saliva slowly changes starch to sugar. Which of the following statements is most probably true?
1. A piece of bread held in the mouth for a long time becomes sweet.
2. Spaghetti in the mouth causes an increase in the flow of saliva.
3. If you eat a potato, the enzyme is in your saliva.
4. If you eat sugar, it can turn to starch in the mouth.
5. A cookie tastes sweet because it contains starch.

Answer and Analysis
If the saliva in the mouth changes the starch in the bread to sugar, you might expect that the bread would begin to taste sweet. Choice 1 is correct. None of the other choices is suggested by the information given.

Analysis

These questions are more complicated. To answer them, you will have to find the relationships among several different items of information. Some of these items will not be given; you will be expected to know things that are general knowledge. It is possible to identify five somewhat different kinds of skills that belong to the general category of analysis:
- Recognizing unstated assumptions
- Using several related pieces of information
- Distinguishing fact from opinion
- Distinguishing cause from effect
- Drawing conclusions from data

Here are some examples of questions requiring analysis:

Question

A doctor discovers that a patient has blood pressure of 170/110. He tells the patient that medication, accompanied by a reducing diet and limited exercise, will bring the blood pressure down. What has the doctor assumed without actually stating it?

1.   Blood pressure of 170/110 is dangerous to the health of the patient.
2.   Medication can bring down blood pressure.
3.   Medication will reduce the patient's weight.
4.   The patient has not been exercising at all.
5.   Blood pressure varies greatly in the population at large.

Answer and Analysis

Surely the doctor would not bother with the problem if he did not assume that the patient's blood pressure is too high for continued good health, so the answer is Choice 1. Choice 2 is true, but it is not unstated; the doctor told the patient that medication would work. Since there is no reason to believe that the medication is used for weight reduction, Choice 3 is wrong. Choice 4 is wrong because the prescription for limited exercise might just as easily mean that the patient has been exercising too much. Choice 5 is true, but irrelevant.

If you are asked to find an unstated assumption, do *not* select one that is (a) stated in the information given; (b) untrue; (c) ambiguous; or (d) irrelevant.

Question

Corals are tiny animals that obtain their energy from their close association with green algae. Fish that eat corals do not live in deep water because

1.   the pressure is too great in deep water
2.   the fish that live in deep water eat them
3.   sunlight does not penetrate into deep water
4.   there are no currents in deep water to carry nutrients to them
5.   it is too cold in deep water

Answer and Analysis

This is one of the questions in which you are expected to know a few facts and to put some ideas together. You should know that green algae need sunlight to grow, and that corals use energy for growth. The answer is Choice 3. Some of the other answers may be true, but they are irrelevant.

Question

Someone sees a high waterfall on the side of a cliff and comments about it. Which of the following comments is probably based on opinion rather than fact?

1. The waterfall is about 30 meters high.
2. The valley into which it falls was carved by a glacier.
3. The rock in the mountain is a form of granite.
4. The speed of the water at the bottom of the fall is about 25 meters per second.
5. A photograph of the fall would be really beautiful.

Answer and Analysis

"Based on fact" is not the same as "factual." A statement is probably based on fact if it can be derived from one or more facts. Choices 1 and 4 could be determined by measurement or calculation—facts. Choices 2 and 3 could be determined from facts by any competent geologist. Since beauty is in the eye of the beholder, Choice 5 is an opinion.

Question

It is found that, when a stream becomes more muddy, the population of catfish increases. Three possible explanations are offered:

A. More catfish tend to make the water muddy.
B. Catfish thrive on invertebrates that live in mud.
C. Other fish cannot live in muddy water, so catfish have less competition.

Which of these explanations is (are) feasible?

1. A only
2. B only
3. C only
4. A and B only
5. B and C only

Answer and Analysis

This question requires you to tell the difference between cause and effect. Is it possible that explanation A is true? No; the water became muddy before the catfish population increased, and a cause can never come after its effect. In both explanation B and explanation C, the water is already muddy, and both are reasonable hypotheses, so the answer is Choice 5.

This type of question can be tricky. If one event follows another, the one that occurs first may or may not be the cause of the second, even if the second invariably follows the first. The crowing of the rooster does not make the sun rise. In the example given, the sequence of the two events stated in the question establishes only that B and C are possible explanations, not that they must necessarily be true.

Question

A chemical factory manufacturing a detergent discovers that its product contains a material that is considered a biohazard. Of the following, which can be considered a conclusion based on data?
1. The amount of reactant *A* is twice as great as that of reactant *B*.
2. The temperature of the reaction is 140°C.
3. The pH of the reaction mixture is 5.4.
4. The problem can be solved by adding an alkali.
5. There is a contaminant in reactant *A*.

Answer and Analysis

Fact or conclusion? All the statements except Choice 4 are data, testable and presumably confirmed by measurement. Putting all the known facts together, the engineer might use his knowledge of the process to obtain an overall picture of what is happening. He can then draw the conclusion in Choice 4.

A conclusion is a general statement that is not obtained from direct observation. It comes from intelligent application of known principles to measurement data.

Evaluation

We all have our own beliefs and ideas, and most of our beliefs and general thought processes are not scientific. But then, this is how it should be. Science cannot tell you what career to choose or whom to marry, or whether to go to church on Sunday, or who to vote for, or what kind of music to listen to. What science can do, however, is provide highly reliable and accurate answers to questions.

On the GED Examination, evaluation questions test your ability to apply the rules of scientific analysis to questions. Before you can do this, though, you need to understand a little about some of the many different kinds of statements that you will encounter.

Fact or Datum

A fact (datum) is something that can be observed and proved to be true.

EXAMPLE

If you measure a piece of wood and it is precisely 8 feet long, you have established a fact. If, however, someone estimates and tells you that the piece is 8 feet long even though it has not been measured, then you have an estimation, not a fact. Another kind of statement is an opinion, as when someone remarks that the piece of wood is an attractive color. Again, you do not have a fact.

You may be asked to determine whether a statement is a valid fact. Sloppy techniques can produce a statement that looks like a fact, but which cannot be supported by evidence or by the experimental process. You will need to be able to identify such statements.

Hypothesis

A hypothesis is an educated guess, the possible answer to a question. It is a purely tentative statement that may be modified or even disproved when more information becomes available.

EXAMPLE

If you find that a type-A shrub in the sunlight grows better than another type-A shrub in the shade, you might propose the hypothesis that type-A shrubs need sunlight for optimum growth. This hypothesis can be tested by a controlled experiment. The most common mistake that people make is to accept a hypothesis as a fact without realizing the need for an experiment to provide proof.

You may have to distinguish between a fact and a hypothesis.

Conclusion

A conclusion may be the result of a controlled experiment. A hypothesis becomes a conclusion when you have tested and verified the initial statement.

EXAMPLE

If the type-A shrub really does grow better in the sunlight during a carefully designed experiment, then it is a reasonable conclusion that this particular plant should be grown in the sun.

You may be asked whether it is reasonable to draw a certain conclusion from a given set of data. You will have to be able to distinguish between a hypothesis and a conclusion.

Generalization

A generalization is a conclusion that can apply to a wide variety of situations.

EXAMPLE

Many experiments with green plants have indicated that all of them, whether a tiny alga cell or an enormous redwood tree, need some sunlight in order to live.

If you are asked whether a certain generalization is reasonable, look to see if it applies to many situations.

Value Judgment

A value judgment is an opinion based on cultural or emotional factors rather than on scientific evidence. Opinions have an important place in our lives, but they cannot be allowed to affect the process of arriving at a scientific conclusion.

EXAMPLE

A certain landowner decided that he should kill every snake on his property because he didn't like snakes. He also killed squirrels and chipmunks for the same reason—he didn't like them.

You will be asked to distinguish value judgments from scientifically valid statements.

Logical Fallacy

A fallacy is a wrong conclusion that results when you use information incorrectly. The most common logical fallacy goes by the imposing name *post hoc ergo propter hoc*, which means "followed by, therefore caused by."

EXAMPLE

I drink a glass of milk for breakfast every morning, and I always get sleepy. Does the milk make me sleepy? Maybe. Or maybe I would become sleepy even if I didn't drink the milk. The way to avoid this kind of fallacy is to perform a controlled experiment and test the possible relationship.

The examples below will give you some idea of the sorts of questions that will test your ability to evaluate scientific statements.

Question

A proposal to build a dam on a river is opposed by a group of citizens, offering various reasons. Which of the following reasons is based on a value judgment rather than scientific information?

1. The river should be preserved because it is a habitat for much beautiful wildlife.
2. The cost of the dam will be too high for the amount of electricity it produces.
3. It is not possible to dam the river at the site selected because of the surface features of the land.
4. The proposed site is on a fault, and the dam could be destroyed by an earthquake.
5. The river carries so much silt that the lake formed by it would soon fill up and render the dam useless.

Answer and Analysis

The word *beautiful* in Choice 1 is a giveaway, specifying a value judgment. Whoever makes that argument sees an esthetic value in the preservation of wildlife. All the other objections are based on arguments that can be subjected to rigid testing, using established scientific principles.

Question

The following graph shows the average growths of two groups of rats. The solid line represents a group raised under standard conditions by a supplier of laboratory animals; the dashed line, a group raised in a laboratory and treated with pituitary extract.

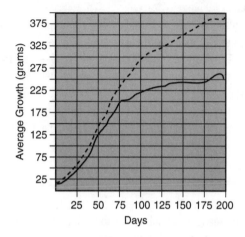

—— Average growth of 38 untreated rats (control)
- - - - Average growth of 38 rats injected with
       anterior pituitary extract (experimental)

What is a proper conclusion from the experiment?

1. It is known that pituitary extract stimulates growth, and the experiment confirms it.

2. The difference between the control group and the experimental group is so clear that it can be concluded that pituitary extract stimulates growth.

3. The growths of the two groups are too similar to show that there is any difference in average growth.

4. The experiment is useless because there is no reason to believe that the same result would be obtained with human beings.

5. The experiment is inconclusive because there was no attempt to control the heredity of the animals or the conditions of their nurture.

Answer and Analysis

Whether an experiment should have some obvious use is a value judgment that is not at issue here, so Choice 4 is wrong. Choice 1 is wrong because it suggests that the outcome of the experiment was prejudiced in advance. At first this looks like a nice, neat experiment; the difference in growth is marked, and so Choice 3 is wrong. However, Choice 2 is wrong because the controls are inadequate. The rats were not necessarily of the same breed, nor were they raised in the same place. They could differ also in their hereditary endowments, their feeding, and any number of other factors. The results of this experiment could lead to a hypothesis, but not a conclusion, so the answer is Choice 5.

Question

Over the last hundred years, people have been burning more and more fossil fuel, which releases carbon dioxide into the atmosphere. This excess CO_2 is a cause of global warming, which, according to ecologists, is one of the most serious problems facing us today. Carbon dioxide in the upper atmosphere traps the Sun's heat, in much the same way that the panes of glass hold heat in a greenhouse.

Which graph best represents what most likely happens to the temperature of the Earth's atmosphere as the amount of carbon dioxide in the atmosphere increases over a period of many years?

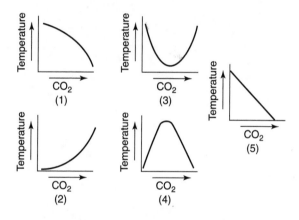

Answer and Analysis

Graph (2) shows that, as the amount of carbon dioxide increases, the average temperature of the atmosphere also increases.

6

INTERPRETING LITERATURE AND THE ARTS

BASIC READING SKILLS

Reading consists of a complex combination of skills. The writer sets forth his or her ideas using the medium of language consisting of printed words. If the writer has stated the ideas clearly, they have been well organized and well developed. You, the reader, must draw meaning from the ideas expressed on the printed page. In addition, there may be ideas that are implied rather than openly stated. For example, a woman dressed in black is described as *grieving*. The implication is that she has lost a loved one, even if this fact is not stated in so many words.

Reading requires the use of a number of skills so you can decode or derive from the language used the meaning intended by the writer, whether it is explicitly stated or suggested by implication.

These skills are basically three in number.

You read to find the main idea of the selection.

You find the main idea in a variety of places. It may be stated directly in the first sentence (easy to find). It may be stated in the final sentence to which the others build up (a bit harder to find). It may have to be discovered within the passage (most difficult); an example (note the underscored words) occurs in the following paragraph:

> Several students were seriously injured in football games last Saturday. The week before, several more were hospitalized. <u>Football has become a dangerous sport.</u> The piling up of players in a scrimmage often leads to serious injury. Perhaps some rule changes would lessen the number who are hurt.

You may also find that the main idea is not directly expressed, but can only be inferred from the selection as a whole.

> The plane landed at 4 P.M. As the door opened, the crowd burst into a long, noisy demonstration. The waiting mob surged against the police

guard lines. Women were screaming. Teenagers were yelling for autographs or souvenirs. The visitor smiled and waved at his fans.

The main idea of the paragraph is not expressed, but it is clear that some popular hero, movie or rock star is being welcomed enthusiastically at the airport.

To find the main idea of a passage, **ask yourself any or all of these questions:**

1. What is the *main idea* of the passage? (Why did the author write it?)
2. What is the *topic sentence* of the paragraph or paragraphs (the sentence that the other sentences build on or flow from)?
3. What *title* would I give this selection?

You read to find the details that explain or develop the main idea.

How do you do this? You must determine how the writer develops the main idea. He or she may give examples to illustrate that idea, or may give reasons why the statement that is the main idea is true, or may give arguments for or against a position stated as the main idea. The writer may define a complex term and give a number of aspects of a complicated belief (such as democracy). He or she may also classify a number of objects within a larger category. Finally, the writer may compare two ideas or objects (show how they are similar) or contrast them (show how they are different).

In the paragraph immediately above, you can see that the sentence "You must determine how the writer develops the main idea" *is* the main idea. Six ways in which the writer can develop the main idea follow. These are the details that actually develop the main idea of the paragraph.

To find the main details of a passage, **the questions to ask yourself are these:**

1. What examples illustrate the main point?
2. What reasons or proof support the main idea?
3. What arguments are presented for or against the main idea?
4. What specific qualities are offered about the idea or subject being defined?

5. Into what classifications is a larger group broken down?
6. What are the similarities and differences between two ideas or subjects being compared or contrasted?

You read to make inferences by putting together ideas that are expressed to arrive at other ideas that are not.

In other words, you draw conclusions from the information presented by the author. You do this by locating relevant details and determining their relationships (time sequence, place sequence, cause and effect).

How do you do this? You can put one fact together with a second to arrive at a third that is not stated. You can apply a given fact to a different situation. You can predict an outcome based on the facts given.

To make inferences from a passage, ask yourself the following questions:
1. From the facts presented, what conclusions can I draw?
2. What is being suggested, in addition to what is being stated?
3. What will be the effect of something that is described?
4. What will happen next (after what is being described)?
5. What applications does the principle or idea presented have?

READING CURRENT LITERATURE

The basic reading skills apply to current and earlier literature alike. Current literature is easier to read. The content presents fewer problems since you are more likely to have shared the same experiences as the writer. Also, you are generally more familiar with the language of the writer. Since the selections are drawn from sources that you read quite frequently—newspapers and magazines, for example—they should be no more difficult than the usual materials geared to the high school graduate.

READING EARLIER LITERATURE

Earlier literature differs from current literature in a number of ways. The settings are certainly different because they go back at least fifty to two hundred years. Also, the style of writing is different; sentences are longer and more complicated. The vocabulary is less familiar. Some of the subject matter may be dated for today's reader. On the other hand, fine earlier literature deals with the eternal emotions of love, hate, greed, loyalty, self-sacrifice, joy, fear, among others. And many themes are eternal—the relationship of man to his fellow man and woman, of man to God, of man to nature, of man to his family, of man to his country.

Reading earlier literature requires patience but it can be greatly rewarding. Try to imagine the unfamiliar setting. Reread the difficult sentences. Get the meaning of the unfamiliar word from its context. Find the application to life today of the theme of the selection. Continued practice will make these worthwhile tasks easier and the literature more satisfying.

LOCATING THE MAIN IDEA

Depending upon the type of passage—poetry, fiction, essay, drama—the technique of finding the main idea may vary. In the essay, for example, the main idea may very well appear as a straightforward statement, usually expressed in the topic sentence. In this particular case, the trick is to find the topic sentence. In works of fiction, poetry, or drama, the main idea might be found in a line of dialogue or exposition, or within a long, flowing line of verse.

Prose

In reading *prose*, the main unit is the paragraph. Since all the paragraphs you will encounter on the GED examination have been chosen for their "loaded" content—that is, because they contain a number of ideas offering possibilities for questions—it is important that you learn how to locate the main idea. This, in turn, will enable you to understand many of the subordinate (less important) elements of the paragraph—all of which may also be the basis for examination questions.

The topic sentence containing the main idea is used in five standard patterns:

1.   The topic sentence, expressing the main idea, may introduce the paragraph and be followed by sentences containing details that explain, exemplify, prove, or support the idea, or add interest.

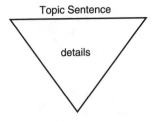

Topic Sentence

details

EXAMPLE

In *Alice in Wonderland*, Lewis Carroll created a world of fantasy out of essentially real creatures, transformed into whimsy by the odd patterns of a dream. Sitting with her sister by a stream, Alice sees a rabbit; as she dozes off, the rabbit becomes larger, dons a waistcoat and a pocket watch, and acquires human speech.

2. The topic sentence may appear at the end of the paragraph, with a series of details leading to the main idea.

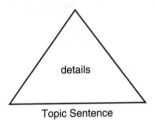

details

Topic Sentence

EXAMPLE

The small, darting rabbit on the riverbank becomes a huge White Rabbit, complete with waistcoat and pocket watch. The cards in a discarded deck become the Queen of Hearts and her court. The real world of Alice Liddell becomes, through the odd patterns of the dream, the fantasy world of *Alice in Wonderland*.

3. The selection may begin with a broad generalization (topic sentence) followed by details that support the main idea and lead to another broad generalization that is called the "summary sentence" (conclusion).

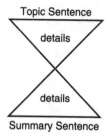

EXAMPLE

<u>The elements of the real world become, through the strange, shifting patterns of the dream, objects and creatures of curiosity and whimsy.</u> A scurrying rabbit becomes a humanized White Rabbit; a deck of cards becomes the court of the Queen of Hearts; a kitten becomes a chess Queen. In *Alice in Wonderland* reality becomes fantasy and, for a while, fantasy becomes reality.

4. The topic sentence may appear in the body of the paragraph.

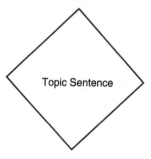

EXAMPLE

When Alice goes through the looking glass, she enters a garden where the flowers speak. In a dark forest, a fawn befriends her. <u>The dream world reverses the events of the real world.</u> The Lion and the Unicorn come off their shield and do battle. The Red Queen, originally a kitten of Alice's pet cat Dinah, gives Alice instructions in etiquette.

5. The selection may contain *no expressed topic sentence* but consist of a series of sentences giving details and implying a central thought.

EXAMPLE

A deck of cards becomes a royal court. A kitten becomes a chess Queen. A scurrying wild creature becomes a sophisticated courtier, a White Rabbit in vest and pocket watch. A proper Victorian tea party becomes the setting for rude remarks and outrageous behavior.

Poetry

Poetry is a form of literature that is difficult to define. Dictionary definitions are very complicated. One states that a poem is a rhythmical composition, sometimes rhymed, expressing experiences, ideas, or emotions in a style more concentrated, imaginative, and powerful than that of ordinary speech or prose. Another dictionary defines poetry as writing that formulates a concentrated imaginative awareness in language chosen and arranged to create a specific emotional response through meaning, sound, and rhythm. A desk encyclopedia defines poetry as a meaningful arrangement of words into an imaginative emotional discourse, always with a strong rhythmic pattern.

All these definitions stress certain common elements.

1. The content is an experience of the poet, usually emotional, filtered through the poet's imagination.
2. The poet uses a special language that is concentrated, using words that suggest more than their exact meaning.
3. The poet creates rhythmic and sound patterns that contribute to the experience described. He or she frequently, but not necessarily, uses rhyme.

With these elements in mind, let us analyze the poem "Ozymandias" by Percy Bysshe Shelley.

WHAT REMAINS OF A ONCE POWERFUL KING
I met a traveler from an antique land
Who said: "Two vast and trunkless legs of stone
Stand in the desert... Near them, on the sand,
Half sunk, a shattered visage lies, whose frown
And wrinkled lip, and sneer of cold command,
Tell that its sculptor well those passions read
Which yet survive, stamped on these lifeless things,

The hand that mocked them, and the heart that fed;
And on the pedestal these words appear:
'My name is Ozymandias, king of kings:
Look on my works, ye Mighty, and despair!'
Nothing beside remains. Round the decay
Of that colossal wreck, boundless and bare
The lone and level sands stretch far away."

The poet meets someone who describes something seen in a desert. It is the colossal wreck of a statue of a powerful king that has decayed over time. The remains consist of several parts—two legs, a shattered face, and the pedestal on which the statue once stood. The poet wants to portray a scene of utter desolation. Only the shattered statue survives amidst the emptiness of the boundless, bare desert sands. The poem gains its power by means of irony—the opposite of what we expect for a powerful king, not a royal palace but a broken statue of a king, is described. The poet creates, in a few words, the character of the king—his frown, his wrinkled lip, his sneer of authority. All of these details lead to the lesson the poet wishes to teach the Mighty: life is brief; human desires are vain; power leads to despair. He does this in 14 lines and 111 words.

Technically the poem has faulty rhyme—*stone* and *frown*, *appear* and *despair*, and the word order in "Nothing beside remains" is unusual. Nevertheless, an emotional response from us results from the picture the poet creates and the message engraved on the pedestal: nothing lasts forever, not even the power of a mighty king.

DETERMINING TONE AND MOOD

Tone is the aspect of the author's style that reveals attitude toward the subject. *Mood* is the atmosphere, or emotional effect, created by the manner in which the author presents the material.

To determine the tone or mood of a passage, consider the feelings or attitudes that are expressed. Examine, for example, the following passages:

EXAMPLE

The room was dark—so dark that even after giving her eyes a while to accustom themselves to the blackness, she could still see nothing. Something soft—she hoped it was only a cobweb—brushed her lip.

And the throbbing sound, attuned to her own heavy heartbeat, became stronger and faster.

EXAMPLE

The room was dark—not dark as it is when your eyes are just not used to blackness, but really *dark* dark. Then some soft creepy thing brushed her lip, and she found herself hoping very hard that it was only a cobweb. And then there was that sound—baBoom, baBoom, baBoom—getting faster and louder all the time like her own heart going thump, thump, thump.

Consider the contrasting moods of the two passages above. The first passage presents a sustained mood of suspense and fear. The woman in the room can see nothing; something strange touches her; she hears a heavy and mysterious sound. We have the feeling that something is going to happen; the indication is that what will happen is dangerous, evil, or deadly.

The second paragraph relates essentially the same event. But we are distracted somewhat from what is happening by several devices. First, we are brought informally into the story—we know what a room is like when it's *really* dark. And the quality of darkness is also expressed informally—it is not pitch dark, or night dark, but "dark dark." "Then something creepy" is felt, and the sounds of the noise and the woman's heart are described—baBoom. The feeling conveyed by these devices is somehow made less frightening by the familiarity of the language, and the general impression is less one of total fear than of "scariness"—an easier emotion to deal with. Thus, we have the impression from this second passage that whatever happens will probably not be all that bad or, if it is, it will somehow be easier to overcome.

INFERRING CHARACTER

Character is often implied by a person's words or actions, rather than by direct description. This has always been particularly true of drama, where the reader of a play is often called upon to interpret a character's personality without benefit of stage directions or other descriptive material. In the modern novel, too, the trend has been away from utilizing long descriptive passages and more toward allowing the characters' actions, speech, or thoughts (often called "inner dialogue") to reveal their personalities. The reader must rely, therefore, on the hints offered by the playwright or novelist to interpret character—and even then, a wide range of interpretation may be possible.

The following scene from *Life with Father* features Father and his son Clarence.

EXAMPLE

CLARENCE (desperately): I have to have a new suit of clothes— you've got to give me the money for it.

(Father's *account book reaches the table with a sharp bang as he stares at Clarence with astonishment.*)

FATHER: Young man, do you realize you're addressing your father?

(Clarence *wilts miserably and sinks into a chair.*)

CLARENCE: I'm sorry, Father—I apologize—but you don't know how important this is to me. (Clarence's *tone of misery gives* Father *pause.*)

FATHER: A suit of clothes is so—? Now, why should a —? (*Something dawns on* Father *and he looks at* Clarence.) Has your need for a suit of clothes anything to do with the young lady?

CLARENCE: Yes, Father.

FATHER: Why, Clarence! (*Suddenly realizes that women have come into* Clarence's *emotional life and there comes a yearning to protect this inexperienced and defenseless member of his own sex.*) This comes as quite a shock to me.

CLARENCE: What does, Father?

FATHER: Your being so grown up! Still, I might have known that if you're going to college this fall—yes, you're at an age when you'll be meeting girls. Clarence, there are things about women I think you ought to know! (*He goes up and closes the doors, then comes down and sits beside* Clarence, *hesitating for a moment before he speaks.*) Yes, I think it's better for you to hear this from me than to have to learn it for yourself. Clarence, women aren't the angels that you think they are! Well, now—first, let me explain this to you. You see, Clarence, we men have to run this world and it's not an easy job. It takes work, and it takes thinking. A man has to be sure of his facts and figures. He has to reason things out.

Now, you take a woman—a woman thinks—I'm wrong right there—a woman doesn't think at all! She gets stirred up! And she gets stirred up over the damnedest things! Now I love my wife just as much as any man, but that doesn't mean I should stand for a lot of folderol! By God! I won't stand for it!

CLARENCE: Stand for what, Father?

FATHER (to himself): That's the one thing I will not submit myself to. (*Has ceased explaining women to* Clarence *and is now explaining himself.*) Clarence, if a man thinks a certain thing is wrong to do he shouldn't do it. Now that has nothing to do with whether he loves his wife or not.

What action is taking place? A son is asking his father for money to buy a suit. What is the relationship between father and son? Father scolds his son for doing so; the son is miserable and apologizes. Obviously, the first thing we learn about Father is his lack of understanding of his son's needs. He acts like a dictator and causes his son to "wilt miserably." Next, after realizing his son's newly found interest in girls, he takes it upon himself to teach Clarence about women. Father acts like a know-it-all. "It's better for you to hear this from me than to have to learn it yourself." Then he reveals his prejudices against women: "a woman doesn't think at all!" Finally, his thinking becomes disorganized, he starts telling Clarence about women and ends up trying to convince himself how he should deal with them. The conversation, which started out as a request for money from a son to his father, ends in a useless discussion that reveals Father's prejudices.

We are left with a devastating picture of Father's character—a person who is dictatorial, lacking in understanding of his son's needs, filled with prejudices, self-deceptive, and disorganized, who regards himself as all knowing.

We learn all this from a cleverly written page of dialogue between father and son.

INFERRING SETTING

A number of factors are involved in the setting of a selection. These include not only *place* (physical location, type of locale—noisy, crowded, tranquil, etc.), but *time* (of day, of season, of historical period). See what clues to the setting you can find in the following passage.

EXAMPLE

He knew she would be late, but he could not keep himself from hurrying, pushing his way impatiently through the strolling, multilingual crowd. The Germans, their sunburned necks garlanded with camera straps, bargained gutturally with the indifferent women at their stalls, thinking to strike a sharp bargain on the price of a straw handbag or a painted box. The women let them struggle with the unfamiliar numbers, knowing exactly how much they would ultimately settle for. Three American girls, distinguishable by their short hair and madras skirts above sandalled feet and bare legs, dawdled along, giggling at the pleadings of two persistent *pappagalli* who seemed determined to improve international relations at all costs.

The sidestreet leading to the Signoria was hardly less busy, and he found it easier to dodge the small motorbikes bouncing noisily along the cobbled roadway than to struggle against the crowds pouring out of the great museum and onto the narrow sidewalks. He hated these annual floods of holiday-makers and culture-seekers who jammed the streets, the hotels, and the small restaurants so that the year-round residents found it necessary to retreat more than ever to the interiors of their cool, stone houses and their small, closed social circles. The more fortunate natives, of course, headed for Viareggio or the beaches of the South or the Riviera.

He finally found a table at the back of the cafe—a little too close to the bar but partially screened by a box hedge—and ordered a drink. The ancient *piazza* was mostly in shade now, except for the very tops of the towers which had been turned by the sun from the faded buff of the old stone to a rich gold against the blue sky.

What can we tell of the setting described?

Place: We can immediately pick up a number of clues. Obviously the setting is a city (crowds, sidewalks, a market, a museum). It is also not in the United States, since American girls are particularly distinguishable. By the mention of the Riviera as a nearby vacation spot, we know that we are somewhere in western Europe—but not Germany (the Germans are not familiar with the language). We can narrow the location down even further (although you are not expected to have all this extra information): two foreign words, *pappagalli* and *piazza*, might lead to the educated guess that the country is Italy.

Time: (1) Period—although the city itself is old (cobbled streets, narrow sidewalks, towers in an ancient piazza), the period is more recent. Motorbikes, barelegged girls, camera-carrying tourists all indicate the modern era. (2) Season—we can assume by the dress of the tourists, and by the fact that the natives usually head for the beach during this season, that it is summer. (3) Time of day—The piazza is in shade, except for the tops of the towers. It is unlikely, therefore, to be midday. Since the main character orders a drink in a cafe-bar, and since we have nowhere been given to understand that he has a drinking problem, we can assume it is late afternoon (cocktail time) and he has an appointment with someone for a predinner drink.

You should be made aware that the above passage was prepared solely to give you practice in inferring setting, and that you are not likely to find too many passages on the actual examination that concentrate on such description. However, you should learn to pick up small clues here and there that will give you an idea of the setting in a descriptive passage. Remember that, more often than not, the locale will be inferred rather than actually stated.

Practice in Reading Current and Earlier Prose

WHAT IS ABOUT TO HAPPEN TO BORIS?

The light carriage swished through the layers of fallen leaves upon the terrace. In places, they lay so thick that they half covered the stone balusters and reached the knees of Diana's stag. But the trees were bare; only here and there a single golden leaf trembled high upon the black twigs. Following the curve of the road, Boris's carriage came straight upon the main terrace and the house, majestic as the Sphinx herself in the sunset. The light of the setting sun seemed to have soaked into the dull masses of stone. They reddened and glowed with it until the whole place became a mysterious, a glorified abode, in which the tall windows shone like a row of evening stars.

Boris got out of the britska in front of the mighty stone stairs and walked toward them, feeling for his letter. Nothing stirred in the house. It was like walking into a cathedral. "And," he thought, "by the time that I get into that carriage once more, what will everything be like to me?"

1. The title that expresses the main idea of this passage is
   (1) "The Lure of Autumn"
   (2) "Sphinx in the Sunset"
   (3) "A Mysterious Cathedral"
   (4) "A Terrifying Surprise"
   (5) "An Important Visit"

2. From the description of the house, we may most safely conclude that the house
   (1) is sometimes used as a place of worship
   (2) is owned by a wealthy family
   (3) was designed by Egyptian architects
   (4) is constructed of modern brick
   (5) is a dark, cold-looking structure

3. This story probably takes place in
   (1) the British Isles
   (2) the Far East
   (3) eastern Europe
   (4) southern United States
   (5) the Mediterranean

4. We may most safely conclude that Boris has come to the house in order to
   (1) secure a job
   (2) find out about his future
   (3) join his friends for the holidays
   (4) attend a hunting party
   (5) visit his old family home

5. In this passage, which atmosphere does the author attempt to create?
   (1) pleasant anticipation
   (2) quiet peace
   (3) carefree gaiety
   (4) unrelieved despair
   (5) vague uncertainty

6. From this passage, which inference can most safely be drawn?
   (1) The house was topped by a lofty tower.
   (2) Boris is tired from his journey.

(3) There is only one terrace before the house is reached.

(4) The most imposing feature of the house is the door.

(5) Boris intends to stay at the house for only a short time.

Answer Key

1. **5**   2. **2**   3. **3**   4. **2**   5. **5**   6. **5**

Summary of Prose Interpretation

You should:

1. *Read the selection carefully.*

2. *In **selecting a title** that expresses the main idea, go back to the selection constantly. Arrive at the correct answer by a process of elimination.* Eliminate the one or more possibilities that are clearly incorrect. Eliminate the possibilities that are based on minor details; there will be one or two of these. From the remaining choices, you must select the one that expresses the main rather than the subordinate idea.

3. *In **drawing inferences**, find the clues in the passage from which you can draw the proper conclusion.* The clue may be a name, a place, an adjective, an object, an unusual word. You may have to reread the selection a few times before you locate the clue or the two details that can be linked to make a clue.

4. *In **determining purpose**, ask yourself why the author wrote the passage; what he or she wanted you, the reader, to understand or feel.* After you have read the passage several times, try to define the *total impression* you get from your reading. The purposes of authors at various times may be to inform, to arouse anger, to poke fun at, to evoke pity, to amuse, and to urge to action, among others. Which of these predominates?

5. *In **determining mood**, try to find words that either create an atmosphere or evoke an emotion.* This is related to the author's purpose but may not necessarily be his or her main purpose. There are two main guides to determining atmosphere: selection of details and use of adjectives and adverbs.

Reading Poetry

Reading poetry requires a special set of skills because the poet uses both a special language and special writing techniques.

In poetry, words are not used in their normal, literal senses. Rather, they are used in such a way that you, the reader, must call on your imagination to fully understand them. Let's consider an example.

"I almost blew my top."

Here the words *blew* and *top* do not have their regular meanings, but are used figuratively to express the idea "I almost went crazy."

> *Skill One.* In poetry, words are often used in a figurative sense. Do not take these words literally. Use your imagination in order to understand them as the poet uses them.

In poetry, meaning is frequently compressed into a few words by the use of figures of speech such as metaphors.

"The road was a ribbon of moonlight."

In seven words, the poet Walter de la Mare tells us that the time is night, the moon was shining, and the road is a lighted area surrounded by darker ones.

"The moon was a ghostly galleon."

In six words, the poet tells us that the moon is like a ship, the sky is like an ocean, and the moon creates an eerie, supernatural feeling as it moves across the sky.

> *Skill Two.* In poetry, words often compress or condense extended meanings and pictures into a few words, usually by the use of figures of speech such as metaphors. Add to the words you read the implied meanings and pictures they create.

In poetry, meaning is closely related to rhythm. For this reason it helps to read poetry aloud.

> *Skill Three.* Read the poem aloud paying attention to the rhythm, because the rhythm of the poem will help you understand its meaning.

In poetry, in addition to rhythm, which is always present, you will frequently encounter rhyme. Rhyme, too, often helps to convey meaning. In Edgar Allan Poe's poem "The Raven," the rhyme is repeated in *door, more, Lenore, forevermore,* and *nevermore.*

"'Tis some visitor,' I muttered, 'tapping at my chamber door: Only this and nothing more.'"

The sound itself adds to the atmosphere of mystery.

Skill Four. As you read the poem aloud, note the rhyme as well as the rhythm, since both add to the meaning and feelings expressed.

In poetry, the poet uses sounds in addition to rhyme to help convey meaning. The poet John Masefield describes the effect of the wind with a series of "w" and "wh" sounds. He wants to return

"To the gull's *w*ay and the *wh*ales's *w*ay *wh*ere the *w*ind's like a *wh*etted knife."

Another technique is the use of words whose sounds correspond to their meaning. Here is the way one poet describes the movement of the waters of a river:

"And rushing and flushing and brushing and gushing, And flapping and rapping and clapping and slapping..."

Skill Five. As you read the poem aloud, note the sounds of the words as well as their rhyme and their rhythm, since each adds to the meaning and feelings expressed by the poet.

In poetry, the poem itself has a certain shape or form. The poem can be in a very definite form, such as the sonnet, or in a very loose form. "The New Colossus," by Emma Lazarus, which follows, is a sonnet with a definite rhythm and a definite rhyme scheme. The form of "The New Colossus" is appropriate because it lends itself to the main ideas expressed in each of the two stanzas of the poem.

Skill Six. As you read the poem, study its form and structure. If it is divided into stanzas or paragraph units, try to determine what each stanza adds to the meaning of the poem. The poem's form is another aid to your understanding its meaning.

Read the following poem carefully and answer the questions based on it. Compare your answers with the answer key.

Practice in Reading Poetry

WHAT DOES THE NEW STATUE REPRESENT?

The New Colossus

Not like the brazen giant of Greek fame,
With conquering limbs astride from land to land;
Here at our sea-washed, sunset gates shall stand
A mighty woman with a torch, whose flame
Is the imprisoned lightning, and her name
Mother of Exiles. From her beacon-hand
Glows world-wide welcome; her mild eyes command
The air-bridged harbor that twin cities frame.
"Keep, ancient lands, your storied pomp!" cries she
with silent lips. "Give me your tired, your poor,
Your huddled masses yearning to breathe free,
The wretched refuse of your teeming shore.
Send these, the homeless, tempest-tost, to me.
I lift my lamp beside the golden door!"

—Emma Lazarus

1. The main idea of the poem is that
    (1) the ancient lands of Europe should serve as a beacon to America
    (2) the Greek statue serves as a model for the American statue
    (3) the mighty are asked to come to these shores
    (4) America welcomes all persecuted freedom-lovers
    (5) the lamp guides those who come to the golden door

2. In the choices below, the incorrectly paired words are
   (1) brazen—of brass
   (2) sunset—east
   (3) beacon—guiding light
   (4) refuse—trash
   (5) pomp—splendor

3. The "mighty woman" and "Mother of Exiles" is the
   (1) United States of America
   (2) city of New York
   (3) Statue of Liberty
   (4) Plymouth Rock
   (5) Golden Gate

4. The title of this poem, "The New Colossus," implies
   (1) similarity to the old
   (2) replacement of the old
   (3) difference from the old
   (4) inferiority to the old
   (5) acceptance of the old

5. The *incorrectly* matched phrase from the poem with the figure of speech or poetic device it demonstrates is
   (1) "Her mild eyes"—epithet
   (2) "Keep, ancient lands, your storied pomp!" cries she—personification
   (3) "shall stand a mighty woman"—inversion
   (4) "world-wide welcome"—alliteration
   (5) "flame is the imprisoned lightning"—simile

6. The form of the poem is that of
   (1) a ballad
   (2) an octet
   (3) an ode
   (4) a sestet
   (5) a sonnet

Answer Key

1. **4**   2. **2**   3. **3**   4. **3**   5. **5**   6. **5**

Summary of Interpretation of Poetry

The skills needed in reading and interpreting poetry call for you to:

1. Try to get the extended meaning of words used figuratively by using your imagination to add to the usual meanings of the words.

2. Since poetry compresses meaning and description into a few words, fill in the suggested meanings and pictures they create by studying the figures of speech used, such as similes and metaphors.

3. Read the poem aloud, since the rhythm will help you determine its meaning.

4. Note the rhymes used, since they will also help you get meaning and feeling from the poem.

5. Note the sounds of the words, since they reinforce meaning.

6. Study the form of the poem, since its subdivisions (stanzas) can help you understand it better.

Note: First, read the poem through quickly to get an overall idea of its meaning and feeling. Then read it more slowly and carefully.

Reading Drama

The playwright does not speak directly to the reader in modern drama, as do the novelist and short story writer. Sometimes the playwright sets the scene for those who produce or read the play, and sometimes he or she includes instructions to the actors about mood or action. For the most part, however, the playwright leaves it to the actor and the reader to figure out appearance, character, actions, and feelings. The only real help the playwright should and must give is through the dialogue, the conversation between the characters. From this dialogue alone, you must *imagine the setting*, *visualize the action*, including "hearing" the speech of the actors, and *draw conclusions about their character and motives*. In addition, you must understand the nature of the essence of drama, which is conflict between ideas or characters. This is made clear only through the dialogue. A final point: you may also be asked to predict what is likely to happen on the basis of what you have read.

An analysis of the following scene from a modern American play will illustrate the skills you need to read and understand drama. Reading it aloud will help.

Practice in Reading Drama

HOW DOES WILLY LOMAN'S FAMILY REACT TO HIS DEATH?

REQUIEM

CHARLEY: It's getting dark, Linda. (*Linda doesn't react. She stares at the grave.*)

BIFF: How about it, Mom? Better get some rest, heh! They'll be closing the gate soon. (*Linda makes no move. Pause.*)

HAPPY (*deeply angered*): He had no right to do that. There was no necessity for it. We would've helped him.

BIFF: Come along, Mom.

LINDA: Why didn't anybody come?

CHARLEY: It was a very nice funeral.

LINDA: But where are all the people he knew? Maybe they blame him.

CHARLEY: Naa. It's a rough world, Linda. They wouldn't blame him.

LINDA: I can't understand it. At this time especially. First time in thirty-five years we were just about free and clear. He only needed a little salary. He was even finished with the dentist.

CHARLEY: No man only needs a little salary.

LINDA: I can't understand it.

BIFF: There were a lot of nice days. When he'd come home from a trip, or on Sundays, making the stoop, finishing the cellar, when he built the extra bathroom, and put up the garage. You know something, Charley, there's more of him in that front stoop than in all the sales he ever made.

CHARLEY: Yeah, he was a happy man with a batch of cement.

LINDA: He was so wonderful with his hands.

BIFF: He had the wrong dreams. All, all, wrong.

HAPPY: (*almost ready to fight Biff*): Don't say that.

BIFF: He never knew who he was.

CHARLEY (*stopping Happy's movement and reply. To Biff*): Nobody dast blame this man. You don't understand. Willy was a salesman. And for a salesman, there is no rock bottom to the life. He don't put a bolt to a nut, he don't tell you the law or give you medicine. He's the man way out there in the blue riding on a smile and a shoeshine. And when they start not smiling back—that's an earthquake. And then you get yourself a couple of spots on your hat, and you're finished. Nobody dast blame this man. A salesman has got to dream, boy. It comes with the territory.

BIFF: Charley, the man didn't know who he was.

HAPPY (*infuriated*): Don't say that.

BIFF: Why don't you come with me, Happy?

HAPPY: I'm not licked that easily. I'm staying right here in this city, and I'm gonna beat this racket! (*He looks at Biff, his chin set.*) The Loman Brothers!

BIFF: I know who I am, kid.

HAPPY: All right, boy. I'm gonna show you and everybody else that Willy Loman did not die in vain. He had a good dream. It's the only dream you can have—to come out number-one man. He fought it out here, and this is where I'm gonna win it for him.

1. "Requiem" most closely means
   (1) prayer
   (2) regret
   (3) argument
   (4) repetition
   (5) request

2. What has happened prior to this scene?
   (1) The Lomans had an unhappy marriage.
   (2) The brothers did not get along.
   (3) Willy Loman had many friends.
   (4) The Loman family had an easy life.
   (5) Willy Loman was buried.

3. From the dialogue, we can conclude that
   (1) the members of the family differed in their view of Willy Loman.
   (2) the brothers will stick together.
   (3) the family was not tightly knit.
   (4) there was a generation gap in the family.
   (5) everyone blames Willy for his action.

4. Happy defends Willy by saying
   (1) he wanted to be popular.
   (2) he was a family man.
   (3) he wanted to be a top salesman.
   (4) he wanted to build his house.
   (5) he didn't care for himself.

5. The member of the family who differs from the rest is
   (1) Linda
   (2) Biff
   (3) Charley
   (4) Happy
   (5) Willy

6. The irony of the situation is that, at the time of Willy's death, the family is
   (1) splitting up
   (2) united in tragedy
   (3) appreciative of Willy
   (4) in good shape financially
   (5) mutually supportive

Answer Key
1. **1**   2. **5**   3. **1**   4. **3**   5. **2**   6. **4**

Summary of Interpretation of Drama Reading

The skills needed in reading and interpreting drama call for you to:

1. Try to imagine the setting. If no stage directions are given, deduce from the speech and dialogue of the characters where the action is taking place.

2. Visualize the action. As the characters speak, figure out *what they are doing* while they are speaking.

3. Determine their motives. Why are the characters speaking as they do? *Why are they doing what they do?*

4. Determine their character and personality. What sort of person talks and acts the way he does? Why?

5. Determine the conflict that is taking place. Since the essence of drama is conflict, who or what is in conflict with whom or what? Is the conflict physical? Is it emotional? Is it a conflict of ideas?

6. Try to predict on the basis of all of the above what is most likely to happen next.

7. Read the scene aloud, trying to project yourself into the character of each of the roles.

READING COMMENTARY ON THE ARTS

Selections that fall under the term *commentary* are limited to the aspects of contemporary writing that deal with the arts—music, art, theater, movies, television, literature, and dance. They are further limited to selections in which the author comments critically on the arts, discussing the value of the content and the style of these means of expression.

In reading commentaries, try to determine the point of view of the writer and whether his or her evaluation of the artist, the musician, the author, the playwright, the film, the television program, or the dancer is favorable or unfavorable. Also look for the insights of the critic into the meaning and emotion conveyed by the artist or the medium.

The writing style will be that of the author of a piece of popular literature, so sentence structure and vocabulary will be relatively simple. *Here is a helpful hint.* Since critics who comment on the arts are describing their reactions, they resort to many adjectives that express their judgment.

Here are a couple of dozen of such adjectives: *adept, authentic, candid, credible, dynamic, eloquent, exquisite, graphic, inane, inept, laudable, lucid, naive, poignant, prosaic, spontaneous, superb, superlative, tedious, timeless, tiresome, trite, vivacious, witty.*

Practice in Reading Commentary on the Arts

WHAT DID THE CREATOR OF THE MUPPETS CONTRIBUTE TO CHILDREN'S TELEVISION?

He built an empire on a discarded green coat and a Ping-Pong ball. Jim Henson, creator of Kermit the Frog and a menagerie of other furry creatures known as the Muppets, revolutionized puppetry and reinvented children's television.

The Muppets charmed audiences of all ages on *Sesame Street*, possibly the most influential children's show ever, and later on *The Muppet Show*, which became the mostly widely watched TV program in the world, attracting 135 million viewers in 100 countries.

Henson succeeded with craftsmanship and showmanship and salesmanship. But above all, he constantly challenged the status quo.

Henson was one of the first producers to use television not merely as a medium but as a tool to enhance his performances.

While earlier puppet programs, such as *Kukla, Fran, and Ollie*, simply pluncked a camera in front of a traditional stage, Henson used a variety of camera lenses to create illusions which made his Muppets more agile and antic.

He also taught his puppeteers to work while using a TV monitor. For the first time, they could see not only their performances as they were unfolding, but also what the viewers could see.

That insight led Henson to create a new, softer-looking style of puppet that was extremely expressive in TV closeups.

Henson's unconventional approach to life came through in his Muppets—a word he coined for the crossbreed of marionettes and puppets he developed in the mid-50s.

While companies like Disney were creating model characters that lived up to the era's model of perfection, such as Bambi, Henson's creatures, such as the proud Miss Piggy, the grumpy Oscar the Grouch, and the uncontrollable Animal, were wildly irreverent.

Henson also applied this irreverent approach to his work. He promoted productivity, not by demanding results, but by encouraging his associates to have fun. He promoted silliness, even chaos, on the set. In fact, he was most satisfied with a scene when it had grown so funny that no one could perform it without busting up, former associates say.

Despite his childlike enthusiasm, Henson was also a pragmatist who tackled situations by approaching them from new angles. He was a problem solver and had a knack for sidestepping complexity and finding a simpler, purer way of doing things.

1. The contributions of Jim Henson, according to the article,
   (1) retained earlier approaches
   (2) added little to current programming
   (3) climbed on the bandwagon of children's television
   (4) imitated Kukla, Fran, and Olllie
   (5) broke new ground in puppetry

2. The reinventing of children's TV was exemplified by the worldwide success of
   (1) *Sesame Street*
   (2) *The Muppet Show*
   (3) *Kukla, Fran, and Ollie*
   (4) Kermit the Frog
   (5) the status quo

3. The most important reason for the success of Jim Henson was
   (1) his craftsmanship
   (2) his showmanship
   (3) his salesmanship
   (4) his unconventional approach
   (5) his charm

4. Henson pioneered in using television
   (1) as a medium
   (2) to improve performance
   (3) as a traditional stage
   (4) to teach tried-and-true methods
   (5) to preserve the familiar puppets

5. Henson's Muppets
   (1) sought perfection
   (2) imitated Disney's creations
   (3) were disrespectful
   (4) were ideal role models
   (5) were static and serious

6. Jim Henson was all of the following EXCEPT
   (1) a man of childlike enthusiasm
   (2) a searcher for simple solutions
   (3) a pragmatist
   (4) an irreverent innovator
   (5) a conformist

Answer Key

1. **5**   2. **2**   3. **4**   4. **2**   5. **3**   6. **5**

7

MATHEMATICS

AN OVERVIEW

BASIC FACTS

The Mathematics section of the GED test contains approximately 55 questions, most of which are word problems. You will have 90 minutes to answer them. All problems offer multiple-choice answers, and you don't have to show any of your computational work.

You are not permitted to use a calculator. This means you must have a solid grasp of multiplication, division, addition, and subtraction facts.

THE "FORMULAS" SHEET

Students are usually relieved when they first hear that a 1 1/2-page collection of mathematical formulas will be included in every test booklet. That is, until they actually examine the sheet and see how complicated-looking the information appears. The sheet can be a worthwhile aid, but first you must learn how and when to apply the information listed there. Such learning is only accomplished through hard work and dedication. Once it's done, however, you'll be pleasantly surprised to find you won't even need the sheet—much of it will already be committed to memory. You'll be able to move through the test more quickly and confidently.

WORD PROBLEMS USING BASIC OPERATIONS

Almost all of the questions on the GED will be word problems. Read carefully and rely on your common sense to tell you what operations to use. Be aware of certain words and phrases that tell you what to do:

- **Sum, total,** and **all together** usually mean addition.
- **How much more, how much less, find the difference,** and **deduct** indicate subtraction.

EXAMPLE

Carl purchased a computer for $589. In addition, he chose to buy a two-year service contract for $75 and a tech-support option for $35. What is the total cost of Carl's computer purchase?

The words **total** and **in addition** should clue you in to the fact that this is an addition problem:

$$
\begin{array}{rl}
589 & \text{for the computer} \\
75 & \text{for the service contract} \\
+\;\;\;35 & \text{for tech-support option} \\
\hline
\$699 & \text{for the computer purchase}
\end{array}
$$

EXAMPLE

The Glenridge Elementary School had an enrollment of 352 first-graders and 413 second-graders. How many more second-graders were there than first-graders?

$$
\begin{array}{rl}
413 & \text{second-graders} \\
-\;\;352 & \text{first-graders} \\
\hline
61 & \text{more second-graders}
\end{array}
$$

Multiplication is not often associated with particular words or phrases. Rely on your mathematical sense to determine whether to multiply.

Practice—Solving Word Problems

1. Geri cycled a 36-mile loop every day for two weeks. What is the total number of miles she rode during that period?
2. In 1939 there were 4,212 people who lived in the town of Twin Forks. By 1999 there were 32,118 people residing there. What is the difference between Twin Forks' population in1999 and 1939?

Answers
1. **504**   2. **27,906**

Multistep Word Problems

Multistep problems ask you to use more than one operation to find an answer. You might, for example, need to add a set of numbers, then multiply the sum by another number.

EXAMPLE

The Wilson children were each given a weekly allowance. Tanya, the oldest, received $15, Ed got $10, and Lakisha, the youngest, got $8. Find the total amount the children received after four weeks.

Step one: Find the total allowance for **one** week by adding the amounts of each child.

$$
\begin{array}{r}
15 \\
10 \\
+\ \ 8 \\
\hline
\$33 \quad \text{for one week}
\end{array}
$$

Step two: Multiply one week's total allowance by 4 (for 4 weeks)

$$
\begin{array}{r}
33 \\
\times\ \ 4 \\
\hline
\$132 \quad \text{combined allowance for 4 weeks}
\end{array}
$$

Gross and **net** are two words you will encounter frequently.
Gross is a total amount **before** deducting taxes, expenses, etc.
Net is the amount remaining **after** deducting taxes, expenses, etc.

EXAMPLE

Tracy's **gross** salary is $450 per week. After her employer deducts $150 for taxes and medical insurance, her **net** salary is $300.

Practice—Multistep Word Problems
1. Each month, the Bluesteins pay a home mortgage of $860 and a $218 payment on their car loan. What is the cost of these expenses for one year?
2. Sue is an endurance athlete who likes to run and bike. She can run 6 miles per hour and can bike at 22 miles per hour. In three hours, how much farther can she travel biking than running?

Answers

1. **$12,936**   2. **48**

SETUPS

Throughout the GED, you will have to respond to setup questions. You won't have to find an answer to the problem, but, instead, will be asked to choose the setup of operations that will allow you to solve it. Setups are usually "friendly" questions; since you don't need to do any calculation to answer them, they take up less time.

EXAMPLE

Bill, Jodi, and Sue decided to share evenly the cost of a computer package that includes the following items: computer and keyboard—$724, monitor—$212, and printer—$159. Which expression below represents what each person had to contribute to the purchase?

(1) $(\$724 + \$212 + \$159) + 3$

(2) $\dfrac{3}{(\$724 + \$212 + \$159)}$

(3) $3(\$724 + \$212 + \$159)$

(4) $\dfrac{(\$724 + \$212 + \$159)}{3}$

(5) $(3 + \$724) + (3 + \$212)$

The answer is (4) because it's the only one that adds the cost of the computer components together, then divides them among the three people sharing the expense.

PARENTHESES

Parentheses ( ) are a very important part of setups and mathematical computation, in general. They serve to enclose and isolate parts of mathematical sentences. *Do the operations in parentheses first.* Here are some examples of how parentheses work:

$$3(26 + 41)$$

tells you to add 26 + 41, then multiply the sum (67) by 3.
Answer: 201

$$(95 + 26) - (81 + 14)$$

tells you, **first**, to add 95 + 26 = 121 and 81 + 14 = 95
then, **second**, to subtract 121 − 95
Answer: 26

Practice—Setups and Parentheses

1. Find the value of 4(46 + 23 − 8)

2. Find the value of $\dfrac{5(19 + 3)}{11}$

3. Serena took her family out to a fast-food restaurant. The bill was $18.24 and the tax was $3.11. Serena gave the cashier $25 to pay the bill. Which of the following expression represents the change Serena received?

(1) (20 + 5) + (18.24 − 3.11)

(2) $\dfrac{(18.24 - 3.11)}{25}$

(3) 25 − (18.24 + 3.11)

(4) (18.24 − 3.11) − 25

Answers

1. **244**   2. **10**   3. **3**

EXPONENTS

Consider this number: 6^3

The little 3 that seems to be floating in the air is called an **exponent**. 6 is called the **base number**. What you're being told to do here is multiply **6 × 6 × 6**. It can also be stated as "6 to the third power."

$$6^3 = 6 \times 6 \times 6$$
$$6 \times 6 = 36 \times 6 = 216$$
$$6^3 = 216$$

Any number to the first power is equal to itself.

EXAMPLE

$$18^1 = 18$$

Sometimes on the GED, you might have to deal with more complex exponent problems like this one:

$$5^4 + 6^2 - 8^1 =$$

Convert each base/exponent pair into a separate number and then perform the operations.

$$5^4 = 5 \times 5 \times 5 \times 5 = 625$$
$$6^2 = 6 \times 6 = 36$$
$$8^1 = 8$$
$$625 + 36 - 8 = 653$$

Practice—Exponents
Find the value of the following.

1. 7^3
2. 10^4
3. 16^3
4. 28^1

Answers
1. **343**   2. **10,000**   3. **4096**   4. **28**

SQUARE ROOTS

The square root sign $\sqrt{\ }$ looks like a cross between a checkmark and a division sign. When you see this: $\sqrt{49}$, you're being asked to find a number that, multiplied by itself, will equal 49. Since $7 \times 7 = 49$, 7 is the square root of 49 or $\sqrt{49} = 7$.

Here's how to find square roots of larger numbers.

EXAMPLE

Find $\sqrt{441}$

Step one: Narrow down using multiples of 10.

You know that $10 \times 10 = 100$, but that's too low. Next, try $20 \times 20 = 400$—very close to 441. $30 \times 30 = 900$, which is way over. The square root of 441 must be a number more than 20 and less than 30. So we know $\sqrt{441} = 2\_$

Step two: Find the exact number for the ones' digit.

441 ends in a "1." Therefore, the number you choose to accompany your 20, when multiplied by itself, must end in one. For example, $1 \times 1 = 1$ (that works, so it could be 21.) $2 \times 2 = 4$ (no) $3 \times 3 = 9$ (no), $4 \times 4 = 1\underline{6}$ (ends in "6"—no) and so on—up to $9 \times 9 = 8\underline{1}$ (ends in "1"—yes). You have two numbers to choose from—21 or 29. Which one is a better guess? 21, of course, because 29 is so close to 30 and you've already seen that 30^2 is 900, which is way over.

Step three: Try it. $21 \times 21 = 441$

Answer: $21 = \sqrt{441}$

EXAMPLE

The value of $\sqrt{34}$ is between what pair of whole numbers?

(a) 16 and 17
(b) 5 and 6
(c) 2 and 3
(d) 9 and 10
(e) 6 and 7

This can be done in your head. Since $5 \times 5 = 25$ is too low and $6 \times 6 = 36$ is just a bit too high, the number has to be between the two. The actual $\sqrt{34}$ is 5.830518... but (b) will answer this question.

Answer: (b)

Practice—Square Roots

Solve.

1. $\sqrt{121}$
2. $\sqrt{289}$
3. $\sqrt{529}$

Answers

1. **11**   2. **17**   3. **23**

ORDER OF OPERATIONS

Do you remember learning *PEMDAS* or "Please Excuse My Dear Aunt Sally?" This is a way of remembering the order of operations for solving complicated mathematical sentences.

PEMDAS or "Please Excuse My Dear Aunt Sally"
1st—**P** stands for **parentheses**
2nd—**E** stands for **exponents**
3rd—**M** stands for **multiplication**
4th—**D** stands for **division**
5th—**A** stands for **addition**
6th—**S** stands for **subtraction**

If you have a problem that asks you to do addition, multiplication, and some work in parentheses, first you would do the work in parentheses, then the multiplication, and finally, the addition. Memorize the order and follow it.

EXAMPLE

Solve: $\dfrac{(5+3)^2}{4} + 27$

Step one: **P** (parentheses) always comes first, so do all work in parentheses.

$5 + 3 = 8$. Now the problem looks like this:

$$\frac{8^2}{4} + 27$$

Step two: **E** (exponents) comes second, so do $8 \times 8 = 64$

$$\frac{64}{4} + 27$$

Step three: **D** (division) is the next operation in the order that has to be performed in this particular problem, so do $64 \div 4 = 16$

$$16 + 27$$

Step four: **A** (addition) is the last step for this problem. So do $16 + 27 = 43$

Answer: 43

Practice—Order of Operations
Evaluate using order of operations.

1. $(43 - 19) + (16 - 14)4$

2. $\frac{48}{3} - 6$

3. $\frac{(6 + 7 + 2)^3}{3}$

Answers
1. **32**   2. **10**   3. **1125**

MEAN AND MEDIAN

Finding the *mean* and *median* of a group of numbers are two operations you must learn for the GED. They both tell you to find the *average* for a group of numbers, but each is a bit different from the other.

> **Mean** is interchangeable with the word **average**. Add all of the numbers given, then divide by the amount of numbers.

EXAMPLE

Tanya is a waitress at the Mercer Street Café. Last week, she worked five days and earned the following tips:

> Monday: $26
> Tuesday: $32
> Wednesday: $18
> Thursday: $40
> Friday: $39

Find the mean (average) amount of her daily tips for the five days she worked.

Step one: Add all of the numbers

$$(26 + 32 + 18 + 40 + 39) = 155$$

Step two: Count how many numbers you just added and divide by the amount of the numbers.

$$5 \overline{)155} \quad 31$$

Answer: Mean amount of tips for the days worked that week is $31. It's true that Tanya never earned $31 on any of the given days she worked that week. The mean indicates that an **average** day's tips for her comes to about **$31**.

Median is the middle number in a group of numbers arranged in order. Sometimes this is a very simple operation—just line the numbers up in order and pick the one in the middle. Other times, it's a bit more complicated.

EXAMPLE

For the marking period, Joe's test scores are 86, 66, 75, 81, and 68. What is his median score for the marking period?

Step one: Line the numbers up in order:

66   68   75   81   86

Step two: Choose the middle number: 75

EXAMPLE

For the next marking period, Joe's test scores are 62, 88, 90, 85, 75, and 83. What is his median score for the marking period?

Step one: Line the numbers up in order:

62   75   83   85   88   90

Step two: Choose the middle number—but there's a problem. There is no middle number because there are an even amount of numbers. In these situations, *choose the **two** middle numbers* and average those two:

62   75   83   85   88   90

The two middle numbers are 83 and 85.

Sub-step one: 83 + 85 = 168

Sub-step two: 168 ÷ 2 = 84

Answer: Joe's median score for the marking period is **84**.

Practice—Mean and Median

1. Kwan is a bike messenger who works three days a week. On Wednesday, he pedaled 32 miles, on Thursday 48 miles, and on Friday 34 miles. What is the mean distance he pedaled during those days?

2. Cara is a real estate broker who does a survey of properties for sale on Beach Street. The prices for four homes are $96,000; $92,900; $101,500; and $91,000. Find the median sale price for the homes on Beach Street.

Answers

1. **38**   2. **$94,450**

NOT ENOUGH INFORMATION IS GIVEN

Sometimes, a question is purposely misleading. It fails to provide enough information for you to calculate the answer.

EXAMPLE

Forestry workers plant trees at the rate of 12 per hour. At that rate, how long will it take two workers to plant 8 acres of cleared land?

(a) 86 hours
(b) 14 hours
(c) 43 hours
(d) 16 hours
(e) not enough information given

The answer is (e). You would need to know how many trees need to be planted in order to calculate an answer.   The size of the land is not relevant information.

> **Note:** Don't be frequently tempted by the "not enough information is given" response. It is used on only a few occasions during the course of a GED Math section.

Practice—Not Enough Information Is Given

One of the following questions does not provide enough information; another does.

1.   Gerald works for his uncle 3 days a week, and gets paid $115 a day plus tips. He works two days a week delivering lumber for $90 a day. What is his average daily pay for a typical week?
  (1) $525
  (2) $105
  (3) $185
  (4) $95
  (5) not enough information is given

2. A plumber buys pipe at $1 a foot. From a 15-foot pipe, he cuts a piece 9 feet long to be used on a job. What is the value of the unused portion?

   (1) $16
   (2) 15 – 11
   (3) $6
   (4) $8
   (5) not enough information is given

Answers

1. **5**　　2. **3**

BASIC GEOMETRY

In this section, you will deal with the rectangle, square, rectangular container, and cube.

Perimeter

The perimeter is the distance around a figure. It's the sum of the lengths of all its sides.

EXAMPLE

Find the perimeter of the triangle below.

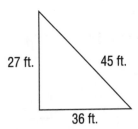

To find perimeter, add the sum of all sides:　27 + 36 + 45 = 108 ft.
Note: Always be aware of the units named in the diagram or asked for in the problem. If it's *feet*, make sure your answer is in *feet*.

EXAMPLE

Find the perimeter of the rectangle below.

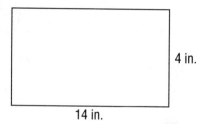

4 in.

14 in.

The formula for finding the perimeter of a rectangle is:

$$P = 2(l) + 2(w)$$
l = length and w = width

The *length* of the rectangle is the longer side and the *width* is the shorter side.

In the rectangle above, the length = 14 in. and the width = 4 in. Now you can use the formula for perimeter:

$P = 2(l) + 2(w)$
$P = 2(14) + 2(4)$
$P = 28 + 8$
$P = 36$ in.

Answer: Perimeter = 36 in.

EXAMPLE

Find the perimeter of the square below.

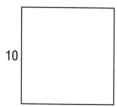

10

The formula for finding the perimeter of a square is:

$$P = 4(s)$$
$$s = \text{side}$$

Unlike a rectangle, all four sides of a square are equal. So, to find a square's perimeter, multiply the one side × 4.

$$P = 4(s) \qquad P = 4(10) \qquad P = 40$$

Note how there is no unit of measure next to the 10. 10 what? You will sometimes see this on the GED. Simply express the answer in terms of a number without a unit of measure.

Answer: $P = 40$

Practice—Finding Perimeter
Find the perimeter of the following figures.

1.

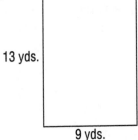

28 in.   28 in.

26 in.

2.

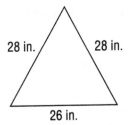

13 yds.

9 yds.

3.

41

Answers

1. **82 in.**   2. **44 yds.**   3. **164 sq. units**

Area

The area of a figure is the measure of flat surface inside its perimeter.

EXAMPLE ONE

A bedroom is 10 ft. long and 12 ft. wide. How many square feet of carpet will be needed to cover its floor?

The bedroom above is rectangular. The formula for the area of a rectangle is:

$$A = l(w) \quad \text{or} \quad A = lw$$

Note: When letters are pushed right next to each other it means multiply.
In this case, **lw** means **length** × **width**

Step one: Draw a diagram. It's always a good idea to draw a diagram from a word problem about geometry to help visualize what you need to solve.

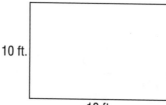

10 ft.

12 ft.

Step two: Using the formula for the area of a rectangle, find the area.

$$A = lw$$
$$A = 10(12)$$
$$A = 120 \; square \text{ feet.}$$

EXAMPLE

Find the area of the square below.

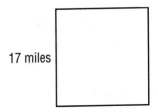

17 miles

Since all the sides of a square are equal, the formula for the area of a square is:

$$A = s^2$$

$$A = s^2$$
$$A = 17^2$$
$$A = 17 \times 17$$
$$A = 289$$

Answer: *A* = 289 sq. miles

Practice—Area

1.

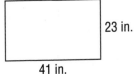

23 in.

41 in.

(a) find perimeter
(b) find area

2.

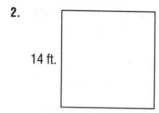

14 ft.

    (a) find perimeter
    (b) find area

3. How many 1-ft. by 1-ft. square blocks would be required to pave a patio with a length of 20 ft. and a width of 12 ft.?

Answers
1. (a) **128 in.**   (b) **903 sq. in.**
2. (a) **56 ft.**   (b) **196 sq. ft.**
3. **240**

Volume

Volume is the measure of the amount of space inside a three-dimensional figure such as a rectangular container, cube, or sphere. It tells how much these figures can hold.

EXAMPLE

Find the volume for the rectangular container below.

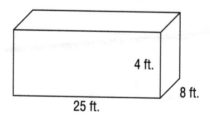

4 ft.

8 ft.

25 ft.

The formula for volume of a rectangular container is:

$$V = lwh$$
$$V = \text{volume}$$
$$l = \text{length}$$
$$h = \text{height}$$
$$w = \text{width}$$
$$(V = l \times w \times h)$$

$V = 25 \times 8 \times 4 = 800$ **cubic** ft. or 800 ft. **cu.** or 800 ft.^{3}

Note: A rule in math called the **associative property** states that it doesn't matter in what order you multiply any three numbers together, the answer will always be the same. So, for finding volume, don't worry about which is the height, length, or width. Just multipy three numbers in any order.

EXAMPLE

A cube-shaped container holds sand. How many cubic feet of sand will it hold if one of its sides is 8 feet?

The formula for volume of a cube is:

$$V = s^3 \qquad v = \text{volume} \qquad s = \text{side}$$

Since all sides of a cube are equal, there is no difference between its length, width, and height. Just multiply any side to the third power.

Step one: Draw a diagram.

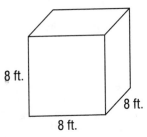

8 ft.

8 ft.

8 ft.

Step two: Do the multiplication.

$$8 \times 8 \times 8 = 512 \text{ cu. ft.}$$

Practice—Volume

1.   Find the volume of the figure below.

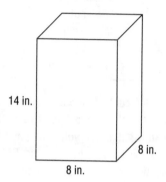

14 in.

8 in.

8 in.

2.   What is the difference in volume between a 13-ft. cube and a 10-ft. cube?

Answers

1. **896 cu. in.**   2. **1,197 cu. ft.**

FRACTIONS

WRITING FRACTIONS

A **fraction** of something means a part of that thing; for example, a pizza pie has eight slices. If you take one slice, that equals $\frac{1}{8}$ (one eighth) of the pie. Two slices equals $\frac{2}{8}$ (two eighths), three slices equals $\frac{3}{8}$ (three eighths), and so on.

In the fraction $\frac{3}{8}$, the top number (3) is called the **numerator**. It tells how many parts you have. The bottom number (8) is called the **denominator** and tells you how many equal parts there are in the whole.

$$\underline{3} \leftarrow \text{numerator}$$
$$8 \leftarrow \text{denominator}$$

Consider the square below:

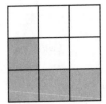

It's one whole divided into nine equal parts. If four of those parts are shaded, as in the diagram above, the shaded area represents $\frac{4}{9}$ of the square.

Fraction Types

There are three types of fractions you need to become familiar with: proper fractions, improper fractions, and mixed numbers.

- *Proper fractions* have numerators that are smaller than their denominators and are always less than one. $\frac{1}{3}$, $\frac{5}{6}$, and $\frac{11}{12}$ are proper fractions.

- *Improper fractions* have numerators that are larger than or equal to their denominators. $\frac{7}{3}$, $\frac{9}{6}$, and $\frac{12}{12}$ are improper fractions.

- *Mixed numbers* have a whole number included to the left of the fraction.

    $3\frac{1}{2}$ (three and one-half)

    $5\frac{5}{6}$ (five and five-sixths) are mixed numbers

Practice—Writing Fractions

Put an I for improper fraction, P for proper fraction, and M for mixed number on the blank lines next to each number below.

1. _____ $\frac{3}{8}$

2. _____ $\frac{8}{5}$

3. _____ $9\frac{3}{11}$

Answers

1. **P**   2. **I**   3. **M**

EQUIVALENT FRACTIONS AND REDUCING TO LOWEST TERMS

Four slices of pizza make up $\frac{4}{8}$ of a pie, which happens also to be $\frac{1}{2}$ the pie. Therefore, we say $\frac{4}{8}$ is **equivalent** (equal) to $\frac{1}{2}$. Even though the numbers in both the numerator and denominator are higher, the value of $\frac{4}{8}$ and $\frac{1}{2}$ are the same. Notice in the fraction $\frac{4}{8}$ that both numerator and denominator can be divided by 4.

$$\frac{4 \div 4 = 1}{8 \div 4 = 2}$$

This process is called **reducing to lowest terms**. Simply find the largest number that can be used to divide both numerator and denominator, then divide.

EXAMPLE

Reduce the following fractions to lowest terms.

$$\frac{5}{25} \qquad\qquad \frac{6}{9}$$

$$\frac{5 \div 5 = 1}{25 \div 5 = 5} \qquad\qquad \frac{6 \div 3 = 2}{9 \div 3 = 3}$$

Practice—Reducing to Lowest Terms

Reduce the following fractions to lowest terms.

1. $\frac{4}{8}$

2. $\frac{12}{16}$

3. $\frac{40}{50}$

Answers

1. $\frac{1}{2}$ 2. $\frac{3}{4}$ 3. $\frac{4}{5}$

RAISING FRACTIONS TO HIGHER TERMS

When solving problems with fractions, the **answer** must be expressed in lowest terms. However, when working with fractions to solve a problem, you will often have to do the exact opposite—raise them to higher terms while keeping them equivalent. To do this, multiply both the numerator and denominator by the same number.

In virtually all situations where you will raise to higher terms, the denominator will already be determined. You'll just need to figure out the numerator.

EXAMPLE

Convert $\frac{2}{3}$ to sixths

$$\frac{2}{3} = \frac{?}{6} \qquad \frac{2 \times 2}{3 \times 2} = \frac{4}{6}$$

Practice—Raising to Higher Terms

Add the appropriate numerator so that the fractions will be equivalent.

1. $\frac{5}{8} = \frac{}{24}$

2. $\frac{3}{8} = \frac{}{16}$

3. $\frac{4}{5} = \frac{}{20}$

Answers

1. **15**   2. **6**   3. **16**

CONVERTING IMPROPER FRACTIONS TO MIXED NUMBERS

Sometimes the solution to a problem will be expressed as an improper fraction, which then must be converted to a mixed number.

EXAMPLE

$$\frac{11}{4} = 2\frac{3}{4}$$

Remember that fractions are division problems, so $\frac{11}{4}$ can be written as $11 \div 4$ or $4\overline{)11}$.

$$\begin{array}{r} 2\ r3 \\ 4\overline{)11} \end{array}$$ 2 r3 is the same as $2\frac{3}{4}$

Practice—Converting Improper Fractions to Mixed Numbers
Convert the following improper fractions to mixed or whole numbers. Reduce where necessary.

1. $\frac{15}{2}$

2. $\frac{27}{3}$

3. $\frac{26}{4}$

4. $\frac{56}{7}$

Answers

1. $7\frac{1}{2}$ 2. **9**   3. $6\frac{1}{2}$ 4. **8**

ADDING AND SUBTRACTING FRACTIONS

Adding and subtracting fractions when the denominators are the same is a simple process. It looks like this:

$$\frac{1}{5} + \frac{3}{5} = \frac{4}{5} \qquad \frac{5}{7} - \frac{3}{7} = \frac{2}{7}$$

Notice the denominators stay the same and the numerators either increase or decrease.

Practice—Adding and Subtracting Fractions with Same Denominator

Solve the following and, where necessary, reduce to lowest terms.

1. $\frac{5}{8} - \frac{3}{8}$

2. $\frac{1}{6} + \frac{3}{6}$

3. $\frac{3}{11} + \frac{5}{11}$

Answers

1. $\frac{1}{4}$ 2. $\frac{2}{3}$ 3. $\frac{8}{11}$

LOWEST COMMON DENOMINATOR

When denominators **differ**, however, fractions can't be added or subtracted until all the denominators are converted to the same number, known as the **lowest common denominator** or **LCD**.

EXAMPLE

Find $\frac{5}{8} + \frac{1}{4}$

The two fractions have different denominators so you can't add them in their present state. Since $\frac{5}{8}$ can't be reduced to quarters, the lowest common denominator that can be used for both fractions is eighths. Both four and eight can divide eight evenly.

Step one: Choose the LCD. Here, it's eighths.

Step two: Convert $\frac{1}{4}$ to $\frac{2}{8}$ by raising to higher terms.

Step three: Add $\frac{5}{8} + \frac{2}{8}$

Answer: $\frac{7}{8}$

EXAMPLE

Find $\frac{1}{2} + \frac{1}{6} + \frac{1}{8}$

Step one: Choose the LCD.

This is a bit more difficult here. None of the denominators in the problem ($\bar{2}$, $\bar{6}$, or $\bar{8}$) can be used as an LCD. You canconvert $\frac{1}{2}$ to $\frac{4}{8}$ but you can't convert $\frac{1}{6}$ to eighths ($\bar{8}$) because six doesn't divide evenly into eight—there's a remainder of two. And $\frac{1}{2}$ can be converted to $\frac{3}{6}$, but, eighths can't be converted to sixths. You must choose the lowest number all three denominators ($\bar{2}$, $\bar{6}$, and $\bar{8}$) can divide into evenly. This is often a trial-and-error process. You already know 6 and 8 don't work. How about 10? 2 divides 10 evenly, but neither 6 nor 8 does so. How about 12? Both 2 and 6 divide it evenly, but 8 doesn't. How about 16? Both 2 and 8 work, but 6 doesn't. Eventually, you will reach 24. It is the lowest number that all three denominators can divide equally. Therefore, 24 is the LCD used for solving the problem. This may seem like a long process, but with some practice, finding the LCD will come more quickly to you.

Step two: Convert $\frac{1}{2}$ to $\frac{12}{24}$, $\frac{1}{6}$ to $\frac{4}{24}$, and $\frac{1}{8}$ to $\frac{3}{24}$

Step three: Add $\frac{12}{24} + \frac{4}{24} + \frac{3}{24}$

Answer: $\frac{19}{24}$

Practice—Adding and Subtracting Using LCD

Find the LCD, then add or subtract. Reduce answers to lowest terms where necessary.

1. $\dfrac{2}{7} + \dfrac{3}{21}$

2. $\dfrac{5}{6} - \dfrac{1}{3}$

3. $\dfrac{1}{4} + \dfrac{1}{6}$

4. $\dfrac{5}{7} + \dfrac{3}{4}$

Answers

1. $\dfrac{3}{7}$ 2. $\dfrac{1}{2}$ 3. $\dfrac{5}{12}$ 4. $1\dfrac{13}{28}$

COMPARING AND ORDERING FRACTIONS

To compare and order fractions with different denominators: (1) find the LCD; (2) convert fractions by raising to higher terms, where necessary; (3) compare the numerators.

EXAMPLE

Find the larger of the two fractions:

$$\frac{2}{5} \qquad \frac{1}{3}$$

Step one: Find the LCD: $\overline{15}$

Step two: Convert: $\dfrac{2}{5} = \dfrac{6}{15} \qquad \dfrac{1}{3} = \dfrac{5}{15}$

Step three: Compare: $\dfrac{6}{15}\left(\dfrac{2}{5}\right)$ is larger than $\dfrac{5}{15}\left(\dfrac{1}{3}\right)$ by $\dfrac{1}{15}$

Answer: $\dfrac{2}{5}$ **is larger**

EXAMPLE

Arrange the following fractions in order from greatest to least:

$$\frac{7}{8} \quad \frac{5}{6} \quad \frac{7}{12} \quad \frac{3}{4}$$

Step one: Find the LCD: use $\overline{24}$

Step two: Convert: $\frac{7}{8} = \frac{21}{24}$ $\frac{5}{6} = \frac{20}{24}$ $\frac{7}{12} = \frac{14}{24}$ $\frac{3}{4} = \frac{18}{24}$

Step three: Compare and arrange in order:

$$\frac{7}{8}\left(\frac{21}{24}\right) \quad \frac{5}{6}\left(\frac{20}{24}\right) \quad \frac{3}{4}\left(\frac{18}{24}\right) \quad \frac{7}{12}\left(\frac{14}{24}\right)$$

Practice—Comparing and Ordering Fractions

Choose the larger fraction in each pair.

1. $\frac{5}{8}$ $\frac{9}{16}$

2. $\frac{5}{12}$ $\frac{4}{9}$

3. $\frac{1}{3}$ $\frac{2}{7}$

Answers

1. $\frac{5}{8}$ 2. $\frac{4}{9}$ 3. $\frac{1}{3}$

WORKING WITH MIXED NUMBERS

Addition

EXAMPLE

$$14\frac{3}{4} + 2\frac{3}{5}$$

Step one: Using LCD, convert the fractions so they can be added.

$$14\frac{3}{4} = 14\frac{15}{20}$$
$$+ 2\frac{3}{5} = 2\frac{12}{20}$$
$$\overline{\phantom{+ 2\frac{3}{5} = } 16\frac{27}{20}}$$

Step two: Convert the fraction to a mixed number

$$\frac{27}{20} = 1\frac{7}{20}$$

and carry the whole number 1 over to the whole-number column, adding it to the 16.

$$16 + 1\frac{7}{20} = 17\frac{7}{20}$$

Subtraction and "Borrowing"

To subtract mixed numbers, you must be able to "borrow." Here's how to do it.

EXAMPLE

$$5\frac{1}{6} - 2\frac{5}{6}$$

$$5\frac{1}{6}$$

$$-2\frac{5}{6}$$

The problem here is that you can't subtract 5 from 1. You need to borrow from the column to the left, just as you do in working with whole numbers. You borrow 1 from 5, which then becomes 4. Then convert the borrowed one into 6ths. Remember: $1 = \frac{6}{6}$. Add those borrowed $\frac{6}{6}$ to the $\frac{1}{6}$, which now becomes $\frac{7}{6}$.

$$^4\cancel{5}\frac{1}{6} + \frac{6}{6} = 4\frac{7}{6}$$

$$-2\frac{5}{6}$$

$$2\frac{2}{6} = 2\frac{1}{3}$$

Always convert the borrowed 1 into whatever the denominator specifies. If it's 8ths, add $\frac{8}{8}$, or if it's 12ths, add $\frac{12}{12}$ to the existing fraction.

Practice—Adding and Subtracting with Mixed Numbers

Add or subtract. Express answers as mixed numbers where appropriate. Reduce to lowest terms.

1. $\dfrac{7}{9} + \dfrac{5}{9}$

2. $12\dfrac{1}{8} - 5\dfrac{5}{8}$

3. $\dfrac{3}{4} + \dfrac{5}{6}$

4. $41\dfrac{1}{3} - 18\dfrac{5}{9}$

Answers

1. $1\dfrac{1}{3}$ 2. $6\dfrac{1}{2}$ 3. $1\dfrac{7}{12}$ 4. $22\dfrac{7}{9}$

Multiplication

In one important way, multiplication is a much easier process than adding and subtracting fractions. You don't need to worry about finding a common denominator—simply multiply the numerators of the fractions by each other and then do the same for the denominators. Reduce to lowest terms where necessary.

EXAMPLE

Find $\dfrac{5}{8} \times \dfrac{1}{3}$

$$\dfrac{5 \times 1}{8 \times 3} = \dfrac{5}{24}$$

When multiplying fractions, all mixed numbers must be converted to improper fractions, and all whole numbers must use $\dfrac{}{1}$ as a denominator. See the following example.

EXAMPLE

Find $5\dfrac{3}{4} \times 7$

Step one: Convert to improper fractions

$$5\dfrac{3}{4} = \dfrac{23}{4} \qquad 7 = \dfrac{7}{1}$$

Step two: Multiply

$$\frac{23}{4} \times \frac{7}{1} = \frac{161}{4}$$

Step three: Divide and convert to a mixed number

$$\frac{161}{4} = 40\frac{1}{4}$$

Converting Mixed Numbers to Improper Fractions

How did we get $\frac{23}{4}$ from $5\frac{3}{4}$ in Step one above? Here's how.

Step one: Multiply the denominator of the fraction by the whole number to its left.

$$5\frac{3}{4} \quad (5 \times 4 = 20)$$

Step two: Take the product of Step one (20) and add it to the numerator.

$$(20 + 3 = 23)$$

Step three: Place the "new" numerator (<u>23</u>) over the same denominator (4).

$$5\frac{3}{4} = \frac{23}{4}$$

Practice—Converting Mixed Numbers to Improper Fractions
Convert the following to improper fractions.

1. $2\frac{3}{8}$
2. $14\frac{1}{2}$
3. $9\frac{6}{7}$

Answers

1. $\frac{19}{8}$ 2. $\frac{29}{2}$ 3. $\frac{69}{7}$

Using Cross-Cancelling in Multiplication

This process reduces the size of the numerators and denominators, making multiplication easier. Here's how to do it:

Look at the the the numerator and its diagonal denominator. See whether there is a number that divides evenly into both. Choose the **highest** number common to both, then divide them by that number. Cross the old numbers out and replace them with the newer (smaller) numbers. Then multiply horizontally (across) to find the answer.

EXAMPLE

Find $\dfrac{5}{18} \times \dfrac{9}{20}$

Step one: Look for diagonal relationships. Both 18 and 9 can be divided evenly by 9; both 20 and 5 can be divided evenly by 5.

Step two: Cross out the old numbers and replace them with the new ones.

$$\frac{^{1}\cancel{5}}{_{2}\cancel{18}} \times \frac{\cancel{9}^{1}}{20_{4}}$$

Step three: Multiply across using the new numbers.

$$\frac{1}{2} \times \frac{1}{4} = \frac{1}{8}$$

Practice—Multiplication of Fractions

Solve, using cross-canceling where possible. Reduce where necessary.

1. $\dfrac{1}{4} \times \dfrac{5}{8}$

2. $\dfrac{5}{6}\left(\dfrac{8}{15}\right)$

3. $\dfrac{1}{8}\left(4\dfrac{2}{3}\right)$

Answers

1. $\dfrac{5}{32}$ 2. $\dfrac{4}{9}$ 3. $\dfrac{7}{12}$

TRIANGLES

You already know how to calculate the perimeter of a triangle by adding up its sides. Finding its area is a bit more complicated. First, you must be able to identify two parts of the triangle—the base and the height.

The base is usually the "bottom" of the triangle, the side perpendicular to its height. The corner where the base and height lines meet make a 90-degree angle or square corner.

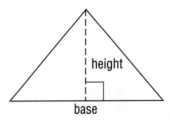

The height is almost always indicated by a vertical (up and down) dotted line. Only when the triangle is a **right triangle** is the height not marked by a dotted line. Study the diagrams below to become acquainted with base and height.

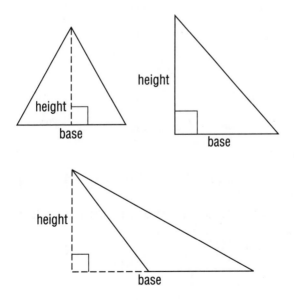

Area of a Triangle

The formula for area of a triangle is

$$A = \frac{1}{2}\,bh$$

It's easier to separate this formula into two steps so that is looks like this:

$$\frac{1}{2}\,(b \times h)$$

Do the work in parentheses first by finding the product of the base times the height, then multiply the product by $\frac{1}{2}$.

EXAMPLE

Find the area of the following triangle.

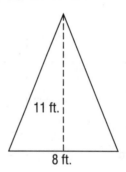

$$A = \frac{1}{2}\,(b \times h) \qquad A = \frac{1}{2}\,(8 \times 11) \qquad A = \frac{1}{2}\,(88)$$

$A = 44$ sq. ft. (remember that area is always expressed in **square** units).

Practice—Area of a Triangle

Find the area of the following triangles.

1.

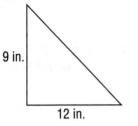

9 in.

12 in.

3.

35 yds.

32 yds.

2.

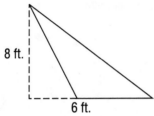

8 ft.

6 ft.

4.

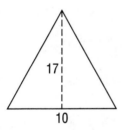

17

10

Which expression represents the area of triangle 4?

(a) $17(10 + 2)$

(b) $\dfrac{17}{2} \times \dfrac{1}{10}$

(c) $\dfrac{1}{2}(17 + 10)$

(d) $\dfrac{17 \times 10}{2}$

(e) $\dfrac{1}{2}(17 - 10)$

Answers

1. **54 sq. in.**   2. **24 sq. ft.**   3. **560 sq. yds.**   4. **(d)**

STANDARD MEASUREMENTS

Many of the GED math questions will test your knowledge of measurement conversions. You should make yourself very familiar with those listed below.

Time
1 year = 12 months = 52 weeks = 365 days
1 week = 7 days
1 day = 24 hours
1 hour = 60 minutes
1 minute = 60 seconds

Liquid Measure
1 pint = 16 ounces (oz.)
1 quart = 32 oz.
1 gallon = 4 quarts

Length
1 ft. = 12 in.   1 yd = 3 ft. = 36 in.

Weight
1 lb. = 16 oz.   1 ton = 2,000 lbs.

Sometimes, you'll need to convert larger units of measure to smaller ones, and vice versa. Some terms can be expressed in two different ways: (1) In two units of measure, and (2) as a fraction or mixed number. Become familiar with both.

EXAMPLE

Convert 40 ounces to quarts.

Answer 1: 40 oz. = 1 qt. 8 oz. (32 oz. is one quart—8 oz. is the "remainder")

Answer 2: 40 oz. = $1\frac{1}{4}$ qts. (32 oz. is one quart—$\frac{8}{32}$ is $\frac{1}{4}$ qt.)

EXAMPLE

Convert $2\frac{1}{2}$ days to hours.

$$2\frac{1}{2}(24) = \frac{5}{2} \times \frac{24}{1} = 60 \text{ hours}$$

Part-to-Whole Relationships

A fraction is representative of a part-to-whole relationship. When converting units of measure this $\frac{\text{part}}{\text{whole}}$ setup is useful.

EXAMPLE

Convert 45 minutes to hours

You know that 45 minutes is less than one hour; therefore, it's going to be a fraction (or part) of the whole hour, which is made up of 60 minutes. To solve, set up a fraction with the part (45) as numerator and the whole (60) as denominator. Then reduce.

$$\frac{45}{60} = \frac{3}{4} \text{ hour}$$

Practice—Standard Units of Measure

1. Convert 6,500 lbs. to: (a) tons   (b) tons and lbs.
2. Convert 18 months to: (a) years   (b) years and months

Using the *part* relationship, convert each of the following measures to a fraction of the whole units indicated.

3. 1 qt. = _____ gallons
4. 28 in. = _____ yd.

Using multiplication, convert the following.

5. $6\frac{1}{2}$ tons = _____ lbs.
6. 5 years = _____ months

Answers

1. (a) **3 tons, 500 lbs.**   (b) $3\frac{1}{4}$ **tons**

2. (a) **1 year, 6 months**   (b) $1\frac{1}{2}$ **years**

3. $\frac{1}{4}$ 4. $\frac{7}{9}$ 5. **13,000**   6. **60**

The Metric System of Measure

On the GED, you won't be asked to make precise conversions from the standard system to the metric system. But you should familiarize yourself with the following:

Liquid Measure

liter: about 1 qt.

milliliter: $\frac{1}{1000}$ of a liter

Weight

gram: $\frac{1}{28}$ of an ounce

milligram: $\frac{1}{1000}$ of a gram

kilogram: 1000 grams (2.2 lbs)

Length

meter: 39 inches

millimeter: $\frac{1}{1000}$ of a meter

kilometer: 1000 meters ($\frac{6}{10}$ of a mile)

WORD PROBLEMS WITH FRACTIONS

Part-to-Whole Relationship

The part-to-whole relationship is an important part of setting up solutions to word problems. Here's how to use it.

EXAMPLE

There were 42 people taking the GED exam at Grovesville Center, 28 of whom were men. Find the fractional part of men taking the test.

The **part** you're seeking is the number of men taking the test—28. The **whole** is the total number of people taking the test—42.

$$\frac{\text{part}}{\text{whole}} = \frac{28}{42} = \frac{2}{3}$$

Answer: $\frac{2}{3}$ of those taking the test were men.

Sometimes, the **whole** won't be stated; you'll have to figure it out by adding the parts.

EXAMPLE

Jerry packed his suitcase with 10 pairs of black socks, 12 pairs of white socks, and 2 pairs of striped socks. What fractional part of the socks he packed was white?

The **part** is 12, but the **whole** isn't stated. You must add 10, 12, and 2 to get it.

$$\frac{12}{10 + 12 + 2} = \frac{12}{24} = \frac{1}{2}$$

Practice—The Part-to-Whole Relationship

Solve.

1. The Kingsford field hockey team consisted of 27 girls, 18 of whom were seniors. What fractional part of the team was comprised of seniors?

2. A fourth-grade class at Bucksville Elementary School took a poll regarding its favorite ice cream flavors. Fifteen class members chose chocolate as their favorite, 8 chose vanilla, 2 chose pistachio and 5 chose various other flavors. Which expression can be used to find the fractional part of the class favoring chocolate?

   (a) $\frac{15}{4} + \frac{(8 + 5 + 2)}{4}$

   (b) $\frac{30}{15}$

   (c) $\frac{15}{15 + 8 + 2 + 5}$

   (d) $\frac{(8 + 2 + 15) - 15}{4}$

Answers

1. $\dfrac{2}{3}$ 2. **(c)**

"Of" Means "Multiply"

This may sound strange, but it's an important thing to remember. The word "of," especially when it appears in a fraction problem, almost always means you need to multiply.

EXAMPLE

At a free concert, $\dfrac{1}{6}$ of the 636 people who attended were senior citizens. How many senior citizens attended?

$$\dfrac{1}{6} \text{ of } 636 = \dfrac{1}{6} \times \dfrac{636}{1} = \dfrac{636}{6} = 106 \text{ senior citizer}$$

Practice—"Of" Means "Multiply"

Solve.

1. The Granville PTA spends $\dfrac{1}{4}$ of its annual budget on scholarship funds. If the PTA's budget is \$18,240, what fractional part is contributed to scholarship funds?

2. LeeAnn took a history test consisting of 75 questions, $\dfrac{2}{5}$ of which were multiple choice while the rest were short-answer. How many questions were short-answer?

Answers

1. **4560**   2. **45**

Ratio

Ratio is just another way to express a fractional part of something. It looks a little different (example: the ratio 1:3 is actually $\dfrac{1}{3}$) and sounds different (you would say 1:3 as "a ratio of one to three") but it acts just like a fraction.

EXAMPLE

There are 54 workers in an office, 18 of whom are men. What is the ratio of men to women in the office?

Step one: The number of women is not stated, so it must be figured out.

$$54 \text{ (total)} - 18 \text{ men} = 36 \text{ women}$$

Step two: Set the ratio up in the order it was asked for (men : women) or 18 : 36

Step three: Convert the ratio to a fraction and reduce $\frac{18}{36} = \frac{1}{2}$

Step four: Change back to a ratio when expressing the answer

Answer: 1 : 2 is the ratio of men to women.

Practice—Ratio

1. A computer printer is $119 and its ink cartridge is $17. What is the ratio of the price of the cartridge to the printer?
2. A student takes an exam with 100 questions on it and answers five questions incorrectly. What is the ratio of the number of questions he answered correctly to the number he answered incorrectly?

Answers
1. **7 : 1**   2. **19 : 1**

Probability

The probability of rolling a 3 using one die (one cube of dice) is said to be 1 in 6 or $\frac{1}{6}$. The numerator represents how many chances there are that a certain event will happen (in this case, rolling a 3) and the denominator represents the total number of possiblities. In this case, there are six different numbers (including the 3) that could come up. It's another use of the part-to-whole relationship.

EXAMPLE

A cooler is packed with 8 cans of ginger ale, 4 cans of root beer, and 12 cans of cola. What is the probability that a person reaching into the cooler will pull out a cola?

Step one: Get a denominator by calculating the total number of possibilities.

$$8 + 4 + 12 = 24$$

use $\frac{}{24}$ as a denominator

Step two: Get a numerator that represents the number of colas there are in the cooler.

$$\frac{12}{24} = \frac{1}{2}$$

Answer: The probability of pulling out a cola is $\frac{1}{2}$.

A root beer?

Step one: Get a denominator $\frac{}{24}$

Step two: Get a numerator $\frac{4}{24} = \frac{1}{6}$

Answer: The probability of pulling out a root beer is $\frac{1}{6}$.

A ginger ale? $\frac{8}{24} = \frac{1}{3}$

Answer: The probability of pulling out a ginger ale is $\frac{1}{3}$.

Practice—Probability

1. There are 6 limes, 5 lemons, and 4 tangerines in a bag. What is the probability of choosing a lemon the first time?
2. There are ten "number" keys on a computer keyboard and 36 "letter" keys. If a person presses a key at random, what is the likelihood that it will be the number 7?
3. You are trying to guess a person's birth date. What is the probability that the person was born in a month beginning with the letter "J?"

Answers

1. $\frac{1}{3}$ 2. $\frac{1}{46}$ 3. $\frac{1}{4}$

DECIMALS

Decimals are just like fractions—they are a way of showing part of a whole number. For example, $\frac{7}{10}$ is written as .7 or 0.7. You can read .7 as "seven tenths," but, more commonly, it is read as "point seven."

Actually, you've been using the decimal system for a long time, perhaps without realizing it. If you have a quarter, two dimes, and three pennies, you know you have $.48 or 48 cents. This .48 represents 48 cents out of one dollar, or $\frac{48}{100}$ or **.48 out of 1.00**.

DECIMAL PLACES

An important part of working effectively with decimals is understanding the **decimal place-value system**. As you move further to the right of the decimal point, the value of the numbers grows smaller. Study the chart below and memorize the values for each place to the right of the decimal point.

. _____ _____ _____ _____ _____
(10ths)　　(100ths)　　(1,000ths)　(10,000ths)　(100,000ths)

DECIMALS AND FRACTIONAL EQUIVALENTS

Study these fractional equivalents of decimals to better understand the system.

$$.1 = \frac{1}{10}$$

$$.14 = \frac{14}{100}$$

$$.235 = \frac{235}{1,000}$$

$$.7894 = \frac{7894}{10,000}$$

$$.90023 = \frac{90023}{100,000}$$

Practice—Writing Decimal Equivalents to Fractions

Write the following fractions as decimals. Refer to the place-value chart above if necessary.

1. $\frac{9}{10}$

2. $\frac{33}{100}$

3. $\frac{507}{1,000}$

Answers

1. **.9**   2. **.33**   3. **.507**

USING ZEROS WITH DECIMALS

Putting a zero to the **right** of a decimal number does not change its value at all. For example, .7 is equal to .70 or .700 or even .70000000! Which is worth more, seven dimes (.7 or $\frac{7}{10}$) or seventy cents (.70 or $\frac{70}{100}$)? Of course, their value is equal.

However, putting a zero to the left of a number (in between the number and the decimal point) **changes** its value by making it ten times smaller. For example, .07 is ten times smaller than .7. Which is larger, seven dimes (.7) or seven pennies (.07)? Seven dimes (.70) is larger than seven pennies (.07).

Which is larger, .4 or .396? Clearly, .4 is larger. This is often confusing to GED students at first. Try setting these decimals up as fractional equivalents and then compare.

$$.4 = \frac{4}{10} \qquad .396 = \frac{396}{1,000}$$

If you raise to higher terms for purposes of comparing fractions, you will see that:

$$\frac{4}{10} = \frac{400}{1,000} \text{ is larger than } \frac{396}{1,000} \text{ or } .400 \text{ is larger than } .396$$

Practice—Writing and Comparing Decimals with Fractions

Write the decimal equivalent of the following fractions.

1. $\dfrac{5}{1,000}$

2. $\dfrac{60}{100}$

3. $\dfrac{47}{100}$

Write "L" if the first decimal of the pair is larger, "S" if it is smaller, and "E" if the pair is equal.

4. .703   .0788
5. .493   .6
6. 1.08   2.003

Arrange the following sets of decimals in size order from smallest to largest.

7. 1.8, 1.743, .992, 1.089, 1.81
8. 71.049, 71.2, 70.98, 71.203, 71.0491

Answers
1. **.005**   2. **.6**   3. **.47**   4. **L**   5. **S**   6. **S**
7. **.992, 1.089, 1.743, 1.8, 1.81**
8. **70.98, 71.049, 71.0491, 71.2, 71.203**

ADDING AND SUBTRACTING DECIMALS

These operations are the same as working with whole numbers. Here's what it looks like.

EXAMPLE

$5.04 + 12.62 + .88$ $23.214 - 8.906$

```
   12.62              23.214
    5.04            -  8.906
 +   .88              14.308
   18.54
```

Notice: (1) how the place-value columns are perfectly aligned
 (2) that the decimal points are moved directly below in the answers.

The only complication with addition and subtraction is this:

EXAMPLE

$3.9 + 5 + 4.007$

It might be set up:
$$\begin{array}{r} 5 \\ 4.007 \\ +\ \underline{3.9} \end{array}$$

It **should** be set up:
$$\begin{array}{r} 5.000 \\ 4.007 \\ +\ \underline{3.900} \\ 12.907 \end{array}$$

Notice how the zeros are added to keep the place–value columns looking aligned to eliminate confusion and to help when there is carrying. This is especially true for subtraction when there is borrowing.

EXAMPLE

$5 - 3.03$

It **should** be set up:
$$\begin{array}{r} 5.00 \\ -\ \underline{3.03} \\ 1.97 \end{array}$$

Practice—Adding and Subtracting Decimals
Solve the following.
1. $4.09 + 55.369 + 5.6$
2. $300 - 186.82$
3. $88 + 903.01 + .06 + 12.173$

Answers
1. **65.059**   2. **113.18**   3. **1003.243**

MULTIPLYING DECIMALS

You learned in basic operations that it is best to arrange the larger number on top when multiplying, but when working with decimals this is not always the case. Place the number with the *most* digits on top—there's less work to do.

EXAMPLE

Solve   5.4 × 2.13

The number 5.4 is clearly larger than 2.13, but 2.13 has more digits. The problem should be set up this way, then solved using the following steps.

Step one: Don't align the decimals here. Just multiply.

$$\begin{array}{r} 2.13 \\ \times\ 5.4 \\ \hline 852 \\ 1065 \\ \hline 11502 \end{array}$$

Step two: Count the number of digits to the right of the decimal point in both multiplying numbers. Here, there are three (1 and 3 from 2.13 and 4 from 5.4).

Step three: Put your pen just past the last digit to the right. Here, it's the two. Now move the decimal point to the left the number of digits you counted in Step two (here, it's three). Place the decimal point there.

Answer: 11.502.

Practice—Multiplying Decimals
Solve.

1. 4.65(38)

2. .913(4.4)

3. 10.04(.03)

Answers

1. **176.7**   2. **4.0171**   3. **.3012**

DIVIDING DECIMALS

When the decimal is in the dividend, all that's needed to be done is to duplicate it (carefully and precisely) directly above to the "shelf" of the dividing sign. Then, divide as you normally would. The decimal is already placed correctly in the answer.

EXAMPLE

91.8 ÷ 54

```
                      1.7    ← quotient
                             ← shelf
   divisor →  54 ) 91.8      ← dividend
                 − 54
                  378
                − 378
                    0
```

When the decimal is in the divisor, the process becomes a bit more complicated. You cannot proceed with decimals there. Follow the steps below.

EXAMPLE

30.176 ÷ 7.36

```
                       4.1
   7.36. ) 30.17.6
         − 2944
            736
          − 736
              0
```

Step one: Move the decimal point in the divisor all the way to the right, making it a whole number. Count the number of places you've moved it. Here, it would be two.

Step two: Now move the decimal in the dividend the same number of spaces as you moved it in Step one.

Step three: Place a decimal on the "shelf" of the dividend just as you did in Example One above. Divide.

Note: Sometimes, you will need to move the decimal point in the dividend, but you will already be at the right end of the number. When this happens, create places to the right by adding zeros. See the following example.

EXAMPLE

$62 \div 1.25$

```
                49.6
        1.25 ) 62.00.0
             − 520
               1200
             − 1125
                 750
               − 750
                   0
```

The example above also illustrates another very important concept in division. Previously, you would have ended the division at the second zero in 6200 and expressed the answer as 49 r75. But now that you know how to work with decimals, this rough method of dividing is no longer necessary. Simply add zeros to the right side of the dividend until either:

    (1) the dividend divides evenly (as it did in Example Three)
        or
    (2) you have carried out the division to the decimal place specified by the question and the answer can then be **rounded off**.

Practice—Dividing Decimals

Solve using division. Round off answers to the nearest hundredth, where necessary.

1. $223.2 \div 12$
2. $34.44 \div 32.8$
3. $129 \div 5.14$
4. $\dfrac{67}{14}$

Answers
  1. **18.60**   2. **1.05**   3. **25.10**   4. **4.79**

SCIENTIFIC NOTATION

Scientific notation is a method used by scientists to convert very large or very small numbers to more manageable ones. You will almost certainly be required to do one conversion to scientific notation on the GED. It's an easy operation.

EXAMPLE

A space satellite can transmit from a distance of 46,000,000 miles away. What is the number written in scientific notation?

> *Step one:* Starting at the "imaginary" decimal point to the *right* of the last zero, move the decimal point until only one digit remains to its *left*.

> 46,000,000 becomes 4.6

> *Step two:* Count the number of places the decimal was moved left. It's 7 places, which is expressed this way:

> $$10^7$$

> *Step three:* Express the full answer in scientific notation this way:

> 46,000,000 miles = **4.6 $\times$ 10^7**

EXAMPLE

A microorganism is .000056 inch long. What is its length in scientific notation?

> *Step one:* Move the decimal point to the *right* until there is one digit other than zero to the *left* of the decimal.

> .000056 becomes 5.6

> *Step two:* Count the number of places moved to the right—it's 5, which is expressed this way, using a *negative sign* with the exponent:

> $$10^{-5}$$

> *Step three:* Express the full answer in scientific notation this way:

> .000056 = **5.6 $\times$ 10^{-5}**

Consider these other examples to help you get the concept:

$$783,000,000 = 7.83 \times 10^8$$
$$500,000,000 = 5 \times 10^8$$
$$.00000923 = 9.23 \times 10^{-6}$$
$$.0005134 = 5.134 \times 10^{-4}$$

Practice—Scientific Notation

Express in scientific notation.

1. 83,000,000
2. .000012
3. 5,160,000,000
4. .0000006

Answers

1. **8.3×10^7**   2. **1.2×10^{-5}**   3. **5.16×10^9**   4. **6×10^{-7}**

CIRCLES AND CYLINDERS

Now that you know how to multiply decimals, you can work with circles. First, there are important concepts you must understand and vocabulary you must memorize.

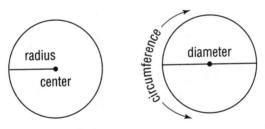

- The **circumference (c)** is the distance around the circle. It's another word for "perimeter."
- The **center** of a circle is its exact middle.
- The **radius (r)** of a circle is a straight line that runs from the exact center of the circle to its circumference.
- The **diameter (d)** is the distance across the circle from a point on the circumference to its opposite side, passing through the center. It is **twice the length of the radius** or **$d = 2r$**.

Calculating Radius, Diameter, and Circumference of a Circle

Learn the following:

> **radius = $\frac{d}{2}$** (radius = diameter ÷ 2)
>
> **diameter = 2r**
>
> **$c = \pi d$** (pi × diameter)

π = **pi (pronounced "pie")**. It is a letter from the Greek alphabet. It represents the number **3.14** and is essential for working with circles. Memorize it.

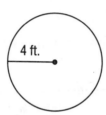

EXAMPLE

Calculate the radius, diameter, and circumference of the above circle.

- radius = 4 ft. (this is stated in the diagram—no calculation is necessary)
- diameter = 2r or 2(4) = 8 ft.
- circumference = πd or 3.14(4) = 12.56 ft.

Calculating the Area of a Circle

The formula for calculating the area of a circle is

$$A = \pi(r^2) \text{ or } \pi \times r^2$$

EXAMPLE

Find the area of the following circle.

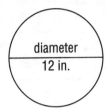

Step one: Find the radius. If $d = 12$ inches, then $r = \dfrac{d}{2}$ or 6 inches

Step two: Square the radius (r^2) $6 \times 6 = 36$ inches

Step three: Multiply $\pi \times r^2$
$3.14 \times 36 = 113.04$ **square** inches (even though a circle is round, area is still expressed in terms of **square** units.)

Practice—Calculating the Dimensions of Circles
Find the radius (r), diameter (d), circumference (c), and area (a) of the following circles. Round to the nearest hundredth, where necessary.

1.

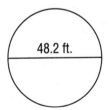

2.

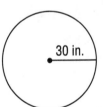

Answers
1. $r = 30$ inches, $d = 60$ inches, $c = 188.4$ inches, $a = 282.6$ inches
2. $r = 4.82$ feet, $d = 96.4$ feet, $c = 302.70$ feet, $a = 7294.97$

Calculating the Volume of Cylinders

Like cubes and rectangular containers, cylinders are three-dimensional figures, which are measured by volume. The formula for volume of a cylinder is:

> $$V = (\pi\, r^2)\, h \qquad \text{or}$$
> $$\text{volume} = (\pi \times \text{radius}^2) \times \text{height}$$

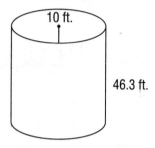

EXAMPLE

Find the volume of the above cylinder.

> *Step one:* Find the area on the top (or bottom) circle of the cylinder.
> $$A = \pi r^2 = 3.14 \times 10^2 = 314$$

Step two: $A \times h = 314 \times 46.3 = 14{,}538.2$ cubic (cu.) ft. (Always
express a volume answer in **cubic** units.)

Practice—Volume of Cylinders

Find the volume for the following cylinder.

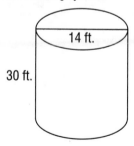

Answer
4615.8 cubic feet

PERCENTS

Working with percents is one of the more frequently tested skills on the GED, so it's essential that you become familiar with it.

The percent sign (%) following a number means that the number is a fraction of 100. For example, if you read about the construction of a bridge and the newspaper says, "The project is 60% complete," it means that if the entire bridge-building job were divided into 100 equal parts, 60 of them are complete or $\frac{60}{100}$ of the project is complete or $\frac{3}{5}$ of the project is complete.

CHANGING PERCENTS TO DECIMALS

This is a simple procedure. Replace the % sign with a decimal point and move it two places to the left.

EXAMPLE

Change 52% to a decimal (move two places to the left)—52% = .52

EXAMPLE

Change 3% to a decimal (move two places to the left)—3% = .03 (add a zero to occupy the place)

Notice that when there is a decimal point already included in the percent, begin at the decimal point and move it two places to the left.

EXAMPLE

Change 140% to a decimal (move two places to the left)—140% = 1.40

EXAMPLE

Change .5% to a decimal (begin at the decimal point and move two places to the right)—.5% = .005 (it's $\frac{1}{2}$ of 1%)

Practice—Converting Percents to Decimals

Convert the following to decimals.

1. 23%

2. 6%

3. 138%

4. 8.5%

Answers

1. **.23**   2. **.06**   3. **13.8**   4. **.085**

COMPARING AND ORDERING FRACTIONS, DECIMALS, AND PERCENTS

This activity is a summary of all you've learned about conversions. Consider the following examples.

EXAMPLE

Which of the following two numbers have the same value?

$$3\frac{3}{8} \qquad 33\% \qquad 37.5\% \qquad 3.33 \qquad \frac{3}{8}$$

(1) $3\frac{3}{8}$ and 3.33

(2) 33% and 3.33

(3) 37.5% and $3\frac{3}{8}$

(4) $\frac{3}{8}$ and 33%

(5) 37.5% and $\frac{3}{8}$

(1) $3\frac{3}{8}$ and 3.33 (no, but close, $3\frac{3}{8}$ = 3.375)

(2) 33% and 3.33 (no, 33% = 3.375)

(3) 37.5% and $3\frac{3}{8}$ (no, 37.5% = .375, $3\frac{3}{8}$ = 3.375)

(4) $\frac{3}{8}$ and 33% (no, 33% = $\frac{1}{3}$)

(5) 37.5% and $\frac{3}{8}$ (yes, both equal $\frac{3}{8}$ or .375 or 37.5%)

EXAMPLE

The following table indicates what part of his or her 12 oz. bottle each infant drank.

Tina—60%
LaShaun—.7
Lina—$\frac{2}{3}$

Which of the following lists the infants according to how much they drank from *least to greatest*?

(1) Tina, Lina, LaShaun
(2) LaShaun, Tina, Lina
(3) LaShaun, Lina, Tina
(4) Lina, LaShaun, Tina
(5) not enough information is given

Convert all numbers to the same scale, choosing the easiest method possible. Here, it would be decimals.

LaShaun—.7 (no conversion necessary)
Tina—60% =.60 or .6
Lina—$\frac{2}{3}$ = .66

Now, the answer is obvious: Tina (.6), Lina (.66), LaShaun (.7) or Choice (1).

Practice—Comparing and Ordering Decimals, Fractions and Percents

Choose the correct answer.

1. Which of the following is not the same as 3.25?

(1) $3\frac{25}{100}$
(2) 325%
(3) 3.25%
(4) $3\frac{1}{4}$
(5) 3.250

2. Ed is a sales agent who gets 16% of his salary from commission. Juana gets $\frac{1}{5}$ of her salary from commission and Bill gets $\frac{3}{8}$ of his salary from commission.

    Which of the following lists the sales agents according to the size of their commissions from smallest to largest?

    (1) Ed, Juana, Bill
    (2) Bill, Ed, Juana
    (3) Juana, Ed, Bill
    (4) Bill, Juana, Ed
    (5) Juana, Bill, Ed

Answers

1. **3**   2. **1**

SOLVING WORD PROBLEMS WITH PERCENTS

All word problems that involve percents, no matter how complicated they may seem, can be reduced to one of these three operations:

---

1. Finding a percent of a number
    30% of 86 = ?

2. Finding what percent one number is of another
    40 is ?% of 100

3. Finding a number when a percent of it is given
    30 is 40% of ?

GED students sometimes find it difficult to tell the difference among these three operations and when to apply each to a problem. An aid designed to help you with this difficulty is **the percent triangle**. Once it is understood and memorized, it will guide you through every operation with percents.

The Percent Triangle

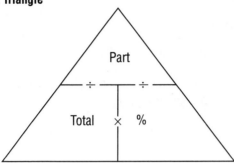

Here's how to use it:

EXAMPLE

What is 30% of 86?

> *Step one:* Decode the problem by labeling its parts. In this problem, you have a **total (86)** and a **% (30%)**. 30% will become .30 (always convert percents to decimals in calculations).

> *Step two:* Using the labeled parts, find the operation on the percent triangle. Notice that **total** and **%** are next to each other at the base of the triangle.

> *Step three:* Perform the operation (either × or ÷) indicated by the separation line between the parts in Step two.

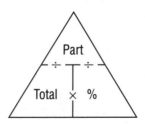

In this case, the × sign separates **total** and %.

$$86 \times .3 = 25.8$$

Answer: 30% of 86 = 25.8

EXAMPLE

32 is what percent of 128?

Step one: Decode and label. 32 is a **part** and 128 is a **total**.

Step two: Find the operation on the triangle. The sign that separates **total** and **part** is a ÷ sign.

Step three: Perform the operation. **Be careful here!** In Example One, the operation was multiplication, so it makes no difference how the numbers are arranged, the answer will always be the same. But when it comes to division, there is a huge difference in the answer if you choose the wrong dividends and divisors. Follow this one simple rule and you shouldn't have problems: When dividing using the triangle, *always place the **part** first.*
Therefore, in this example, you would find 32 ÷ 128.

$$128\overline{)32.00}^{\,.25}$$

The problem asks for a percent. Simply convert .25 to 25%. Does that make sense? Is $32\frac{3}{7}$ (25%) of 128? Yes.

Practice—Basic Word Problems with Percents
Label and solve.

1. 40% of 68 is ?
2. 90 is ? % of 135
3. 86 is 12.5% of ?

Answers
1. **27.2**   2. **67%**   3. **688**

WORD PROBLEMS WITH PERCENTS

Don't be intimidated by the length or complexity of percent word problems. Simply repeat the process you just learned. Reduce the sentences down to a short one, label, then perform the operations according to the triangle.

EXAMPLE

Alan earns a salary of $1,420. The rent he pays on his apartment is 44% of his salary. How much is his rent?

Step one: Reduce—all this problem is asking you to find is: 44% of $1,420.

Step two: % × total

Step three: Perform the operation—.44 × 1420 = $624.80
Answer: $624.80

EXAMPLE

Lee and Huan went to dinner at the Riverside Restaurant. Not including tax, the bill came to $34.50. The sales tax on the meal was $2.07. What percent of the meal was the sales tax?

Step one: Reduce—$2.07 is ? % of $34.50?

Step two: **Part ÷ total**

Step three: Perform the operation— $34.00\overline{)2.07.00}^{.06}$
Answer: .06 = 6%

Practice—Basic Word Problems II
Solve the following.
1. John bought 140 pieces of plywood for a construction job, but 40% of them were warped and had to be returned. How many pieces did John return?
2. Keira invested $43,608 in a mutual fund that paid $432.96 in interest at the end of the year. What was the percent of interest Keira earned from her initial investment?
3. The Baileys drove 280 miles during the first leg of a trip to visit their cousins. The distance represented 32% of the trip. How many miles is the entire trip?

Answers
1. **56**   2. **1%**   3. **875**

MULTISTEP PROBLEMS WITH PERCENTS

Most of the problems involving percents on the GED Math section will be multistep. They require careful attention to wording, but they are usually not much more complicated than the problems in the last exercise.

EXAMPLE

Michelle is a waitress who earns $7 per hour and receives 10% of all tips collected by her and the other waitresses by the end of the day. If she works a six-hour shift and $482.50 is the total collected by the end of the day, what are Michelle's total earnings for the day?

Step one: Calculate her hourly earnings—$7 × 6 = $42

Step two: Calculate her tips—10% of $482.50 = $48.25

Step three: Add $42 + $48.25 = $90.25

EXAMPLE

A home-entertainment system, originally priced at $1,250, is on sale for 15% off. One week later, the price of the system is reduced an additional 10% off the discounted price. What is the final sale price of the system?

The "double discount" is a frequently-asked question. Avoid the temptation to add the two discounts together (35%) and then find 65% of $1,250. Here's the right way to do it.

Step one: Find the sale price of the first discount—$1,250 × .85 = $1,062.50

Step two: Find the sale price of the second discount—$ 1,062.50 × .80 = $850
Answer: $850

Practice—Multistep Percent Problems
Solve the following.

1. A businesswoman spends $\frac{1}{5}$ of her travel allotment on airfare and

    $\frac{3}{10}$ on hotel accommodations. What percent of her allotment is left?

2. Last year's Fourth of July parade was attended by 25,000 people, but this year attendance was only 21,000. What was the percentage of decrease in attendance?

Answers

1. **50%**   2. **16%**

TABLES, GRAPHS, AND CHARTS

Many questions on the GED—not only in the Math section, but in the Science and Social Studies sections, as well—test your ability to read tables, charts, and graphs.

TABLES

Tables are the simplest forms of graphic representation. Usually, you'll be asked to answer more than one question based on information in the table. Take care to read all the information provided.

SCHEDULE FOR TRAIN LEAVING CENTERVILLE AT 4:05 P.M.			
Destination	**Arrival Time**	**Departure Time**	**Fare**
Roxbury	4:20 P.M.	4:22 P.M.	$1.50
Lanesville	4:43 P.M.	4:45 P.M.	$2.10
Hampton	5:10 P.M.	5:12 P.M.	$4.50
Cheshire	5:31 P.M.	5:33 P.M.	$5.25
(double the fare for round-trip price)			

EXAMPLE

The following questions are based on the table.

1. Which is the least expensive destination to travel to from Centerville?

    Look at the "fare" column—it costs only $1.50 to travel to Roxbury.

    Answer: Roxbury

2. How long does it take to travel from Lanesville to Cheshire?

   This is a "clock" question. It's usually best to use an hour marker to help you answer it. The train departs from Lanesville at 4:45, from 4:45 to 5:00 is 15 minutes, and from 5:00 to 5:31 (arrival time in Cheshire) is 31 minutes. Add the two sums together (15 + 31) to get 46 minutes.

   Answer: 46 minutes

3. The fare to Roxbury is what percent of the fare to Cheshire?

   This is a basic percent word problem. Just be careful to select the right numbers. When working with tables and charts, it can be helpful to use the straight edge of a piece of paper to read across a row.

   Step one: Reduce—$1.50 is ? % of $4.50?

   Step two: Solve—$1.50 ÷ $4.50 = .33 = 33%

   Answer: 33%

4. James lives in Centerville and commutes to and from a job in Cheshire five days a week. What expression can be used to calculate the cost of his weekly commutation?

   Always read "the fine print." In this case, it tells you that round trips are double the price listed in the "fare" column. Therefore the expression is: **5 (2 × $5.25)**—the "5" represents five days per week.

KINGSFIELD COMMUNITY RECREATION PROGRAM		
Activity	**Number of Participants**	**Enrollment Fee (per person)**
Volleyball League	24	$30
Softball League	108	$10
Ballroom Dancing	32	$10
Cooking Class	15	$100
First Aid and CPR	25	$50

Practice—Tables

Use the chart above to answer the following questions.

1. Which activity attracted the smallest number of participants?

2. What is the difference in total enrollment fees between the cooking class and the softball league?

3.   How many of the programs grossed over $1,000 in enrollment fees?

Answers

1. **Cooking**   2. **$420**   3. **3**

BAR GRAPHS

Bar graphs use vertical (up and down) and horizontal (across) "bars" to represent quantities. It's essential that you read all labels and legends ("the fine print"), looking carefully at the base and sides of the graph to see what the bars are measuring and how much they're increasing or decreasing.

EXAMPLE

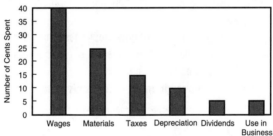

ACME CO.—PER DOLLAR EXPENDITURES

Before answering any questions, familiarize yourself with the graph and what it means. The Acme Co. may have gross income well over a million dollars, but the graph illustrates how much the company had to pay out *per dollar* in expenses, divided into six different categories. So, as an example, for every dollar the Acme Co. grossed, it had to pay out 15¢ in taxes.

1.   How many cents of each dollar did the company use to pay for materials?

Use the edge of a paper to line up the top of the "materials" bar with the numbers on the left side of the chart. It's very close to 25¢ spent.

Answer: 25¢

2. How much are the combined expenses of taxes and "uses in business" equal to?

    Taxes = 15¢

    Use in business = 5¢

    15 + 5 = 20¢

    Answer: 20¢ spent per dollar

3. The combined expenses of depreciation, dividends, and use in business represent what percentage of the number of cents spent on wages?

    10 + 5 + 5 = 20   (combined expenses)

    20 is ? % of 40?   40 (wages)

    20 is half of 40 or 50%

    Answer: 50%

4. If the Acme Co. reduced its wage payroll by laying off five managers, what would be the new number of cents per dollar spent on wages?

    There is no indication of how much these managers are paid nor is there a dollar amount given that reflects total wages. The answer can't be calculated.

    Answer: not enough information is given

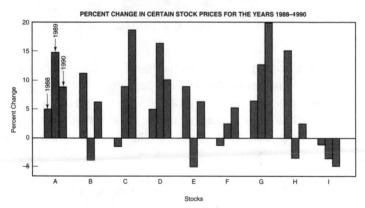

PERCENT CHANGE IN CERTAIN STOCK PRICES FOR THE YEARS 1988–1990

Practice—Bar Graphs

Use the graph above to answer the following questions.

1. Which stocks showed *increases* for every year charted?

2. Which stock had the greatest percentage of change from one year to the next?

3. The percent of change for Stock G in 1990 was how much greater than the percent of change for Stock D in 1988?

Answers

1. **C, F, G**   2. **H**   3. **15%**

LINE GRAPHS

Line graphs almost always measure how things increase or decrease over time.

There is often more than one line on a graph, which can cause some confusion. Proceed slowly and carefully.

EXAMPLE

The graph below shows the conversion of farm and forest acreage to housing developments in Granite County.

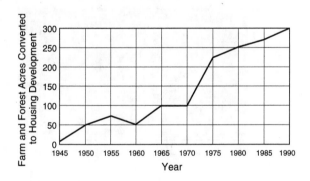

1. How many acres of farm and forest were converted to housing developments in 1955?

You can't tell **exactly** because the line crosses 1955 about one-third of the way between 50 and 60 acres. But an estimate of 70 acres would be correct.

Answer: 70 acres

2. During which five-year period was there no increase in conversion?

That's easy. Look for the place where the line runs horizontally for five years—between 1965 and 1970.

Answer: 1965–1970

3. During which five-year period were conversions greatest?
    Look for the steepest rise in the line.
    Answer: 1970–1975

4. During which year were the most forest acres converted?
    Look carefully at the fine print. There is no special distinction
    between farm and forest conversion. Therefore, there is **not
    enough information** given to calculate the answer.

5. What is the difference between the number of acres converted in
    1945–1950 and those converted in 1970–1975?
    The 1945–1950 conversions are approximately 45 acres, and the
    1970–1975 conversions are approximately 125 acres. 125 – 45 = 80.
    Answer: approximately 80 acres

Practice—Line Graph

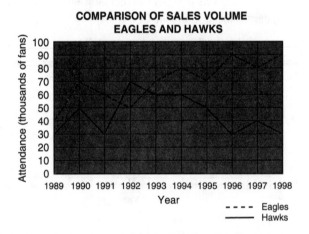

The Hawks and Eagles are minor-league baseball teams. The graph represents the paid attendance record of each team over a ten-year period. The
following questions are based on information in the above graph.

1. During which year did the Hawks' attendance exceed that of the
    Eagles?

2. In 1996 how many more fans attended Eagles games than Hawks
    games?

3. By what percent did the Eagles' attendance increase from 1989 to
    1993?

Answers

1. **1992**   2. **60,000 more**   3. **75%**

PIE CHARTS

Pie charts (sometimes called **circle graphs**) represent the way in which something is divided into parts. As always, try to get the big picture while paying attention to the fine print.

EXAMPLE

Annual Expenses for the Golden Tree Landscaping Corp.

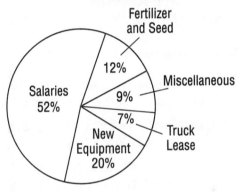

1. What part of Golden Tree's annual expenses does New Equipment and Fertilizer and Seed represent?

   (1) about $\frac{1}{2}$

   (2) about 20%

   (3) about $\frac{1}{3}$

   (4) about 40%

   First, add the two sections:

   $$20\% + 12\% = 32\%.$$

   32% is very close to 33%. You know that 33% of anything is $\frac{1}{3}$.

   Answer: (3) about $\frac{1}{3}$

2. Golden Tree establishes a relationship with a new equipment sales company that gives them a 25% discount on all purchases. What would the recalculated percentage of expense be for new equipment using the new supplier?

   New equipment consumes 20% of expenses. If the company now gets a 25% (or $\frac{1}{4}$ off) discount on its purchases, then the percentage will be reduced by $\frac{1}{4}$. $\frac{1}{4}$ of 20% = 5% and 20 − 5 = 15%

   Answer: 15%

3. Which section of the chart accounts for equipment repair?

   Since none of the sections specify "Equipment Repair," it must be assumed that "Miscellaneous" (which means "other various unnamed items") accounts for it.

   Answer: Miscellaneous

4. If Golden Tree's expenses for one year total $62,000, how much does the company pay *per month* for the truck lease?

   Step one: Calculate the annual amount paid for the truck lease.
   $62,000 × .07 = $4,340

   Step two: Calculate the monthly amount of the lease.
   $4,340 ÷ 12 (for 12 months of the year) = $361.66

   Answer: $361.66

Practice—Pie Charts

Distribution of $62,000 Grant for School Improvement

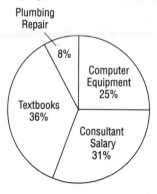

Answer the following questions based on the information provided in the chart.

1. How many dollars of the grant were spent on plumbing repair?
2. All of the money allotted to computer equipment went to the purchase of five of the same computer systems. How much did each system cost?
3. What expression represents the difference in dollars between money spent on textbooks and that spent on computer equipment?
4. If the grant increased by $21,500 for the following year, how much money would be allotted for consultant salary?

Answers

1. **$4,960**   2. **$3,100**   3. **.11 (62,000)**   4. **$25,885**

ALGEBRA

THE NUMBER LINE AND POSITIVE AND NEGATIVE NUMBERS

Consider the number line above. The arrows at each end mean the line extends infinitely in each direction, so that any number imaginable can be found on it. Notice that 0 is at the midpoint of the line.

Up to this point, you have only dealt with positive numbers, but it's now time to introduce negative numbers, which are marked by a "–" sign. The further a number is to the **right** of the number line, the **greater** its value. For example, 3 > 0 (this symbol, >, means "is greater than") because it's further to the right on the number line. Likewise, 0 > –3 (0 is greater than –3) and –2 > –3.

Finding Points on the Number Line

On the GED, you'll be asked to identify points on the number line.

EXAMPLE

Which point represents 3.5?
Answer: *B*—it's halfway between 3 and 4.

EXAMPLE

Which point represents –5?
Answer: *C*—it's right above the –3 marker.

EXAMPLE

Which point approximates $\sqrt{28}$?

$\sqrt{28}$ isn't a whole number. $5 \times 5 = 25$ and $6 \times 6 = 36$ Therefore, $\sqrt{28}$ has to be between 5 and 6.
Answer: *A* is between 5 and 6.

Practice—Finding Points on the Number Line

From the above number line, choose the correct letter for the following.
1. .5
2. –3.5
3. $\sqrt{16}$

Answers
1. **E**   2. **D**   3. **C**

Adding Signed Numbers

Here are the rules that tell how to add signed numbers. Memorize them.

- If the signs are the same (–,– or +,+) **add** the two numbers and label the answer with that sign.

EXAMPLES

$7 + 3 = 10$ (Both signs are positive, add, label answer positive.)
$-5 + (-3) = -8$ (Both signs negative, add, label answer negative.)

- If the signs are different (+,− or −,+), **subtract**. Forgetting for a moment the positive and negative signs, compare the numbers and choose **the larger of the two**. Label the answer with the sign of the "larger" number.

EXAMPLES

$-6 + 5 = -1$ (Signs different, subtract, $6 - 5 = 1$, compare, 6 is larger than 5, 6 has a negative sign, attach it to answer: −1).

$12 + (-7) = 5$ (Signs different, subtract, $12 - 7 = 5$, 12 is larger and positive so attach sign to answer: +5 or 5).

- When adding **more than two** signed numbers, follow the above rules to get a sum for the first two numbers, then continue to use rules for adding subsequent numbers.

EXAMPLES

$-5 + (-14) + (-6) = -25$
  Step one: $-5 + (-14) = -19$
  Step two: $-19 + (-6) = -25$ (Same signs, add, label negative)

$5 + (-12) + 7 = 0$
  Step one: $5 + (-12) = -7$
  Step two: $-7 + 7 = 0$ (Different signs, subract $7 - 7 = 0 - 0$ never takes a sign)

Practice—Adding with Signed Numbers

Add the following.

1. $12 + (-8)$
2. $-14 + (-6)$
3. $-40 + 13$
4. $-2 + (-19)$

Answers

1. **4**   2. **−20**   3. **−27**   4. **−21**

Subtracting Signed Numbers

Here are the three steps that will help you to subtract signed numbers.
Memorize them.

Step one: Change the subtraction problem to an addition
problem.

Step two: Change the sign of the second number.

Step three: Follow the rules of addition you just learned.

EXAMPLE

$$-16 - 6 = -22$$

Step one: Change subtraction to addition.

$$-16 + 6$$

Step two: Change sign of second number.

$$-16 + (-6)$$

Step three: Follow rules of addition. (Same signs, add, $16 + 6 = 22$,
same sign, attach to answer)

Answer: –22

EXAMPLE

$$12 - (-7) = 19$$

Step one: $12 - (-7)$ becomes $12 + (-7)$

Step two: $12 + (-7)$ becomes $12 + 7$

Step three: $12 + 7 = 19$

Answer: 19

Practice—Subtracting Signed Numbers

Solve.

1. $-5 - 4$
2. $16 - (-18)$
3. $12 - 23$
4. $-20 - 16$

Answers

1. **–9**   2. **34**   3. **–11**   4. **–36**

Multiplying and Dividing Signed Numbers

Good news. The rules for these operations are much simpler than for addition and subtraction. They are:

> 1. Signs **alike**—answer is **positive**
>
> 2. Signs **different**—answer is **negative**

Look carefully at the following examples and see how the rules work.

$$-3(5) = -15 \qquad\qquad 3(-5) = -15$$

$$-3(-5) = 15 \qquad\qquad \frac{-15}{3} = -5$$

$$\frac{15}{-3} = -5 \qquad\qquad (3)(-5)(2) = -30$$

$$\frac{-5}{-3} = 5 \qquad\qquad (3)(-5)(-2) = 30$$

Practice—Adding and Dividing Signed Numbers

Solve.

1. $\dfrac{24}{-8}$

2. $\dfrac{1}{4}(-3)$

3. $(-.5)(-6.1)$

Answers

1. **–3**   2. $-\dfrac{3}{4}$ 3. **3.05**

WORKING WITH VARIABLES

In a mathematical sentence, a variable is a letter that represents a number. Consider this sentence: $x + 4 = 10$. Here, it's easy to figure out that x represents 6. However, problems with variables on the GED will become much more complex than that, and there are many rules and procedures that need to be learned.

Before you learn to solve equations with variables, you need to perform basic operations with them. Here's some vocabulary that will be helpful.

3*y* is called a **monomial**
The 3 in 3*y* is called a **coefficient**
The *y* is called a **variable**

Adding and Subtracting with Variables

Consider the following statements:

$$x + x = 2x \quad \text{but} \quad x + 1 = x + 1$$
$$3x + x = 4x \quad \text{but} \quad 3x + 1 = 3x + 1$$
$$4y + 3y = 7y \quad \text{but} \quad 4y + 3 = 4y + 3$$
$$3r - 6r = -3r \quad \text{but} \quad 3r - 6 = 3r - 6$$
$$3rx + 3rx = 6 \quad \text{but} \quad 3r + 3rx = 3r + 3rx$$

Remember: *x* is the same as 1*x*

As you can see, only those monomials that have the same variables can be added to or subtracted from each other.

Sometimes, you'll see problems like this:

Evaluate: $a + 3b + 3a$
  Answer: $4a + 3b$

Evaluate: $5b + 3c - 2b + c$
  Answer: $3b + 4c$

Do the addition and subtraction with like terms (the ones with exactly matching variables). Anything that stands alone, leave alone.

Practice—Adding and Subtracting with Variables
Add or subtract the following. If the terms can't be added or subtracted, recopy them.
1. $5x + 12x$
2. $-14a - (-3a)$
3. $25 + 6a$
4. $12st + (-6st)$
5. $3y + 6$
6. $7xy + 8x$

Answers
1. **17x**   2. **–11a**   3. **25 + 6a**   4. **6st**   5. **3y + 6**   6. **7xy + 8x**

Multiplying and Dividing with Variables

Once again, the rules are different with these operations. You *must* multiply and divide monomials with numbers as well as monomials with different variables. Carefully consider the following examples:

Multiplication

$3(4x) = 12x$ $\qquad$ $3x(4y) = 12xy$

$3x(4yz) = 12xyz$ $\qquad$ $\frac{1}{7}(5x) = \frac{5x}{7}$

$\frac{1}{2}(4a) = \frac{4a}{2} = 2a$

As you can see from the examples above, multiply the coefficients and include the variables.

Division

$\frac{12x}{4} = 3x$ $\qquad$ $\frac{12x}{4x} = 3$ $\qquad$ $\frac{12xy}{4x} = 3y$

(The variables cancel each other out.)

Practice—Multiplying and Dividing with Variables
Solve.

1. $5(5x) =$

2. $\frac{14s}{7} =$

3. $-5y(6x) =$

4. $\frac{72x}{9x} =$

5. $13x(5y) =$

Answers
1. **25x**   2. **2s**   3. **–30xy**   4. **8**   5. **65xy**

Variables and Exponents

Multiplication
Consider the following:

$$x + x = 2x \text{ but } x(x) = x^2 \text{ and } x^2(x^3) = x^5$$
$$2(4x) = 8x \text{ but } 2x(4x) = 8x^2$$
$$2x^2(4x) = 8x^3$$
$$x(4x^3) = 4x^4$$
$$5x^3(4x^5) = 20x^8$$
$$4x^3y^2(5x^2y) = 20x^5y^3$$
$$3x^5y^3z^4(6x^3yz^2) = 18x^8y^4z^6$$

What you *should* see from the above examples is that when multiplying variables with exponents, you *add* the exponents, as long as the bases are the same.

Division
Consider the following:

$$\frac{12x^6y^4}{3x^3y^2} = 4x^3y^2 \qquad \frac{9a^8b^2c^7}{3a^5c} = 3a^3b^2c^6$$

When dividing variables with exponents, **subtract** the exponents.

Practice—Variables and Exponents
Solve.

1. $x(x^3)$

2. $4x(5x)$

3. $\dfrac{16x^4}{4x}$

4. $\dfrac{25s^3}{s}$

Answers
1. x^4 2. $20x^2$ 3. $4x^3$ 4. $25s^2$

Working with Parentheses

You already know that $5(6a)$ means $5 \times 6a$, but consider this more complicated statement:

$$5(6a + c)$$

It must be rewritten like this:

$$5(6a) + 5(c) \quad \text{which is} \quad 30a + 5c$$

Each term **inside** the parentheses must be multiplied by the one directly outside. Then the operation specified (in this case, addition) must be carried out.

Consider two more examples:

$3b(6b - 2ac)$ becomes $18b^2 - 6abc$

$\frac{1}{3}(6x + 7)$ becomes $\frac{6x}{3} + \frac{7}{3} = 2x + \frac{7}{3}$

Practice—Parentheses
Rewrite the following, as in the above examples.

1. $3(5a - 6)$

2. $2(2a + 7)$

3. $5(6r + 7s - t)$

Answers
1. $15a - 18$ 2. $4a + 14$ 3. $30r + 35s - 5t$

Finding Values When Variables Are Given

Consider the following:

EXAMPLE

Find the value of z if $z = 3x + y^2$ where $x = 6$ and $y = -4$

    Step one: Replace the variables with numbers

    $z = 3(6) + (-4)^2$

    Step two: perform the operations in proper order (remember PEMDAS from page 188).

    Answer: $z = 18 + 16$ or $z = 34$

Practice—Finding Values with Given Variables

Solve.

1. $c = 4a - 3b$, if $a = 8$ and $b = 5$. Find c.

2. $s = 3q^2 + 2r$, if $q = 6$ and $r = .5$. Find s.

3. $z = 3x^2(y + 8)$, if $x = 10$ and $y = -12$. Find z.

Answers

1. **17**   2. **109**   3. **−1200**

One-Step Equations

Here's an example of a one-step equation.

$$x + 5 = 29$$

Your goal is to figure out what number can replace x so that both sides of the equation will equal 29. The boundary line of each **side** of the equation is the = sign. So $x + 5$ is on the left side of this equation and 29 is on the right.

To reach your goal in any simple equation, you must reduce one side of the equation to just one variable and the other side to just one number. You accomplish this by performing any of the four basic operations to both sides of the equation. Just remember this:

> What you do to one side of the equation, you must do to the other side.

Here's how it works:

EXAMPLE

$x + 5 = 29$ solve for x

$$x + 5 = 29$$

Step one: $\underline{-5 \quad -5}$

Step two: $x \quad\; = 24$

Step three: Check $24 + 5 = 29$

Step one: Since you want to reduce the left side of the equation to just x, you've got to get rid of the "+ 5" in "$x + 5$." The way to get rid of it is to perform its inverse (opposite) by subtracting 5 from that side of the equation. *Remember*, what you do to one side of the equation, you must do to the other side. Therefore, you do 29 – 5.

Step two: Draw a line across the bottom of the entire equation and do the subtraction problems for each side. The result on the left is "$x + 0$." There is no need to write the 0. You have accomplished your goal of reducing one side of the equation to just one variable—x. The result on the right side is 24. Therefore, $x = 24$

Step three: Check. Simply replace the variable with the number, do the math, and make sure both sides of the equation are equal.

The procedure is the same for all other simple equations. Consider the following example.

EXAMPLE

$a - 19 = 12$ Solve for a.

$$
\begin{array}{r}
a - 19 = 12 \\
+\,19 \quad +19 \\
\hline
a \quad\;\; = 31
\end{array}
$$ Check: $31 - 19 = 12$

Practice—One-step Equations
Solve for the variable.
1. $51 = x + 20$
2. $x - 43 = 12$
3. $38 = b + 14$
4. $r - 81 = 16$

Answers
1. $x = 31$ 2. $x = 55$ 3. $b = 24$ 4. $r = 97$

Multistep Equations

These equations are just a bit more complicated because they combine two or three of the procedures just learned into one problem. Consider the following:

EXAMPLE

$5m + 8 = 48$

$$5m + 8 = 48$$
$$\underline{\quad -8 \quad -8}$$
$$\frac{5m}{5} = \frac{40}{5} \qquad m = 8$$

EXAMPLE

$$\frac{3p}{8} + 17 = 38$$

$$\frac{3p}{8} + 17 = 38$$
$$\underline{\quad -17 = -17}$$
$$\frac{8}{3} \times \frac{3p}{8} = 21 \times \frac{8}{3}$$
$$p = 56$$

Practice—More Complex Equations

Solve for the variable and check.

1. $12a + 6 = 42$
2. $7x - 14 = 14$
3. $\dfrac{r}{9} + 8 = 12$
4. $116 = 15c + 11$
5. $\dfrac{1}{8}m - 27 = 16$

Answers

1. $a = 3$ 2. $x = 4$ 3. $r = 36$ 4. $c = 7$ 5. $m = 344$

INEQUALITIES

> means **is greater than** $5 > 4$

< means **is less than** $6 < 8$

≥ means **is greater than or equal to**

   $5 \geq 5$ and all positive numbers added to it

≤ means **is less than or equal to**

   $3 \leq 3$ and all positive numbers subtracted from it

Memorize the meanings of the inequality signs.

Practice—Simple Inequalities

True or False.

1. $\frac{1}{4} > \frac{1}{8}$

2. $3(5) < 14$

3. $-.5 > 0$

Answers

1. **True**   2. **False**   3. **False**

Equations with Inequalities

On the GED, you will certainly have to solve equations with inequalities. Proceed exactly as you would with the equations just learned, replacing the = sign with whatever inequality sign is in the equation.

EXAMPLE

$$3s - 4 > 11$$
$$\underline{+4 \quad +4}$$
$$\frac{3s}{3} > \frac{15}{3}$$

Answer: $s > 5$

What this means is that s can be checked with any number **greater than** 5. It could be 5.1 or 5,000,000.

Let's use 6.

$$3(6) - 4 > 11 = 18 - 4 > 11$$

$14 > 11$ is a true statement. It works.

Practice—Equations with Inequalities

Solve and check.

1. $\frac{x}{3} < 12$

2. $5y - 2 > 23$

Answers

1. $x < 36$ 2. $y > 5$

MULTIPLYING BINOMIALS

$x + 6$ is an example of a binomial. You won't be asked to identify one, nor define the difference between a monomial and a binomial, but you will need to know how to multiply two binomials. It's very much like multiplying regular numbers. Consider this example:

$$(x + 4) \ (x + 3)$$

Step one: Set up like a two-digit multiplication problem

$$
\begin{array}{r}
x + 4 \\
\times \ \ x + 3 \\
\hline
+ \ 3x + 12 \\
+ \ x^2 + 4x \\
\hline
x^2 + 7x + 12
\end{array}
$$

Step two: Starting with the lower right term (+3), multiply the two top terms, right (4) then left (x). Put the products to each computation in the column where they belong.

$$4 \times 3 = 12 \quad \text{and} \quad x \times 3 = 3x$$

Step three: Now do the same for the lower left term. Just as in numeral multiplication, skip a one-digit space at the far right when entering the second row of products.

$$4 \times x = 4x \quad \text{and} \quad x \times x = x^2$$

Step four: Again, as in numerical multiplication, add the results in columns going downward.

Practice—Multiplying Binomials
Solve.

1. $(x+2)(x+4)$
2. $(x-6)(x+3)$
3. $(x-8)(x-5)$

Answers
1. x^2+6x+8 2. $x^2-3x-18$ 3. $x^2-13x+40$

FACTORING QUADRATIC EXPRESSIONS

This is the reverse operation of multiplying binomials. You will probably have one problem like this on the test, so it's best to be prepared. A quadratic expression looks like this:

$$x^2+10x+16$$

Here's how to factor it.

EXAMPLE

Factor $x^2+10x+16$

$(x\ \ )(x\ \ )$ will always be your starting point because $x(x)=x^2$.
    You now need to find **one set** of two numbers that, when multiplied, will equal +16 and when added will equal +10.

$16\times1=16$ but $16+1=17$—No
$4\times4=16$ but $4+4=8$—No
$8\times2=16$ *and* $8+2=10$—**Yes**

The factors for the quadratic expression $x^2+10x+16$ are:

$$(x+8)(x+2)$$

A check will prove it.

EXAMPLE

Factor x^2+2x-8

$-8\times1=-8$ but $-8+-1=-7$—No
$-4\times2=-8$ but $-4+(-2)=-2$—No
$4\times-2=-8$ *and* $4+(-2)=+2$—**Yes**
Answer: $(x+4)(x-2)$

Practice—Factoring Quadratic Expressions

Factor the following.

1. $x^2 + 9x + 18$
2. $x^2 - 7x + 10$
3. $x^2 - 49$

Answers

1. $(x + 3)(x + 6)$ 2. $(x - 5)(x - 2)$ 3. $(x + 7)(x - 7)$

QUADRATIC EQUATIONS

The quadratic equation problems you'll see on the GED all look similar to this:

$x^2 - 12x + 27 = 0$ Solve for x

The key here is that you must come up with **two** different numbers for x that will make the equation work.

EXAMPLE

$x^2 - 12x + 27 = 0$ Solve for x

Step one: Factor the left side of the equation $(x - 9)(x - 3)$

Step two: Simply reverse the signs on the two numbers in each binomial factor. −9 becomes 9, −3 becomes 3
Answer: $x = 9, 3$

A check of both numbers replacing x is time-consuming. Know the process.

Practice—Quadratic Equations

Solve for x.

1. $x^2 + 15x + 56 = 0$
2. $x^2 - 7x - 30 = 0$
3. $x^2 + 8x - 9 = 0$

Answers

1. **(−7, −8)**   2. **(10, −3)**   3. **(−9, 1)**

ALGEBRA AND WORD PROBLEMS

Proportions

This operation is the next logical step after "ratio." In its simplest form, the idea is to make two ratios equal, when one of the four parts is unknown.

EXAMPLE

$7 : 2 = x : 6$ solve for x

Step one: Set up ratios as fractions

$$\frac{7}{2} = \frac{x}{6}$$

Step two: Cross-multiply and set up the products as two numbers separated by an = sign:

$$7 \times 6 = 42 \quad \text{and} \quad 2 \times x = 2x$$

Set up as $2x = 42$

Step three: Finish the equation by dividing

$$\frac{\cancel{2}x}{\cancel{2}} = \frac{\cancel{42}^{21}}{\cancel{2}^{1}}$$

$$7:2 = 21:6$$

Answer: $x = 21$

What this means is that 7 has the same numerical relationship to 2 as 21 does to 6.

Let's say you were baking a cake that required you to put in seven cups of milk to two cups of flour. If you wanted to bake a larger cake (in this case, three times larger), you would still follow the same recipe ratio of 7 parts to 2 parts by using 21 cups of milk and 6 cups of flour.

EXAMPLE

The scale on a map is 1 inch to every 150 miles. How far apart in miles are two cities that are 6 inches apart on the map?

Step one: $1:150 = 6:x$

Step two: $\dfrac{1}{150} = \dfrac{6}{x}$

Step three: $900 = x$, making *Step four* unnecessary

Answer: 900 miles

Practice—Proportions

1. On a construction job, a carpenter uses 26 feet of lumber to build 2 door frames. If he is going to build 5 door frames, how much lumber does he need?

2. The scale on a road map indicates that $\frac{1}{4}$ inch equals 20 miles. How far apart in miles are two towns that are $3\frac{1}{2}$ inches away on the map?

Answers

1. **65 feet**   2. **280 miles**

SETUPS USING VARIABLES

This is, perhaps, the most common type of problem seen on the GED, so understanding it is really important. You should rely on your common sense to guide you.

EXAMPLE

Sally can plant x tomato seedlings per row and there are y rows in her garden. Write an algebraic expression that represents the total amount of seedlings that could be planted in the garden.

It should occur to you that this is very much like an "area" question ($l \times w$). What might help you to picture the solution is **to put numbers in place of the variables**. In this case, say Sally can plant 10 seedlings per row and there are 12 rows in the garden. The total number of seedlings would be represented by 10(12) or **xy**.

Answer: xy

EXAMPLE

A class of fourth-graders voted for class president. P students voted for Jake, Q students voted for Ming, and R students voted for Louisa. What fractional part of the class voted for Louisa?

Fractional part is a good clue that this problem should be set up as a fraction and that you're looking for a part-to-whole relationship. Compute the *whole* or total of the class by adding each variable ($P + Q + R$). Remember that the *part* in a part-whole relationship goes on top.

Answer: $\dfrac{R}{P + Q + R}$

Practice—Setups with Variables

Choose the correct expression for each of the following.

1. A fisherman purchases two fishing rods at *b* dollars each and a lure for *c* dollars. He pays with a $20 bill. What is the amount of change returned?
   - (1) $2b - c + 20$
   - (2) $20 + (2b - c)$
   - (3) $20 + 2(b - c)$
   - (4) $20 - (2b + c)$
   - (5) $\dfrac{2b + c}{20}$

2. Tom is *b* years old. How old will he be in 12 years?
   - (1) $b - 12$
   - (2) $b + 12$
   - (3) $12b$
   - (4) $b + 12 - x$
   - (5) $12 - b$

3. Lina grosses $11,000 per month at her yogurt store. Each month she pays out *f* dollars for rental of the building, *g* for electric use, and *h* for other expenses. How much does she net per month?
   - (1) $11(f + g + h)$
   - (2) $11{,}000 - (f + g + h)$
   - (3) $(f - g - h)11{,}000$
   - (4) $(11{,}000 - h) - (f + g)$
   - (5) not enough information is given

Answers

1. **4**   2. **2**   3. **2**

CONVERTING WORDS INTO ALGEBRAIC EQUATIONS

This is an important skill. To help master it, here is a list of commonly used phrases with numbers and their algebraic translations. Read the left-hand column and cover the right-hand column. Using *x* as a variable to replace the phrase "a number," predict what the right column will say.

Words	Algebraic Expression
5 plus a number	$5 + x$
12 decreased by a number	$12 - x$
The sum of a number and 6	$x + 6$
16 less than a number	$x - 16$
2.5 more than a number	$2.5 + x$
13 minus a number	$13 - x$
A number increased by 8	$x + 8$
The product of 13 and a number	$13x$
A number divided by 4	$\dfrac{x}{4}$
3 times a number	$3x$
18 divided by a number	$\dfrac{18}{x}$
5 times a number decreased by 7	$5x - 7$
A number times itself	x^2
The square root of a numberless 6	$\sqrt{x} - 6$
14 increased by a number, all multiplied by 8	$8(14 + x)$
8 minus a number, all divided by that same number	$\dfrac{8 - n}{n}$

CONVERTING WORDS TO EQUATIONS AND SOLVING

You've learned how to solve simple and complex equations. This operation asks you to convert sentences into equations and then solve them. Look for the words **is** or **equals**; they mark the place in the equation where the = sign belongs.

EXAMPLE

Three times a number increased by 14 is 23. Convert and solve.
Let $3x$ stand for "3 times a number"
Let $+ 14$ stand for "increased by 14"
Let $= 23$ stand for "is 23."
Put it all together and solve the equation.

$$3x + 14 = 23$$
$$\underline{\quad -14 \quad -14}$$
$$\frac{3x}{3} = \frac{9}{3}$$

Answer: $x = 3$

Practice—Solving Simple Word Equations

Convert and solve for the variable.

1. A number decreased by 16 = 39.
2. 90 divided by a number is 18.

Answers

1. $x = 55$ 2. $x = 5$

MULTISTEP ALGEBRAIC WORD PROBLEMS

For some students, these are the most difficult questions on the GED. All these problems need to be converted to multistep equations that then need to be solved.

EXAMPLE

Dolores and her brother Jim have a paper route. Dolores delivers twice as many papers as Jim does. Together, they deliver 117 papers. How many papers does Jim deliver? How many does Dolores deliver?

Step one: Build a box.

$$
\boxed{
\begin{aligned}
2x &= \text{Dolores} \\
x &= \text{Jim}
\end{aligned}
}
$$

We don't know how many papers either person delivered, but we do know Dolores delivered twice as many as Jim did. In virtually all of these problems, one of the unknowns, usually the smallest, will be represented by x.

Step two: Write an equation based on the information given.

$$2x + x = 117$$

Step three: Solve the equation.

$$2x + x = 117 \text{ becomes } \frac{3x}{3} = \frac{117}{3} \qquad x = 39$$

Step four: Return to the box and apply the information to the question asked.

Answer: Jim delivered **39** papers; Dolores delivered 2(39) or **78** papers

EXAMPLE

Three soccer players led the Rhinos in scoring for the season. Henri scored twice as many goals as Fred, and Angelo scored 18 more goals than Fred. If the three combined to score 78 goals, how many did Henri score?

Step one: Build a box.

> Henri = 2x
> Fred = x
> Angelo = $x + 18$

Step two: $2x + x + (x + 18) = 78$

Step three:
$$4x + 18 = 78$$
$$\underline{-18 \quad -18}$$
$$\frac{4x}{4} = \frac{78}{4}$$
$$x = 15$$

Step four: Henri scored 2(15) or **30** goals.

Practice—Multistep Word Problems
Solve.
1.   At Oasis College, three times as many freshmen live on campus as those who commute. If there are 988 freshmen, how many commute?
2.   A soda vendor sold large sodas for $3 and small sodas for $2. If he sold 182 large sodas and his gross profit for the day was $894, how many small sodas did he sell?

Answers
1. **247**   2. **174**

COORDINATE GEOMETRY

Finding Points on the Rectangular Coordinate Grid

Study the diagram below.

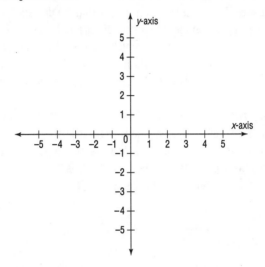

Here, two number lines are set up perpendicular to each other. The horizontal line is the **x-axis** and the vertical line is the **y-axis**. Memorize that.

The diagram below is a more dressed-up version called a **rectangular coordinate grid**. You must learn to locate points on the grid using two numbers: the **x-coordinate** and the **y-coordinate**.

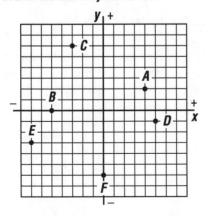

EXAMPLE

Find the coordinates of Point *A*

> *Step one:* Locate the *x*-coordinate (it comes first alphabetically and must be listed first in the answer). Using the darkened *x*-axis zero line as a guide, count the number of ticks (or boxes) on the number line you need to move horizontally (across) from the exact center (0,0) of the graph to the vertical line on which Point *A* is located. It's four horizontal ticks from the center, so the *x*-coordinate is **4**.

> *Step two:* Find the *y*-coordinate. Again, start at dead center but move vertically (up) along the *y*-axis to the horizontal line on which Point *A* is located, counting the ticks as you go. It's two vertical ticks from the center, so the *y*-coordinate is **2**.

> **Answer: Coordinates for Point *A* (4,2)**

EXAMPLE

Find coordinates for Point *B*

> *Step One:* Find the *x*-coordinate. Counting from dead center, *B* is five ticks away. Notice, though, that it is five steps to the **left** of 0, putting it on the negative side of the number line. The *x*-coordinate is –5.

> *Step two:* Find the *y*-coordinate. Since Point *B* lies directly on the *x*-axis and does not rise above or sink below the 0 line, its *y*-coordinate is 0.

> **Answer: Coordinates for Point *B* (–5,0)**

Here are coordinates for four more points on the above grid. Try to calculate the coordinates yourself first, and then check your accuracy.

Point *C* (–3,6)   Point *E* (–7, –3)

Point *D* (5, –1)   Point *F* (0, –6)

Practice—Finding Points on the Grid

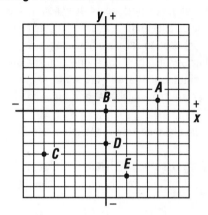

Identify the coordinates of the five points on the grid above.

1. Point *A*
2. Point *B*
3. Point *C*
4. Point *D*
5. Point *E*

Answers

1. **(5, 1)**   2. **(0, 0)**   3. **(–6, –4)**   4. **(0, –3)**   5. **(2, –6)**

Finding the Distance between Points

This may look complicated, but it's a very simple operation.

EXAMPLE

Find the distance between Points *A* and *B*

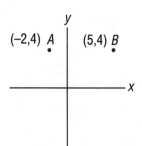

Don't worry because the grid is gone—you don't need it. Since y-coordinates of both points are +4, they both rest on that imaginary horizontal line parallel to the x-axis. To find the distance between the points, you just need to calculate how many ticks there are between the x coordinates. Disregard any + or – sign and **add the sum of the pair of coordinates that aren't the same**. In this case, the pair of y-coordinates are the same (4,4) and the x-coordinates aren't the same (–2,5). Drop the signs and add: 2 + 5 = 7

Answer: The distance between Points *A* and *B* is 7

Practice—Finding Distance Between Points

Using the graph below, find the distance between the following sets of points:

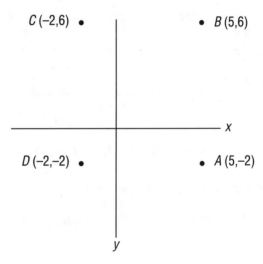

1. *A* and *B*
2. *D* and *C*
3. *C* and *B*
4. *D* and *A*

Answers

1. **8**   2. **7**   3. **7**   4. **7**

Finding the Slope of a Line

This is another operation that looks complicated but isn't. The formula for calculating slope is included on the formula sheet (see pages 306–307) and looks like this:

slope of a line (m) $\qquad m = \dfrac{y_2 - y_1}{x_2 - x_1}$

Here's how to apply it.

EXAMPLE

What is the slope of the line that passes through A and B?

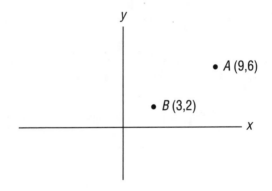

Step one: Write down the formula for slope.

$$m = \frac{y_2 - y_1}{x_2 - x_1}$$

Step two: Replace the letter symbols with the appropriate coordinates. There is no way to tell from the problem which are the $_2$'s and which are the $_1$'s. It's your choice, as long as you remain consistent by assigning one set of coordinates to a number and don't mix them. If, in this case, you decide A will be the $_2$'s and B will be the $_1$'s, then the slope solution will look like this:

$$m = \frac{6 - 2}{9 - 3} = \frac{4}{6} = \frac{2}{3}$$

Step three: Do the math and reduce.

Answer: slope is $\dfrac{2}{3}$

If you chose the coordinates for Point B as $_1$'s and A as $_2$'s, the answer would still be the same.

$$m = \frac{2 - 6}{3 - 9} = \frac{-4}{-6} = \frac{2}{3}$$

Practice—Finding the Slope of a Line

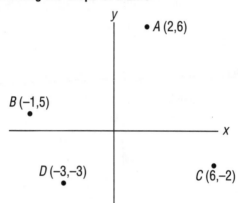

Find the slopes of the lines passing through the following points on the graph.

1. AC
2. AB
3. AD
4. BD

Answers

1. –2   2. $\frac{1}{3}$ 3. $1\frac{4}{5}$ 4. 4

Finding a Coordinate When the Slope Is Given

This is a relatively simple algebra problem that won't be accompanied by a coordinate graph.

EXAMPLE

Find y if the slope of a line passing through points A $(5,y)$ and B $(2,3)$ is equal to 1.

Step one: Set up the formula for slope of a line:

$$m = \frac{y_2 - y_1}{x_2 - x_1}$$

Step two: Insert the slope and the given coordinates. Use y as a variable for the unknown. Again, it's your choice as to whether it's a y_1 or y_2. In this case, we'll make it a $_2$.

$$1 = \frac{y - 3}{5 - 2}$$

Step three: Solve as an equation.

$$1 = \frac{y - 3}{5 - 2} \quad = \quad \frac{(3)}{1}1 = \frac{y - 3}{3}\frac{(3)}{1} \quad = \quad \begin{array}{c} 3 = y - 3 \\ +3 \quad +3 \\ \hline 6 = y \end{array}$$

Answer: $y = 6$

Practice—Finding a Coordinate When Slope Is Given

1. Find x if the slope of a line passing through Points A (4,3) and B (x,7) equals 4.

Answer

1. **5**

GEOMETRY

ANGLES

Learn the following vocabulary.

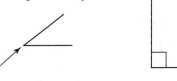

vertex of an angle

right angles
90° exactly

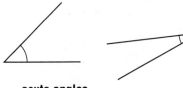

acute angles
less than 90°

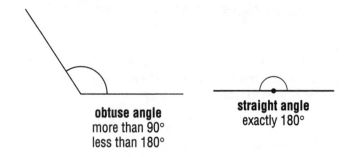

obtuse angle
more than 90°
less than 180°

straight angle
exactly 180°

On the GED, angles might be referred to in a few different ways.

The angle above might be referred to as ∠*CBA* or ∠*ABC*. Notice how the letter *B*, the one that marks the vertex, is always in the middle of the three letters.

The angle above might be referred to as ∠*x* or m of ∠*x*, with **m** meaning **the measure of** ∠*x*.

Practice—Identifying Angles

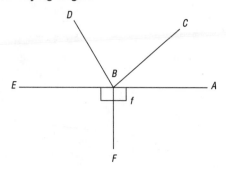

Refer to the above diagram to answer the following.

1. What is m $\angle f$? (How many degrees?)
2. What kind of angle is $\angle ABC$?
3. What kind of angle is $\angle ABD$?
4. What kind of angle is $\angle EBC$?
5. What is m $\angle EBD$ + m $\angle ABD$?
6. What kind of angle is $\angle ABE$?
7. What is m $\angle ABC$ if it is equal to $\frac{1}{2}$ m $\angle EBF$?

Answers
1. **90°**   2. **acute**   3. **obtuse**   4. **obtuse**
5. **180°**   6. **straight angle**   7. **45°**

Complementary and Supplementary Angles
Two or more angles are *complementary* if their sum is equal to 90 degrees.

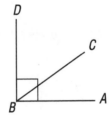

m $\angle ABC$ = 33°
m $\angle CBD$ = <u>57°</u>
            90°
$\angle ABC$ and $\angle CBD$ are *complementary*

Two or more angles are *supplementary* if their sum is equal to 180°.

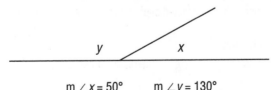

m $\angle x$ = 50°   m $\angle y$ = 130°
        (130 + 50 = 180)
    x and y are *supplementary*

Bisectors

Any line that *bisects* an angle divides the measure of the angle *in half*.

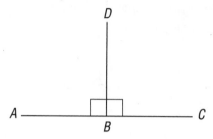

$m \angle ABC = 180°$
$\overline{BD}$ bisects $\angle ABC$
$m \angle CBD = 90°$ $m \angle ABD = 90°$

Vertical Angles

Vertical angles, the ones that appear *opposite* to each other, are equal.

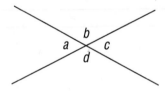

$\angle a$ is vertical to $\angle c$ and $\angle b$ is vertical to $\angle d$
$\angle a = \angle c$
$\angle b = \angle d$

If, in the above diagram $\angle a = 60°$, then $\angle b = 120°$ (supplementary) and $\angle d = 120°$ (vertical) and $\angle c = 60°$ (vertical).

These concepts will be tested over and over in various ways. Know them.

Practice—Angles

To answer questions 1–3, refer to the diagram below.

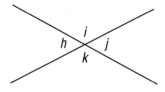

1. What two angles, when separately added to ∠*j*, will equal 180°?
2. What is the sum of all angles in the diagram?
3. What other angle is equal to ∠*i*?

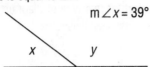

m∠*x* = 39°

4. In the diagram above, what is m ∠*y*?

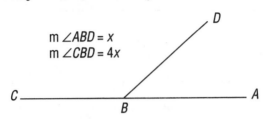

m ∠ABD = x
m ∠CBD = 4x

5. In the diagram above, what is m ∠*CBD*? (Hint: 4x + x =180)

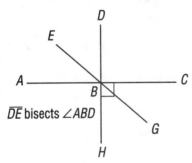

$\overline{DE}$ bisects ∠ABD

Questions 6 and 7 refer to the diagram above.

6. What is m ∠*CBG*?
7. Which *two* expressions are true?
   (1) m ∠DBC = 2(∠ABH)
   (2) m ∠DBH = $\dfrac{∠ABH}{2}$
   (3) m ∠ABC = m of 2(∠CBH)
   (4) 2(∠CBG) = $\dfrac{∠ABC}{2}$

Answers

1. *I, K*   2. **360°**   3. *K*   4. **141°**
5. **144°**   6. **45°**   7. **3, 4**

Transversals

A **transversal** is a line that cuts across a set of parallel lines. You won't have to know a definition for this type of diagram, but you must thoroughly understand the concepts it illustrates.

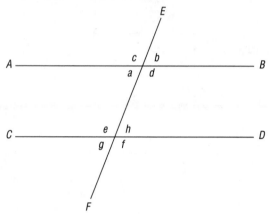

In the above diagram, $\overline{AB} \parallel \overline{CD}$ ($\parallel$ means $\overline{AB}$ is parallel to $\overline{CD}$.) $\overline{EF}$ is the transversal.

We know that because of the rule of vertical (opposite) angles:

$$\angle c = \angle d \quad \text{and} \quad \angle a = \angle b$$
$$\angle e = \angle f \quad \text{and} \quad \angle g = \angle h$$

Also: $\quad \angle b = \angle g \quad \text{and} \quad \angle c = \angle f$
$$\angle c = \angle e \quad \text{and} \quad \angle b = \angle h$$

Practice—Transversals

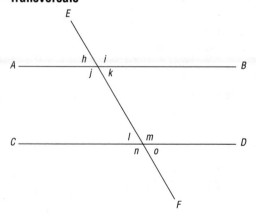

In the above diagram, $\overline{AB}$ is ‖ to $\overline{CD}$.

1. Name all other angles equal to ∠*h*.
2. Name all other angles equal to ∠*n*.
3. If m ∠*o* = 36°, what is m ∠*i*?
4. If m ∠*n* = 117°, what is m ∠*h*?
5. If m ∠*h* = 63°, then what is m ∠*h* + ∠*n* + ∠*o*?

Answers

1. ***K, L, O***   2. ***M, I, J***   3. **144°**   4. **63°**   5. **243°**

Triangles

There are four types of triangles you need to know about.

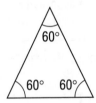

Equilateral triangle—All sides are equal. All angles equal 60°.

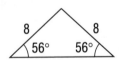

Isoceles triangle (pronounced *I-sosaleez*)—Two sides are equal. Two angles are equal.

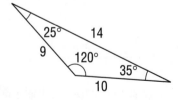

Scalene triangle (pronounced *skayleen*)— No sides are equal. No angles are equal.

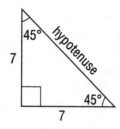

Right triangle—one of the angles is always 90°.

The other two angles can be equal to each other or different, but their sum will always equal 90°.

The two sides that make up the right angle *can* be equal but don't have to be.

The third side, the one opposite the right angle, is always longer than the other two and is called the *hypotenuse.*

> The sum of all angles of a triangle always add up to 180°.

This is a fact that will help you to solve several questions on the GED. Memorize it.

Practice—Triangles

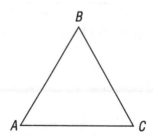

1. In △*ABC* above, ∠*A* = 70° and ∠*B* = 40°. What is the measure of ∠*C*?
2. What kind of triangle is △*ABC*?
3. What kind of triangle is △*DEF* if it has a hypotenuse?

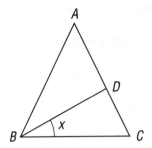

4. △*ABC*, above, is an equilateral triangle. $\overline{AD}$ bisects ∠*ABC*. What is m ∠*x*?

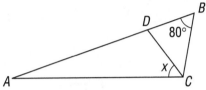

5. △*ABC*, above, is a scalene triangle. ∠*B* = 80°, $\overline{CD}$ bisects ∠*ACB*. What is m ∠*x*?
   (1) 50°
   (2) 25°
   (3) 55°
   (4) 35°
   (5) not enough information is given

Answers
1. **70°**   2. **isosceles**   3. **right triangle**   4. **30°**   5. **5**

Relationships Between Sides and Angles

In a triangle, **the sides opposite two equal angles are also equal**.

EXAMPLE

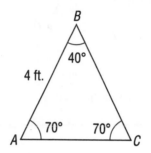

Find $\overline{BC}$

$\overline{BC}$ is **opposite** $\angle A$ $\overline{AB}$ is **opposite** $\angle C$

m $\angle A$ = m $\angle C$ Find $\overline{BC}$

m $\angle A$ = m $\angle C$, so $\overline{AB}$ = $\overline{BC}$; if $\overline{AB}$ = 4 ft., then $\overline{BC}$ = 4 ft.

In a triangle, **the angles opposite two equal sides are equal**.

EXAMPLE

Find x in both figures.

Figure One

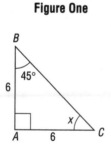

Figure Two

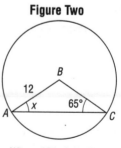

Where *AB* is the radius
of the circle

In Figure One, $\overline{AB}$ = $\overline{AC}$. Therefore, $\angle B$ (opposite $\overline{AC}$) = m $\angle C$ (opposite $\overline{AB}$).

Answer: x = 45°

In Figure Two, $\overline{AB}$ and $\overline{BC}$ are both radii (plural of "radius") of the circle. Therefore, $\overline{AB} = \overline{BC}$. So, m $\angle C$ (opposite $\overline{AB}$) = m $\angle A$ (opposite $\overline{BC}$).

   Answer: $x = 65°$

In all triangles except the equilateral, **the longest side is opposite the largest angle and the shortest side is opposite the smallest angle.**

EXAMPLE

In $\triangle ABC$, m $\angle A = x$, m $\angle B = 1.5x$, and m $\angle C = 2.5x$. Which side is the longest?

Step one: It might help to draw a diagram. Don't worry about where you place the angles or the scale of the drawing; it'll work out.

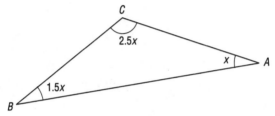

Since the longest side is opposite the largest angle, it has to be $\overline{AB}$.

   Answer: $\overline{AB}$

Practice—Relationships Between Sides and Angles

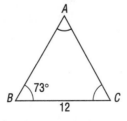

1.   In the triangle above, if $\overline{AB} = \frac{3}{4}(\overline{AC})$ and m $\angle A = \angle C$, what is the length of $\overline{AB}$?

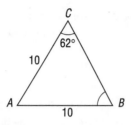

2. In △*ABC* above, find m ∠*B*.

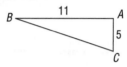

3. The perimeter of △*ABC* above = 29. Which angle is largest?

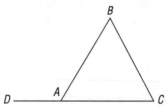

4. In △*ABC* above m ∠*B* = 50° and $\overline{AB}$ = $\overline{BC}$. What is m ∠*DAB*?

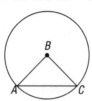

5. $\overline{BC}$ and $\overline{AB}$ are the radii of the circle above. If m ∠*C* = 60°, what kind of triangle is △*ABC*?

Answers

1. **12°** 2. **62°** 3. ∠*A* 4. **115** 5. **equilateral**

Right Triangles and the Pythagorean Theorem

Using a formula known as the Pythagorean theorem can help you to figure out the length of unknown sides of right triangles. It's listed on the formula sheet, but you should memorize it anyway.

Pythagorean theorem: $c^2 = a^2 + b^2$
where **c** always represents the hypotenuse and **a** and **b** represent the other sides of a right triangle.

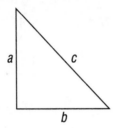

EXAMPLE

What is the length of *EF*?

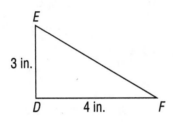

Step one: Replace the formula with numbers from the diagram.

$c^2 = a^2 + b^2$ becomes $c^2 = 3^2 + 4^2$
(it doesn't matter which side you use as **a** or **b**)

Step two: Continue the equation by solving the exponents.

$c^2 = 3^2 + 4^2$ becomes $c^2 = 9 + 16 = c^2 = \sqrt{25}$

Step three: Find the square root of c^2

$$\sqrt{25} = 5$$

Answer: $\overline{EF} = 5$ in.

EXAMPLE

What is the length of *AC*?

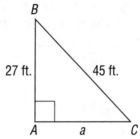

Step one: $c^2 = a^2 + b^2$ becomes $45^2 = 27^2 + b^2$

Step two: $2025 = 729 + b^2$
$$\underline{-729 \quad -729}$$
$$1296 = \qquad b^2$$

Step three: Find the square root of b^2

$$\sqrt{1296} = 36$$

Answer: $\overline{AC}$ **= 36 ft.**

EXAMPLE

Kyla hikes .6 mile due north across a meadow. She then turns and hikes .8 mile due east. How far is she from her starting point?

The "due north" and "due east" phrases are immediate tip-offs that you're working with right triangles and the Pythagorean theorem. Remember that.

Step one: Draw a diagram.

Starting point

Step two: $c^2 = a^2 + b^2$ becomes $c^2 = .6^2 + .8^2$

$$c^2 = .36 + .64 = c^2 = 1$$

Step three: $c = \sqrt{1} = 1$

Answer: 1 mile

Practice—Pythagorean Theorem

1. What is the length of $\overline{BC}$ in the diagram below?

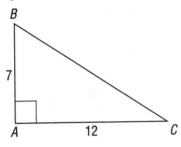

   (1) 15
   (2) 13.6
   (3) $\sqrt{193}$
   (4) 95
   (5) not enough information is given

2. A telephone pole is 40 ft. high and perpendicular to the ground. It needs to be supported by a wire staked into the dirt 30 ft. from the base of the pole and attached to its top. How long is the wire?

3. In the diagram below, what is the length of $\overline{DF}$?

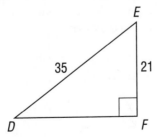

4. A sailboat takes off from its mooring and sails due south for 12 miles, then due east for 16 miles and drops anchor. How far is it from its mooring?

Answers

1. **3**   2. **50 ft.**   3. **28**   4. **20 miles**

GEOMETRY AND PROPORTION

These questions are frequently asked and each is somewhat different from the other. The solutions all rely on your knowledge of geometry and proportion.

EXAMPLE

On line segment $\overline{AC}$, $\overline{BC}$ = 18 inches. $\overline{AB} : \overline{BC}$ = 2:3. What is the length, in inches, of $\overline{AB}$?

Step one: $x : 18 = 2:3$ or $\dfrac{x}{18} = \dfrac{2}{3}$

Step two: Cross-multiply, then solve the proportion.

$$3x = 36 \qquad \dfrac{3x}{3} = \dfrac{36}{3}$$
$$x = 12$$

Answer: $\overline{AB}$ = 12 inches

EXAMPLE

A tree casts a shadow of 96 ft. at the same time that a man's shadow measures 8 ft. How tall is the tree?

Shadow questions are proportion questions. Set up the proportions in the correct order and solve.

Step one: height of tree : shadow of tree
               x :   72

           height of man : shadow of man
               6   :   8

Step two: Convert to fractional proportions, cross-multiply, and solve.

$$\frac{x}{72} = \frac{6}{8} \text{ (reduce) } \frac{x}{72} = \frac{3}{4} \text{ (cross-multiply } 288 = 4x)$$

$$\frac{288}{4} = \frac{4x}{4}$$

$$x = 72$$

Answer: 72 ft.

EXAMPLE

Based on a survey answered by 900 people, the pie graph above shows where holiday shoppers buy the majority of their gifts. How many people surveyed purchased the majority of their gifts at small shops?

Be careful. The segments of the pie are represented by *degrees*, not percentages. There are 360° in a circle, so:

Step one: Create a proportion.

Small shop degrees : total degrees
40°   :   360°

small shop buyers : total buyers
x   :   900

Step two: Solve.

$$\frac{40}{360} = \frac{x}{900} \text{ (reduce) } \frac{1}{9} = \frac{x}{900}$$

$$\frac{9x}{9} = \frac{900}{9}$$

$$x = 100$$

Answer: 100 people

Practice—Geometry and Proportion

1.   A   B   C
   •————————————————•———————————————————————•

   If line segment $\overline{AC}$ = 120 ft. and the ratio of $\overline{AB} : \overline{BC}$ = 3:5, what is the length of $\overline{AB}$?

2.   A 35-foot telephone pole casts a shadow 21 ft. tall at the same time that a lamppost's shadow measures 12 ft. How tall is the lamppost?

3.

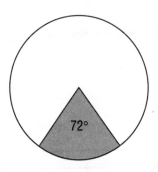

   The shaded area of the chart represents the number of Acme employees who bring their children to day-care centers before work. If there are 465 employees at Acme, how many do not bring their children to day-care centers before coming to work?

Answers
1. **45 feet**   2. **20 feet**   3. **372**

GEOMETRY AND ALGEBRA

To answer these challenging problems, you must know facts, formulas and procedures from both disciplines.

EXAMPLE

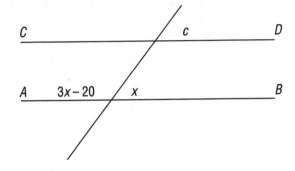

In the diagram above, find the measure of $\angle c$.

The key fact that will allow you to solve this problem is that a straight angle = 180°. You should recognize that $3x - 20$ and x are supplementary.

Step one: Set up an equation and solve for x.

$$3x - 20 + x = 180$$
$$4x - 20 = 180$$
$$\underline{+20 \qquad +20}$$
$$\frac{4x}{4} = \frac{200}{4}$$
$$x = 50°$$

Step two: Find m $\angle c$ based on the measure of $\angle x$

That's easy. The diagram is a transversal—$\angle c = \angle x$

Answer: m $\angle c = 50°$

EXAMPLE

In a triangle, the largest angle is 18 more than twice the smallest angle. The other angle is 18 more than the smallest angle. What is the size of the *largest* angle?

The key fact here is that the sum of all angles in a triangle is always 180°.

Step one: Build a box.

> Largest ∠ = $2x + 18$
> Middle ∠ = $x + 18$
> Smallest ∠ = x

Step two: Set up an equation and solve for *x*. Add all the angles together with their sum equaling 180°.

$$2x + 18 + x + 18 + x = 180 \text{ becomes}$$
$$4x + 36 = 180$$
$$\underline{-36 \quad -36}$$
$$\frac{4x}{4} = \frac{144}{4}$$
$$x = 36$$

Step three: Find the measure of the largest angle. Go back to the box for the "largest angle" sentence: Largest ∠ = $2x + 18$ and replace *x* with 36.

Answer: largest angle is 90°

Practice—Geometry and Algebra

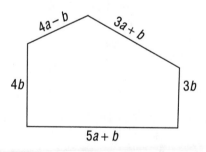

1. What is the perimeter of the figure above?

Questions 2 and 3 are based on the diagram below.

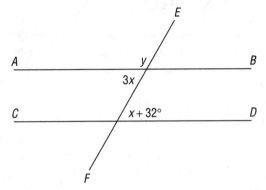

2. Solve for x. (Hint: set up equation using rules of transversals: $3x = x + 32$)

3. What is m $\angle y$?

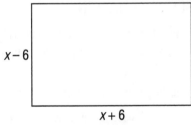

4. If the area of the above rectangle equals 108 sq. ft., find both its length and width.

5. In a scalene triangle, the measure of the largest angle is four more than two times the smallest and the other angle is two more than the smallest. What is the measure of the largest angle?

Answers
1. **$12a + 8b$**   2. **$x = 16$**   3. **$y = 132$**   4. **18, 6**   5. **91°**

TEST-TAKING STRATEGIES

A sure strategy for success on the Mathematics section of the GED is to learn how to quickly solve every type of problem you might be likely to find there. That means familiarizing yourself with all concepts, formulas, and operations.

Achieving that level of familiarity with the material is not always possible. Furthermore, it's certainly not necessary in order to pass the test. Though requirements vary from state to state, it's safe to say that if you answer at least 30 out of the 56 problems in the section correctly, you'll pass (check with the appropriate agency in your state or region to find out the exact requirements).

Though they are no replacement for knowing the material, here are some test-taking strategies specific to the Math section that should prove helpful.

THE TWO-STEP EVALUATION

"What am I being asked to find?" and "How do I find it?" are the two most important questions you need to answer when approaching any math problem.

Step one: After reading each question, say to yourself,

"I need to find......."

It could be the value of x, the length of side $\overline{AB}$ in $\triangle ABC$, or the percent of questions Susan answered incorrectly on a test. Whatever it is, do not proceed with any calculations or attempt to eliminate any of the choices until you feel confident you know what you're being asked to find.

If you're in doubt, carefully reread the problem, paying special attention to the *last sentence*, which tells you specifically what you need to find. If you're still unsure, immediately skip to the next problem.

Step two: Once you are certain of what you need to find, say to yourself,

"I find the answer by doing this: ......"

Avoid reviewing the multiple choices before beginning calculation. There are four wrong answers there that can serve to mislead you. Instead, pause a moment and think carefully. Ask yourself the following:

- Is this a single- or multistep problem?
- What operations and formulas will I use?
- What information given in the problem will be useful?
- Is there a diagram, and, if so, how can it help?
- Do I need to draw my own diagram?
- Is there important information *missing* from the problem that can't be figured out? If so, immediately choose (5) *not enough information is given*, and move to the next problem.
- Is there unnecessary information that must be ignored?

With practice, the answers to these questions will come to you quickly. Begin working, doing your calculations on scrap paper. The scrap paper will *not* be collected, but get in the habit of writing neatly and precisely anyway. Neatness helps in avoiding errors and can aid in making you feel more confident about your work.

Come up with an answer and carefully compare it with the multiple choices. You should find a match among the five offered.

Quick review:
> *Step one:* "I need to find…."
> *Step two:* "I find the answer by doing this: …"

Try using this way of approaching a problem in the example below.

EXAMPLE

Parking meters in Springfield read: "12 minutes for 5 cents. Maximum deposit—50 cents." What is the maximum time, in hours, that a driver may be legally parked at one of these meters?

(1) 1
(2) 1.2
(3) 120
(4) 2
(5) not enough information is given

Step one: What are you being asked to find?

> "I need to find the maximum hours a driver can park."

Not maximum deposit—that's given. Not maximum minutes, even though the information is provided in minutes. You need to find the maximum hours a driver can park, using the information provided.

Step two: How do you find the answer?

"I find the maximum hours a driver can park by doing this:"

Now it's time to think, using the questions listed above. This is a multistep problem. You're given a maximum *deposit*, and from that information you can calculate a maximum *time*. You'll also need to convert maximum minutes to hours. You know 5 cents buys a driver 12 minutes of parking time, so:

(1) 12 min. $\times$ 10 (the number of 5-cent deposits in 50 cents) = 120 min. Now, you need to convert 120 minutes to hours:

(2) $\dfrac{120 \text{ min.}}{60 \text{ min.}}$ = 2 hours

Answer: (4) 2

If you'd reviewed the multiple choices first, you might have been misled. Choice (5) looks tempting because the problem doesn't mention a "maximum *time*" and choice (3) seems appealing because it's the correct number of minutes, not hours. Again, attempt to solve the problem before looking at the answer choices.

Try this two-step evaluation strategy with every problem on the Mathematics section. It should help to keep you focused during a time when anxiety tends to creep in.

SKIPPING AND RETURNING

The questions on the Mathematics section do *not* increase in difficulty; more difficult questions alternate with easier ones in a random pattern throughout the test. It is a far better strategy to direct your time and attention to all the questions you feel confident in answering quickly and correctly than to spend excessive time trying to solve very difficult questions you have a greater chance of getting wrong. Therefore, you should be ready to make a quick judgment about each problem using the Two-step Evaluation.

If you
- are unsure of what you're being asked to find

  or

- you know what you have to find but are unsure how to proceed

or

- you know what to find and how to proceed, but feel it will take a while to get a correct answer,

  skip the problem and go to the next one.

You may find yourself skipping more than half the problems on the test your first time around. That's O.K.

Establish a system for recording your skips. On your answer grid, put a checkmark to the left of each problem you skip and be especially mindful of the problem numbers *at all times* whether skipping or entering answers. You don't want to make the discovery more than halfway through the section that you just entered an answer on the grid space (31) for problem (32)! Careful attention to the question numbers will avoid this problem.

After you finish the last question on your first time through, return to those questions you skipped. Now attempt the ones you know how to solve but initially judged to be too time-consuming. Do not obsess over any one problem. If you divide the 90 minutes allotted for the section by 56 problems, that allows you an average of about $1\frac{1}{2}$ minutes per question. If you feel two minutes have slipped away and you're still not even close to an answer, make your best guess and *move on.* Mark the answer grid with a different symbol—perhaps an *X*—and return to the question later, if you have time.

PLUGGING IN

There will be a handful of occasions when, after doing a Two-step Evaluation, you decide it's quicker and easier to use the multiple choices to get an answer to the problem instead of calculating an answer on your own. *Plugging in* is a strategy in which you choose what looks like a correct answer from the multiple choices and plug it in to a formula or operation to see if it works.

EXAMPLE

Which of the following is a solution to the inequality:

$$3x + 7 > 23 ?$$

(1) 4   (4) 5

(2) 6   (5) 4.5

(3) 2

Using the Two-step Evaluation, you'd say to yourself, I need to find the value for "*x*," which can be gotten by setting up and solving this multistep equation,

or...

you could go directly to the multiple choices, pick what looks like a correct answer, and plug it in to the inequality. Choice (1) looks good; try plugging it in on paper or in your head.

$$3(4) + 7 > 23 \ldots 12 + 7 > 23 \ldots 19 > 23?$$

Close, but wrong. Try another—choice (4). It's easy to do and you don't have to deal with the decimal that's in choice (5).

$$3(5) + 7 > 23 \ldots 22 > 23$$

Really close, but still not large enough to make the inequality a true statement. However, you now know the answer must be choice (2) because it's the only number larger than choice (5).

Answer: (2) 6

ELIMINATING

Eliminating choices you *know* are wrong so that you can spend more time considering choices that *might* be right is a standard test-taking strategy. Consider this:

EXAMPLE

A hockey team won *x* games, lost *y* games, and tied *z* games. What fractional part of the games played were won?

(1) $\dfrac{x}{x + y + z}$

(2) $\dfrac{x}{xyz}$

(3) $\dfrac{x}{xy}$

(4) $\dfrac{x}{x + y}$

(5) $\dfrac{x}{x - y - z}$

Since x represents the number of games won, it has to be in the numerator. All choices have x as a numerator, so you can't eliminate any yet. But the denominator has to represent a **sum** of all the games, which means **addition** would have to be included. Therefore, choices (2), (3), and (5) can be eliminated. You've narrowed the possibilities down to only two possible choices and, by doing so, have more than doubled your chances of getting the answer correct, even if you have to guess between choices (1) and (4). The correct answer, of course is (1) because it represents the sum of *all* games.

MAKING AN EDUCATED GUESS

It's important to remember that the penalty for a wrong answer is the same as it is for a blank answer. **You have nothing to lose by guessing; it's essential that you fill in every answer on the grid, leaving no blanks.** Sometimes, you might be unsure of how to reach a solution to a problem. In these situations, making an educated guess using common sense and elimination is the only logical strategy you can use.

EXAMPLE

Martin has a piece of lumber 9 ft. 8 in. long. He wishes to cut it into four equal lengths. How far from the edge should he make his first cut?

(1) 2.5 ft.
(2) 2 ft. 5 in.
(3) 2.9 ft.
(4) 29 ft.
(5) 116 in.

The wording in this problem might be confusing to some. "How far from the edge" is an overly complicated way of asking, "How long would the first of the four pieces be?" Also, there are numerous conversions to consider: feet to inches, feet to feet and inches, feet and inches to feet and inches in a decimal setup, etc. Even if you aren't quite sure this problem requires you to divide 9 ft. 8 in. by 4, you can eliminate choices (4) and (5). Common sense tells you that the board is just a bit less than 10 feet. Choice (4)—29 ft.—is almost three times longer than the board's length, and choice (5)—116 inches—is exactly equal to its length. It's impossible to make cuts anywhere on the board using these answers. All the other answers are close. A 60% chance of getting a correct answer (eliminating 2 out of 5 choices, then guessing) is better than a 20% chance (eliminating none and guessing). The correct answer is **(2)**.

PRACTICE TEST

This section is designed to give you practice in taking the Mathematics test of the High School Equivalency Examination. In taking this practice test, give yourself the benefit of good working conditions. Select a quiet place and allow yourself 90 minutes for the test. If you finish in less time, use the remaining time to check your work.

After you have completed the test, use the answer key to find your score and then study the solutions and explanations. You may discover new ways to attack problems. Also you will obtain help on the questions that you could not answer, and you will be able to correct any errors that you have made.

Remember that you do not have to get a perfect score to pass the test. If you find that you are weak on a certain topic, review the material in the text on that topic.

FORMULAS	
Description	**Formula**
AREA (A) of a:	
square	$A = s^2$; where s = side
rectangle	$A = lw$; where l = length, w = width
parallelogram	$A = bh$; where b = base, h = height
triangle	$A = \frac{1}{2} bh$; where b = base, h = height
circle	$A = \pi r^2$; where π = 3.14, r = radius
PERIMETER (P) of a:	
square	$P = 4s$; where s = side
rectangle	$P = 2l + 2w$; where l = length, w = width

FORMULAS (continued)	
Description	**Formula**
triangle	$P = a + b + c$; where a, b, and c are the sides
circumference (C) of a circle	$C = \pi d$; where $\pi = 3.14$, d = diameter
VOLUME (V) of a:	
cube	$V = s^3$; where s = side
rectangular container	$V = lwh$; where l = length, w = width, h = height
cylinder	$V = \pi r^2 h$; where $\pi = 3.14$, r = radius, h = height
Pythagorean theorem	$c^2 = a^2 + b^2$; where c = hpotenuse, a and b are legs of a right triangle
distance (d) between two points in a plane	$d = \sqrt{(x_2 - x_1)^2 + (y_2 - y_1)^2}$; where (x_1, y_1) and (x_2, y_2) are two points in a plane
slope of a line (m)	$m = \dfrac{y_2 - y_1}{x_2 - x_1}$, where (x_1, y_1) and (x_2, y_2) are two points in a plane
mean	mean = $\dfrac{x_1 + x_2 + ... + x_n}{n}$ where the x's are the values for which a mean is desired, and n = number of values in the series
median	median = the point in an ordered set of numbers at which half of the numbers are above and half of the numbers are below this value
simple interest (i)	$i = prt$; where p = principal, r = rate, t = time
distance (d) as function of rate and time	$d = rt$; where r = rate, t = time
total cost (c)	$c = nr$; where n = number of units, r = cost per unit

1. In a theater audience of 650 people, 80% were adults. How many children were in the audience?
   - (1) 130
   - (2) 150
   - (3) 450
   - (4) 500
   - (5) 520

2. On a certain map 1 inch represents 60 miles. If two towns are 255 miles apart, what is the distance, in inches, between the towns on the map?
   - (1) 4
   - (2) $4\frac{1}{4}$
   - (3) $4\frac{1}{2}$
   - (4) $4\frac{5}{6}$
   - (5) $4\frac{7}{8}$

3. A carpenter has a board 4 feet 3 inches in length. He cuts off a piece 2 feet 8 inches in length. The length of the piece that is left is
   - (1) 1 ft. 5 in.
   - (2) 2 ft. 7 in.
   - (3) 2 ft. 5 in.
   - (4) 1 ft. 7 in.
   - (5) 2 ft. 3 in.

4. A cardboard crate is 5 feet long, 3 feet wide, and 2 feet tall. What is its holding capacity?
   - (1) 45 cu. ft.
   - (2) 37 cu. ft.
   - (3) 9 cu. ft.
   - (4) 30 cu. ft.
   - (5) 10 cu. ft.

5. A suitable metric unit to use in stating a man's weight is the
   - (1) liter
   - (2) millimeter

(3) kilogram
(4) cubic meter
(5) centimeter

6. If O is the center of the circle and m $\angle B = 52°$, find m $\angle O$.

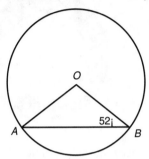

(1) 52°
(2) 76°
(3) 80°
(4) 94°
(5) not enough information is given

7. On line segment $\overline{AC}$, $AB : BC = 3 : 5$ and $BC = 20$ inches.

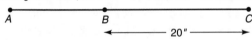

The length, in inches, of $\overline{AB}$ is
(1) 3
(2) 10
(3) 12
(4) 15
(5) 16

8. The diagram below represents a cross section of a pipe. If the diameter of the outer circle is $7\frac{1}{2}$ inches and the diameter of the inner circle is $4\frac{1}{2}$ inches, what is the thickness of the pipe?

(1) 1 in.

(2) $1\frac{1}{4}$ in.

(3) $1\frac{1}{2}$ in.

(4) 2 in.

(5) 3 in.

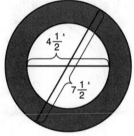

9. Mr. Gray's weekly salary was increased from $400 per week to $500 per week. The percent increase in his salary was

(1) 20%

(2) 25%

(3) 80%

(4) 100%

(5) 125%

10. A shopper buys a loaf of bread at x cents and 2 pounds of coffee at y cents per pound. If she pays with a $5.00 bill, the number of cents she receives in change is

(1) $500 - x - y$

(2) $500 - (x - y)$

(3) $500 - x + y$

(4) $500 - x - 2y$

(5) $x + y - 500$

11. The area of a rectangular living room is 240 square feet. If the length of the room is 20 feet, what is the perimeter, in feet, of the room?

(1) 12

(2) 32

(3) 50

(4) 64

(5) not enough information is given

12. The Center Movie House charges $2 for matinee performances and $4 for evening performances. On one day 267 matinee tickets and 329 evening tickets were sold. An expression that represents the total receipts, in dollars, for that day is

(1) $4(267) + 2(329)$
(2) $2(267) + 4(329)$
(3) $6(267 + 329)$
(4) $2(267 + 329) + 4(267 + 329)$
(5) $4(267 + 329)$

13. A crew of painters can paint an apartment in $4\frac{1}{2}$ hours. What part of the apartment can they paint in $2\frac{1}{2}$ hours?

(1) $\frac{5}{9}$

(2) $\frac{5}{7}$

(3) $\frac{2}{3}$

(4) $\frac{5}{6}$

(5) $\frac{7}{8}$

14. Which of the following expresses 2,347,516 in scientific notation?

(1) 2.347516×10^5
(2) 23.47516×10^5
(3) 234.7516×10^4
(4) 23.47516×10^6
(5) 2.347516×10^6

15. The expression $x^2 - 5x + 6$ may be written as

(1) $(x + 3)(x + 2)$
(2) $(x + 3)(x - 2)$
(3) $(x - 3)(x - 2)$
(4) $(x - 3)(x + 2)$
(5) $x(5x + 6)$

16. A class has 32 students. On a certain day x students are absent. What fractional part of the class is present on that day?

(1) $\dfrac{x}{32}$

(2) $\dfrac{32 - x}{x}$

(3) $\dfrac{x}{32 - x}$

(4) $\dfrac{32 - x}{32}$

(5) $\dfrac{32 - x}{32 + x}$

17. At Adams High School 402 students are taking Spanish and French. If twice as many students take Spanish as take French, how many students take Spanish?

(1) 134
(2) 150
(3) 200
(4) 258
(5) 268

18. According to the graph below, which of the following statements is correct?

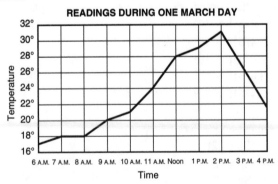

READINGS DURING ONE MARCH DAY

(1) The change in temperature between 7 A.M. and noon was 8°.
(2) The highest temperature reached during the day was 32°.
(3) The change in temperature between 8 A.M. and noon was –10°.
(4) The temperature did not change between 7 A.M. and 8 A.M.
(5) The temperature at noon was 30°.

19. A shipment of 2,200 pounds of sugar is packed in 40-ounce bags. How many bags are needed for the shipment?

(1) 640

(2) 750

(3) 780

(4) 800

(5) 880

20. A ship sails 8 miles due east and then 15 miles due north. At this point, how many miles is the ship from its starting point?

(1) 17

(2) 19

(3) 20

(4) 24

(5) 25

21. A book salesman earns 12% commission on sales. Last month he sold a set of 300 textbooks at $20 per book, a group of 20 art books at $50 per book, and a shipment of 400 novels at $25 per book. What was his commission for the month?

(1) $204

(2) $1,700

(3) $2,040

(4) $17,000

(5) $20,400

22. Mrs. Alvin bought 120 shares of RST Corporation at $32.75 per share and sold these shares a year later at $36.50 per share. Her profit before paying commission and taxes was

(1) $400

(2) $450

(3) $480

(4) $520

(5) $560

23. Mr. and Mrs. Donato went on a vacation motor trip. When the trip started, the odometer reading in their car was 8,947 miles. When the trip was completed the odometer reading was 9,907 miles. How many gallons of gas, to the nearest gallon, were used on the trip?

(1) 36

(2) 38

(3) 40

(4) 41

(5) not enough information is given

24. In a class of 34 students, there are 6 more girls than boys. How many girls are in the class?

(1) 14

(2) 15

(3) 18

(4) 20

(5) 22

25. The number of miles per hour needed to cover 120 miles in x hours may be expressed as

(1) $\dfrac{120}{x}$

(2) $\dfrac{x}{120}$

(3) $120x$

(4) $120 + x$

(5) $x - 120$

26. In 5 years the population of a town decreased from 3,500 to 2,800. The percent of decrease was

(1) 20%

(2) 25%

(3) 30%

(4) 40%

(5) 70%

27. Mr. Fox's will provided that his wife receive $\frac{1}{2}$ of his estate, and his three sons divide the rest equally. If each son's share was $8,000, what was the value of the estate?

(1) $24,000
(2) $32,000
(3) $40,000
(4) $48,000
(5) $50,000

28. Joshua earns $72 for typing 20 pages. At the same rate, how much does he earn for typing 15 pages?

(1) $48
(2) $54
(3) $60
(4) $72
(5) $84

29. A woman buys a Thanksgiving Day turkey weighing 19 pounds 6 ounces. If the turkey sells for $0.88 per pound, how much change does the woman receive from a $20 bill?

(1) $1.95
(2) $2.05
(3) $2.95
(4) $3.95
(5) $4.15

30. Frank had x dollars. He bought y articles for z dollars each. The number of dollars Frank had left was

(1) $yz - x$
(2) $yx - z$
(3) $x - yz$
(4) $x + yz$
(5) $xy + z$

Questions 31 and 32 are based on the following information.

The fare schedule for Checker Taxi is shown below:

First one-fifth mile   1 dollar
Each one-fifth mile after the first   20 cents

31. How much would a 3-mile trip cost (not including tip)?
   (1) $2.00
   (2) $2.50
   (3) $3.00
   (4) $3.80
   (5) $5.00

32. If a passenger has exactly $10.00, how many miles can she ride and still be able to give the driver a tip of $1.00?
   (1) 7 or less
   (2) more than 7 but no more than 8
   (3) more than 8 but no more than 9
   (4) more than 9 but no more than 10
   (5) more than 10

---

33. In the diagram below, a semicircle surmounts a rectangle whose length is $2a$ and whose width is a. A formula for finding A, the area of the whole figure, is

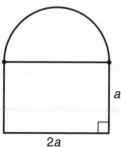

2a

   (1) $A = 2a^2 + \dfrac{1}{2}\pi a^2$
   (2) $A = 2\pi a^2$
   (3) $A = 3\pi a^2$
   (4) $A = 2a^2 + \pi a^2$
   (5) not enough information is given

34. The graph indicates the way a certain man spends his day. Which one of the following statements is correct?

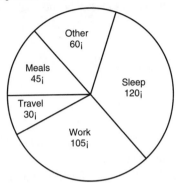

(1) The man works 8 hrs. per day.

(2) The man spends 1 hr. more on meals than he does on travel.

(3) The man sleeps 7 hrs. per day.

(4) The man spends half his time on work and travel.

(5) The man spends 4 hrs. on meals.

35. A storage oil tank in the form of a cylinder is full of oil. The radius of the base of the tank is 7 feet and the height of the tank is 6 feet. Find the number of gallons of oil in the tank if each cubic foot of space holds 7 gallons of oil.

[Use $\pi = \dfrac{22}{7}$.]

(1) 924

(2) 3,234

(3) 5,000

(4) 6,468

(5) 7,200

36. If $y = 2x^2(z - 3)$, find the value of y if $x = 5$ and $z = 7$.

(1) 54

(2) 150

(3) 180

(4) 200

(5) 400

37. On a motor trip Mr. Shore covered $\frac{2}{7}$ of his total trip distance during the first day by driving 384 miles. The total distance to be covered, in miles, was

(1) 98
(2) 1,244
(3) 1,306
(4) 1,344
(5) 1,500

38. The table below gives the annual premiums for a life insurance policy taken out at various ages.

AGE IN YEARS	PREMIUM PER $1,000
22	$18
30	$22
38	$28
46	$38

If the policy is fully paid up after 20 years, how much is saved by taking out a $10,000 policy at age 30 rather than at age 46?

(1) $160
(2) $320
(3) $400
(4) $3,200
(5) $4,000

39. In a right triangle, the ratio of the two acute angles is 3 : 2. The number of degrees in the larger acute angle is

(1) 36
(2) 54
(3) 72
(4) 90
(5) not enough information is given

40. If $3x - 1 < 5$, then x must be

(1) greater than 2
(2) less than 2
(3) greater than 3
(4) less than 0
(5) greater than 5

41. If $\overleftrightarrow{AB} \parallel \overleftrightarrow{GH}$, m $\angle BDE = 100°$, $\overrightarrow{DJ}$ bisects $\angle BDE$, $\overrightarrow{EJ}$ bisects $\angle DEH$, find m $\angle J$.

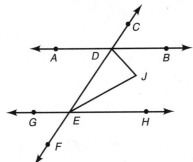

    (1) 40°
    (2) 60°
    (3) 65°
    (4) 75°
    (5) 90°

42. A chair was marked for sale at $315. This was a discount of 25% off the original price. What was the original price of the chair?
    (1) $236.50
    (2) $390
    (3) $420
    (4) $450
    (5) $520

43. There are 48 couples at a dance. Each couple consists of 1 male and 1 female. Mr. Fowler selects a female dancing partner for the next dance at random. What is the probability that Mr. Fowler selects his wife?
    (1) $\dfrac{1}{50}$

    (2) $\dfrac{1}{48}$

    (3) $\dfrac{2}{48}$

    (4) $\dfrac{1}{2}$

    (5) $\dfrac{2}{3}$

44. Which inequality is true?

(1) $\frac{4}{5} > \frac{2}{3} > \frac{5}{7}$

(2) $\frac{5}{7} > \frac{2}{3} > \frac{4}{5}$

(3) $\frac{4}{5} > \frac{5}{7} > \frac{2}{3}$

(4) $\frac{2}{3} > \frac{4}{5} > \frac{5}{7}$

(5) $\frac{5}{7} > \frac{4}{5} > \frac{2}{3}$

45. If p pounds of oranges can be bought for c cents, how many pounds can be bought for 98 cents?

(1) $\frac{98c}{p}$

(2) $98cp$

(3) $\frac{cp}{98}$

(4) $\frac{98p}{c}$

(5) $\frac{p}{98c}$

46. A man invests $6,000 in a stock that pays dividends amounting to 5% annually on his investment. How much more must he invest in a stock that pays 6% annually in dividends so that his annual income from both investments will be $900?

(1) $3,000

(2) $5,000

(3) $8,000

(4) $10,000

(5) $12,000

47. A tree is 24 feet tall and casts a shadow of 10 feet. At the same time a tower casts a shadow of 25 feet. What is the height, in feet, of the tower?

(1) 45

(2) 60

(3) 75

(4) 80

(5) 84

48. Mr. Capiello is on a diet. For breakfast and lunch together, he consumes 40% of his allowable number of calories. If he still has 1,200 calories left for the day, his daily calorie allowance is

(1) 2,000
(2) 2,200
(3) 2,400
(4) 2,500
(5) 2,800

49. If $3x - y = 11$ and $2y = 8$, then $x =$

(1) 3
(2) 4
(3) $4\frac{1}{2}$
(4) 5
(5) 6

50. Ms. Ruiz pays \$4,800 in income taxes. If this is 15% of her annual income, what is her annual income?

(1) \$25,000
(2) \$30,000
(3) \$32,000
(4) \$36,000
(5) \$40,000

51. A square has sides that each measure n feet in length. A larger square has sides that are each 2 feet larger than the smaller square's and an area that is 48 square feet greater. Which equation represents a comparison between the area of the smaller square and that of the larger square?

(1) $n^2 = (n + 2)^2 + 48$
(2) $(n + 2)^2 = n^2 + 48$
(3) $n^2 + (n + 2)^2 = 48$
(4) $n^2 - (n + 2)^2 = 48$
(5) $(n + 4)^2 - n^2 = 48$

52. A man earns 6% interest annually on an investment of $8,000. He is then taxed at a rate of 23% on his earnings. What is his net profit on the investment after taxes?
  (1) around $300
  (2) almost $410
  (3) around $650
  (4) almost $370
  (5) not enough information is given

53. A family spent $\frac{1}{4}$ of its income for rent and $\frac{1}{5}$ of its income for food. What percent of its income remains?
  (1) 40%
  (2) 45%
  (3) 50%
  (4) 52%
  (5) 55%

54. The perimeter of a triangle is 42 inches. If one side of the triangle is 6 inches longer than the first side and the third side is double the size of the first side, find the length of the first side.
  (1) 8 in.
  (2) 9 in.
  (3) 10 in.
  (4) 12 in.
  (5) 15 in.

55. On the number line below, $\sqrt{7}$ is located at point

  (1) A
  (2) B
  (3) C
  (4) D
  (5) E

56. A certain recipe that will yield 4 portions calls for $1\frac{1}{2}$ cups of sugar. If the recipe is used to yield 10 portions, the amount of sugar needed, in cups, is

(1) $3\frac{1}{2}$

(2) $3\frac{3}{4}$

(3) 4

(4) $4\frac{1}{4}$

(5) $4\frac{3}{4}$

Answer Key

1. **1**	13. **1**	24. **4**	35. **4**	46. **4**
2. **2**	14. **5**	25. **1**	36. **4**	47. **2**
3. **4**	15. **3**	26. **1**	37. **4**	48. **1**
4. **4**	16. **4**	27. **4**	38. **4**	49. **4**
5. **3**	17. **5**	28. **2**	39. **2**	50. **3**
6. **2**	18. **4**	29. **3**	40. **2**	51. **2**
7. **3**	19. **5**	30. **3**	41. **5**	52. **4**
8. **3**	20. **1**	31. **4**	42. **3**	53. **5**
9. **2**	21. **3**	32. **3**	43. **2**	54. **2**
10. **4**	22. **2**	33. **1**	44. **3**	55. **3**
11. **4**	23. **5**	34. **2**	45. **4**	56. **2**
12. **2**				

Answer Analysis

1. **1** If 80% of the audience were adults, 100% − 80% = 20% were children.

   20% = 0.20, and 0.20(650) = 130

2. **2** Let x = number of inches between the towns on the map.

   Set up a proportion:

   $$\frac{1 \text{ in.}}{60 \text{ mi.}} = \frac{x \text{ in.}}{225 \text{ mi.}}$$

   $$60x = 255$$

   $$x = \frac{255}{60} = 4\frac{1}{4}$$

3. **4**   4 ft. 3 in.   3 ft.15 in.
$$\underline{-2 \text{ ft. 8 in.}} = \underline{-2 \text{ ft. 8 in.}}$$
1 ft. 7 in.

4. **4** $v = lwh$. The container is 5 ft. long × 3ft. wide × 2 ft. high.
(5 × 3 × 2 = 30 cu. ft.)

5. **3**   Of the metric units listed, only the kilogram is a unit of weight.

6. **2**

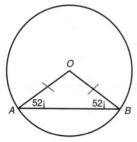

$OA = OB$, since each is a radius.
$m\angle A = m\angle B = 52°$
$m\angle A + m\angle B + m\angle O = 180°$
$52 + 52 + m\angle O = 180$
$104 + m\angle O = 180$
$m\angle O = 180 - 104 = 76°$

7. **3**

Let $x = AB$.
Then $\dfrac{3}{5} = \dfrac{x}{20}$, so $5x = 60$ and $x = 12$.

8. **3**

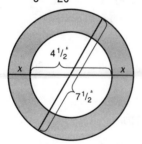

Let x = thickness of the pipe.
Then $x + x + 4\dfrac{1}{2} = 7\dfrac{1}{2}$
so $2x = 3$ and $x = 1\dfrac{1}{2}$ in.

9. **2** Percent increase = $\dfrac{\text{actual increase}}{\text{original amount}}$

Actual increase: $500 − $400 = $100

Percent increase: $\dfrac{100}{400} = \dfrac{1}{4} = 25\%$

10. **4** The shopper gives the storekeeper $5.00, or 500 cents. From this amount the storekeeper takes out x cents for the bread and $2y$ cents for the coffee.

The result is $500 − x − 2y$.

11. **4** Draw a diagram:

Since $A = lw = 240$, then $20w = 240$, and $w = 12$. Then $P = 2(l + w) = 2(20 + 12) = 2(32) = 64$.

12. **2** To find the total receipts, find the receipts of the matinee performances and add to these the receipts of the evening performances.

$2(267) + 4(329) = $ total receipts

13. **1** The part of the apartment painted in $2\frac{1}{2}$ hours =

$\dfrac{2\frac{1}{2}}{4\frac{1}{2}} = \dfrac{5}{2} \div \dfrac{9}{2} = \dfrac{5}{2} \times \dfrac{2}{9} = \dfrac{5}{9}$

14. **5** To write a number in scientific notation, write it as the product of a number between 1 and 10 and a power of 10.

In this case, the number between 1 and 10 is 2.347516. In going from 2.347516 to 2,347,516, move the decimal point 6 places to the right. Therefore, $2{,}347{,}516 = 2.347516 \times 10^6$.

15. **3** The expression $x^2 − 5x + 6$ factors as $(x − 3)(x − 2)$. If you can't factor, check each choice by multiplying out.

16. **4** If there are 32 students in the class and x students are absent, then $32 − x$ students are present.

The fractional part of the students present is $\dfrac{32 − x}{32}$.

17. **5** Let x = number of students taking French,

and $2x$ = number of students taking Spanish.

$x + 2x = 402$

$3x = 402$

$x = 402 \div 3 = 134$

$2x = 2(134) = 268$

18. **4** Note on the graph that the temperature neither rose nor fell, that is, it did not change, between 7 A.M. and 8 A.M.

19. **5** Since there are 16 oz. in 1 lb.
2,200 lb. = 2,200 × 16 = 35,200 oz.
35,200 ÷ 40 = 880

20. **1** Use the Pythagorean theorem.
$x^2 = 8^2 + 15^2$
$= 64 + 225$
$= 289$
$x = \sqrt{289} = 17$

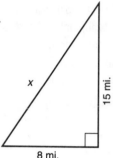

21. **3** Textbook sales: 300 × $20 = $6,000
Art book sales: 20 × $50 = $1,000
Novel sales: 400 × $25 = $10,000
Total sales = $17,000
Commission: 12% of $17,000 = $2,040

22. **2** Profit per share:
$36.50 − $32.75 = $3.75
Total profit: 120 × $3.75 = $450

23. **5** You could subtract to find the number of miles driven, but since the number of miles per gallon is not given, the problem cannot be solved.

24. **4** Let x = number of boys,
and $x + 6$ = number of girls.
$x + x + 6 = 34$
$2x + 6 = 34$
$2x = 34 − 6 = 28$
$x = 28 ÷ 2 = 14$
$x + 6 = 14 + 6 = 20$ girls

25. **1** Use the relationship
Rate × Time = Distance
or Rate = $\dfrac{\text{Distance}}{\text{Time}}$
In this case, distance = 120 mi. and time = x
Therefore, the number of miles per hour is $\dfrac{120}{x}$.

26. **1** Percent decrease = $\dfrac{\text{actual decrease}}{\text{original number}}$

Actual decrease: $3{,}500 - 2{,}800 = 700$

Percent decrease: $\dfrac{700}{3{,}500} = \dfrac{1}{5} = 20\%$

27. **4** $\$8{,}000 = 1$ son's share

$3 \times \$8{,}000 = \$24{,}000$, amount left to three sons

$\$24{,}000 = \dfrac{1}{2}$ of the estate

$2(\$24{,}000) = \$48{,}000$, value of the full estate

28. **2** Let $x =$ amount Joshua earns for typing 15 pages.

Set up a proportion:

$$\frac{\text{pages typed}}{\text{dollars earned}} \cdot \frac{20}{72} = \frac{15}{x}$$

$20x = 15 \times 72 = 1{,}080$, and

$x = 1{,}080 \div 20 = \$54.$

29. **3** 6 oz. $= \dfrac{6}{16} = \dfrac{3}{8}$ lb.

19 lb. costs $19(\$0.88) = \$16.72$

$\dfrac{3}{8}$ lb. costs $\dfrac{3}{8}(\overset{0.11}{\cancel{\$0.88}}) = \$0.33$

$19\dfrac{3}{8}$ lb. costs $\$16.72 + \$.33 = \$17.05$

Change $= \$20.00 - \$17.05 = \$2.95.$

30. **3** Frank spent yz dollars.

Subtract yz from x. The result is $x - yz$.

31. **4** Note that, after the first $\dfrac{1}{5}$ mi., the fare amounts to \$1 per mile. Therefore, a 3-mi. trip would cost \$2 for the second and third miles. The first $\dfrac{1}{5}$ mi. would cost \$1, and each of the next $\dfrac{4}{5}$s would cost 20 cents each, for a total of \$1.80. The entire 3-mi. trip would cost $\$2.00 + \$1.80 = \$3.80.$

32. **3** Taking \$1 tip from the \$10 available leaves \$9 for the actual travel. The first $\dfrac{1}{5}$ mi. costs \$1, leaving \$8. Since the fare is \$1 per mile thereafter, the trip could be as long as $8\dfrac{1}{5}$ mi.

33. **1** Area of rectangle $= (2a)(a) = 2a^2.$

Radius of semicircle $= \dfrac{1}{2}(2a) = a.$

The formula for the area of a circle is $A = \pi r^2.$

Area of semicircle = $\frac{1}{2}(\pi a^2)$.

Area of whole figure = $2a^2 + \frac{1}{2}\pi a^2$.

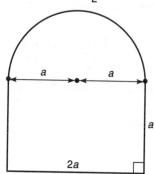

34. **2**   The man spends $\frac{45}{360} = \frac{1}{8}$ day on meals. $\frac{1}{8}$ day = $\frac{1}{8} \times 24 = 3$ hrs.

The man spends $\frac{30}{360} = \frac{1}{12}$ day on travel. $\frac{1}{12}$ day = $\frac{1}{12} \times 24 = 2$ hrs.

The man spends 1 hr. more on meals than on travel. Each of the other statements is incorrect. For example, consider statement (1).

$\frac{105°}{360°} = \frac{7}{24}$, $\frac{7}{24} \times 24 = 7$

Each day, the man works 7 hrs., not 8 hrs.

35. **4**   Use the formula for the volume of a cylinder: $V = \pi r^2 h$.

In this case, $\pi = \frac{22}{7}$, $r = 7$, and $h = 6$.

$$V = \frac{22}{7} \times 7 \times 7 \times 6$$
$$= 924 \text{ cu. ft.}$$

$924 \times 7 = 6{,}468$

36. **4** $y = 2x^2(z - 3)$
$$= 2(5)(5)(7 - 3)$$
$$= 2(5)(5)(4)$$
$$= 200$$

37. **4**   Let x = total distance to be covered.

$\frac{2}{7}x = 384$

$2x = 7(384) = 2{,}688$

$x = 2{,}688 \div 2 = 1{,}344$

38. **4** At age 30, the policy costs 22(10) = $220 per year.
At age 46, the policy costs 38(10) = $380 per year.
Thus, $380 – $220 = $160 saved per year.
In 20 years, the savings is 160(20) = $3,200.

39. **2**

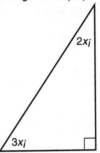

Let $3x$ = measure of the larger angle,
and $2x$ = measure of the smaller angle.

$3x + 2x = 90$
$5x = 90$
$x = 90 \div 5 = 18$
$3x = 3(18) = 54°$

40. **2** $3x - 1 < 5$
$3x < 6$
$x < 2$

x must be less than 2.

41. **5**

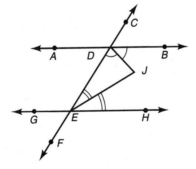

m$\angle BDE = 100°$
Since $\overleftrightarrow{AB} \parallel \overleftrightarrow{GH}$, $\angle BDE +$ m$\angle DEH = 180°$
$100 +$ m$\angle DEH = 180$
m$\angle DEH = 180 - 100 = 80°$
m$\angle JDE = \frac{1}{2}$ m$\angle BDE = 50°$

$$m\angle DEJ = \frac{1}{2}m\angle DEH = 40°$$

$$m\angle J + 50 + 40 = 180$$

$$m\angle J = 180 - 50 - 40 = 90°$$

42. **3** $25\% = \frac{1}{4}$. Selling price of chair was $\frac{3}{4}$ of original selling price.

Let x = original selling price.

$$\frac{3}{4}x = \$315$$

$$x = \$315 \div \frac{3}{4} = \$315 \times \frac{4}{3} = \$420$$

43. **2**   Probability =

number of successful outcomes
number of possible outcomes

In this case, the number of successful outcomes is 1 since, of the 48 women present, only 1 woman is Mr. Fowler's wife. The number of possible outcomes is 48 since there are 48 possible women partners.

Probability = $\frac{1}{48}$

44. **3** $\frac{4}{5} > \frac{5}{7}$ because $4 \times 7 > 5 \times 5$

$\frac{5}{7} > \frac{2}{3}$ because $5 \times 3 > 7 \times 2$

Thus, $\frac{4}{5} > \frac{5}{7} > \frac{2}{3}$ is correct.

Alternative Method:

Convert the three fractions to decimals, to the nearest hundredth.

$$\frac{5}{7} = 0.71, \ \frac{4}{5} = 0.80, \ \frac{2}{3} = 0.67$$

Therefore, $\frac{4}{5} > \frac{5}{7} > \frac{2}{3}$

45. **4**   Set up a proportion.

$$\frac{pounds}{cents} \cdot \frac{p}{c} = \frac{x}{98}$$

Then $98p = cx$, and $x = \frac{98p}{c}$.

46. **4**   \$6,000 at 5% = \$6,000 × 0.05 = \$300 income.

The man needs \$900 − \$300 = \$600 more in income.

6% of the new amount needed = \$600.

Let x = new amount needed.

$$0.06x = 600$$

$$x = 600 \div 0.06 = \$10,000$$

47. **2**

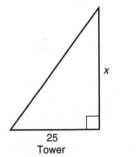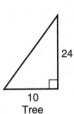

25
Tower

10
Tree

Let x = height of tower.

Set up a proportion.

$$\frac{\text{height of object}}{\text{length of shadow}} : \frac{x}{25} = \frac{24}{10}$$

$10x = 25(24) = 600$

$x = 600 \div 10 = 60$

48. **1** If Mr. Capiello has consumed 40% of his allowable calories, he has 60% left.

Let x = his daily allowance of calories

$0.60x = 1,200$

$x = 1,200 \div 0.60 = 2,000$

49. **4** Since $2y = 8$, then $y = 4$.

$3x - y = 11$

$3x - 4 = 11$

$3x = 15$ and $x = 5$

50. **3** Let x = Ms. Ruiz's annual income.

$15x = \$4,800$

$$x = \frac{\$4,800}{0.15} = \frac{\$480,000}{15}$$

$= \$32,000$

51. **2** Area of enlarged square = $(n + 2)(n + 2)$

Area of original square = n^2

Use this relationship:

Enlarged square area = original square area + 48

$$(n + 2)^2 = n^2 + 48.$$

52. **4**   6% of 8000 = 480 (.06 × 8000 = 480)

$480 is taxed at 23%, 100% − 23% = 77%.

480 × .77 = $369.60 left after taxes, or almost $370.

53. **5**   Fractional part of income spent on rent and food:

$$\frac{1}{4} + \frac{1}{5} = \frac{5}{20} + \frac{4}{20} = \frac{9}{20}$$

$1 - \frac{9}{20} = \frac{11}{20}$, remaining income, $\frac{11}{20} = 0.55 = 55\%$.

54. **2**   Let x = length of first side.

Then $x + 6$ = length of second side,

and $2x$ = length of third side.

$$x + x + 6 + 2x = 42$$
$$4x + 6 = 42$$
$$4x = 42 - 6 = 36$$
$$x = 36 \div 4 = 9 \text{ in.}$$

55. **3**   Since $2^2 = 4$ and $3^2 = 9$, $\sqrt{7}$ is between 2 and 3. On the number line, only point C lies between 2 and 3.

56. **2**   Let x = number of cups of sugar needed. Set up a proportion:

$$\frac{\text{number of portions}}{\text{cups of sugar}} : \frac{4}{1.5}$$

Then $4x = 10(1.5) = 15$, and $x = \frac{15}{4} = 3\frac{3}{4}$.

8

A PRACTICE EXAMINATION

The direction sheets, mathematics formulas,* and question formats of this examination are constructed like the actual test you will take. The examination consists of five parts.

Tests	Questions	Time Allowance
Test 1: The Writing Skills Test, Part I	55	1 hour, 15 minutes
The Writing Skills Test, Part II	Essay	45 minutes
Test 2: The Social Studies Test	64	1 hour, 25 minutes
Test 3: The Science Test	66	1 hour, 35 minutes
Test 4: The Interpreting Literature and the Arts Test	45	1 hour, 5 minutes
Test 5: The Mathematics Test	56	1 hour, 30 minutes
	Total:	7 hours, 35 minutes

For this examination, we have included an answer sheet and a self-appraisal chart. Mark yourself on each test, checking your answers against the answer key. Read the answer explanations to be sure you understand the correct answer choices. After you have calculated the scores for all five tests, refer to the self-appraisal materials to determine your subject area strengths and weaknesses as well as your total GED score.

The main purpose of the test is to help you discover your strengths and your weaknesses. IMPORTANT: You should spend more time studying those chapters that deal with the tests in which you are weakest.

SIMULATE TEST CONDITIONS

To make conditions similar to those on the actual examination, do not take more time than that allowed for each test.

---

*Directions and mathematics formulas are reprinted by permission of the GED Testing Service of the American Council on Education.

ANSWER SHEET—PRACTICE EXAMINATION

Test 1: The Writing Skills Test

1. ① ② ③ ④ ⑤
2. ① ② ③ ④ ⑤
3. ① ② ③ ④ ⑤
4. ① ② ③ ④ ⑤
5. ① ② ③ ④ ⑤
6. ① ② ③ ④ ⑤
7. ① ② ③ ④ ⑤
8. ① ② ③ ④ ⑤
9. ① ② ③ ④ ⑤
10. ① ② ③ ④ ⑤
11. ① ② ③ ④ ⑤
12. ① ② ③ ④ ⑤
13. ① ② ③ ④ ⑤
14. ① ② ③ ④ ⑤
15. ① ② ③ ④ ⑤
16. ① ② ③ ④ ⑤
17. ① ② ③ ④ ⑤
18. ① ② ③ ④ ⑤
19. ① ② ③ ④ ⑤

20. ① ② ③ ④ ⑤
21. ① ② ③ ④ ⑤
22. ① ② ③ ④ ⑤
23. ① ② ③ ④ ⑤
24. ① ② ③ ④ ⑤
25. ① ② ③ ④ ⑤
26. ① ② ③ ④ ⑤
27. ① ② ③ ④ ⑤
28. ① ② ③ ④ ⑤
29. ① ② ③ ④ ⑤
30. ① ② ③ ④ ⑤
31. ① ② ③ ④ ⑤
32. ① ② ③ ④ ⑤
33. ① ② ③ ④ ⑤
34. ① ② ③ ④ ⑤
35. ① ② ③ ④ ⑤
36. ① ② ③ ④ ⑤
37. ① ② ③ ④ ⑤
38. ① ② ③ ④ ⑤

39. ① ② ③ ④ ⑤
40. ① ② ③ ④ ⑤
41. ① ② ③ ④ ⑤
42. ① ② ③ ④ ⑤
43. ① ② ③ ④ ⑤
44. ① ② ③ ④ ⑤
45. ① ② ③ ④ ⑤
46. ① ② ③ ④ ⑤
47. ① ② ③ ④ ⑤
48. ① ② ③ ④ ⑤
49. ① ② ③ ④ ⑤
50. ① ② ③ ④ ⑤
51. ① ② ③ ④ ⑤
52. ① ② ③ ④ ⑤
53. ① ② ③ ④ ⑤
54. ① ② ③ ④ ⑤
55. ① ② ③ ④ ⑤

Test 2: The Social Studies Test

1. ① ② ③ ④ ⑤
2. ① ② ③ ④ ⑤
3. ① ② ③ ④ ⑤
4. ① ② ③ ④ ⑤
5. ① ② ③ ④ ⑤
6. ① ② ③ ④ ⑤
7. ① ② ③ ④ ⑤
8. ① ② ③ ④ ⑤
9. ① ② ③ ④ ⑤
10. ① ② ③ ④ ⑤
11. ① ② ③ ④ ⑤
12. ① ② ③ ④ ⑤

13. ① ② ③ ④ ⑤
14. ① ② ③ ④ ⑤
15. ① ② ③ ④ ⑤
16. ① ② ③ ④ ⑤
17. ① ② ③ ④ ⑤
18. ① ② ③ ④ ⑤
19. ① ② ③ ④ ⑤
20. ① ② ③ ④ ⑤
21. ① ② ③ ④ ⑤
22. ① ② ③ ④ ⑤
23. ① ② ③ ④ ⑤
24. ① ② ③ ④ ⑤

25. ① ② ③ ④ ⑤
26. ① ② ③ ④ ⑤
27. ① ② ③ ④ ⑤
28. ① ② ③ ④ ⑤
29. ① ② ③ ④ ⑤
30. ① ② ③ ④ ⑤
31. ① ② ③ ④ ⑤
32. ① ② ③ ④ ⑤
33. ① ② ③ ④ ⑤
34. ① ② ③ ④ ⑤
35. ① ② ③ ④ ⑤
36. ① ② ③ ④ ⑤

37. ① ② ③ ④ ⑤   47. ① ② ③ ④ ⑤   56. ① ② ③ ④ ⑤
38. ① ② ③ ④ ⑤   48. ① ② ③ ④ ⑤   57. ① ② ③ ④ ⑤
39. ① ② ③ ④ ⑤   49. ① ② ③ ④ ⑤   58. ① ② ③ ④ ⑤
40. ① ② ③ ④ ⑤   50. ① ② ③ ④ ⑤   59. ① ② ③ ④ ⑤
41. ① ② ③ ④ ⑤   51. ① ② ③ ④ ⑤   60. ① ② ③ ④ ⑤
42. ① ② ③ ④ ⑤   52. ① ② ③ ④ ⑤   61. ① ② ③ ④ ⑤
43. ① ② ③ ④ ⑤   53. ① ② ③ ④ ⑤   62. ① ② ③ ④ ⑤
44. ① ② ③ ④ ⑤   54. ① ② ③ ④ ⑤   63. ① ② ③ ④ ⑤
45. ① ② ③ ④ ⑤   55. ① ② ③ ④ ⑤   64. ① ② ③ ④ ⑤
46. ① ② ③ ④ ⑤   55. ① ② ③ ④ ⑤

Test 3: The Science Test

1. ① ② ③ ④ ⑤   24. ① ② ③ ④ ⑤   47. ① ② ③ ④ ⑤
2. ① ② ③ ④ ⑤   25. ① ② ③ ④ ⑤   48. ① ② ③ ④ ⑤
3. ① ② ③ ④ ⑤   26. ① ② ③ ④ ⑤   49. ① ② ③ ④ ⑤
4. ① ② ③ ④ ⑤   27. ① ② ③ ④ ⑤   50. ① ② ③ ④ ⑤
5. ① ② ③ ④ ⑤   28. ① ② ③ ④ ⑤   51. ① ② ③ ④ ⑤
6. ① ② ③ ④ ⑤   29. ① ② ③ ④ ⑤   52. ① ② ③ ④ ⑤
7. ① ② ③ ④ ⑤   30. ① ② ③ ④ ⑤   53. ① ② ③ ④ ⑤
8. ① ② ③ ④ ⑤   31. ① ② ③ ④ ⑤   54. ① ② ③ ④ ⑤
9. ① ② ③ ④ ⑤   32. ① ② ③ ④ ⑤   55. ① ② ③ ④ ⑤
10. ① ② ③ ④ ⑤   33. ① ② ③ ④ ⑤   56. ① ② ③ ④ ⑤
11. ① ② ③ ④ ⑤   34. ① ② ③ ④ ⑤   57. ① ② ③ ④ ⑤
12. ① ② ③ ④ ⑤   35. ① ② ③ ④ ⑤   58. ① ② ③ ④ ⑤
13. ① ② ③ ④ ⑤   36. ① ② ③ ④ ⑤   59. ① ② ③ ④ ⑤
14. ① ② ③ ④ ⑤   37. ① ② ③ ④ ⑤   60. ① ② ③ ④ ⑤
15. ① ② ③ ④ ⑤   38. ① ② ③ ④ ⑤   61. ① ② ③ ④ ⑤
16. ① ② ③ ④ ⑤   39. ① ② ③ ④ ⑤   62. ① ② ③ ④ ⑤
17. ① ② ③ ④ ⑤   40. ① ② ③ ④ ⑤   63. ① ② ③ ④ ⑤
18. ① ② ③ ④ ⑤   41. ① ② ③ ④ ⑤   64. ① ② ③ ④ ⑤
19. ① ② ③ ④ ⑤   42. ① ② ③ ④ ⑤   65. ① ② ③ ④ ⑤
20. ① ② ③ ④ ⑤   43. ① ② ③ ④ ⑤   66. ① ② ③ ④ ⑤
21. ① ② ③ ④ ⑤   44. ① ② ③ ④ ⑤
22. ① ② ③ ④ ⑤   45. ① ② ③ ④ ⑤
23. ① ② ③ ④ ⑤   46. ① ② ③ ④ ⑤

Test 4: The Interpreting Literature and Arts Test

1. ① ② ③ ④ ⑤
2. ① ② ③ ④ ⑤
3. ① ② ③ ④ ⑤
4. ① ② ③ ④ ⑤
5. ① ② ③ ④ ⑤
6. ① ② ③ ④ ⑤
7. ① ② ③ ④ ⑤
8. ① ② ③ ④ ⑤
9. ① ② ③ ④ ⑤
10. ① ② ③ ④ ⑤
11. ① ② ③ ④ ⑤
12. ① ② ③ ④ ⑤
13. ① ② ③ ④ ⑤
14. ① ② ③ ④ ⑤
15. ① ② ③ ④ ⑤

16. ① ② ③ ④ ⑤
17. ① ② ③ ④ ⑤
18. ① ② ③ ④ ⑤
19. ① ② ③ ④ ⑤
20. ① ② ③ ④ ⑤
21. ① ② ③ ④ ⑤
22. ① ② ③ ④ ⑤
23. ① ② ③ ④ ⑤
24. ① ② ③ ④ ⑤
25. ① ② ③ ④ ⑤
26. ① ② ③ ④ ⑤
27. ① ② ③ ④ ⑤
28. ① ② ③ ④ ⑤
29. ① ② ③ ④ ⑤
30. ① ② ③ ④ ⑤

31. ① ② ③ ④ ⑤
32. ① ② ③ ④ ⑤
33. ① ② ③ ④ ⑤
34. ① ② ③ ④ ⑤
35. ① ② ③ ④ ⑤
36. ① ② ③ ④ ⑤
37. ① ② ③ ④ ⑤
38. ① ② ③ ④ ⑤
39. ① ② ③ ④ ⑤
40. ① ② ③ ④ ⑤
41. ① ② ③ ④ ⑤
42. ① ② ③ ④ ⑤
43. ① ② ③ ④ ⑤
44. ① ② ③ ④ ⑤
45. ① ② ③ ④ ⑤

Test 5: The Mathematics Test

1. ① ② ③ ④ ⑤
2. ① ② ③ ④ ⑤
3. ① ② ③ ④ ⑤
4. ① ② ③ ④ ⑤
5. ① ② ③ ④ ⑤
6. ① ② ③ ④ ⑤
7. ① ② ③ ④ ⑤
8. ① ② ③ ④ ⑤
9. ① ② ③ ④ ⑤
10. ① ② ③ ④ ⑤
11. ① ② ③ ④ ⑤
12. ① ② ③ ④ ⑤
13. ① ② ③ ④ ⑤
14. ① ② ③ ④ ⑤
15. ① ② ③ ④ ⑤
16. ① ② ③ ④ ⑤
17. ① ② ③ ④ ⑤
18. ① ② ③ ④ ⑤
19. ① ② ③ ④ ⑤

20. ① ② ③ ④ ⑤
21. ① ② ③ ④ ⑤
22. ① ② ③ ④ ⑤
23. ① ② ③ ④ ⑤
24. ① ② ③ ④ ⑤
25. ① ② ③ ④ ⑤
26. ① ② ③ ④ ⑤
27. ① ② ③ ④ ⑤
28. ① ② ③ ④ ⑤
29. ① ② ③ ④ ⑤
30. ① ② ③ ④ ⑤
31. ① ② ③ ④ ⑤
32. ① ② ③ ④ ⑤
33. ① ② ③ ④ ⑤
34. ① ② ③ ④ ⑤
35. ① ② ③ ④ ⑤
36. ① ② ③ ④ ⑤
37. ① ② ③ ④ ⑤
38. ① ② ③ ④ ⑤

39. ① ② ③ ④ ⑤
40. ① ② ③ ④ ⑤
41. ① ② ③ ④ ⑤
42. ① ② ③ ④ ⑤
43. ① ② ③ ④ ⑤
44. ① ② ③ ④ ⑤
45. ① ② ③ ④ ⑤
46. ① ② ③ ④ ⑤
47. ① ② ③ ④ ⑤
48. ① ② ③ ④ ⑤
49. ① ② ③ ④ ⑤
50. ① ② ③ ④ ⑤
51. ① ② ③ ④ ⑤
52. ① ② ③ ④ ⑤
53. ① ② ③ ④ ⑤
54. ① ② ③ ④ ⑤
55. ① ② ③ ④ ⑤
56. ① ② ③ ④ ⑤

PRACTICE EXAMINATION

TEST 1: WRITING SKILLS, PART I

Directions

Alloted Time: 75 minutes

The Writing Skills test is intended to measure your ability to use clear and effective English. It is a test of English as it should be written, not as it might be spoken. This test includes both multiple-choice questions and an essay. These directions apply only to the multiple-choice section; a separate set of directions is given for the essay.

The multiple-choice section consists of paragraphs with numbered sentences. Some of the sentences contain errors in sentence structure, usage, or mechanics (spelling, punctuation, and capitalization). After reading the numbered sentences, answer the multiple-choice questions that follow. Some questions refer to sentences that are correct as written. The best answer for these questions is the one that leaves the sentence as originally written. The best answer for some questions is the one that produces a sentence that is consistent with the verb tense and point of view used throughout the paragraph.

You should spend no more than 75 minutes on the multiple-choice questions and 45 minutes on your essay. Work carefully, but do not spend too much time on any one question. You may begin working on the essay part of this test as soon as you complete the multiple-choice section.

To record your answers, mark the numbered space on the answer sheet beside the number that corresponds to the question in the test.

FOR EXAMPLE:

Sentence 1: **We were all honored to meet governor Phillips.**

What correction should be made to this sentence?

(1) insert a comma after <u>honored</u>   ① ② ● ④ ⑤
(2) change the spelling of <u>honored</u> to <u>honered</u>
(3) change <u>governor</u> to <u>Governor</u>
(4) replace <u>were</u> with <u>was</u>
(5) no correction is necessary

In this example, the word "governor" should be capitalized; therefore, answer space 3 would be marked on the answer sheet.

Questions 1 to 9 refer to the following paragraph.

(1) A combination of attributes make vegetable gardening a national hobby with both young and old. (2) For an ever-increasing number of individuals seed catalogs and the thoughts of spring gardening provide a happy escape from the winter doldrums. (3) Vegetable gardeners unanimously agree that many home-grown vegetables picked at their peak of maturity have quality. seldom found in vegetables purchased from commercial markets. (4) From Spring to late Fall, a well-planned and maintained garden can provide a supply of fresh vegetables, thus increasing the nutritional value of the family diet. (5) Freezers make it possible to preserve some of the surplus vegetables to be enjoyed at a later date other vegetables can be stored for a few months in a cool area. (6) Not to be overlooked is the finger-tip convenience of having vegetables in the backyard; this in itself justifies home gardening for many individuals. (7) In addition, vegetable gardening provides excercise and recreation for both urban and suburban families. (8) Although your initial dollar investment for gardening may be nominal, one cannot escape the fact that gardening requires manual labor and time. (9) Neglecting jobs that should be performed on a regular basis may result in failure and a negative feeling toward gardening.

1. Sentence 1: **A combination of attributes make vegetable gardening a national hobby with both young and old.**

   What correction should be made to this sentence?
   (1) insert a comma after <u>attributes</u>
   (2) change <u>make</u> to <u>makes</u>
   (3) capitalize vegetable gardening
   (4) reverse <u>with</u> and <u>both</u>
   (5) no correction is necessary

2. Sentence 2: **For an ever-increasing number of individuals seed catalogs and the thoughts of spring gardening provide a happy escape from the winter doldrums.**

   What correction should be made to this sentence?
   (1) remove the hyphen from <u>ever-increasing</u>
   (2) change <u>number</u> to <u>amount</u>
   (3) insert a comma after <u>individuals</u>
   (4) insert a comma after <u>catalogs</u>
   (5) no correction is necessary

3. Sentence 3: **Vegetable gardeners unanimously agree that many home-grown vegetables picked at their peak of maturity have <u>quality. seldom</u> found in vegetables purchased from commercial markets.**

Which of the following is the best way to write the underlined portion of this sentence? If you think the original is the best way, choose option (1).
- (1) quality. seldom
- (2) quality. Seldom
- (3) quality seldom
- (4) quality; seldom
- (5) quality, seldom

4. Sentence 4: **From Spring to late Fall, a well-planned and maintained garden can provide a supply of fresh vegetables, thus increasing the nutritional value of the family diet.**

What correction should be made to this sentence?
- (1) remove capitals from <u>Spring</u> and <u>Fall</u>
- (2) remove the hyphen from <u>well-planned</u>
- (3) remove the comma after <u>vegetables</u>
- (4) change <u>thus</u> to <u>however</u>
- (5) no correction is necessary

5. Sentence 5: **Freezers make it possible to preserve some of the surplus vegetables to be enjoyed at a later <u>date other</u> vegetables can be stored for a few months in a cool area.**

Which of the following is the best way to write the underlined portion of this sentence? If you think the original is the best way, choose option (1).
- (1) date other
- (2) date, other
- (3) date. Other
- (4) date, while other
- (5) date; while other

6. Sentence 6: **Not to be overlooked is the finger-tip convenience of having vegetables in the backyard; this in itself justifies home gardening for many individuals.**

What correction should be made to this sentence?
- (1) insert a comma after <u>overlooked</u>
- (2) change the spelling of <u>vegetables</u> to <u>vegtables</u>
- (3) replace the semicolon after <u>backyard</u> with a comma
- (4) change the spelling of gardening to <u>gardning</u>
- (5) no correction is necessary

7. Sentence 7: **In addition, vegetable gardening provides excercise and recreation for both urban and suburban families.**

   What correction should be made to this sentence?
   (1) remove the comma after <u>addition</u>
   (2) change the spelling of <u>excercise</u> to <u>exercise</u>
   (3) insert a comma after <u>recreation</u>
   (4) change <u>for both</u> to <u>both for</u>
   (5) no correction is necessary

8. Sentence 8: **Although your initial dollar investment for gardening may be nominal, one cannot escape the fact that gardening requires manual labor and time.**

   What correction should be made to this sentence?
   (1) change <u>Although</u> to <u>Because</u>
   (2) remove the comma after <u>nominal</u>
   (3) change <u>one</u> to <u>you</u>
   (4) change <u>requires</u> to <u>require</u>
   (5) no correction is necessary

9. Sentence 9: **Neglecting jobs that should be performed on a regular basis may result in failure and a negative feeling toward gardening.**

   What correction should be made to this sentence?
   (1) insert a comma after <u>jobs</u>
   (2) insert a comma after <u>basis</u>
   (3) change <u>may result</u> to <u>results</u>
   (4) change <u>and</u> to <u>despite</u>
   (5) no correction is necessary

<u>Questions 10 to 19</u> refer to the following paragraph.

(1) In coming years, families will need to learn to turn to their computers for assistence. (2) With the increasing amounts of information a family is required to process, the home computer will become a necessity for both decision making and family record storage and retrieval. (3) A home communications revolution is predicted with the arrival of the home computer. It will serve as a source and processor of information. (4) A virtually infinite amount of information from many sources will be at the instantaneous disposal of the family for more efficient decision making. (5) The computer will plan meals, turn lights on at appropriate times, keep track

of family members' schedules, calculate budget information, and oversee credit, spending, and bank accounts. (6) Just as home equiptment frees the homemaker from the labor of housekeeping, the computer releases family members from some repetitious managerial duties. (7) The home terminal may serve as a home education center for children's homework and part of the lifelong learning program of parents and elderly family members. (8) The change that will have the most immediate effect on family decision making will be increased discretionary time. (9) For economic reasons, many families will decide to use they're "free" time to hold a second job. (10) With the increasing interest in personal development, a segment of the time might be allotted by some to develop alternative interests through lifelong educational programs that will facilitate career changes, to increase skills for effective citizenship, and learning new skills to enhance their family living.

10. Sentence 1: **In coming years, families will need to learn to turn to their computers for assistence.**

    What correction should be made to this sentence?
    (1) remove the comma after <u>years</u>
    (2) change <u>will need</u> to <u>need</u>
    (3) change the spelling of <u>their</u> to <u>they're</u>
    (4) change the spelling of <u>assistence</u> to <u>assistance</u>
    (5) no correction is necessary

11. Sentence 2: **With the increasing amounts of information a family is required to process, the home computer will become a necessity for both decision making and family record storage and retrieval.**

    What correction should be made to this sentence?
    (1) change <u>With the</u> to <u>Despite</u>
    (2) change <u>is</u> to <u>are</u>
    (3) remove the comma after <u>process</u>
    (4) change the spelling of <u>necessity</u> to <u>neccesity</u>
    (5) no correction is necessary

12. Sentence 3: **A home communications revolution is predicted with the arrival of the home <u>computer. It</u> will serve as a source and processor of information.**

    Which of the following is the best way to write the underlined portion of the sentence? If you think the original is the best way, choose option (1).
    (1) computer. It
    (2) computer, It

(3) computer, it
(4) computer it
(5) computer; It

13. Sentence 4: **A virtually infinite amount of information from many sources will be at the instantaneous disposal of the family for more efficient decision making.**

What correction should be made to this sentence?
(1) insert a comma after <u>information</u>
(2) insert a comma after <u>sources</u>
(3) insert a comma after <u>family</u>
(4) change the spelling of <u>efficient</u> to <u>eficient</u>
(5) no correction is necessary

14. Sentence 5: **The computer will plan meals, turn lights on at appropriate times keep track of family members' schedules, calculate budget information, and oversee credit, spending, and bank accounts.**

What correction should be made to this sentence?
(1) remove comma after <u>meals</u>
(2) insert comma after <u>times</u>
(3) change <u>members'</u> to <u>member's</u>
(4) change the spelling of <u>schedules</u> to <u>skedules</u>
(5) no correction is necessary

15. Sentence 6: **Just as home equiptment frees the homemaker from the labor of housekeeping, the computer releases family members from some repetitious managerial duties.**

What correction should be made to this sentence?
(1) change <u>Just</u> as to <u>Although</u>
(2) change the spelling of <u>equiptment</u> to <u>equipment</u>
(3) remove the comma after <u>housekeeping</u>
(4) change <u>releases</u> to <u>will have released</u>
(5) no correction is necessary

16. Sentence 7: **The home terminal may serve as a home education center for children's homework and part of the lifelong learning program of parents and elderly family members.**

If you rewrote sentence 7 beginning with
<u>Children's homework and part of the lifelong learning program of parents and elderly family members</u>
the next words should be

(1) are served
(2) may serve
(3) may be served
(4) serve
(5) will serve

17. Sentence 8: **The change that will have the most immediate effect on family decision making will be increased discretionary time.**

    What correction should be made to this sentence?
    (1) change <u>will have</u> to <u>having</u>
    (2) change the spelling of <u>effect</u> to <u>affect</u>
    (3) change <u>family</u> to <u>family's</u>
    (4) change <u>will be</u> to is
    (5) no correction is necessary

18. Sentence 9: **For economic reasons, many families will decide to use they're "free" time to hold a second job.**

    What correction should be made to this sentence?
    (1) remove the comma after <u>reasons</u>
    (2) change the spelling of <u>families</u> to <u>familys</u>
    (3) change the spelling of <u>they're</u> to <u>their</u>
    (4) change <u>to</u> to <u>and</u>
    (5) no correction is necessary

19. Sentence 10: **With the increasing interest in personal development, a segment of the time might be allotted by some to develop alternative interests through lifelong educational programs that will facilitate career changes, to increase skills for effective citizenship, and learning new skills to enhance their family living.**

    What correction should be made to this sentence?
    (1) change the spelling of <u>development</u> to <u>developement</u>
    (2) change the spelling of <u>through</u> to <u>thorough</u>
    (3) remove the comma after <u>changes</u>
    (4) change learning to <u>to learn</u>
    (5) no correction is necessary

<u>Questions 20 to 28</u> refer to the following paragraphs.

(1) To lessen the threat of faulty car repair work or repair frauds, they're a number of constructive steps you can take. (2) While these measures can't offer full protection they are wise insurance against dented pocketbooks and expanded time schedules.

(3) First, never wait until a small problem becomes a big and costly one. (4) Always take your car in for a check at the first sign of trouble.

(5) But before you take the car in, make a list of all problems and "symptoms" so you are prepared to describe the trouble as accurately and specifically as possible.

(6) Don't just ask to have the car put in "working order," (7) that kind of general statement can lead directly to unnecessary work.

(8) On your initial visit, make certain you get a copy of the work authorization that you sign or a general estimate of the total cost of the repairs. (9) Don't leave until you do.

(10) Ask the repair garage to telephone you when the exact work to be done has been determinned. (11) When you recieve the call, say you now want to return to the station to obtain another work order itemizing the cost of each repair to be made.

20. Sentence 1: **To lessen the threat of faulty car repair work or repair frauds, they're a number of constructive steps you can take.**

    What correction should be made to this sentence?
    (1) change <u>lessen</u> to <u>lesson</u>
    (2) remove the comma after <u>frauds</u>
    (3) change the spelling of <u>they're</u> to <u>there are</u>
    (4) change <u>can</u> to <u>might</u>
    (5) no correction is necessary

21. Sentence 2: **While these measures can't offer full protection they are wise insurance against dented pocketbooks and expanded time schedules.**

    What correction should be made to this sentence?
    (1) change <u>while</u> to <u>nevertheless</u>
    (2) insert a comma after <u>protection</u>
    (3) change <u>insurance</u> to <u>insurence</u>
    (4) insert a hyphen in <u>pocketbooks</u>
    (5) no correction is necessary

22. Sentence 3: **First, never wait until a small problem becomes a big and costly one.**

    What correction should be made to this sentence?
    (1) change <u>first</u> to <u>firstly</u>
    (2) remove the comma after <u>first</u>

(3) change the spelling of <u>until</u> to <u>untill</u>

(4) change <u>becomes</u> to <u>will become</u>

(5) no correction is necessary

23. Sentence 4: **Always take your car in for a check at the first sign of trouble.**

What correction should be made to this sentence?

(1) change <u>always</u> to <u>allways</u>

(2) change <u>take</u> to <u>you should take</u>

(3) change <u>your</u> to <u>your'e</u>

(4) insert a comma after <u>check</u>

(5) no correction is necessary

24. Sentence 5: **But before you take the car in, make a list of all problems and "symptoms" so you are prepared to describe the trouble as accurately and specifically as possible.**

What correction should be made to this sentence?

(1) change <u>take</u> to <u>will take</u>

(2) remove the comma after <u>in</u>

(3) change <u>are</u> to <u>will be</u>

(4) change the spelling of <u>specifically</u> to <u>specificaly</u>

(5) no correction is necessary

25. Sentences 6 and 7: **Don't just ask to have the car put in "working <u>order," that</u> kind of general statement can lead directly to unnecessary work.**

Which of the following is the best way to write the underlined portion of these sentences? If you think the original is the best way, choose option (1).

(1) order," that

(2) order" that

(3) order": that

(4) order". that

(5) order." That

26. Sentence 8: **On your initial visit, make certain you get a copy of the work authorization that you sign or a general estimate of the total cost of the repairs.**

What correction should be made to this sentence?

(1) change the spelling of <u>initial</u> to <u>initail</u>

(2) remove the comma after <u>visit</u>

(3) insert a comma after <u>sign</u>
(4) change the spelling of <u>estimate</u> to <u>estemate</u>
(5) no correction is necessary

27. Sentence 10: **Ask the repair garage to telephone you when the exact work to be done has been determinned.**

What correction should be made to this sentence?
(1) insert a comma after <u>you</u>
(2) change <u>when</u> to <u>while</u>
(3) change <u>has been</u> to <u>will have been</u>
(4) change the spelling of <u>determinned</u> to <u>determined</u>
(5) no correction is necessary

28. Sentence 11: **When you recieve the call, say you now want to return to the station to obtain another work order itemizing the cost of each repair to be made.**

What correction should be made to this sentence?
(1) change the spelling of <u>recieve</u> to <u>receive</u>
(2) remove the comma after <u>call</u>
(3) insert a comma after <u>order</u>
(4) change <u>to be made</u> to <u>that will have been made</u>
(5) no correction is necessary

<u>**Questions 29 to 37**</u> **refer to the following paragraphs.**

(1) Total dollars available, family tastes storage and preparation facilities, end use, and item cost all affect a buying decision. (2) Unit pricing can help by taking the guesswork out of the price factor and simplifying cost comparisons.

(3) Unit price is just what its name implies—the price per unit. (4) To be more specific, unit pricing gives you the cost per ounce or per pound or per 100 or per square foot. (5) This price per unit enables you to readily find the best buy dollarwise among several items in different size packages with different total prices.

(6) Thousands of retail food chain stores now have unit pricing programs. (7) Such programs are required by local laws in several areas, but generally the programs are voluntary.

(8) Stores that offer unit pricing generally use a shelf tag system—a label on the shelf edge below the item gives the name of the item, the size, the total price, and the unit price.

(9) When unit pricing was first introduced there were some problems with the shelf tag system since just keeping the tags on the shelves in the right location can be difficult. (10) But as unit pricing has gained acceptance, some of these mechanical problems have been overcome, and the label information has become more usable from the shoppers standpoint.

29. Sentence 1: **Total dollars available, family tastes storage and preparation facilities, end use, and item cost all affect a buying decision.**

    If you rewrote sentence 1 beginning with <u>A buying decision is affected</u> the next words should be
    (1) because of
    (2) by
    (3) depending on
    (4) however
    (5) therefore

30. Sentence 1: **Total dollars available, family tastes storage and preparation facilities, end use, and item cost all affect a buying decision.**

    What correction should be made to this sentence?
    (1) insert a comma after <u>tastes</u>
    (2) change <u>all</u> to <u>each</u>
    (3) change <u>affect</u> to <u>effect</u>
    (4) change the spelling of <u>buying</u> to <u>bying</u>
    (5) no correction is necessary

31. Sentence 2: **Unit pricing can help by taking the guesswork out of the price factor and simplifying cost comparisons.**

    What correction should be made to this sentence?
    (1) change <u>can</u> to <u>could</u>
    (2) change <u>by taking</u> to <u>to take</u>
    (3) insert a hyphen in <u>guesswork</u>
    (4) insert a comma after <u>factor</u>
    (5) no correction is necessary

32. Sentences 3 and 4: **Unit price is just what its name implies—the price per unit. <u>To be more specific,</u> unit pricing gives you the cost per ounce or per pound or per 100 or per square foot.**

Which of the following is the best way to write the underlined portion of these sentences? If you think the original is the best way, choose option (1).

(1) . To be more specific
(2) , To be more specific
(3) ; To be more specific
(4) : To be more specific
(5) —To be more specific

33. Sentence 5: **This price per unit enables you to readily find the best buy dollarwise among several items in different size packages with different total prices.**

    What correction should be made to this sentence?
    (1) change <u>you</u> to <u>one</u>
    (2) insert comma before and after <u>dollarwise</u>
    (3) change among to <u>between</u>
    (4) change <u>size</u> to <u>sized</u>
    (5) no correction is necessary

34. Sentences 6 and 7: **Thousands of retail food chain stores now have unit pricing programs. Such programs are required by local laws in several areas, but generally the programs are voluntary.**

    The most effective combination of sentences 6 and 7 would include which of the following groups of words?
    (1) and such programs
    (2) although such programs
    (3) whereas such programs
    (4) programs that are
    (5) programs some being

35. Sentence 8: **Stores that offer unit pricing generally use a shelf tag <u>system—a label</u> on the shelf edge below the item gives the name of the item, the size, the total price, and the unit price.**

    Which of the following is the best way to write the underlined portion of this sentence? If you think the original is the best way, choose option (1).
    (1) system—a label
    (2) system. a label
    (3) system; a label

(4) system: a label
(5) system, a label

36. Sentence 9: **When unit pricing was first introduced there were some problems with the shelf tag system since just keeping the tags on the shelves in the right location can be difficult.**

What correction should be made to this sentence?
(1) change <u>was</u> to <u>had been</u>
(2) insert a comma after <u>introduced</u>
(3) change <u>there</u> to <u>their</u>
(4) insert commas before and after <u>in the right location</u>
(5) no correction is necessary

37. Sentence 10: **But as unit pricing has gained acceptance, some of these mechanical problems have been overcome, and the label information has become more usable from the shoppers standpoint.**

What correction should be made to this sentence?
(1) change the spelling of <u>acceptance</u> to <u>acceptence</u>
(2) remove the comma after <u>acceptance</u>
(3) change the spelling of <u>usable</u> to <u>useable</u>
(4) add an apostrophe after <u>shoppers</u>
(5) no correction is necessary

<u>Questions 38 to 47</u> refer to the following paragraphs.

(1) You are going to move. (2) That statement will ring true for most Americans. (3) You will be the exception if you maintain your present residence for the rest of your life. (4) About one in five persons moves each year, put another way, the average person moves once every five years.

(5) Again dealing in averages most moves of household goods are completed without difficulty, although some are not. (6) The moving experience can be uneventful, but it should be recognized that many of the factors involved can lead to frustrations uncertainties, and expected courses of action that suddenly must be changed.

(7) Most moves involve fulfilment of a positive development. (8) A promotion has come through, (9) or perhaps an opportunity to move to a better climate. (10) Maybe there's a long-sought chance to be closer to the home folks or the grandchildren.

(11) On the other side of the coin, a familar neighborhood is being left behind. (12) The personal effort that must be put into a move can leave family members exhausted just at the time when they need to be at their sharpest.

38. Sentences 1 and 2: **You are going to move. That statement will ring true for most Americans.**

    The most effective combination of sentences 1 and 2 would include which of the following groups of words.
    (1) would be a statement that will ring
    (2) is a statement that will ring
    (3) might be a statement that will ring
    (4) being a statement that will ring
    (5) will be a statement that will ring

39. Sentence 3: **You will be the exception if you maintain your present residence for the rest of your life.**

    What correction should be made to this sentence?
    (1) change <u>will be</u> to <u>are</u>
    (2) change the spelling of <u>exception</u> to <u>exeption</u>
    (3) insert a comma after <u>exception</u>
    (4) change <u>your</u> to <u>you're</u>
    (5) no correction is necessary

40. Sentence 4: **About one in five persons moves each <u>year, put</u> another way, the average person moves once every five years.**

    Which of the following is the best way to write the underlined portion of this sentence? If you think the original is the best way, choose option (1).
    (1) year, put
    (2) year, although put
    (3) year, and put
    (4) year, because put
    (5) year, or put

41. Sentence 5: **Again dealing in averages most moves of household goods are completed without difficulty, although some are not.**

    What correction should be made to this sentence?
    (1) insert a comma after <u>averages</u>
    (2) insert a hyphen in <u>household</u>
    (3) change the spelling of <u>difficulty</u> to <u>dificulty</u>

(4) remove the comma after <u>difficulty</u>

(5) no correction is necessary

42. Sentence 6: **The moving experience can be uneventful, but it should be recognized that many of the factors involved can lead to frustra-tions uncertainties, and expected courses of action that suddenly must be changed.**

What correction should be made to this sentence?

(1) change the spelling of <u>experience</u> to <u>experiance</u>

(2) remove the comma after <u>uneventful</u>

(3) change <u>but</u> to <u>and</u>

(4) insert a comma after <u>frustrations</u>

(5) no correction is necessary

43. Sentence 7: **Most moves involve fulfilment of a positive development.**

What correction should be made to this sentence?

(1) change <u>most moves</u> to <u>most every move</u>

(2) change <u>involve</u> to <u>could involve</u>

(3) change the spelling of <u>fulfilment</u> to <u>fulfillment</u>

(4) change the spelling of <u>development</u> to <u>developement</u>

(5) no correction is necessary

44. Sentences 8 and 9: **A promotion has come <u>through, or</u> perhaps an opportunity to move to a better climate.**

Which of the following is the best way to write the underlined portion of these sentences? If you think the original is the best way, choose option (1).

(1) through, or

(2) through. or

(3) through : or

(4) through ; or

(5) through—or

45. Sentence 10: **Maybe there's a long-sought chance to be closer to the home folks or the grandchildren.**

What correction should be made to this sentence?

(1) change <u>there's</u> to <u>they're is</u>

(2) remove the hyphen from <u>long-sought</u>

(3) add an apostrophe to <u>folks</u>

(4) change the spelling of <u>grandchildren</u> to <u>grandchildern</u>
(5) no correction is necessary

46. Sentence 11: **On the other side of the coin, a familar neighborhood is being left behind.**

What correction should be made to this sentence?
(1) remove the comma after <u>coin</u>
(2) change the spelling of <u>familar</u> to <u>familiar</u>
(3) change the spelling of <u>neighborhood</u> to <u>nieghborhood</u>
(4) change <u>is being</u> to <u>has been</u>
(5) no correction is necessary

47. Sentence 12: **The personal effort that must be put into a move can leave family members exhausted just at the time when they need to be at their sharpest.**

What correction should be made to this sentence?
(1) insert commas around that <u>must be put into a move</u>
(2) change <u>can</u> to <u>could</u>
(3) change the spelling of <u>exhausted</u> to <u>exausted</u>
(4) insert a comma after <u>time</u>
(5) no correction is necessary

<u>Questions 48 to 55</u> refer to the following paragraphs.

(1) In fishing, the first step for the angler is to upgrade his equipment so that the availible range of lures, line weights, distances, etc., is substantially increased. (2) Usually a spinning reel and rod are selected as the next phase in advancement.

(3) The spinning reel consists of a stationery spool carrying a length of monofilament line, a bail or pickup device to direct the line onto the reel and a crank that rotates the pickup device restoring the line to the spool.

(4) In operation, the lure, attached to the monofilament line and dangling several inches beyond the rod tip is cast by swinging the rod from a position slightly behind the shoulder through a forward arc to a position in front at approximately eye level.

(5) Proper timing of the finger pressure on the line as it leaves the reel, combined with the rod acceleration, control the distance the lure will travel.

(6) Lures as light as a sixteenth of an ounce with two-pound test monofilament line will provide enjoyable sport with any of the panfish, heavier lures and lines will more than adequately subdue far larger fish.

(7) Lures are available in a near infinite range of weights, sizes, shapes, and colors and include such items as spoons, spinners, jogs, plugs, and bugs as well as natural baits.

(8) With adequate spinning gear, anyone is prepared to pursue the fascinating and challenging game fish. (9) This category includes the world-famous and aristocratic salmon, the trout, the chars, the grayling, the basses, and the pike family.

48. Sentence 1: **In fishing, the first step for the angler is to upgrade his equipment so that the availible range of lures, line weights, distances, etc., is substantially increased.**

    What correction should be made to this sentence?
    (1) change the spelling of <u>availible</u> to <u>available</u>
    (2) remove the comma after <u>lures</u>
    (3) remove the period after <u>etc.</u>
    (4) change the spelling of <u>substantially</u> to <u>substantialy</u>
    (5) no correction is necessary

49. Sentence 2: **Usually a spinning reel and rod are selected as the next phase in advancement.**

    If you rewrote sentence 2 beginning with <u>The next phase in advancement</u> the next words would be
    (1) are selected a spinning
    (2) are selecting a spinning
    (3) selects a spinning
    (4) is the selection of a spinning
    (5) will be selecting a

50. Sentence 3: **The spinning reel consists of a stationery spool carrying a length of monofilament line, a bail or pickup device to direct the line onto the reel, and a crank that rotates the pick-up device restoring the line to the spool.**

    What correction should be made to this sentence?
    (1) change the spelling of <u>stationery</u> to <u>stationary</u>
    (2) change the spelling of <u>length</u> to <u>lenth</u>
    (3) remove the comma after <u>line</u>
    (4) insert a comma after <u>device</u>
    (5) no correction is necessary

51. Sentence 4: **In operation, the lure, attached to the monofilament line and dangling several inches beyond the rod tip is cast by swinging the rod from a position slightly behind the shoulder through a forward arc to a position in front at approximately eye level.**

    What correction should be made to this sentence?
    (1) change the spelling of <u>attached</u> to <u>attatched</u>
    (2) insert a comma after <u>tip</u>
    (3) insert a comma after <u>shoulder</u>
    (4) change the spelling of <u>approximately</u> to <u>approximatly</u>
    (5) no correction is necessary

52. Sentence 5: **Proper timing of the finger pressure on the line as it leaves the reel, combined with the rod acceleration, control the distance the lure will travel.**

    What correction should be made to this sentence?
    (1) insert a comma after <u>pressure</u>
    (2) insert a comma after <u>line</u>
    (3) insert commas before and after <u>reel</u>
    (4) change <u>control</u> to <u>controls</u>
    (5) no correction is necessary

53. Sentence 6: **Lures as light as a sixteenth of an ounce with two-pound test monofilament line will provide enjoyable sport with any of the <u>panfish, heavier</u> lures and lines will more than adequately subdue far larger fish.**

    Which of the following is the best way to write the underlined portion of this sentence? If you think the original is the best way, choose option (1).
    (1) panfish, heavier
    (2) panfish: heavier
    (3) panfish; heavier
    (4) panfish. heavier
    (5) panfish. Heavier

54. Sentence 7: **Lures are available in a near infinite range of weights, sizes, shapes, and colors and include such items as spoons, spinners, jogs, plugs, and bugs as well as natural baits.**
    What correction should be made to this sentence?
    (1) change <u>near</u> to <u>nearly</u>
    (2) change the spelling of <u>infinite</u> to <u>infinate</u>
    (3) remove the comma after <u>shapes</u>

(4) remove the comma after <u>plugs</u>
(5) no correction is necessary

55. Sentences 8 and 9: **With adequate spinning gear, anyone is prepared to pursue the fascinating and challenging game fish. This category includes the world-famous and aristocratic salmon, the trout, the chars, the grayling, the basses, and the pike family.**

The most effective combination of sentences 8 and 9 would include which of the following groups of words?
(1) and this category includes
(2) since this category includes
(3) which category includes
(4) which include
(5) and including

TEST 1: WRITING SKILLS, PART II

This part of the Writing Skills test is intended to determine how well you write. You are asked to write an essay that explains something, presents an opinion on an issue, or concentrates on retelling a personal experience.

PROMPT

As a child we have many experiences ranging from funny to unfortunate. In the Mark Twain story, *Tom Sawyer*, we find young Tom in many unforgettable situations, such as being lost in a cave to returning in time for his own funeral. Each of us has a personal story from childhood that seems to be told over and over at family reunions, birthdays, or around friends. Perhaps your personal experience happened on a fishing trip, at school, or on a camp out.

DISCUSSION QUESTION

Think of a personal childhood experience that seems to be told over and over again. It may be funny, sad, exciting, or just something out of the ordinary. What personal experience comes to mind?

Directions

Write an essay of about 200 words in which you recount this personal event. Give supporting details in your essay. You have 45 minutes to write on this topic.

CHECK YOURSELF

- Read carefully the prompt, discussion question, and directions.
- Decide if the prompt is expository, persuasive, or narrative.
- Plan your essay before you begin.
- Use scratch paper to prepare a simple outline.
- Write your essay on the lined pages of a separate answer sheet.
- Read carefully what you have written and make needed changes.
- Check for focus, elaboration, organization, conventions, and integration.

TEST 2: SOCIAL STUDIES

Directions

Alloted Time: 85 minutes

The Social Studies test consists of multiple-choice questions intended to measure general social studies concepts. The questions are based on short readings that often include a graph, chart, or figure. Study the information given and then answer the question(s) following it. Refer to the information as often as necessary in answering the questions.

You should spend no more than 85 minutes answering the questions. Work carefully, but do not spend too much time on any one question. Be sure you answer every question. You will not be penalized for incorrect answers.

To record your answers, mark the numbered space on the answer sheet beside the number that corresponds to the question in the test.

FOR EXAMPLE:

Early colonists of North America looked for settlement sites that had adequate water supplies and were accessible by ship. For this reason, many early towns were built near

(1) mountains

(2) prairies

(3) rivers

(4) glaciers

(5) plateaus

The correct answer is "rivers"; therefore, answer space 3 would be marked on the answer sheet.

Questions 1 to 3 are based on the following passage.

The governor is empowered to veto single items of the budget bill, appending to each a message, and to return the same to the legislature if it is still in session. Such items can be enacted over his veto. This authority, not possessed by the president of the United States, lays a heavy responsibility on the governor for the integrity of the budget in all its parts.

All bills passed within the last ten days of a legislative session fall under what is called the "30-day" rule. None can become a law unless within 30 days (Sundays included) it has been signed by the governor.

The veto power is not used sparingly. More than one out of four bills falls to the deadly stroke of the executive pen.

1. The passage indicates that the governor
   (1) vetoes about one-fourth of the bills
   (2) vetoes about three-fourths of the bills
   (3) vetoes all bills during the legislative session
   (4) vetoes no bills during the legislative session
   (5) uses the veto power very sparingly

2. The "30-day" rule applies to
   (1) the time limit for exercising the veto
   (2) the pocket veto
   (3) the amount of time in which to appeal the governor's action
   (4) bills passed within the last ten days of a legislative session
   (5) the limitation on passing a law over the governor's veto

3. The governor's veto power is greater than that of the president in that the governor has the ability to
   (1) take as much time as he wishes before signing a bill
   (2) veto a bill in less than 10 days
   (3) ignore all bills during the last month of the legislature
   (4) veto single items of the budget bill
   (5) override the two-thirds vote of the legislature

Questions 4 to 6 are based on the following passage.

The consumer's first line of defense is information. Before you buy any product—especially before you make a major purchase of any kind—get all the information you can about the manufacturer's guarantee or warranty provisions.

Remember, a guarantee is a statement by the manufacturer or vendor that he stands behind his product or service. Guarantees and warranties usually have limitations or conditions, so get all promises in writing.

Before you buy any product or service covered by a guarantee or warranty, make sure you resolve these questions:

—What, exactly, is covered?

—Whom should you call when you need repairs under the warranty?

—Must repairs be made at the factory or by an "authorized service representative" to keep the warranty in effect?

—Who pays for parts, for labor, for shipping charges?

—How long does the warranty last?

—If pro rata reimbursement is provided, what is the basis for it?

—If the warranty provides for reimbursement, is it in cash or credit toward a replacement?

Keep the warranty and sales receipt for future reference.

4. The advice given to the consumer in this passage deals chiefly with
   (1) business ethics
   (2) unconditional guarantees
   (3) product safety
   (4) unwarranted promises
   (5) pre-purchase information

5. Guarantees and warranties, the passage implies, should be
   (1) conditional
   (2) in writing
   (3) made by the salesman
   (4) cancelable
   (5) dependent on the use of the product

6. Warranties usually include all of the following EXCEPT
   (1) what is covered
   (2) who does the repairs
   (3) where the repairs are made
   (4) who pays for expenses incurred in doing the repairs
   (5) return of monies paid

Questions 7 and 8 are based on the following chart.

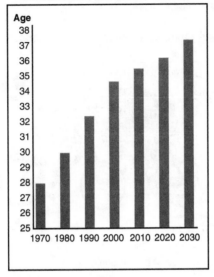

MEDIAN AGE IN THE UNITED STATES

7. Which situation will be most likely to occur after the period shown in the graph?
   (1) Advertisers will increase their emphasis on youth.
   (2) The size of the average family will increase.
   (3) School districts will build more elementary schools.
   (4) The cost of the Social Security program will rise.
   (5) Population will begin to decline.

8. Which factor would most likely reverse the direction of the trend indicated by the graph?
   (1) development of a cure for cancer
   (2) a large increase in the birth rate
   (3) a prolonged period of economic depression
   (4) an increase in infant mortality
   (5) pollution control

9. Government policies designed to foster economic growth by encouraging greater consumption would probably meet with the greatest opposition from which group?
   (1) labor leaders
   (2) business executives

(3) military leaders
(4) environmentalists
(5) individual entrepreneurs

Questions 10 and 11 are based on the following cartoon.

10. What is the main idea of the cartoon?
   (1) The world lacks sufficient energy resources to survive much longer.
   (2) Concerns of environmentalists have had little impact on the actions of industrialists.
   (3) The struggle between energy and the environment cannot be resolved.
   (4) The need to produce energy comes into conflict with the need to preserve the environment.
   (5) A stalemate has been arrived at between industrialists and environmentalists.

11. In dealing with the situation referred to in the cartoon during the late 1970s, the United States federal government generally followed a policy that
   (1) gave priority to energy demands over environmental concerns
   (2) sided with environmentalists against corporations
   (3) sought new energy sources outside the United States
   (4) attempted to divert national attention to other issues
   (5) dealt evenhandedly with industrialists and environmentalists

12. The presidents of the United States from the time of World War II to the present have been most influential in the area of
   (1) civil rights

   (2) urban affairs
   (3) foreign affairs
   (4) states' rights
   (5) human rights

Questions 13 and 14 are based on the following passage.

Not all place names on maps refer to visible locations. When a name refers to a specific place, it can be easy to get a mental picture of it. When you see a name such as Arctic Circle, Antarctic Circle, Tropic of Cancer, or Tropic of Capricorn, you do not get a mental picture in the same way. These imaginary markers on the Earth's surface usually appear on maps as dotted blue lines. When you travel across one of them, you cannot detect it with the human eye or feel it against your skin.

The Tropics of Cancer and Capricorn are named after constellations of stars. Historians believe that ancient Roman geographers were the first to refer to these two imaginary lines as Cancer and Capricorn.

The Tropic of Cancer runs parallel to the equator at latitude 23°27'N. It marks the northernmost point at which the sun appears directly overhead at noon. The name refers to the constellation Cancer (the Crab), which first becomes visible in the Northern Hemisphere on June 20, 21, or 22, near the summer solstice.

The Tropic of Capricorn runs parallel to the equator at about latitude 23°27'S. It designates the southernmost point at which the sun appears directly overhead at noon. The name refers to the constellation Capricorn (the Goat), which first becomes visible in the Southern Hemisphere on December 21 or 22, near the winter solstice.

13. The Arctic and Antarctic Circles are
   (1) mental pictures
   (2) imaginary markers
   (3) dotted blue lines
   (4) visible locations
   (5) easily detected

14. The Tropic of Cancer and the Tropic of Capricorn are similar in that they
   (1) are specific places
   (2) are of recent origin
   (3) mark the same points
   (4) run parallel to the equator
   (5) were named by navigators

Questions 15 and 16 are based on the following passage.

Fourscore and seven years ago our fathers brought forth on this continent a new nation, conceived in liberty, and dedicated to the proposition that all men are created equal.

Now we are engaged in a great civil war, testing whether that nation, or any nation so conceived and so dedicated, can long endure. We are met on a great battlefield of that war. We have come to dedicate a portion of that field as a final resting-place for those who here gave their lives that that nation might live. It is altogether fitting and proper that we should do this.

But, in a larger sense, we cannot dedicate—we cannot consecrate—we cannot hallow—this ground. The brave men, living and dead, who struggled here, have consecrated it far above our poor power to add or detract.

—Abraham Lincoln

15. In the first paragraph, the speaker refers to
    (1) the Declaration of Independence
    (2) the Articles of Confederation
    (3) the United States Constitution
    (4) the Northwest Ordinance
    (5) the Monroe Doctrine

16. The purpose of the speech was to
    (1) commemorate a battle
    (2) remember the founding of our nation
    (3) dedicate a cemetery
    (4) deplore civil war
    (5) seek political support in an election

Questions 17 to 19 are based on the following chart, which lists some characteristics of Nations *A* and *B*.

Factors of Production	Nation A	Nation B
Land (natural resources)	Relative scarcity	Relative abundance
Labor	Relative abundance	Relative abundance
Capital	Relative abundance	Relative scarcity
Business management	Relative abundance	Relative scarcity

17. Which economic decision would most probably be in the best interests of Nation *A*?
    (1) permitting an unfavorable balance of payments
    (2) seeking foreign markets
    (3) attracting investments from foreign nations
    (4) encouraging immigration
    (5) increasing imports

18. During the early 19th century, which nation most nearly resembled Nation *A*?
    (1) the United States
    (2) Great Britain
    (3) Russia
    (4) Turkey
    (5) China

19. If Nation *B* wishes to industrialize, how can it best encourage its own citizens to invest their capital in domestic industries?
    (1) by permitting an unfavorable balance of payments and seeking colonies
    (2) by permitting an unfavorable balance of payments and encouraging immigration
    (3) by attracting investments from foreign nations and encouraging immigration
    (4) by instituting high protective tariffs and giving tax concessions to business
    (5) by lowering taxes on imports

20. "Our policy in regard to Europe . . . is not to interfere in the internal concerns of any of its powers"—President Monroe, 1823

    "It must be the policy of the United States to support free peoples who are resisting attempted subjugation by armed minorities or by outside pressures."—President Truman, 1947

    The most valid conclusion to be drawn from these statements is that
    (1) President Truman followed President Monroe's theory of foreign relations
    (2) during the 19th and 20th centuries, the United States was not interested in international affairs
    (3) during the 19th century, events in Europe did not affect the United States

(4) President Truman changed the policy of President Monroe

(5) conditions were different in 1947 from those in 1823

Questions 21 and 22 are based on the following graphs.

Of all women with children under 6 and living with their husbands, how many work?

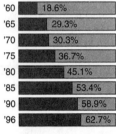

'60	18.6%
'65	29.3%
'70	30.3%
'75	36.7%
'80	45.1%
'85	53.4%
'90	58.9%
'96	62.7%

Of all working women with children under 6 and living with their husbands, how many work...

	FULL TIME	PART TIME
'60	69.6%	30.4%
'65	68.8%	31.2%
'70	64.9%	35.1%
'75	64.9%	35.1%
'80	64.9%	35.1%
'85	65.7%	34.3%
'90	64.2%	35.8%
'96	62.8%	37.2%

Source: Bureau of Labor Statistics

Of all woman who work, how many have children under 6 years old?

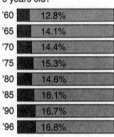

'60	12.8%
'65	14.1%
'70	14.4%
'75	15.3%
'80	14.6%
'85	16.1%
'90	16.7%
'96	16.8%

21. The period with the greatest increase in the percentage of working women having children under 6 and living with their husbands was

(1) '60–'65

(2) '70–'75

(3) '80–'85

(4) '85–'90

(5) '90–'96

22. The percentage of women working part time remained steadiest between

(1) '60 and '70

(2) '70 and '80

(3) '75 and '85

(4) '80 and '90

(5) '90 and '96

Question 23 is based on the following graph.

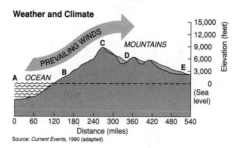

23. Which area, as illustrated in the graph, would be warmest and driest?
- (1) A
- (2) B
- (3) C
- (4) D
- (5) E

Question 24 is based on the following diagram.

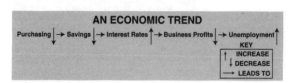

24. Which is occurring in the economy illustrated above?
- (1) increase in real income
- (2) devaluation of currency
- (3) growth
- (4) recession
- (5) recovery

---

25. "All forms of life developed from earlier forms. In every case the fittest survived and the weak died out. It is the same for people and nations."

This passage expresses a view most often found in
- (1) fundamentalism
- (2) social Darwinism

(3) liberalism

(4) utopian socialism

(5) egalitarianism

Questions 26 to 28 are based on the following graph.

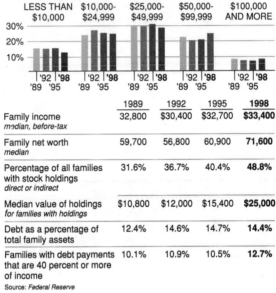

A Snapshot of Family Finances

Percentage of families in each income group. In 1998 dollars.

	1989	1992	1995	**1998**
Family income *median, before-tax*	32,800	$30,400	$32,700	**$33,400**
Family net worth *median*	59,700	56,800	60,900	**71,600**
Percentage of all families with stock holdings *direct or indirect*	31.6%	36.7%	40.4%	**48.8%**
Median value of holdings *for families with holdings*	$10,800	$12,000	$15,400	**$25,000**
Debt as a percentage of total family assets	12.4%	14.6%	14.7%	**14.4%**
Families with debt payments that are 40 percent or more of income	10.1%	10.9%	10.5%	**12.7%**

Source: *Federal Reserve*

26. The largest percent of families was in the income group of
    (1) less than $10,000
    (2) $10,000 to $25,000
    (3) $25,000 to $50,000
    (4) $50,000 to $100,000
    (5) $100,000 and over

27. The largest increase in income between 1989 to 1998 was in the group
    (1) less than $10,000
    (2) $10,000 to $25,000
    (3) $25,000 to 50,000
    (4) $50,000 to $100,000
    (5) $100,000 and over

28. According to the table, the following rose every year from 1989 to 1998:
   (1) family income
   (2) family net worth
   (3) families with stock holdings
   (4) family debt
   (5) debt payments 40% or more of income

Questions 29 to 31 are based on the following passage.

We must pursue a course designed not merely to reduce the number of delinquents. We must increase the chances for young people to lead productive lives.

For these delinquent and potentially delinquent youth, we must offer a New Start. We must insure that the special resources and skills essential for their treatment and rehabilitation are available. Because many of these young men and women live in broken families, burdened with financial and psychological problems, a successful rehabilitation program must include family counseling, vocational guidance, education and health services. It must strengthen the family and the schools. It must offer courts an alternative to placing young delinquents in penal institutions.

—Lyndon B. Johnson

29. The emphasis in this speech is on
   (1) diagnosis and research
   (2) prevention and rehabilitation
   (3) rehabilitation and research
   (4) treatment and diagnosis
   (5) research and diagnosis

30. The main purpose of this speech is to
   (1) provide federal financial aid
   (2) give advice to broken families
   (3) support research and experimentation
   (4) praise "halfway houses"
   (5) advocate legislation to combat juvenile delinquency

31. The passage implies that
   (1) delinquents cannot lead productive lives
   (2) detention of delinquents is unnecessary
   (3) delinquency is caused by family problems

(4) the federal government must assume responsibility for preventing juvenile delinquency

(5) courts must place young delinquents in the proper penal institutions

Questions 32 and 33 are based on the following cartoon.

THE GREASED PIG

PRICES

ECONOMIC CONTROLS

Buffalo Evening News

32. Which statement best summarizes the main idea of the cartoon?

(1) Prices should be regulated by a committee of private business people.

(2) Competition among major industries has led to economic chaos.

(3) Strict price-and-wage controls would assure a stable economy.

(4) Government has been unable to deal effectively with a major economic problem.

(5) Deregulation leads to lower prices.

33. A likely response to the problem referred to in the cartoon would be an increase in the

(1) interest rates on bank loans

(2) amount of government spending

(3) amount of money in circulation

(4) number of loans approved by banks

(5) number of housing starts

<u>Question 34</u> is based on the following graph.

1992 Presidential Election Results

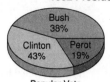

Popular Vote

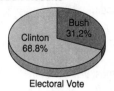

Electoral Vote

34. Which generalization is supported by the information provided by the graph?
   (1) The electoral vote often fails to reflect the popular vote.
   (2) The House of Representatives settles presidential elections in which third-party candiates participate.
   (3) The electoral college system weakens the two-party system.
   (4) Electoral college members often vote against their party's candidates.
   (5) Electoral votes result in closer elections.

<u>Questions 35 to 37</u> are based on the following graph.

Average Amount of Time Each Day Spent Doing Each Activity
(*hours:minutes*)

	Children 2 to 7	Children 8 to 18
Watching TV	1:59	3:16
Listening to CDs or tapes	0:21	1:05
Reading	0:45	0:44
Listening to the radio	0:24	0:48
Using the computer	0:07	0:31
Playing video games	0:08	0:27
Using the Internet	0:01	0:13

Percentage of Children Who Use a Computer Each Day

All children	42%
2–7 years old	26
8–18 years old	51
White	45
Black	39
Hispanic origin	28
Low income	29
Middle Income	40
High income	50

35. The survey mentions all of the following media EXCEPT

    (1) TV

    (2) reading

    (3) radio

    (4) Internet

    (5) movies

36. The most likely computer user according to the graph would be

    (1) an 8- to 18-year-old white

    (2) a low-income 2- to 7-year-old

    (3) a middle-income Hispanic

    (4) a high-income 2- to 7-year-old

    (5) a 2- to 7-year-old Black

37. The dominant medium for children from 2 to 18 is

    (1) TV

    (2) reading

    (3) radio

    (4) computer

    (5) Internet

---

38. A primary source is an eyewitness account of an event or events in a specific time period. Which would be an example of a primary source of information about life in the 18th-century American colonies?

    (1) a diary of a colonial shopkeeper

    (2) a painting of the colonial period by a 20th century artist

    (3) a novel about the American Revolutionary War

    (4) a reproduction of furniture used during the colonial period

    (5) a social history of the period

Questions 39 and 40 are based on the following graph.

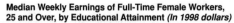

Median Weekly Earnings of Full-Time Female Workers, 25 and Over, by Educational Attainment *(In 1998 dollars)*

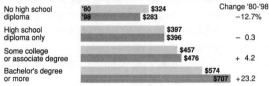

		Change '80-'98
No high school diploma	'80 $324 / '98 $283	−12.7%
High school diploma only	$397 / $396	− 0.3
Some college or associate degree	$457 / $476	+ 4.2
Bachelor's degree or more	$574 / $707	+23.2

Women's Median Earnings by Race and Educational Attainment, 1998

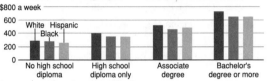

Sources: *Bureau of Labor Statistics, RFA Dismal Sciences*

39. Between 1980 and 1998, weekly earnings fell the most for women with
    (1) no high school diploma
    (2) a high school diploma
    (3) some college study
    (4) an associate degree
    (5) a bachelor's degree

40. By background, women's earnings for whites and Hispanics exceeded that of blacks who had
    (1) no high school diploma
    (2) a high school diploma
    (3) an associate degree
    (4) a bachelor's degree
    (5) more than a bachelor's degree

Questions 41 to 43 are based on the statements made by Speakers *A, B, C, D,* and *E.*

Speaker *A:*   Government could not function very well without them. The flow of information they provide to Congress and the federal agencies is vital to the functioning of our democratic system.

Speaker *B:*   Yes, but the secrecy under which they generally operate makes me suspicious that they are influencing lawmakers in improper ways.

Speaker *C:*   Don't forget that they not only try to influence Washington opinion but also attempt to shape public opinion across the nation in order to create a favorable climate for their views.

Speaker *D:*   That's true. Any politician who ignores 40,000 letters does so at great risk. We have to pay attention to them whether we accept their views or not.

Speaker *E:*   I agree with Speaker *C.* Public opinion is essential to the functioning of our American way of life.

41. Which group are the speakers most likely discussing?
  (1) lawyers
  (2) reporters
  (3) government workers
  (4) media analysts
  (5) lobbyists

42. Which speaker is most concerned about the impact of the methods used by this group upon democratic government?
  (1) *A*
  (2) *B*
  (3) *C*
  (4) *D*
  (5) *E*

43. Which speaker implies that lawmakers frequently must deal with a great many issues about which they know very little?
  (1) *A*
  (2) *B*
  (3) *C*
  (4) *D*
  (5) *E*

Question 44 is based on the following cartoon.

44. Which statement best summarizes the main point of the above cartoon?
   (1) The citizen's vote is a powerful means of influencing legislators seeking reelection.
   (2) Citizens are dependent upon the legislative branch of government for protection.
   (3) Federal and state legislators usually agree on major campaign issues.
   (4) The public generally does not favor consumer protection legislation.
   (5) Voters are easily fooled by politicians seeking votes.

Questions 45 to 47 are based on the following passage.

The people and groups that provide the stimulation and contact necessary for social development—the socializing agents—usually fall into two classes: (1) those people with authority over the individual, such as parents and teachers, and (2) those in positions of equality with him or her—age peers, such as playmates or a circle of friends. Since the family is the socializing agent during the critical first years of life, it naturally has had great influence. But because of the increased specialization of the functions of the family, the rapidity of social change that tends to divide the generations, and the high degree of mobility and social fluidity, the peer group is of growing importance in modern urban life.

45. Parents, teachers, and age peers share the role of
   (1) people with authority over the individual
   (2) peer group members

(3) the friendly circle
(4) the family circle
(5) socializing agents

46. All of these reasons are given for the increased role of peers in an individual's social development EXCEPT
   (1) social mobility
   (2) social fluidity
   (3) generation gap
   (4) growing number of peers
   (5) specialization of family functions

47. The family, in modern urban life, is
   (1) exerting influence
   (2) growing in importance
   (3) being replaced by the peer group
   (4) filling a broadening role
   (5) influential only in the early years of life

Questions 48 and 49 refer to the following statements made by Speakers *A*, *B*, and *C*.

Speaker *A:*   Increased contact among nations and peoples is characteristic of our times. A single decision by OPEC or a multinational corporation can send ripples of change throughout our global society.

Speaker *B:*   If we are to survive, all passengers on our Spaceship Earth must participate in efforts to solve the issues that threaten humankind—poverty, resource depletion, pollution, violence, and war.

Speaker *C:*   We must understand that no single culture's view of the world is universally shared. Other people have different value systems and ways of thinking and acting. They will not see the world as we do.

48. Which concept is discussed by both Speakers *A* and *B*?
   (1) self-determination
   (2) nationalism
   (3) conservation
   (4) interdependence
   (5) protectionism

49. Speaker *C* indicates a desire to reduce
    (1) ethnocentrism
    (2) globalism
    (3) social mobility
    (4) religious tolerance
    (5) interdependence

Questions 50 and 51 are based on the following cartoon.

"Witnesses for the Prosecution"

50. The cartoon is concerned primarily with determining responsibility for which situation?
    (1) use of poison gas during World War I
    (2) slave labor camps in the Soviet Union during the Stalin era
    (3) the Holocaust in Europe during the 1930s and 1940s
    (4) apartheid practices in South Africa
    (5) the blitzkrieg of World War II

51. The trial symbolized in the cartoon is significant because it was the first time that
    (1) the United Nations International Court of Justice worked effectively
    (2) individuals were prosecuted for crimes against humanity
    (3) war guilt was applied to a whole nation
    (4) international law was enforced
    (5) the United States cooperated with the United Nations

Questions 52 to 54 are based on the following passage.

Organized economic studies date only from the 17th century. Since then, there have been a number of major schools of economic thought. They can be briefly identified as follows:

(1) mercantilism—advocates, in foreign trade, a surplus of exports over imports to accumulate gold and supports development of local industries protected by tariffs from foreign trade competition

(2) laissez-faire—opposes state intervention in economic affairs to allow free trade and competition

(3) Marxism—teaches that value created by labor and profit is surplus value skimmed off by the capitalist who owns the means of production, which should be eventually controlled by the proletariat or the industrial workers

(4) Keynes theory—focuses on the need to create demand by government spending and the curbing of excess demand by tight budget policies

(5) supply-side economics—supports stimulating production rather than demand by drastic tax reductions to increase business investment and advocates a cutback in government spending to eliminate deficits

Each of the following describes an action or proposal relating to the economic policies described above. Indicate which school of economic thought would approve the action.

52. The president recommends drastic cuts in defense and nondefense spending.
   (1) mercantilism
   (2) laissez-faire
   (3) Marxism
   (4) Keynes theory
   (5) supply-side economics

53. Congress is considering a tariff on Japanese imports to protect the United States electronics industry.
   (1) mercantilism
   (2) laissez-faire
   (3) Marxism
   (4) Keynes theory
   (5) supply-side economics

54. A company is bought out by its employees.
   (1) mercantilism
   (2) laissez-faire

(3) Marxism

(4) Keynes theory

(5) supply-side economics

---

55. Cultural diffusion is the spread of one culture to other areas of the world. An example is

(1) an immigrant learning a new language

(2) a child learning to walk

(3) conflict between old and new cultures

(4) the superiority of the United States' culture over all others

(5) a Russian playing basketball

56. "Under a government which imprisons anyone unjustly, the true place for a just man is also a prison."

—Henry David Thoreau

Which does this quotation most strongly support?

(1) social control

(2) conformity

(3) suspension of civil liberties

(4) dictatorship

(5) civil disobedience

Questions 57 and 58 are based on the following cartoon.

57. Which best states the main idea of the cartoon?

(1) The United States establishes immigration policies that meet its specific needs.

(2) There is a surplus of highly trained people in foreign countries.

(3) Highly trained people will be able to pass literacy tests required to enter the United States.

(4) The United States lags behind other nations in technological development.

(5) Untrained people are not welcome in the United States.

58. One similarity between immigration policy suggested in the cartoon and United States immigration policy in the 1920s is that both show a

(1) reluctance to admit non-English speaking people

(2) preference for certain groups

(3) desire to encourage increased immigration

(4) desire to adopt the values of international human rights organizations

(5) desire to increase ethnic diversity

Question 59 is based on the following headline.

NIXON MUST SURRENDER TAPES, SUPREME COURT RULES, 8 TO 0; HE PLEDGES FULL COMPLIANCE
House Committee Begins Debate on Impeachment

---

59. Which feature of the United States constitutional system is best illustrated by the above headline?

(1) checks and balances

(2) executive privilege

(3) power to grant pardons

(4) federalism

(5) the Bill of Rights

Questions 60 and 61 are based on the following graph.

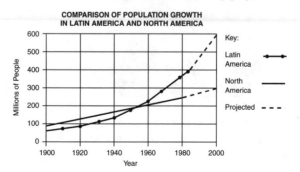

COMPARISON OF POPULATION GROWTH IN LATIN AMERICA AND NORTH AMERICA

60. Based on the information in the graph, which is a valid conclusion about the populations of Latin America and North America?

(1) There has always been a large difference in the population growth of Latin America and North America.

(2) By the year 2000, the population of Latin America is expected to be approximately twice that of North America.

(3) In 1900, the number of people in Latin America was equal to the number of people in North America.

(4) In the early 1980s, the difference in population between the two regions was about 300 million.

(5) The rate of population growth of Latin America has been steadier than that of North America.

61. Which best accounts for the situation shown in the graph?

(1) decline in the standard of living in North America

(2) growing trade surplus of most Latin American nations

(3) improved nutrition and medical care in Latin America

(4) increased death rate in North America due to contagious diseases

(5) increase in democracy in Latin America

Questions 62 and 63 are based on the following cartoon.

Source: The Times Union, July 1991

62. What is the main idea of the cartoon?

(1) The people of developing nations have refused to ask for aid.

(2) Relief workers have died trying to help suffering people in developing nations.

    (3) Industrialized nations have prevented starvation in developing nations.

    (4) People in some developing nations lack the basic necessities, while people in other nations have more than they need.

    (5) Prosperous nations are concerned with the problems of developing nations.

63. The cartoon implies that

    (1) Industrialized nations should help developing nations.

    (2) People in some countries are doomed to a life of poverty.

    (3) The problems of developing nations are no concern of America.

    (4) Americans exploit developing nations.

    (5) Some countries are overpopulated.

---

64. "I believe that it must be the policy of the United States to support free peoples who are resisting attempted subjugation by armed minorities or by outside pressures. I believe that we must assist free peoples to work out their own destinies in their own way. I believe that our help should be primarily through economic and financial aid...."

—Harry S Truman

The recommendation made in this quotation resulted from a perception that the United States needed to

    (1) oppose Communist expansion just after World War II

    (2) prepare for World War I

    (3) fight Nazi aggression in 1941

    (4) justify the withdrawal of United States forces from Korea

    (5) return to a policy of isolationism

TEST 3: SCIENCE

Directions

Alloted Time: 95 minutes

The Science test consists of multiple-choice questions intended to measure the general concepts in science. The questions are based on short readings that often include a graph, chart, or figure. Study the information given and then answer the question(s) following it. Refer to the information as often as necessary in answering the questions.

You will have 95 minutes to answer the questions. Work carefully, but do not spend too much time on any one question. Be sure you answer every question. You will not be penalized for incorrect answers.

To record your answers, mark the numbered space on the answer sheet beside the number that corresponds to the question in the test.

FOR EXAMPLE:

Which of the following is the smallest unit?

(1) solution

(2) molecule

(3) atom

(4) compound

(5) mixture

① ② ● ④ ⑤

The correct answer is "atom"; therefore, space 3 would be marked on the answer sheet.

Questions 1 to 4 refer to the following article.

Scientists have different explanations of how evolution occurred, but they all agree that all living things evolved from other living things. Paleontologists have justified this conclusion from their studies of fossil remains. There is also evidence from other branches of science that there have been changes in organisms, and that these changes are still going on.

While archaeologists have been digging through the remains of ancient civilizations, providing their contribution to our knowledge, the origin of human beings has been the subject of study for the anthropologist. One may study the history of a language, while another investigates the various types of pottery that are unearthed. Physical anthropology is involved with the anatomy of various vertebrates. Of particular interest to physical anthropologists are primates, that is, the group of mammals that includes humans, apes, monkeys, and chimpanzees. With the aid of fossil records, comparisons can be made between the structures of animals from the past and present forms.

1. Which of the following terms includes all the others?
   - (1) human
   - (2) primate
   - (3) monkey
   - (4) ape
   - (5) chimpanzee

2. Evolution is the biological process by which
   - (1) fossils are produced in rocks
   - (2) the anatomy of vertebrates is compared
   - (3) ancient human life is studied
   - (4) new kinds of living things arise
   - (5) chimpanzees give rise to humans

3. Which of the following gives the most direct evidence that different forms of life existed in the past?
   - (1) organic chemistry
   - (2) fossils
   - (3) comparative anatomy
   - (4) archeology
   - (5) laboratory experiments

4. Which of the following discoveries would suggest that the human species is still evolving?
   - (1) The human brain is much larger than the brain of a gorilla.
   - (2) In early stages of development, human embryos have a large tail.
   - (3) There is a strong similarity between the chemistry of humans and that of chimpanzees.
   - (4) The armor of medieval knights is too small for today's average man.
   - (5) Tractors have replaced horses for farm work.

<u>**Questions 5 to 8**</u> **refer to the following information.**

The density of an object can often be used to help identify it. Density is defined as the ratio of the mass of a substance to its volume, or as an equation:

$$\text{Density} = \frac{\text{mass}}{\text{volume}}$$

If the object has a shape such as a block or a cube, then the volume can be determined by multiplying the length times the width times the height or

$$V = l \times w \times h$$

Three samples are provided to a student:

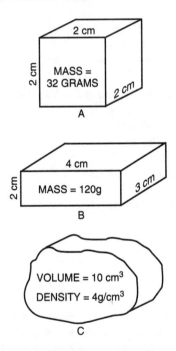

Sample A is a cube 2 cm on a side, with a mass of 32 grams.

Sample B is a 120 gram block with a height of 3 cm, and a width of 2 cm, and a length of 4 cm.

Sample C is an irregularly shaped object with a mass of 4 g/cm3 and a volume of 10 cm.

5. What is the density of sample B?
   (1) 2 g/cm³
   (2) 3 g/cm³
   (3) 4 g/cm³
   (4) 5 g/cm³
   (5) 6 g/cm³

6. Suppose sample A were to be cut into two unevenly sized and shaped pieces. What would be true of the density of the two new, smaller pieces?
   (1) The larger of the two would have a greater density.
   (2) The smaller of the two would have a greater density.
   (3) The two pieces would have the same density, which would be different from the original piece.
   (4) The two pieces would have the same density, which would be the same as the original piece.
   (5) There is not enough information to tell.

7. When a balloon is heated its volume doubles. What happens to its density?
   (1) The density doubles.
   (2) The density quadruples.
   (3) The density stays the same.
   (4) The density is cut in half.
   (5) There is not enough information to tell.

8. What is the mass of sample C?
   (1) 20 g
   (2) 30 g
   (3) 40 g
   (4) 60 g
   (5) 80 g

9. An island may form when material expelled by an undersea volcano gradually builds up and rises above the surface of the water. This has happened in numerous places in the Pacific Ocean. Over time, however, another island may begin to form some distance from the first. It is possible that chains of islands, such as the Hawaiian Islands, were formed in this way. One reason for this may be that
   (1) the volcano moves along the bottom of the ocean
   (2) the plates of earth and rock that cover the interior of planet Earth are slowly moving, taking the islands with them

    (3) when the first island was finished, some leftover lava started
        another island
    (4) volcanoes erupted in places where islands were going to be formed
    (5) volcanic eruptions have had nothing to do with the formation of
        islands

10. The depth of a body of water can be measured by a method called sonar.
Sonar is an acronym for *SO*und *NA*vigation *R*anging, and the method works
on the same principle as radar. Sound waves (sonar beams) are aimed at
the ocean floor, and the times it takes them to bounce back are recorded.
Since we know that the speed of sound in water is approximately 4,800 feet
per second, the depth of the ocean can be determined by measuring how
long it takes a beam to bounce off the ocean floor and return to the ship.

How far, in feet, would a sonar beam travel in $2\frac{1}{2}$ seconds?
    (1) 14,400
    (2) 9,500
    (3) 2,400
    (4) 4,850
    (5) 12,000

Questions 11 to 13 refer to the following passage.

Most of us have played with magnets from the time we were very young.
Magnets may be man-made or occur naturally. The earliest of magnets come
from the ancient Greeks, who used a mineral known as magnetite, which
they noticed could repel or attract certain metals. Interestingly, if a magnet is
broken in half, each piece will then have its own north and south poles.

In general, all magnets, no matter what their shape, have both a north and
south pole. Like poles attract each other; unlike poles repel each other. A
compass works because it uses a freely rotating magnet that be attracted or
repelled by the naturally magnetic poles of the earth.

One of most common applications of magnets is in creating an
electromagnet, which is caused when an electric current moves through a
magnetic material, such as an iron nail.

11. What type of magnet can be controlled by adjusting the flow of electric
current, such as might be used in a scrap yard to pick up, and then drop
large pieces of metal?
    (1) magnetite
    (2) an electromagnet

   (3) a naturally occurring magnet
   (4) a bar magnet
   (5) a magnet with two north poles

12. Which end of a compass will face north?
   (1) the north pole
   (2) the south pole
   (3) either end, depending on whether it is above or below the equator
   (4) it depends what the magnet is made of
   (5) it depends what metals are around the compass

13. Alnico magnets are used in industry because they have a great deal of
strength for their size. What must be true of an alnico magnet?
   (1) It must have an electric current going through it.
   (2) It must be attracted to all metals.
   (3) It must be a naturally occurring magnet.
   (4) It must have both a north and a south pole.
   (5) None of the above must be true.

Questions 14 to 16 refer to the following article.

In one kind of internal-combustion engine, a mixture of gasoline and air is
compressed in a cylinder and then ignited by a spark from a spark plug. The
German engineer Rudolf Diesel developed another type of engine that works
without spark plugs. The intake stroke of this engine admits only air, which is
highly compressed in a cylinder, causing it to heat to a very high temperature.
Heavy fuels, such as oil, are then injected into this hot, compressed air and
are exploded by the heat.

Because diesel engines need such a strong compression stroke, they are heavy
and require the strength of a thick-walled compression chamber to function.
However, they get more energy out of the less expensive fuel they burn
because they can operate at a much higher temperature than a gasoline engine.

14. What is true of the diesel engine but not of the gasoline engine?
   (1) It needs no air supply.
   (2) It has no cylinders.
   (3) It has no spark plugs.
   (4) It uses less expensive types of gasoline.
   (5) It has no pistons.

15. Why are diesel engines used on locomotives?

(1) They can get more heat energy from a less expensive fuel.

(2) Coal-burning engines pollute the air.

(3) It is difficult to store large quantities of gasoline safely in the locomotive.

(4) Electric power is not easily available in remote, rural areas.

(5) Diesel fuel is available in remote, rural areas.

16. Why aren't diesel engines used in airplanes?

(1) Diesel engines are heavy engines.

(2) Diesel oil is very explosive.

(3) Airplanes do not need the power of diesel engines.

(4) Housing the cylinders would take up too much space.

(5) Diesel oil produces more pollutants than other fuels.

Questions 17 to 19 refer to the following article.

All nations agree that cooperative efforts are needed in research to study and predict earthquakes. In July 1956 the first World Conference on Earthquake Engineering was held in Tokyo. Its purpose was to share information about the prediction of earthquakes and methods of constructing buildings and bridges that can withstand the shocks.

What causes earthquakes? The crust of the Earth is a broken mosaic of pieces, bounded by deep cracks called faults. When forces deep inside the Earth move these pieces, tremendous shock waves start from the faults. Shock waves in the crust, from whatever source, can be detected by seismographs all over the world. If the earthquake occurs beneath the ocean, it produces an enormous wave, called a tsunami, that can do much damage when it arrives at a shore.

17. What is the most frequent cause of major earthquakes?

(1) movements within the Earth

(2) folding

(3) landslides

(4) submarine currents

(5) tsunamis

18. How can earthquake destruction be minimized?

(1) more frequent use of seismographs

(2) better construction of buildings

    (3) quicker methods of evacuation

    (4) early detection and warning

    (5) better control of tsunamis

19. Nuclear explosions can be detected by seismographs because they

    (1) cause tsunamis

    (2) occur on geologic faults

    (3) cause earthquakes

    (4) produce shock waves in the crust

    (5) compress the rock

<u>Questions 20 to 23</u> refer to the following article.

All matter is made up of atoms. Atoms contain protons, which have a positive charge; electrons, which have a negative charge; and neutrons, which are neither positively nor negatively charged. Since the atom has the same number of protons and electrons, the atom as a whole is electrically neutral.

The center of the atom, the nucleus, contains the protons and neutrons, while the electrons move outside the nucleus in areas called energy levels. Each energy level has the capacity to hold a maximum number of electrons. The first energy level can hold no more than two electrons, while the second energy level is complete with eight electrons. The third energy level can hold eighteen electrons, except when it happens to be the outer shell, in which case its capacity is only eight electrons. In some atoms, additional energy levels carry additional electrons.

An atom tends to complete the outer shell either by gaining electrons, losing electrons, or sharing electrons. The number of electrons available for such action is called valence. For example, a valence of + 2 means an atom has two electrons to lend. An atom with a valence of −1 needs one electron to complete its outer energy level. The gaining, losing, and sharing of electrons gives rise to the formation of compounds.

The atomic mass of an atom is the sum of the total mass of its protons and neutrons. The proton has a mass of one atomic mass unit. The neutron also has a mass of one atomic mass unit, but the electron adds almost nothing to the mass of an atom and so does not have to be considered in calculating atomic mass. The atomic number tells you the number of protons in the atom.

20. The valence of calcium (Ca) is +2. The valence of chlorine (Cl) is −1. When these elements combine to form calcium chloride, the correct formula for this compound is

(1) CaCl

(2) Ca_2Cl

(3) $CaCl_2$

(4) Ca_2Cl_2

(5) Ca_4Cl_2

21. Lithium has an atomic mass of 7 and an atomic number of 3. How many neutrons are there in the lithium atom?

(1) none

(2) two

(3) three

(4) four

(5) ten

22. The atomic number of an atom is always equal to the total number of

(1) neutrons in the nucleus

(2) neutrons and protons in the atom

(3) protons and electrons in the atom

(4) electrons in the orbits

(5) protons in the nucleus

23. What is the valence of an element that has 11 protons?

(1) +11

(2) −11

(3) +8

(4) +1

(5) −1

Questions 24 to 29 refer to the following article.

Photosynthesis is a complex process involving many steps. Water in the soil is absorbed by the roots of a plant, rises through tubules called xylem, and moves through the stems and into the leaves. Carbon dioxide, diffused from the air through the stomata and into the leaf, comes into contact with the water and dissolves. The solution of carbon dioxide in water then diffuses through the cell walls and into the cells. Organelles within the cell, called chloroplasts, contain chlorophyll, a green pigment that captures light energy from the sun and transforms it into chemical energy. This chemical energy acts to convert the carbon dioxide and water into other compounds. These compounds become more and more complex until finally a sugar is produced. Oxygen is given off as a by-product of the photosynthetic process.

24. Which plant structure is directly involved in the making of sugar?
    (1) stoma
    (2) xylem
    (3) cell wall
    (4) plasma membrane
    (5) chloroplast

25. To carry on photosynthesis, the water of the soil must be transported to the leaf. Which structure conducts soil water to the leaf?
    (1) chlorophyll
    (2) stoma
    (3) xylem
    (4) phloem
    (5) chloroplasts

26. What is/are the main product(s) of photosynthesis?
    (1) chlorophyll only
    (2) sugars and water
    (3) water and oxygen
    (4) oxygen only
    (5) oxygen and sugars

27. Sugar is composed of carbon, hydrogen, and oxygen. In the process of photosynthesis, what is the source of these chemical elements?
    (1) carbon dioxide alone
    (2) water alone
    (3) either the carbon dioxide or the water
    (4) both the carbon dioxide and the water
    (5) neither the carbon dioxide nor the water

28. What is the function of chlorophyll in photosynthesis?
    (1) serves as a source of carbohydrate
    (2) produces carbon dioxide
    (3) changes light energy to chemical energy

   (4) supplies chemical energy
   (5) provides the green color

29. Carbon dioxide enters a plant by way of the
   (1) roots
   (2) xylem
   (3) plasma membrane
   (4) stomata
   (5) intercellular spaces

---

30. In photosynthesis, green plants produce the carbohydrates that become the energy supply of the plants and of the animals that eat them. Photosynthesis can take place only when the plants are in sunlight.

Which statement below is a summary of this process?
   (1) Light and chemical energy are used for growth.
   (2) Chemical energy is converted to light energy.
   (3) Light energy is used for growth.
   (4) Chemical energy is used for growth.
   (5) Light energy is converted to chemical energy.

31. Green plants, in sunlight, absorb carbon dioxide to produce glucose, releasing oxygen in the process. Which of the following would be most likely to increase the rate at which this process goes on?
   (1) Increase the amount of oxygen in the air.
   (2) Add glucose to the soil.
   (3) Move the plants into the shade.
   (4) Reduce the amount of carbon dioxide in the air.
   (5) Increase the amount of carbon dioxide in the air.

Questions 32 to 34 refer to the following article.

In the process of evolution, some individuals in a population of organisms possess physical traits that allow them to have an advantage in survival over other members of their species. These changes may help them better attract mates, find food, hide from predators, or defend themselves. The individuals with a survival advantage will be more likely to pass their genes on to future generations, thus allowing the species to evolve over time.

A bird's bill usually defines the type of food that the bird eats. Some hunting birds have sharp hooked bills. Other birds have slender bills to extract nectar from flowers. The interesting bill of the South American toucan is huge and brightly colored and can be as long as half the length of the the bird's body. This bill is useful in picking fruit.

32. What is the probable reason that African hornbills closely resemble the South American toucan, even though the two species are unrelated?
    (1) The resemblance is purely a coincidence.
    (2) There has been an interchange of genetic material between the two species of birds.
    (3) The two species of birds have evolved from a common ancestor.
    (4) Both species of birds are fruit eaters in tropical rain forests.
    (5) The toucans have migrated from Africa.

33. When the Industrial Revolution introduced great smoke-belching factories into England, a certain species of moth found itself threatened. These white moths lived on the bark of light-colored trees, where they were virtually invisible to predators. When smog from the factories turned everything in the area black with soot, the trunks of the trees were not immune. As time passed, the population of this moth dropped dramatically. The chief reason for the decline may have been that
    (1) because the white moths were now visible against the sooty bark, they were easier for birds to catch
    (2) the soot was poisonous to the moths
    (3) the soot killed off the moth's primary source of food
    (4) the soot destroyed the moth's eggs
    (5) the moths had to find other trees because the old ones were now too dark

34. Snakes are solitary creatures. With a few exceptions, they crawl off to live alone after they hatch. Occasionally a female snake will lay a trail of a special scent called a pheromone. The reason for laying this trail is that the only life process a snake cannot carry on alone is
    (1) respiration
    (2) hibernation
    (3) reproduction
    (4) regulation
    (5) locomotion

35. Potassium is receiving special attention as an important nutritional requirement. Potassium conducts an electric charge that is important in the transmission of nerve impulses and muscle contraction. Such foods as

bananas and dried apricots are rich in potassium. These foods are recommended for persons who lose potassium because their medication causes the loss of body water. Why might the heart malfunction because of loss of potassium?

(1) The heart needs banana and apricot
(2) The heart absorbs much potassium
(3) High blood pressure can be treated
(4) Low blood pressure can be treated
(5) Contraction of heart muscles requires potassium

36. Oxides of carbon, sulfur, and nitrogen, which occur in the stack gases of coal-burning plants, react with atmospheric water to form acids. The pollution caused by stack gases may be responsible for all the following forms of environmental damage EXCEPT

(1) physical deformity of developing fish
(2) corrosion of buildings
(3) death of many forest trees
(4) damage to human lungs
(5) sewage contamination of water supplies

37. The laws that control recombination of genes seem to be much the same for all sexually reproducing organisms. These laws are studied by statistical analysis of large numbers of offspring for several generations. Which of the following organisms would be most useful in experiments to study the laws of recombination of genes?

(1) bacteria
(2) human beings
(3) mice
(4) dogs
(5) oak trees

38. The early atmosphere of the Earth had no oxygen. It was first produced when bacteria developed the green pigment that made photosynthesis possible. In which of the following groups is the sequence in which organisms appeared on Earth presented correctly?

(1) animals, green bacteria, nongreen bacteria
(2) green bacteria, animals, nongreen bacteria
(3) animals, nongreen bacteria, green bacteria
(4) nongreen bacteria, green bacteria, animals
(5) nongreen bacteria, animals, green bacteria

39. The graph below shows the changes in the populations of wolves and moose in a northern forest for a period of 6 years. What is the most reasonable explanation of the facts shown?

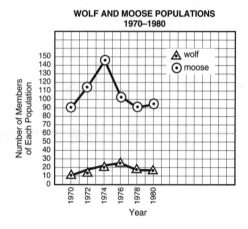

WOLF AND MOOSE POPULATIONS
1970–1980

(1) Moose produce more offspring when there are few wolves.
(2) When there are many moose, there are more recreational hunters.
(3) Wolves produce more offspring when there are many moose.
(4) Both wolf and moose populations vary according to the weather conditions.
(5) Wolf populations have no relationship to the availability of moose.

Question 40 is based on the following diagram.

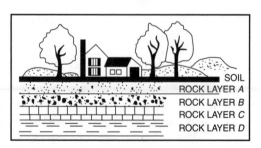

40. When sediments are deposited in the ocean, new layers form on top of preexisting layers. The sediments may eventually turn into fossil bearing rocks. What might a geologist conclude about fossils found in the rock layers shown in the diagram above?
(1) All the fossils are of the same age.

(2) The relative ages of the fossils cannot be determined.

(3) The fossils in rock layer *D* are older than those in layer *A*.

(4) The fossils in rock layer *B* are older than those in layer *C*.

(5) The fossils in rock layer *A* are older than those in layer *B*.

---

41. The AIDS virus is transmitted from an infected person by direct introduction of his or her blood or other body fluids into the body of another person. An individual can contract AIDS by any of the following means EXCEPT

(1) breathing the air expelled by a person with the disease

(2) sexual intercourse with an infected person

(3) using a hypodermic needle that had been used by someone with the disease

(4) receiving a blood transfusion from an infected person

(5) passage of the virus from a pregnant woman into the fetus she is carrying

42. Some corn plants may have genes that make them immune to the poisonous effects of herbicides. These genes can arise spontaneously by mutation, and will then be passed on to future generations. What might a plant breeder do to develop a line of corn that would not be killed by herbicides?

(1) Apply herbicides to cause mutations.

(2) Prevent mutations by careful control of environmental conditions.

(3) Find immune plants by applying herbicides and breeding the survivors.

(4) Withhold all fertilizers and breed the plants that survive.

(5) Withhold all herbicides and breed whichever plants mutate.

43. Since World War II, new varieties of rice have been developed that produce two or three times as much grain when they are grown with heavy doses of chemical fertilizers. A farmer should decide NOT to use these varieties if

(1) he or she is accustomed to growing more familiar varieties of rice

(2) he or she is cultivating only a small plot

(3) his or her farm is in an unusually wet climate

(4) there is no way he or she can obtain the seed of the new varieties

(5) the fertilizer needed costs more than the value of the extra grain

44. Why do you feel cool when you get out of the surf on a dry day?

(1) Evaporating water removes heat from your body.

(2) Evaporation produces heat.

(3) Condensation cools the body.
(4) The air is cooler than the surf water.
(5) Sea breezes make you feel cooler.

<u>**Questions 45 to 49**</u> **refer to the following article.**

Today some plants are cloned to produce millions of offspring from a small piece of the original plant. Plant cloning is possible because each plant cell contains a complete blueprint, in the form of chromosomes, for reproducing itself. After a piece of the plant is placed in a growth medium, special plant growth hormones, called auxins and cytokinin, are added to stimulate the production of new plants. The new plants are genetically identical to the original plant and to each other.

The equipment and process used in cloning are more expensive than those used for other forms of vegetative propagation. The advantage of cloning is that large numbers of plants are produced in a short period of time. For example, a million plants of a new variety can be cloned in about six months. This process is very useful for developing strains of disease resistant crops or plants that not only can survive in a difficult climate but also will produce a large harvest.

45. For which reason is cloning used to reproduce plants?
    (1) Plants with a large degree of genetic variability are produced.
    (2) Plants are produced more cheaply than by other vegetative methods.
    (3) Plants are produced by the sexual process, resulting in seeds.
    (4) A large number of plants are produced in a short period of time.
    (5) Plants with large degrees of variation are produced.

46. It is possible to clone plants that are identical to their parent plants because
    (1) scientists have developed blueprints to make so many different plants
    (2) every plant cell is the same
    (3) chromosomes carry identical genetic blueprints from the parent plant
    (4) hormones are used to induce plants to reproduce
    (5) plants are easy to grow under the correct conditions

47. Which statement describes the hormones auxin and cytokinin?
    (1) They are forms of vegetative propagation.

    (2) They can develop into a zygote.

    (3) They stimulate the production of new plants.

    (4) They inhibit the production of new plants.

    (5) They are forms of asexual reproduction.

48. How is cloning defined?

    (1) a form of sexual reproduction

    (2) a form of vegetative propagation

    (3) an inorganic hormone

    (4) an inorganic component of the growing medium

    (5) an auxin

49. An important difference between plants produced by cloning and plants grown from seed is that

    (1) cloned plants are healthier

    (2) cloned plants are identical to the parent plant

    (3) plants grown from seed are identical to the parent plant

    (4) plants grown from seed are better adapted to the conditions in which the plants are grown

    (5) cloned plants do not need as much care

---

50. If particles are to be considered water soluble, they must dissolve in water. In this case, the resulting solution will be clear. Sometimes, however, some of the substance will settle out of the solution, leaving a residue on the bottom of the container.

Why do we find the instruction "Shake well before using" on the labels of some medicines?

    (1) The liquid is a solution.

    (2) The mixture is not a solution.

    (3) The particles are the size of molecules.

    (4) The particles are not visible.

    (5) Light goes through the solution.

<u>Questions 51 to 53</u> refer to the following article.

Compounds known as bases are bitter to the taste and have a slippery feel. Acids taste sour. Litmus paper can be used to determine whether a substance is acidic or basic; the paper turns blue in a base and red in an acid. If exactly correct quantities of an acid and a base are combined, they react chemically to produce a salt, which is neither acidic nor basic.

51. All of the following are acids EXCEPT
   (1) oranges
   (2) vinegar
   (3) sour cream
   (4) apples
   (5) baking soda

52. Which of the following would turn litmus paper blue?
   (1) alcohol
   (2) soap
   (3) grapefruit
   (4) pure water
   (5) cola

53. Either a base such as ammonia or an acid such as vinegar can clean accumulated dirt from glass. Knowing this, a housekeeper makes a mixture of ammonia and vinegar to clean windows. How will this work?
   (1) There is no way to predict how well the mixture will work.
   (2) The mixture will work better than either substance alone.
   (3) The ammonia will still be effective, but the vinegar will not improve the material.
   (4) The vinegar will still be effective, but the ammonia will not improve the material.
   (5) The mixture will probably not work well at all.

---

54. Which of the following general rules is the best explanation of the way an ice cube cools a drink?
   (1) Cold moves to objects of higher temperature.
   (2) Heat moves to objects of higher density.
   (3) Heat moves to objects of lower density.
   (4) Cold moves to objects of lower temperature.
   (5) Heat moves to objects of lower temperature.

Questions 55 to 58 are based on the following passage and diagram.

When air rises, it expands, and this change makes it cool down. Conversely, when air sinks, it is compressed and becomes warmer. As air cools down, its relative humidity rises; when the relative humidity reaches 100%, moisture condenses out of the air.

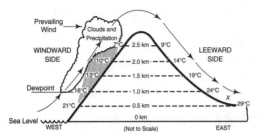

The diagram shows the prevailing wind directions and air temperatures at different elevations on both sides of a mountain.

55. What is the approximate air temperature at the top of the mountain?
   (1) 12°C
   (2) 10°C
   (3) 0°C
   (4) 7°C
   (5) 4°C

56. On which side of the mountain and at what elevation is the relative humidity probably 100%?
   (1) on the windward side at 0.5 km
   (2) on the windward side at 2.5 km
   (3) on the leeward side at 1.0 km
   (4) on the leeward side at 2.5 km
   (5) on the leeward side at 1.5 km

57. How does the temperature of the air change as the air rises on the windward side of the mountain between sea level and 0.5 kilometer?
   (1) The air is warming because of compression of the air.
   (2) The air is warming because of expansion of the air.
   (3) The air is cooling because of compression of the air.
   (4) The air is cooling because of expansion of the air.
   (5) The air is warmed and cooled because of expansion of the air.

58. Which feature is probably located at the base of the mountain on the leeward side (location *X*)?
   (1) a dry, desertlike region
   (2) a jungle
   (3) a glacier
   (4) a large lake
   (5) a river

59. Human activities produce or add all these pollutants EXCEPT
  (1) sound
  (2) pollen
  (3) radiation
  (4) smoke
  (5) carbon oxides

Questions 60 and 61 are based on the following passage and diagram.

The block marked *A* is being pulled uphill at constant speed by the falling weight. Since the speed is constant, the force pulling the block uphill must be equal in magnitude to the force holding it back. This opposing force is called friction.

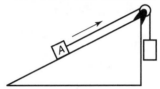

60. How would the situation change if a larger weight were used?
  (1) Nothing would be different.
  (2) Both the block and the weight would accelerate instead of going at a constant speed.
  (3) Both the block and the weight would be going at a higher constant speed.
  (4) The weight would accelerate, but the block would still travel at constant speed.
  (5) Both the block and the weight would slow down.

61. While you are probably most familiar with animals that have an internal skeleton, called an endoskeleton, certain organisms have their skeletons on the outside of their bodies. This exoskeleton is an excellent means of support and protection, but as the animal grows, its skeleton does not. Because of this, the exoskeleton has to be shed or molted now and then.

Animals with an exoskeleton are called invertebrates. Of the animals listed below, which one is *not* an invertebrate?
  (1) lobster
  (2) turtle
  (3) snail
  (4) horseshoe crab
  (5) spider

Questions 62 to 66 refer to the following information.

An experiment was performed to find out whether there are any circumstances in which a wingless type of fruit fly has a selective advantage over the normal kind. Two culture bottles were prepared, using the same kind of food, and were kept next to each other for the entire period of the experiment. Bottle *A* had a small strip of flypaper suspended from its stopper; *B* did not. Four kinds of flies were introduced into each bottle: 10 males and 10 females each of wingless and normal fruit flies.

62. Which of the following is an important control in this experiment?
    (1) the use of both males and females
    (2) placing the flypaper in one bottle only
    (3) using the same kind of food in both bottles
    (4) putting both kinds of flies in each bottle
    (5) taking care that the bottles are well stoppered

63. What is the hypothesis being tested?
    (1) Male fruit flies have a better survival rate than females.
    (2) Flies with wings have a better survival rate than those without.
    (3) There are circumstances in which winglessness confers an advantage in survival.
    (4) Wingless flies have a better survival rate than those with wings.
    (5) All kinds of flies are equally likely to survive.

64. The experiment started with equal numbers of the four kinds of flies in each jar. This is
    (1) an irrelevant fact
    (2) a detail of experimental design
    (3) an assumption
    (4) a general law of nature
    (5) an experimental finding

65. It is known that winglessness in fruit flies sometimes arises by mutation. In the context of this experiment, this is
    (1) an assumption
    (2) a general law of nature
    (3) a hypothesis
    (4) a statement of the problem
    (5) an irrelevant fact

66. What general principle of nature would be explained by finding that most of the flies with wings died on the flypaper?

(1) Flypaper is an effective means of control of insects.

(2) Fruit flies exist in nature in many different forms.

(3) Evolution favors the forms with the best survival values.

(4) The survival value of a trait depends on the environment in which the organism lives.

(5) Processes in natural ecosystems cannot be simulated in the laboratory.

TEST 4: INTERPRETING LITERATURE AND THE ARTS

Directions

Alloted Time: 65 minutes

The Interpreting Literature and the Arts test consists of excerpts from classical and popular literature and articles about literature or the arts. Each excerpt is followed by multiple-choice questions about the reading material.

Read each excerpt first and then answer the questions following it. Refer to the reading material as often as necessary in answering the questions.

Each excerpt is preceded by a "purpose question." The purpose question gives a reason for reading the material. Use these purpose questions to help focus your reading. You are not required to answer these purpose questions. They are given only to help you concentrate on the ideas presented in the reading materials.

You should spend no more than 65 minutes answering the questions. Work carefully, but do not spend too much time on any one question. Be sure you answer every question. You will not be penalized for incorrect answers.

To record your answers, mark the numbered space on the answer sheet beside the number that corresponds to the question in the test.

FOR EXAMPLE:

It was Susan's dream machine. The metallic blue paint gleamed, and the sporty wheels were highly polished. Under the hood, the engine was no less carefully cleaned. Inside, flashy lights illuminated the instruments on the dashboard, and the seats were covered in rich leather upholstery.

The subject ("It") of this excerpt is most likely
(1) an airplane   ① ② ● ④ ⑤
(2) a stereo system
(3) an automobile
(4) a boat
(5) a motorcycle

The correct answer is "an automobile"; therefore, answer space 3 would be marked on the answer sheet.

Questions 1 to 5 refer to the following excerpt from a work of prose nonfiction.

WHAT WAS MARY WHITE'S LAST HOUR LIKE?

The last hour of Mary White's life was typical of its happiness. She came home from a day's work at school, topped off by a hard grind with the copy on the high school annual, and felt that a ride would refresh her. She climbed into her khakis, chattering to her mother about the work she was doing, and
(5) hurried to get her horse and be out on the dirt roads for the country air and the radiant green fields of the spring. As she rode through the town at an easy gallop, she kept waving at passersby. She knew everyone in town. For a decade the little figure with the long pigtail and the red hair ribbon had been familiar on the streets of Emporia, and she got in the way of speaking to
(10) those who nodded at her. She passed the Kerrs, walking the horse, in front of the Normal Library, and waved at them; passed another friend a few hundred feet farther on, and waved at her. The horse was walking, and as she turned into North Merchant Street, she took off her cowboy hat, and the horse swung into a lope. She passed the Tripletts and waved her cowboy hat at
(15) them, still moving gaily north on Merchant Street. A Gazette carrier passed—a high school boy friend—and she waved at him, but with her bridle hand; the horse veered quickly, plunged into the parking lot where a low-hanging limb faced her, and while she still looked back waving, the blow came. But she did not fall from the horse; she slipped off, dazed a bit, staggered, and
(20) fell in a faint. She never quite recovered consciousness.

—W.A. White

1. The passage gives details that create a picture of
   (1) a sad death
   (2) a bookish lady
   (3) an active girl
   (4) a boy-crazy kid
   (5) a pathetic child

2. Mary White was
   (1) small of stature
   (2) big-boned
   (3) tall
   (4) husky
   (5) pretty

3. The picture contains such details as
   (1) jeans, a green ribbon, a pigtail
   (2) riding clothes, sombrero, plait
   (3) overalls, cowboy hat, short hair
   (4) khakis, cowboy hat, red hair ribbon
   (5) bridle, saddle, spurs

4. The death of Mary White can be said to have been caused indirectly by her
   (1) poor horsemanship
   (2) small size
   (3) fast riding
   (4) friendliness
   (5) failure to take proper precautions

5. The main purpose of the author is to
   (1) report the tragic end of a happy life
   (2) stress that it was an accident that killed Mary White
   (3) inform us of the mistake she made in waving with the wrong hand
   (4) show Mary White's bravery in not falling from the horse
   (5) emphasize the unexpectedness of the fatal blow

Questions 6 to 10 refer to the following excerpt from a work of prose fiction.

WHAT CAN A BEREAVED FATHER DO?

Iona sees a hall porter with some sacking, and decides to talk to him.

"Friend, what sort of time is it?" he asks.

"Past nine. What are you standing here for? Move on."

Iona moves on a few steps, doubles up, and abandons himself to his grief. He gives a tug at the reins; he can bear it no longer. "The stables," he thinks, and the little horse, as if it understood, starts off at a trot.

One of the cabdrivers around the stove half gets up, grunts sleepily, and stretches toward a bucket of water.

"Do you want a drink?" Iona asks him.

"Don't I want a drink!"

"That's so? Your good health! But listen, mate—you know, my son is dead...Did you hear? This week, in the hospital...It's a long story."

Iona looks to see what effect his words have, but sees none—the young man is fast asleep again. Just as much as the young one wants to drink, the old man wants to talk. Is it nothing to tell?

"I'll go and look after my horse," thinks Iona; "there's always time to sleep. No fear of that!"

When he is alone, he dares not think of his son; he can speak about him to anyone, but to think of him, and picture him to himself, is unbearably painful.

"That's how it is, my old horse. There's no more Kuzma Ionitch. Now let's say, you had a foal, you were this foal's mother, and suddenly, let's say, that foal went out and left you to live after him. It would be sad, wouldn't it?"

The little horse munches, listens, and breathes over its master's hand...

Iona's feelings are too much for him, and he tells the little horse the whole story.

6. In this story it is ironic that
   (1) the cabdriver wants a drink
   (2) the hall porter tells Iona to move on
   (3) Iona tells his story to his horse
   (4) Iona has run out of food for his horse
   (5) the horse had a foal

7. Iona goes to take care of his horse. He does so most probably to
   (1) have something to do
   (2) protest the high cost of feed
   (3) show his great love for his horse
   (4) prove that he does not resent the cabdriver's action
   (5) remove his feelings of guilt

8. The setting for this story is probably a 19th-century
  (1) American city
  (2) eastern European city
  (3) northern European farm
  (4) American small town
  (5) English city

9. The author's purpose in using the present tense is most probably to
  (1) make the story seem modern
  (2) increase the length of the story
  (3) heighten the reader's sense of immediacy
  (4) write the story as consciously as possible
  (5) reinforce the first-person point of view

10. Iona's situation is brought home to the reader when he
  (1) asks the hall porter for the time
  (2) asks the cabdriver for a drink
  (3) talks to himself
  (4) fights off sleep
  (5) compares himself to a foal's mother

Questions 11 to 15 refer to the following excerpt from a work of prose non-fiction.

HOW DID A MOTHER AND A SON REACT TO A TRAGEDY?

After living nearly two years in Cairo, I had brought my son Guy to enter the University of Ghana in Accra. Guy was seventeen and quick. I was thirty-three and determined. We were Black Americans in West Africa, where for the first time in our lives the color of our skin was
(5) accepted as correct and normal. The future was plump with promise. For two days Guy and I laughed. On the third day, Guy, on a pleasure outing, was injured in an automobile accident. One arm and one leg were fractured and his neck was broken.

July and August stretched out like fat men yawning after a sumptuous
(10) dinner. They had every right to gloat, for they had eaten me up. Gobbled me down. Consumed my spirit, not in a wild rush, but slowly, with the obscene patience of certain victors. I became a shadow walking in the white hot streets, and a dark spectre in the hospital.

Trying utterly, I could not match Guy's stoicism. He lay calm, in a
(15) prison of plaster from which only his face and one leg and arm were visible. His assurances that he would heal and be better than new drove me into a faithless silence.

Admittedly, Guy lived with the knowledge that an unexpected sneeze
could force the fractured vertebrae against his spinal cord, and he would
(20) be paralyzed or die immediately, but he had only an infatuation with life.
He hadn't lived long enough to fall in love with this brutally delicious
experience. He could lightly waft away to another place, if there really
was another place, where his youthful innocence would assure him
wings, a harp, and an absence of nostalgic yearning. My wretchedness
(25) reminded me that, on the other hand, I would be rudderless. We had
been each other's home and center for seventeen years. He could die if
he wanted to and go off to wherever dead folks go, but I, I would be left
without a home.

—Maya Angelou

11. The narrator notes that there are differences between herself
and Guy in both age and
   (1) education
   (2) temperament
   (3) intelligence
   (4) agility
   (5) devotion

12. Which literary device is used in line 9?
   (1) understatement
   (2) hyperbole
   (3) simile
   (4) onomatopoeia
   (5) metaphor

13. The word *they*, as used in line 10, is intended to mean the
   (1) certain victors
   (2) days of July and August
   (3) fat men
   (4) narrator's thoughts
   (5) West Africans

14. The narrator portrays the delicate nature of her son's life with the words
   (1) "seventeen and quick"
   (2) "dark spectre"
   (3) "hadn't lived long"
   (4) "lightly waft away"
   (5) "infatuation with life"

15. What does the imagery in lines 12 and 13 convey about the narrator's situation?

    (1) Her sudden helplessness seemed unreal.

    (2) Her physical health had deteriorated.

    (3) She was a Black American walking freely in a once white-only area.

    (4) She was undefeated by the adversity of life.

    (5) She was uncertain about her future.

Questions 16 to 20 refer to the following poem.

WHAT IS IT LIKE WHEN ELECTRIC POLES REPLACE TREES?

On their sides, resembling fallen timbers without rough
Barks—a hundred feet apart—lie power poles.
Just yesterday, this road was edged
With eucalyptus; in aisles
Between rows of trees, seats for the aged.
Now tree odors hover in the air, residues of life.
The poles are erected. The frigid,
Passionless verticals
Strive
To fill the socket-shaped holes
Left by trees. Identical, cement-wedged
Below, parasitically fastened to live wires above,
Tree imposters, never to be budged
From a telegraphic owl's
Knowitallness, they stand—rigid!
Sad children, wishing to climb, scan the miles
And miles of uninterrupted electric forests for
leaves.

16. Which phrase best expresses the ideas of this poem?

    (1) the new trees

    (2) the promising verticals

    (3) improving the landscape

    (4) on climbing trees

    (5) tree odors

17. The poet seems to resent the power poles'

    (1) rough barks

    (2) new odors

    (3) lifelessness

(4) expensiveness

(5) electric charge

18. In this poem, the children are sad because
(1) the poles are too slippery to climb
(2) the poles are too rigid to climb
(3) they have been forbidden to climb the poles
(4) the poles have replaced the trees
(5) they have grown to love the owls

19. The poet's point of view is expressed by the use of such phrases as
(1) fallen timbers
(2) power poles
(3) passionless verticals
(4) socket-shaped holes
(5) live wires

20. An example of a poetic figure of speech is found in the words
(1) tree odors
(2) cement-wedged
(3) tree imposters
(4) sad children
(5) scan the miles

Questions 21 to 25 refer to the following poem.

WHAT IS THE REACTION OF A TEACHER TO HIS STUDENT'S DEATH?

I remember the neckcurls, limp and damp
  as tendrils;
And her quick look, a sidelong pickerel
  smile;
(5) And how, once startled into talk, the light
  syllables leaped for her,
And she balanced in the delight of her
  thought,
A wren, happy, tail into the wind,
(10) Her song trembling the twigs and small
  branches.
The shade sang with her;
The leaves, their whispers turned to kissing;

And the mold sang in the bleached valleys
(15)   under the rose.
Oh, when she was sad, she cast herself
down into such a pure depth,
Even a father could not find her:
Scraping her cheek against straw;
(20) Stirring the clearest water.
My sparrow, you are not here,
Waiting like a fern, making a spiny shadow.
The sides of wet stones cannot console me,
Nor the moss, wound with the last light.

(25) If only I could nudge you from this sleep,
My maimed darling, my skittery pigeon.
Over this damp grave I speak the words of
my love:
I, with no rights in this matter,
(30) Neither father nor lover.

—Theodore Roethke, *"Elegy for Jane"*

21. The poet wrote this poem mainly to
(1) describe Jane
(2) criticize Jane
(3) mourn Jane
(4) remember Jane
(5) forget Jane

22. The poet's feeling for Jane, as indicated in the poem, is one of
(1) awe
(2) reverence
(3) regret
(4) nostalgia
(5) love

23. To what does the poet repeatedly compare Jane?
(1) a flower
(2) a shooting star
(3) a bird
(4) a small pet
(5) a lovely song

24. The change that takes place in the poem starting on line 21
is that the poet
(1) becomes resigned
(2) recollects further details
(3) compares himself to a father
(4) talks directly to the dead student
(5) becomes more angry at his loss

25. The poem is powerful in its impact on the reader because
the poet feels he
(1) is like a father to Jane
(2) is like a lover to Jane
(3) is like a teacher to Jane
(4) has no right to write the poem
(5) is responsible for her tragedy

Questions 26 to 30 refer to the following excerpt from a play.

HOW DOES THE FAMILY RESPOND TO LINDNER'S OFFER?

WALTER: I mean—I have worked as a chauffeur most of my life—and
my wife here, she does domestic work in people's kitchens.
So does my mother, I mean—we are plain people . . .

LINDNER: Yes, Mr. Younger—

WALTER: [*Really like a small boy, looking down at his shoes and then
up at the man*] And—uh—well, my father, well, he was a
laborer most of his life.

LINDNER: [*Absolutely confused*] Uh, yes—

WALTER: [*Looking down at his toes once again*] My father almost
beat a man to death once because this man called him a
bad name or something, you know what I mean?

LINDNER: No, I'm afraid I don't.

WALTER: [*Finally straightening up*] Well, what I means is that we
come from people who had a lot of pride. I mean—we are
very proud people. And that's my sister over there and
she's going to be a doctor—and we are very proud—

LINDNER: Well—I am sure that is very nice, but—

WALTER: [*Starting to cry and facing the man eye to eye*] What I am
telling you is that we called you over here to tell you that
we are very proud and that this is—this is my son, who
makes the sixth generation of our family in this country,
and that we have all thought about your offer and we have

decided to move into our house because my father—my father—he earned it. [MAMA *has her eyes closed and is rocking back and forth as though she were in church, with her head nodding the amen yes*] We don't want to make no trouble for nobody or fight no causes—but we will try to be good neighbors. That's all we got to say. [*He looks the man absolutely in the eyes*] We don't want your money. [*He turns and walks away from the man*]

LINDNER: [*Looking around at all of them*] I take it then that you have decided to occupy.

BENEATHA: That's what the man said.

LINDNER: [*To MAMA in her reverie*] Then I would like to appeal to you, Mrs. Younger. You are older and wiser and understand things better I am sure...

MAMA: [*Rising*] I am afraid you don't understand. My son said we was going to move and there ain't nothing left for me to say. [*Shaking her head with double meaning*] You know how these young folks is nowadays, mister. Can't do a thing with 'em. Good-bye.

LINDNER: [*Folding up his materials*] Well—if you are that final about it... There is nothing left for me to say. [*He finishes. He is almost ignored by the family who are concentrating on WALTER LEE. At the door LINDNER halts and looks around*] I sure hope you people know what you're doing. [*He shakes his head and exits*]

—Lorraine Hansberry, *A Raisin in the Sun*

26. The story Walter tells about his father almost beating a man to death for calling him a name is
   (1) an anecdote
   (2) a lie
   (3) a warning
   (4) a dream
   (5) an allusion

27. From this point on, the family will
   (1) stay in the ghetto
   (2) try for a new life
   (3) sell their house
   (4) retreat to the South
   (5) fight for causes

28. After this incident, the head of the house will be
  (1) Travis
  (2) Mama
  (3) Walter
  (4) Ruth
  (5) Beneatha

29. Mr. Lindner
  (1) understands the Youngers
  (2) despises the Youngers
  (3) is sympathetic to the Youngers
  (4) is tolerant of the Youngers
  (5) disagrees with the Youngers

30. The word that best describes Walter's family is
  (1) plain
  (2) vicious
  (3) proud
  (4) trouble-making
  (5) uncooperative

Questions 31 to 35 refer to the following passage.

HOW DOES AN INDIAN CHIEF REMEMBER HIS CHILDHOOD?

I have acted in the movies and in Wild West shows, and served as an interpreter between the Indian and the White man. I have met presidents and kings, writers, scientists, and artists. I have had much joy and received many honors, but I have never forgotten my wild, free childhood when I lived in a tepee and heard the calling of the coyotes under the stars . . . when the night winds, the sun, and everything else in our primitive world reflected the wisdom and benevolence of the Great Spirit. I remember seeing my mother bending over an open fire toasting buffalo meat, and my father returning at night with an antelope on his shoulder. I remember playing with the other children on the banks of a clean river, and I shall never forget when my grandfather taught me how to make a bow and arrow from hard wood and flint, and a fishhook from the rib of a field mouse. I am not sentimental but memories haunt me as I review scenes from those days before I was old enough to understand that all Indian things would pass away.

The average American child of today would enjoy the privileges I had out there on the unspoiled prairie one hundred years ago. I was usually awake in time to see the sun rise. If the weather was warm, I went down to the river that flowed near our village and dipped water out of it with my hands for a drink, then plunged into it. The river came down out of the hills, ferrying leaves, blossoms, and driftwood. Fish could be seen in the pools formed near the rapids over which it rippled. Birds nested and flew among the banks, and occasionally I would see a coon or a fox in the brush. Hawks circled overhead, searching the ground for mice or other small animals for their breakfast, or to feed the young in their nests. There were never enough hours in a day to exhaust the pleasure of observing every living creature—from the orb spider spinning his magic and all but invisible web to the bald eagles on their bulky nests atop the tallest trees, teaching fledglings how to eject safely.

—Memoirs of Chief Red Fox

31. The mood of the selection is one of
   (1) nostalgia
   (2) bitterness
   (3) resignation
   (4) envy
   (5) anticipation

32. One of the most important of the chief's memories is that of
   (1) Wild West shows
   (2) many honors
   (3) meeting presidents and kings
   (4) family members
   (5) coyotes

33. The writer's primitive world was characterized by
   (1) evidence of the Great Spirit
   (2) fishhooks
   (3) bow and arrow
   (4) the call of the coyotes
   (5) night winds

34. The writer's love of nature led him to
   (1) observe it closely
   (2) benefit from its warmth
   (3) collect specimens
   (4) search for small animals
   (5) sleep late

35. Nature a hundred years ago was preferable to nature today because it was more

(1) varied

(2) wild

(3) magical

(4) friendly

(5) unspoiled

Questions 36 to 40 refer to the following commentary on the plays *Romeo and Juliet* and *West Side Story*.

HOW DO *ROMEO AND JULIET* AND *WEST SIDE STORY* COMPARE?

What glorious verse falls from the lips of Shakespeare's boys and girls! True, there is a rollicking jazzy vigor in such songs of *West Side Story* as the one of Officer Krupke, but it pales alongside the pyrotechnical display of Mercurio's Queen Mab speech. There is

(5) tenderness in "Maria," but how relatively tongue-tied is the twentieth-century hero alongside the boy who cried, "He jests at scars that never felt a wound." "Hold my hand and we're halfway there," say Maria and Tony to each other, and the understatement touches us. But "Gallop apace, you fiery-footed steeds" and the lines that follow glow with a glory

(10) that never diminishes. The comparisons of language could be multiplied, and always, of course, Shakespeare is bound to win.

Without its great poetry *Romeo and Juliet* would not be a major tragedy. Possibly it is not, in any case; for as has frequently been remarked, Shakespeare's hero and heroine are a little too slender to carry

(15) the full weight of tragic grandeur. Their plight is more pathetic than tragic. If this is true of them, it is equally true of Tony and Maria: for them, too, pathos rather than tragedy. But there is tragedy implicit in the environmental situation of the contemporary couple, and this must not be overlooked or underestimated. Essentially, however, what we see is that

(20) all four young people strive to consummate the happiness at the threshold on which they stand and which they have tasted so briefly. All four are deprived of the opportunity to do so, the Renaissance couple by the caprice of fate, today's youngsters by the prejudice and hatred engendered around them. All four are courageous and lovable. All four

(25) arouse our compassion, even though they may not shake us with Aristotelian fear.

Poets and playwrights will continue to write of youthful lovers whom fate drives into and out of each other's lives. The spectacle will always trouble and move us.

36. The author of the selection implies that
   (1) the songs of *West Side Story* lack strength
   (2) the language of *West Side Story* leaves us cold
   (3) the language of *Romeo and Juliet* lacks the vigor of that of *West Side Story*
   (4) the poetry of *Romeo and Juliet* will prevail
   (5) the speech of *West Side Story* can compete with the verse of *Romeo and Juliet*

37. In comparing the language of *Romeo and Juliet* with that of *West Side Story* the author
   (1) takes no position
   (2) likes each equally
   (3) favors that of *Romeo and Juliet*
   (4) favors that of *West Side Story*
   (5) downplays the differences

38. Both plays share a common weakness. That weakness is
   (1) the stature of their heroes and heroines
   (2) the absence of deep emotion
   (3) their dramatic construction
   (4) the lack of substance of their themes
   (5) the lack of linguistic power

39. The couples in the two plays share all of the following EXCEPT
   (1) a pathetic situation
   (2) lack of opportunity to achieve happiness
   (3) courage
   (4) inability to instill fear in the reader
   (5) inability to arouse pity in the reader

40. The couples in the two plays differ in the nature of
   (1) their plight
   (2) their ultimate fate
   (3) the cause of their tragic situation
   (4) their attractiveness
   (5) their love for one another

Questions 41 to 45 refer to the following article on art.

WHAT IS THE MESSAGE OF CHAGALL'S WORK?

"Your colors sing!" Chagall's teacher, Leon Bakst, had told him. Indeed, Chagall slapped on colors in bold, solid patches, often contrasting them with striking effects. His burning reds, juicy greens and the magic "Chagall blue" give an almost sensual gratification. Yet when I
(5) once asked, "How do you get your blues?" he replied with a typical pixie twinkle, "I buy them in a shop. They come in tubes."

When he entered his 60s, the painter's inventiveness began to run dry. He had become, in the words of one critic, "his own most faithful imitator." At this crucial point, inspiration struck. Chagall turned to
(10) stained glass. He spent days examining the gemlike windows in France's great medieval cathedrals, where plain bits of colored glass were turned into jewels by the sun. In 1957 he made two small windows, depicting angels, for a chapel in Savoy. The next year he met one of France's foremost stained-glass makers, Charles Marq. Chagall began spending up
(15) to 12 hours a day at the Marq workshop in the cathedral town of Reims.

Chagall's stained-glass creations, a staggering total of 11,000 square feet, include windows for churches, a synagogue in Jerusalem, and the General Assembly Building of the U.N. in New York. But when Chagall was approached in 1972 to do three windows in Reims's 13th-century
(20) cathedral, where more than 20 French kings were crowned, he was alarmed. "I adorn a national shrine? Unthinkable." Finally he complied, once more refusing pay.

On entering the dim Gothic nave of Reims Cathedral today, the first thing you perceive in the distance is the sapphire gleam of Chagall's
(25) stained-glass window, depicting, on the left, the sacrifice of Abraham and, on the right, Christ on the cross. In joining Old and New Testaments into a harmonious whole, Chagall reflected his own deep faith in the all-embracing message of Scripture—mankind's ascent through suffering to salvation.

41. The author writes approvingly of which of the following traits in Chagall's character?
(1) his sensuality
(2) his arrogance
(3) his imitativeness
(4) his impish humor
(5) his materialism

42. The article is most concerned with Chagall's
   (1) paintings
   (2) pastels
   (3) murals
   (4) drawings
   (5) stained glass

43. In his paintings, Chagall used
   (1) contrasting colors
   (2) soft solid colors
   (3) Chagall reds
   (4) gemlike radiances
   (5) sapphire gleams

44. According to the article, Chagall believed deeply in
   (1) French kings
   (2) national shrines
   (3) mankind's salvation
   (4) the Old Testament only
   (5) the New Testament only

45. Chagall turned to the medium of stained glass because
   (1) it was more profitable
   (2) he met Charles Marq
   (3) he was invited to work in the Reims Cathedral
   (4) he had come to imitate his own work
   (5) he got magic blues

TEST 5: MATHEMATICS

Directions

Alloted Time: 90 minutes

The Mathematics test consists of multiple-choice questions intended to measure general mathematics skills and problem-solving ability. The questions are based on short readings that often include a graph, chart, or figure.

You should spend no more than 90 minutes answering the questions. Work carefully, but do not spend too much time on any one question. Be sure you answer every question. You will not be penalized for incorrect answers.

Formulas you may need are given below. Only some of the questions will require you to use a formula. Not all the formulas given will be needed.

Some questions contain more information than you will need to solve the problem. Other questions do not give enough information to solve the problem. If the question does not give enough information to solve the problem, the correct answer is "Not enough information is given."

The use of calculators is not allowed.

To record your answers, mark the numbered space on the answer sheet beside the number that corresponds to the question in the test.

EXAMPLE:

If a grocery bill totaling $15.75 is paid with a $20.00 bill, how much change should be returned?

(1) $5.26   ① ② ● ④ ⑤

(2) $4.75

(3) $4.25

(4) $3.75

(5) $3.25

The correct answer is "$4.25"; therefore, answer space 3 would be marked on the answer sheet.

FORMULAS

Description	Formula
AREA (A) of a:	
square	$A = s^2$; where s = side
rectangle	$A = lw$; where l = length, w = width
parallelogram	$A = bh$; where b = base, h = height
triangle	$A = \frac{1}{2}bh$; where b = base, h = height
circle	$A = \pi r^2$; where π = 3.14, r = radius
PERIMETER (P) of a:	
square	$P = 4s$; where s = side
rectangle	$P = 2l + 2w$; where l = length, w = width
triangle	$P = a + b + c$; where a, b, and c are the sides
circumference (C) of a circle	$C = \pi d$; where π = 3.14, d = diameter

FORMULAS continued

Description	Formula
VOLUME (V) of a:	
cube	$V = s^3$; where s = side
rectangular container	$V = lwh$; where l = length, w = width, h = height
cylinder	$V = \pi r^2 h$; where $\pi = 3.14$, r = radius, h = height
Pythagorean relationship	$c^2 = a^2 + b^2$; where c = hypotenuse, a and b are legs, of a right triangle
distance (d) between two points in a plane	$d = \sqrt{\left(x_2 - x_1\right)^2 + \left(y^2 - y_1\right)^2}$; where (x_1, y_1) and (x_2, y_2) are two points in a plane
slope of a line (m)	$m = \dfrac{y_2 - y_1}{x_2,\ y_1}$; where (x_1, y_1) and (x_2, y_2) are two points in a plane
mean	mean $= \dfrac{x_1 + x_2 + \ldots + x_n}{n}$; where the x's are the values for which a mean is desired, and n = number of values in the series
median	median = the point in an ordered set of numbers at which half of the numbers are above and half of the numbers are below this value
simple interest (i)	$i = prt$; where p = principal, r = rate, t = time
distance (d) as function of rate and time	$d = rt$; where r = rate, t = time
total cost (c)	$c = nr$; where n = number of units, r = cost per unit

1. On 5 successive days a deliveryman listed his mileage as follows: 135, 162, 98, 117, 216. If his truck averages 14 miles for each gallon of gas used, how many gallons of gas did he use during these 5 days?
   (1) 42
   (2) 52

(3) 115
(4) 147
(5) 153

2. Parking meters in Springfield read: "12 minutes for 5¢. Maximum deposit 50¢." What is the maximum time, in hours, that a driver may be legally parked at one of these meters?
(1) 1
(2) 1.2
(3) 12
(4) 2
(5) Not enough information is given.

Question 3 is based on the following figure.

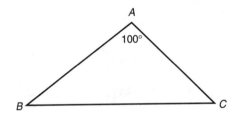

3. If $AB = AC$ and m $\angle A = 100°$, what is the measure of $\angle B$?
(1) 40°
(2) 45°
(3) 50°
(4) 60°
(5) 80°

4. The ABC Department Store had a special sale on shirts. One group sold at $15 per shirt, and another group sold at $18 per shirt. If 432 shirts were sold at $15 each and 368 shirts were sold at $18 each, the number of dollars taken in at the shirt sale may be represented as
(1) 800(15 + 18)
(2) (15)(368) + (18)(432)
(3) (15)(800) + (18)(800)
(4) 33(432 + 68)
(5) (15)(432) + (368)(18)

5. A hockey team won X games, lost Y games, and tied Z games. What fractional part of the games played were won?

  (1) $\dfrac{X}{X+Y+Z}$

  (2) $\dfrac{X}{XYZ}$

  (3) $\dfrac{X}{XY}$

  (4) $\dfrac{X}{X+Y}$

  (5) $\dfrac{X}{X-Y-Z}$

6. One-half the students at Madison High School walk to school. One-fourth of the rest go to school by bicycle. What part of the school population travels by some other means?

  (1) 1/8

  (2) 3/8

  (3) 3/4

  (4) 1/4

  (5) Not enough information is given.

7. Which of the following is a solution of the inequality $2x > 9$?

  (1) 0

  (2) 2

  (3) 3

  (4) 4

  (5) 5

8. Which of the following units would be most appropriate to measure the distance between New York and San Francisco?

  (1) meter

  (2) kilometer

  (3) kilogram

  (4) liter

  (5) centimeter

9. A flagpole casts a shadow 16 feet long. At the same time, a pole 9 feet high casts a shadow 6 feet long. What is the height, in feet, of the flagpole?

  (1) 18

  (2) 19

  (3) 20

(4) 24

(5) Not enough information is given.

10. Martin has a piece of lumber 9 feet 8 inches long. He wishes to cut it into 4 equal lengths. How far from the edge should he make the first cut?

(1) 2.5 ft.

(2) 2 ft. 5 in.

(3) 2.9 ft.

(4) 29 ft.

(5) 116 in.

11. A purse contains 6 nickels, 5 dimes, and 8 quarters. If one coin is drawn at random from the purse, what is the probability that the coin drawn is a dime?

(1) 5/19

(2) 5/14

(3) 5/8

(4) 5/6

(5) 19/5

12. The leaders in the Peninsula Golf Tournament finished with scores of 272, 284, 287, 274, 275, 283, 278, 276, and 281. What is the median of these scores?

(1) 273

(2) 274

(3) 276

(4) 278

(5) 280

13. The cost of a dozen ballpoint pens and 8 pencils is $4.60. If the cost of the pens is 3 for $0.97, what is the cost, in cents, of 1 pencil?

(1) 6

(2) 8

(3) 8.5

(4) 9

(5) 9.5

14. The scale on a map is 1 inch = 150 miles. The cities of Benton and Dover are $3\frac{1}{2}$ inches apart on this map. What is the actual distance, in miles, between Benton and Dover?

(1) 525
(2) 545
(3) 580
(4) 625
(5) Not enough information is given.

Question 15 is based on the following figure.

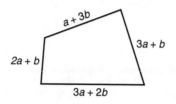

15. What is the perimeter of the figure?
(1) $8a + 5b$
(2) $9a + 7b$
(3) $7a + 5b$
(4) $6a + 6b$
(5) $8a + 6b$

Question 16 is based on the following number line.

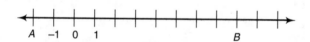

16. On the number line, what is the coordinate of the midpoint of $\overline{AB}$?
(1) −11
(2) 0
(3) 2
(4) 3
(5) 8

17. The Men's Shop advertised a spring sale. David Morris was especially interested in the following sale items.

ties: 3 for $23
shirts: 3 for $43
slacks: $32.75 per pair
jackets: $58.45 each

David bought 6 ties, 3 shirts, 2 pairs of slacks, and 1 jacket. What was his bill?
(1) $157.20
(2) $180.20
(3) $189.95
(4) $202.95
(5) $212.95

18. In which of the following lists are the numbers written in order from greatest to smallest?
(1) 0.80, 19%, 0.080, 1/2, 3/5
(2) 0.80, 1/2, 0.080, 3/5, 19%
(3) 0.80, 3/5, 1/2, 19%, 0.080
(4) 1/2, 0.80, 3/5, 19%, 0.080
(5) 3/5, 1/2, 19%, 0.080, 0.80

19. If an airplane completes its flight of 1,364 miles in 5 hours and 30 minutes, what is its average speed, in miles per hour?
(1) 240
(2) 244
(3) 248
(4) 250
(5) 260

20. The distance between two heavenly bodies is 85,000,000,000 miles. This number, written in scientific notation, is
(1) 8.5×10^{-10}
(2) 8.5×10^{10}
(3) 85×10^{9}
(4) 0.85×10^{-9}
(5) 850×10^{7}

21. What is the value of $3ab - x^2y$ if $a = 4$, $b = 5$, $y = 3$, and $x = 2$?
(1) 18
(2) 24
(3) 48
(4) 54
(5) 72

Questions 22 and 23 are based on the following graph.

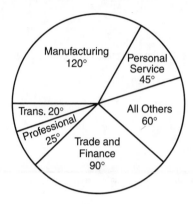

This circle graph shows how 180,000 wage earners in a certain city earned their livings during a given period.

22. The number of persons engaged in transportation in the city during this period was
    (1) 3,600
    (2) 9,000
    (3) 10,000
    (4) 18,000
    (5) 36,000

23. If the number of persons in trade and finance is represented by M, then the number in manufacturing is represented as
    (1) $M \div 3$
    (2) $M + 3$
    (3) $30M$
    (4) $4M \div 3$
    (5) Not enough information is given.

Question 24 is based on the following figure.

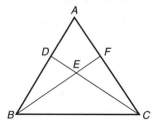

24. If $\overline{BF}$ bisects $\angle ABC$, $\overline{CD}$ bisects $\angle ACB$, m$\angle ABC$ = 68°,
and m$\angle ACB$ = 72°, then m$\angle BEC$ =
- (1) 90°
- (2) 98°
- (3) 100°
- (4) 110°
- (5) 120°

---

25. Bill has $5 more than Jack, and Jack has $3 less than Frank. If Frank has
$30, how much money does Bill have?
- (1) $30
- (2) $27
- (3) $32
- (4) $36
- (5) Not enough information is given.

26. John Davis weighed 192 pounds. His doctor put him on a diet, which
enabled him to lose at least 4 pounds per month. What was John's
weight after 6 months on the diet?
- (1) 160 lb.
- (2) 165 lb.
- (3) 167 lb.
- (4) 168 lb.
- (5) Not enough information is given.

27. Mr. Ames bought a bond for $10,000. The bond yields interest at $8\frac{1}{2}$%
annually. If the interest is paid every 6 months, how much is each
interest payment?
- (1) $400
- (2) $425
- (3) $475
- (4) $500
- (5) $850

28. An aquarium is in the form of a rectangular solid. The aquarium is 3 feet
long, 1 foot 8 inches wide, and 1 foot 6 inches high. What is the volume,
in cubic feet, of the aquarium?
- (1) 6.16
- (2) 6.4
- (3) 7.5

(4) 7.875

(5) 8.64

29. The ratio of men to women at a professional meeting was 9:2. If there were 12 women at the meeting, how many men were at the meeting?

(1) 33

(2) 44

(3) 54

(4) 66

(5) Not enough information is given.

30. What is the slope of the line that passes through point A (2,1) and point B (4,7)?

(1) 1/3

(2) 2/3

(3) 3/2

(4) 2

(5) 3

31. In a basketball game Bill scored three times as many points as Jim. Together they scored 56 points. How many points did Bill score?

(1) 14

(2) 28

(3) 42

(4) 48

(5) Not enough information is given.

Question 32 is based on the following graph.

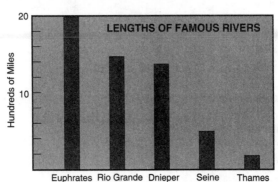

32. The graph shows the lengths of some famous rivers correct to the nearest hundred miles.

Which one of the following statements is correct?
(1) The Thames is more than one-half as long as the Seine.
(2) The Dnieper is 1,200 miles long.
(3) The Euphrates is about 250 miles longer than the Rio Grande.
(4) The Rio Grande is about 1,000 miles longer than the Seine.
(5) The Thames is about 100 miles long.

Question 33 is based on the following graph.

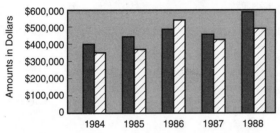

RECEIPTS AND EXPENDITURES

33. The graph shows receipts and expenses for the years indicated. The receipts are designated by shaded bars and the expenses by striped bars.

The year in which receipts exceeded expenses by $100,000 was
(1) 1984
(2) 1985
(3) 1986
(4) 1987
(5) 1988

34. If 1 pencil costs y cents, then 6 pencils will cost, in cents,
(1) $6y$
(2) $\dfrac{y}{6}$
(3) $\dfrac{6}{y}$
(4) $y + 6$
(5) $\dfrac{y}{2}$

35. Mr. Martin earns \$12 per hour. One week Mr. Martin worked 42 hours; the following week he worked 37 hours. Which of the following indicates the number of dollars Mr. Martin earned for the 2 weeks?
   (1) $12 \times 2 + 37$
   (2) $12 \times 42 + 42 \times 37$
   (3) $12 \times 37 + 42$
   (4) $12 + 42 \times 37$
   (5) $12(42 + 37)$

36. The enrollment of a college is distributed as follows:
   360 freshmen
   300 sophomores
   280 juniors
   260 seniors

   The freshman class makes up what percent of the total enrollment?
   (1) 18%
   (2) 20%
   (3) 25%
   (4) 30%
   (5) Not enough information is given.

Question 37 is based on the following figure.

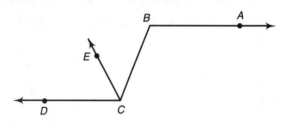

37. In the figure $\overrightarrow{AB}$ II $\overleftrightarrow{CD}$, $\overrightarrow{CE}$ bisects $\angle BCD$, and m$\angle ABC = 112°$. Find m$\angle ECD$.
   (1) 45°
   (2) 50°
   (3) 56°
   (4) 60°
   (5) Not enough information is given.

38. Mrs. Garvin buys a bolt of cloth 22 feet 4 inches in length. She cuts the bolt into four equal pieces to make drapes. What is the length of each piece?

   (1) 5 ft.

   (2) 5 ft. 7 in.

   (3) 5 ft. 9 in.

   (4) 6 ft. 7 in.

   (5) Not enough information is given.

Questions 39 and 40 are based on the following graph.

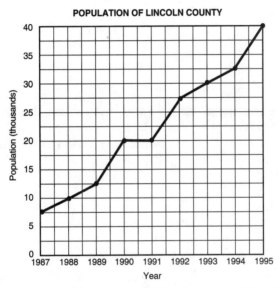

POPULATION OF LINCOLN COUNTY

The graph shows the growth in population in Lincoln County between the years 1987 and 1995.

39. What was the population of Lincoln County in the year 1992?

   (1) 20,000

   (2) 25,000

   (3) 26,000

   (4) 27,500

   (5) 30,000

40. The population of Lincoln County did not change between the years
  - (1) 1988 and 1989
  - (2) 1989 and 1990
  - (3) 1990 and 1991
  - (4) 1991 and 1992
  - (5) 1992 and 1993

---

41. A box is in the form of a rectangular solid with a square base of side x units in length and a height of 8 units. The volume of the box is 392 cubic units. Which of the following equations may be used to find the value of x?
  - (1) $x^2 = 392$
  - (2) $8x = 392$
  - (3) $8x^3 = 392$
  - (4) $8x^2 = 392$
  - (5) $8 + x^2 = 392$

42. There were three candidates at a school board election. Mrs. Clay received twice as many votes as Mr. Dunn, and Mr. Arnold received 66 votes more than Mr. Dunn. How many votes did Mrs. Clay receive?
  - (1) 209
  - (2) 275
  - (3) 320
  - (4) 402
  - (5) Not enough information is given.

Question 43 is based on the following figure.

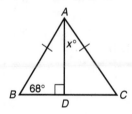

43. If $\overline{AB} = AC$, $\overline{AD} \perp \overline{BC}$, and m$\angle B = 68°$, what is the value of x?
  - (1) 12°
  - (2) 22°
  - (3) 32°
  - (4) 44°
  - (5) 68°

44. A hiker walks 12 miles due north. Then he turns and walks 16 miles due east. At this point, how many miles is the hiker from his starting point?

    (1) 12

    (2) 16

    (3) 18

    (4) 20

    (5) Not enough information is given.

45. The square root of 30 is between which of the following pairs of numbers?

    (1) 3 and 4

    (2) 4 and 5

    (3) 5 and 6

    (4) 6 and 7

    (5) 15 and 16

Question 46 is based on the following figure.

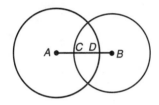

46. The radius of circle A measures 20 inches, and the radius of circle B measures 8 inches. If $CD = 6$ inches, find AB, in inches.

    (1) 22

    (2) 24

    (3) 25

    (4) 28

    (5) Not enough information is given.

Question 47 is based on the following figure.

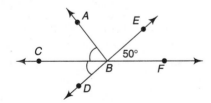

47. $\overleftrightarrow{CF}$ and $\overleftrightarrow{ED}$ intersect at B, m$\angle EBF = 50°$ and $\overrightarrow{CB}$ bisects $\angle ABD$. Find m$\angle ABC$.

(1) 30°
(2) 32°
(3) 40°
(4) 50°
(5) 60°

---

48. A woman buys *n* pounds of sugar at *c* cents a pound. She gives the clerk a $1.00 bill. The change she receives, in cents, is

(1) $nc - 100$
(2) $n + c - 100$
(3) $100 - (n + c)$
(4) $100 - nc$
(5) Not enough information is given.

49. Of a high school graduating class, 85% planned to go to college. If 170 graduates planned to go to college, how many students were in the graduating class?

(1) 200
(2) 250
(3) 340
(4) 400
(5) 500

Question 50 is based on the following figure.

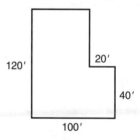

50. Mr. Denby planned to build a house on the plot of ground shown. What is the area, in square feet, of this plot of ground?

(1) 10,000
(2) 10,400
(3) 10,800
(4) 12,000
(5) 104,000

51. If $x = 10$, each of the following is true EXCEPT

  (1) $3x + 1 > 12$

  (2) $2x - 3 < 25$

  (3) $x^2 + 1 > x^2 - 1$

  (4) $4x - 1 = 39$

  (5) $2x - 7 < 7 - 2x$

52. In a right triangle the measure of one acute angle is 4 times as great as the measure of the other acute angle. What is the measure of the larger acute angle?

  (1) $18°$

  (2) $36°$

  (3) $40°$

  (4) $65°$

  (5) $72°$

53. The cost of borrowing a book from a circulating library is $0.50 for the first 3 days and $0.15 per day thereafter. A formula for finding the cost (C), in cents, of borrowing a book for n days ($n \geq 3$) is

  (1) $C = 50 + 15n$

  (2) $C = 50 + 15(n + 3)$

  (3) $C = 50(n - 3) + 15n$

  (4) $C = 50 + 15(n - 3)$

  (5) $C = 50(n + 3) + 15n$

Questions 54 and 55 are based on the following information.

In the figure below line $\overleftrightarrow{PQ}$ is parallel to line $\overleftrightarrow{RS}$.

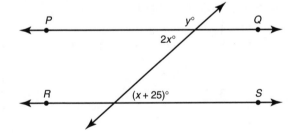

54. What is the value of x?

  (1) 15

  (2) 20

  (3) 25

(4) 30

(5) 35

55. What is the value of y?

(1) 130°

(2) 135°

(3) 140°

(4) 145°

(5) Not enough information is given.

---

56. Given the equation $x^2 - x - 12 = 0$, which of the following give(s) a complete solution of the equation?

(1) 4 only

(2) −4 only

(3) 3 and 4

(4) −3 and 4

(5) −4 and 3

ANSWER KEYS, SUMMARIES OF RESULTS, AND SELF-APPRAISAL CHARTS

TEST 1: WRITING SKILLS, PART I

I. CHECK YOUR ANSWERS, using the following answer key:

1.	**2**	12.	**1**	23.	**5**	34.	**4**	45.	**5**
2.	**3**	13.	**5**	24.	**3**	35.	**3**	46.	**2**
3.	**3**	14.	**2**	25.	**5**	36.	**2**	47.	**5**
4.	**1**	15.	**2**	26.	**5**	37.	**4**	48.	**1**
5.	**4**	16.	**3**	27.	**4**	38.	**2**	49.	**4**
6.	**5**	17.	**5**	28.	**1**	39.	**5**	50.	**1**
7.	**2**	18.	**3**	29.	**2**	40.	**5**	51.	**2**
8.	**3**	19.	**4**	30.	**1**	41.	**1**	52.	**4**
9.	**5**	20.	**3**	31.	**5**	42.	**4**	53.	**5**
10.	**4**	21.	**2**	32.	**1**	43.	**3**	54.	**1**
11.	**5**	22.	**5**	33.	**2**	44.	**1**	55.	**4**

II. SCORE YOURSELF:

Number correct:

Excellent _____

50–55

Good _____

44–49

Fair _____

36–43

III. EVALUATE YOUR SCORE: Did you get at least 38 correct answers? If not, you need more practice for the Writing Skills, Part I test. In any event, you can improve your performance to Excellent or Good by analyzing your errors.

IV. ANALYZE YOUR ERRORS: To determine your areas of weakness, list the number of correct answers you had under each of the following categories (which correspond to the content areas of the Writing Skills, Part I test), and compare your score with the average scores specified in the right-hand column. Review the answer analysis section beginning on page 447 for each of the questions you got wrong, and give yourself more practice in your weak areas with the appropriate material in Unit II before attempting Practice Examination One.

CONTENT AREAS	ITEMS	YOUR SCORE	AVERAGE SCORE
Sentence Structure	3, 5, 12, 16, 25, 29, 32, 34, 38, 40, 44, 49, 53, 55	_____	10
Usage	1, 8, 19, 20, 24, 52, 54	_____	5
Spelling	7, 10, 15, 18, 27–28, 43, 46, 48, 50	_____	7
Punctuation	2, 4, 14, 21, 26, 30, 33, 35–37, 41–42, 51	_____	9
Capitalization	4	_____	1
No correction	6, 9, 11, 13, 17, 22–23, 31, 39, 45, 47	_____	8
	Total	_____	

TEST 2: SOCIAL STUDIES

I. CHECK YOUR ANSWERS, using the following answer key:

1. **1**	14. **4**	27. **4**	40. **3**	53. **1**
2. **4**	15. **1**	28. **3**	41. **5**	54. **3**
3. **4**	16. **3**	29. **2**	42. **2**	55. **5**
4. **5**	17. **2**	30. **5**	43. **1**	56. **5**
5. **2**	18. **2**	31. **3**	44. **1**	57. **1**
6. **5**	19. **4**	32. **4**	45. **5**	58. **2**
7. **4**	20. **4**	33. **1**	46. **4**	59. **1**
8. **2**	21. **1**	34. **1**	47. **1**	60. **2**
9. **4**	22. **2**	35. **5**	48. **4**	61. **3**
10. **4**	23. **5**	36. **1**	49. **1**	62. **4**
11. **1**	24. **4**	37. **1**	50. **3**	63. **1**
12. **3**	25. **2**	38. **1**	51. **2**	64. **1**
13. **2**	26. **3**	39. **1**	52. **5**	

II. SCORE YOURSELF:

Number correct:

Excellent	_____
	57–64
Good	_____
	51–56
Fair	_____
	45–50

III. EVALUATE YOUR SCORE: Did you get at least 45 correct answers? If not, you need more practice for the Social Studies test. In any event, you can improve your performance to Excellent or Good by analyzing your errors.

II. ANALYZE YOUR ERRORS: To determine your specific weaknesses, list the number of correct answers you had under each of the following categories (which correspond to the content areas of the Social Studies test), and compare your score with the average scores specified in the right-hand column. Review the answer analysis section beginning on page 450 for each of the questions you got wrong, and give yourself more practice in your weak area.

CONTENT AREAS	ITEMS	YOUR SCORE	AVERAGE SCORE
Political Science	1–3, 12, 29–31, 34, 41–43, 44, 48–49, 56, 59	_____	9
Economics	4–6, 9, 17–19, 21–22, 24, 26–28, 32–33, 35–37, 39–40, 52–54	_____	13
History	15–16, 20, 25, 38, 50–51, 57–58, 62–63, 64	_____	8
Geography	7–8, 10–11,13–14, 23, 45–47, 55, 60–61	_____	9
	Total	_____	

TEST 3: SCIENCE

I. CHECK YOUR ANSWERS, using the following answer key:

1.	2	15.	1	29.	4	43.	5	57.	4
2.	4	16.	1	30.	5	44.	1	58.	1
3.	2	17.	1	31.	5	45.	4	59.	2
4.	4	18.	2	32.	4	46.	3	60.	2
5.	3	19.	4	33.	1	47.	3	61.	2
6.	3	20.	3	34.	3	48.	2	62.	3
7.	4	21.	4	35.	5	49.	2	63.	3
8.	5	22.	5	36.	5	50.	2	64.	2
9.	2	23.	4	37.	3	51.	5	65.	5
10.	5	24.	5	38.	4	52.	2	66.	4
11.	1	25.	3	39.	3	53.	5		
12.	4	26.	5	40.	3	54.	5		
13.	5	27.	4	41.	1	55.	5		
14.	3	28.	3	42.	3	56.	2		

II. SCORE YOURSELF:

Number correct:

Excellent _____

60–66

Good _____

49–59

Fair _____

40–48

III. EVALUATE YOUR SCORE: Did you get at least 40 correct answers? If not, you need more practice for the Science test. In any event, you can improve your performance to Excellent or Good by analyzing your errors.

IV. ANALYZE YOUR ERRORS: To determine your specific weaknesses, encircle the number of each question that you got wrong. This will reveal the specific science area that needs emphasis in planning your study program. After studying the answer analysis section beginning on page 455 for each of the questions you got wrong, give yourself more practice in your weak areas.

CONTENT AREAS	ITEMS	YOUR SCORE	AVERAGE SCORE
Biology	1–4, 24–39, 41–43, 45–49, 59, 61–66	_____	24
Earth Science	9–13, 17–19, 40, 44, 55–58	_____	7
Chemistry	20–23, 44, 50–52	_____	6
Physics	5–8, 14–16, 53–54, 60	_____	7
	Total	_____	

TEST 4: INTERPRETING LITERATURE AND THE ARTS

I. CHECK YOUR ANSWERS, using the following answer key:

1.	3	10.	5	19.	3	28.	3	37.	3
2.	1	11.	2	20.	3	29.	5	38.	1
3.	4	12.	3	21.	3	30.	3	39.	4
4.	4	13.	2	22.	5	31.	1	40.	3
5.	1	14.	4	23.	3	32.	4	41.	4
6.	3	15.	1	24.	4	33.	1	42.	5
7.	1	16.	1	25.	4	34.	1	43.	1
8.	2	17.	3	26.	3	35.	5	44.	3
9.	3	18.	4	27.	2	36.	4	45.	4

II. SCORE YOURSELF:

Number correct:

Excellent _____
41–45

Good _____
36–40

Fair _____
31–35

III. EVALUATE YOUR SCORE: Did you get at least 31 correct answers? If not, you need more practice for the test on Interpreting Literature and the Arts. In any event, you can improve your performance to Excellent or Good by analyzing your errors.

IV. ANALYZE YOUR ERRORS: To determine your specific weaknesses, first list the number of correct answers you had under each of the following categories and compare your score with the average scores specified in the right-hand column. After studying the answer analysis section beginning on page 460 for each of the questions you got wrong, study the material in the section Basic Reading Skills and the section Reading Prose, Poetry, and Drama to strengthen your weak areas.

READING SKILLS	ITEMS	YOUR SCORE	AVERAGE SCORE
Locating the Main Idea	5, 16, 21, 44	_____	3
Finding Details	2, 3, 12, 17–18, 23–24, 32–33, 38–45	_____	11
Inferring Meaning	13–15, 19–20, 22, 34–35	_____	5
Making Inferences	1, 4, 7, 10, 25, 36–37	_____	5
Determining Tone and Mood	6, 9, 26–27, 31	_____	4
Inferring Character	11, 28–30	_____	3
Inferring Setting	8	_____	1
	Total	_____	

Now, to see how your scores in the content areas of Interpreting Literature and the Arts test compare with the average scores in the right-hand column, list your score for each of the following:

CONTENT AREAS	ITEMS	YOUR SCORE	AVERAGE SCORE
Current Literature	6–10, 16–35	_____	17
Earlier Literature	1–5, 11–15	_____	7
Commentary	36–45	_____	7
	Total	_____	

LITERARY FORMS	ITEMS	YOUR SCORE	AVERAGE SCORE
Prose Fiction	6–15	_____	7
Prose Nonfiction	1–5, 31–35	_____	7
Prose Nonfiction (Commentary)	36–45	_____	7
Poetry	16–25	_____	7
Drama	26–30	_____	3
	Total	_____	

Note: While Commentary on the Arts is a content area in itself, the commentary, as written, is in the form of prose nonfiction.

TEST 5: MATHEMATICS

I. CHECK YOUR ANSWERS, using the following answer key:

1.	2	13.	4	25.	3	37.	3	49.	1
2.	4	14.	1	26.	5	38.	2	50.	2
3.	1	15.	2	27.	2	39.	4	51.	5
4.	5	16.	4	28.	3	40.	3	52.	5
5.	1	17.	5	29.	3	41.	4	53.	4
6.	2	18.	3	30.	5	42.	5	54.	3
7.	5	19.	3	31.	3	43.	2	55.	1
8.	2	20.	2	32.	4	44.	4	56.	4
9.	4	21.	3	33.	5	45.	3		
10.	2	22.	3	34.	1	46.	1		
11.	1	23.	4	35.	5	47.	4		
12.	4	24.	4	36.	4	48.	4		

II. SCORE YOURSELF:

Number correct:

Excellent	_____
	41–45
Good	_____
	36–40
Fair	_____
	31–35

III. EVALUATE YOUR SCORE: Did you get at least 38 correct answers? If not, you need more practice for the Mathematics test. In any event, you can improve your performance to Excellent or Good by analyzing your errors.

IV. ANALYZE YOUR ERRORS: To determine your specific weakness, list the number of correct answers you had under each of the following skill areas, and compare your score with the average scores specified in the right-hand column. After studying the answer analysis section beginning on page 462 for each of the questions you got wrong, give yourself more practice in your weak areas.

CONTENT AREAS	ITEMS	YOUR SCORE	AVERAGE SCORE
Arithmetic	1–2, 4, 6, 8, 10–14, 16–20, 22–23, 25–27, 32–33, 35–36, 38–40, 45	_____	18
Algebra	5, 7, 15, 21, 28–29, 31, 34, 41–42, 48–49, 51–53, 55–56	_____	11
Geometry	3, 9, 24, 30, 37, 43–44, 46–47, 50, 54	_____	7
	Total	_____	

YOUR TOTAL GED SCORE

The Writing Skills Test   _____

The Social Studies Test   _____

The Science Test   _____

The Interpreting Literature
and the Arts Test   _____

The Mathematics Test   _____

                                    Total   _____

ANSWER ANALYSIS

TEST 1: WRITING SKILLS, PART I

1. **2** There is an error in usage. The subject of the sentence is *combination*, which is singular. A singular verb, *makes*, is required for agreement.
2. **3** The error is in punctuation. A comma is needed to set off an introductory phrase.
3. **3** There is a sentence fragment beginning with *seldom*. This is corrected by removing the period and joining the fragment to the rest of the sentence.
4. **1** There is an error in capitalization. Seasons are *not* capitalized.
5. **4** The run-on sentence can be corrected by subordinating the second idea to the first. *Some...vegetables* can be frozen...while *other vegetables can be stored...in a cool area.*
6. **5** No correction is necessary.
7. **2** The correct spelling is *exercise*.
8. **3** The usage error is in the shift in person in two pronouns that refer to the same person. The second-person pronoun *your* in the introductory clause requires a continuation of the second person, *you,* in the main clause.
9. **5** No change is necessary.
10. **4** The correct spelling is *assistance*.
11. **5** No correction is necessary.
12. **1** The original is correct. Two sentences are needed.
13. **5** No correction is necessary.
14. **2** A comma is required to set off items in a series.
15. **2** *Equipment* is the correct spelling.
16. **3** The meaning of the sentence requires *may be served*.
17. **5** No correction is necessary.
18. **3** The correct spelling is *their* rather than *they're*, which is a contraction of *they are*.
19. **4** There is an error in usage. Parallel structure requires the use of infinitives: *to develop, to increase, to learn* (rather than *learning*).
20. **3** The sentence requires the use of *there are* rather than *they are* (they're). *They are a number of...steps* doesn't make sense.
21. **2** A comma is required after the introductory clause "While...protection."
22. **5** No correction is necessary.
23. **5** No correction is necessary.

24. **3** The future tense should be used for an action taking place in the future, that is, *when* you take the car in.

25. **5** Two sentences are necessary to correct the run-on sentence. To accomplish this, a period after *order* and a capitalized *That* are needed.

26. **5** No correction is necessary.

27. **4** The correct spelling is *determined*.

28. **1** The correct spelling is *receive*.

29. **2** The rewritten sentence should read "A buying decision is affected by total dollars...."

30. **1** A comma is needed to set off items in a series.

31. **5** No correction is necessary.

32. **1** The original way is the best among the choices offered.

33. **2** Commas are used to set off words or phrases that interrupt the normal word order of the sentence.

34. **4** The relative pronoun *that* avoids the unnecessary use of the words *such programs*.

35. **3** A semicolon is used to separate independent clauses in a sentence.

36. **2** A comma is used after an introductory clause.

37. **4** An apostrophe must be added after the plural noun *shoppers'* to show possession.

38. **2** Making "You are going to move" the subject of the verb *is* eliminates the need for "That statement" and effectively combines the two sentences.

39. **5** No correction is necessary

40. **5** *Or* is correct because "another way" to state the fact is given.

41. **1** A comma is used after an introductory phrase.

42. **4** A comma is used to set off items in a series.

43. **3** The correct spelling is *fulfillment*.

44. **1** The original is correct because *or* connects two independent clauses (*has come through* is understood after *an opportunity to move to a better climate*).

45. **5** No correction is necessary.

46. **2** The correct spelling is *familiar*.

47. **5** No correction is necessary.

48. **1** The correct spelling is *available*.

49. **4** Rewriting the sentence with *The next phase* as the subject requires a singular verb, *is*, in the present tense.

50. **1** The correct spelling is *stationary* when the reference is to a nonmoving object.

51. **2** A phrase inserted in a sentence is set off by commas. Here the second comma should be inserted after *tip*.
52. **4** The subject, *timing*, is singular and the verb *controls* must agree in number with the subject.
53. **5** This is necessary to correct the run-on sentence.
54. **1** An adverb, *nearly*, is necessary when the word modified is an adjective.
55. **4** The sentences can be combined by using an adjective clause, beginning with *which include*, to describe the noun *game fish*.

TEST 1: WRITING SKILLS, PART II
SAMPLE ESSAY

I remember the day that I fell of the back of my brother's bicycle. The memory is still so vivid in my mind. I will always remember it.

It was a beautiful spring day in 1967 when my older brother and I decided to go bike riding on the same bike. My brother's bicycle was an old Easy Rider with a saddle seat and a fender that went over the back tire. The fender was my "seat." As I straddled the back tire on the fender and we began our journey up a large hill I remember telling him, "I'm slipping off the fender!" "Just hold on," was his reply. I tried but my little seven-year old hands just couldn't do the trick. I slid right onto the asphalt roadway. My hands and knees took the brunt of the force and as I got up I looked down to see two very badly skinned knees. Crying, my brother helped me hobble back to the house where my mother was none too sympathetic with the sight of my terribly skinned knees. In fact, she was upset with me too because I was to wear a short dress the next night for my Bible School Program. She had warned me not to ride on the back of the bike. I suppose I should have listened.

What a day that was in 1967. It still seems like yesterday when I sat straddled on that old bicycle just before slipping off. I'll never forget it.

TEST 2: SOCIAL STUDIES

1. **1** The last paragraph of the passage states clearly that the governor's veto power is not used sparingly, and that more than one out of four bills fails to receive approval.

2. **4** The second paragraph of the selection deals with the "30 day" rule. The first sentence of this paragraph states that all bills passed within the last ten days of the legislative session are covered by this rule.

3. **4** The first sentence of the first paragraph states that the governor has the power to veto single items of the budget bill. This is an authority not possessed by the president of the United States.

4. **5** Nearly all of the selection deals with a plan of action for use before the consumer buys. See the second sentence and also the first words of the third paragraph.

5. **2** The consumer is advised to get all promises in writing.

6. **5** It is specifically mentioned that pro rata (or partial) return of moneys and credit toward a replacement may be part of a warranty.

7. **4** By 2030, increasing numbers of Americans will reach the age that makes them eligible for Social Security benefits.

8. **2** A large increase in the birth rate would cause the average age to become lower since the many babies added to the population would counteract the older Americans.

9. **4** Persons concerned with the natural environment fear that an emphasis on greater production and consumption will mean further pollution of the air (by factory smokestacks and apartment house incinerators) and of rivers, lakes, and streams (by industrial wastes and sewage disposal); and increased problems of solid waste disposal and rising noise levels.

10. **4** There is no movement toward a solution to the energy problem as long as the two cyclists representing energy and environment keep pedaling in different directions.

11. **1** A fivefold increase in the price of imported crude oil from 1973 to 1980 severely affected the U.S. economy and forced a search for alternative domestic sources of energy, despite possible immediate negative effects on the environment.

12. **3** This is directly related to the big change from isolationism to internationalism in U.S. foreign policy. From 1920 to 1940 we had no political or military ties to non-American countries, and we never joined the League of Nations. Since World War II, which ended in 1945, the United States has pursued policies of collective security. President F. D. Roosevelt called for the United Nations, of which we are a charter member. President Truman committed U.S. aid to

Europe through the Marshall Plan, the Truman Doctrine, and NATO. Subsequent presidents have continued economic aid to Asia and Africa, military assistance to Middle East and Asian nations, and commitments to Korea and Vietnam. President Kennedy started the Peace Corps, and President Nixon tried to negotiate peace in Vietnam and in Israel. Each of the other choices involves areas in which the Congress, the Supreme Court, and the states have been more influential than the president.

13. **2** The passage states that the Arctic and the Antarctic are "imaginary markers on the Earth's surface."

14. **4** It is stated that both the Tropic of Cancer and the Tropic of Capricorn run parallel to the equator.

15. **1** The Gettysburg Address was delivered in 1863. Fourscore and seven years earlier—that is, 87 years earlier—the Declaration of Independence had been signed. It declared the liberty of the thirteen colonies and stated that all men are created equal.

16. **3** The speech was delivered at the Gettsyburg cemetery. In the second paragraph, Lincoln states that this is the purpose of the occasion.

17. **2** Lacking land for agriculture, Nation A will use its abundant labor, capital, and management skills to develop industry. The resulting products can be sold to domestic and foreign markets.

18. **2** In the 1800s, Great Britain led the world in manufactures and resembled Nation A in factors of production.

19. **4** Nation B, with its natural resources and labor, must encourage new industries by protectionist tariffs and by tax concessions to attract capital investment.

20. **4** The purpose of the Truman Doctrine, as opposed to President Monroe's policy of noninterference, was to support the governments of Greece and Turkey against direct and indirect Communist aggression. In 1947 Greece was in especially weakened condition following Nazi occupation during World War II, and was under attack by Communist guerrilla bands.

21. **1** From '60 to '65, the increase was 29.3% minus 18.6%, or 10.7%, greater than for any other interval.

22. **2** Between '70 and '80, the percentage of women working part time remained unchanged at 35.1%.

23. **5** Area E is farthest from a large body of water and moisture from the ocean by the prevailing winds would fall as rain before reaching Area E.

24. **4** A recession takes place in the economy when purchasing, saving, and business profits go down. The result is an increase in unemployment and a period of reduced economic activity—a recession.

25. **2** Social Darwinism became popular in the second half of the 19th century. It applied Darwin's theory of natural selection to people and nations, attempting thereby to justify the widening gap between the rich and the poor in the United States.

26. **3** The income group, $25,000 to $49,999, is at or close to 30%, more than any of the others.

27. **4** The largest increase was in the $50,000 to $99,999 group, from 20% to 25%.

28. **3** The number of families with stock holdings increased in each of the years indicated.

29. **2** The purpose of this speech by President Lyndon Johnson was to help troubled young people lead productive lives. In dealing with delinquent and potentially delinquent youth, he was concerned first about preventing them from getting into trouble; then, if they did, in helping them to become useful citizens. These ideas are stated in the first two paragraphs.

30. **5** President Johnson states that he recommends the Juvenile Delinquency Prevention Act of 1967.

31. **3** Family counseling is recommended because so many delinquents "live in broken families, burdened with...problems."

32. **4** Economic controls tried by government have been unable to slow down or catch up with the greased pig of runaway price inflation.

33. **1** Higher interest rates discourage bank loans by business owners and consumers, thereby decreasing the amount of money in circulation and reducing the rate of inflation.

34. **1** Comparing the two graphs reveals that the electoral vote is much different from the popular vote.

35. **5** The movies are not mentioned as a media type.

36. **1** The 8- to 18-year-olds has the highest percentage, 51%, and whites at 45% have a higher computer use than Blacks and Hispanics.

37. **1** As an activity, watching TV is well ahead of the other six mentioned.

38. **1** A primary source is an eyewitness account of an event, such as a description in a diary, or an artifact constructed in a specific time period.

39. **1** With a drop of 12.7%, the weekly earnings fell the most for women with no high school diploma.

40. **3** The graph indicates that median earnings for whites and Hispanics exceeded those for Blacks with an associate degree.

41. **5** Lobbyists are representatives of special-interest groups who attempt to influence congressmen by providing information, preparing bills, and testifying at hearings.

42. **2** (*B*) Lobbyists sometimes use undesirable ways of influencing legislation by giving gifts and campaign contributions. The laws they sponsor may not benefit the general public.

43. **1** (*A*) Thousands of bills in many areas are introduced during each session of Congress. These must be handled by standing committees who try to bring expertise to each subject.

44. **1** Out of concern for their own reelection, legislators (the Boy Scouts in the cartoon) introduce consumer protection bills during an election year.

45. **5** Parents, teachers, and age peers are mentioned in the two classes of socializing agents.

46. **4** In the last sentence, all of the reasons are mentioned except the *number* of peers. The group is mentioned as being of increasing importance.

47. **1** The passage, in the second sentence, refers to the great influence of the family.

48. **4** Speaker *A* is talking about a world made smaller by modern technology. Speaker *B* agrees and adds that the problems of any area now become the problems of all humankind. Both feel that, as the world becomes one community, interdependence is a factor in world survival.

49. **1** Ethnocentrism is the view that one's own culture is superior to all others. Speaker *C* is calling for the appreciation of other people's value systems and ways of life.

50. **3** The extermination of over six million people, nearly all Jews, by the Nazi regime in Germany is called the Holocaust.

51. **2** The Nuremberg Trials after World War II, conducted by the Allies against Germany and Japan, established the principle that individuals are responsible to a higher law than that of individual nations. Acts against humanity could not be defended on the grounds of having to follow orders from a superior.

52. **5** A supply-side economist would welcome cutbacks in government spending to eliminate deficits. An action by the president that sought to cut spending would be supported by a supply-side economist.

53. **1** Mercantilism advocates tariffs to protect local industries from foreign competition.

54. **3** A company is bought out by its employees. This action would be in the direction of the Marxist belief that the means of production should be controlled by the workers.

55. **5** Basketball is a part of U.S. culture that has been adopted by the Russians through the process of cultural diffusion.

56. **5** Thoreau urged his followers to refuse to obey unjust laws, and he himself disobeyed laws that he considered unjust; in other words, he practiced civil disobedience.

57. **1** The Immigration Act of 1965 established occupation as a basic factor in selecting immigrants according to current needs, particularly in technology.

58. **2** Both the immigration policy suggested in the cartoon and the U.S. immigration policy in the 1920s show a preference for certain groups, be they specific nationalities (as in the 1920s) or programmers and electrical engineers (as in the cartoon).

59. **1** President Nixon refused to turn the Watergate tapes over to Congress until the Supreme Court told him that his continued refusal would be an unconstitutional act. This check by the judiciary on the powers of the executive branch of government is an illustration of the system of checks and balances.

60. **2** The graph shows a projected Latin American population of about 600 million people by the year 2000, as opposed to an estimated 300 million for North America (the United States and Canada).

61. **3** Improved nutrition and medical care help account for an increase in the growth rate of the Latin American population.

62. **4** The cartoon shows that people in underdeveloped nations lack basic necessities, whereas people in developed nations have more than they need. The point is made by showing a child in Bangladesh, one of the poorest, most overpopulated nations, who is unable to find drinkable water while an American can choose from an abundance and variety of food.

63. **1** The stark contrast in diet for Americans and Bangladeshi is designed by the cartoonist to arouse our pity for the underfed and to motivate us to do something about the situation.

64. **1** This quotation from a speech on March 12, 1947, has come to be known as the Truman Doctrine. Truman asked for and got $400 million in economic and financial aid to Greece and Turkey to help them resist the "outside pressures" of communism.

TEST 3: SCIENCE

1. **2** Human, monkey, ape, and chimpanzee all belong to the primate group of mammals.

2. **4** Evolution is a process in all of life, not just humans or chimpanzees. Fossils and anatomy provide some of the evidence for evolution.

3. **2** Fossils are the remains of actual living things of the past, so they give the most direct evidence that different forms of life existed.

4. **4** The discovery that today's men are different in size from those of only a few hundred years ago suggests that evolution has not stopped.

5. **3** Use the formula:

$$\text{Density} = \frac{\text{mass}}{\text{volume}}$$

$$\frac{24 \text{ g}}{8 \text{ cm}^3} = 3 \text{ g/cm}^3$$

6. **3** The diagram indicates that the density of sample B is 3 g/cm^3. If the sample were split in half, the density would remain the same. The density of a sample is the ratio of its mass to its volume. When the sample is cut in half, both the mass and the volume of the sample are also reduced by half. As a result, the density remains the same.

7. **4** The mass and volume for different samples of a given substance are directly proportional. This relationship is illustrated by graph 4, which shows a direct relationship between mass and volume. As mass increases, volume increases proportionally.

8. **5** To answer this question, the volumes of samples A and B must first be calculated.

Volume = length × width × height

For A: Volume =
   2 cm × 2 cm × 2 cm = 8 cm^3
For B: Volume =
   3 cm × 2 cm × 1 cm = 6 cm^3
The volume for sample C is given as 12 cm^3. Sample C therefore has the largest volume, and sample B has the smallest volume.

9. **2** According to the theory of continental drift and plate tectonics, the surface of the Earth is moving. The undersea volcanic vent, however, opens deep into the center of the Earth and is stable. One theory about the formation of the Hawaiian Islands suggests that a section of the Earth moves over the volcanic vent, which spews forth enough

material to form an island; then, as a new section of Earth moves over the vent, another island is formed.

10. **5** $2.5 \times 4,800$ ft./sec. = 12,000 ft.

11. **1** An electromagnet is the only type of magnet that can be turned on and off.

12. **4** That Earth is a magnet is proved by the fact that the planet can exert a magnetic force.

13. **5** Lodestone is a well-known natural magnet.

14. **3** In diesel engines the tight-fitting pistons compress air and thus cause the temperature to rise above the kindling temperature of the heavy fuels used. This serves the same purpose as the spark plugs in the gasoline engine.

15. **1** Locomotives can easily carry the heavy diesel engine and thus take advantage of using a less expensive fuel.

16. **1** Because of the strong compression stroke, diesel engines are very heavy and therefore not suitable for airplanes.

17. **1** Earthquakes are the result of the movement of rock masses below the Earth's surface, resulting in breaking rock layers and displacement (fault) of segments of the layer at the breaking point. The folding of rock layers results from the action of lesser forces acting over a longer period of time. The forces produced by landslides are too small to create an earthquake.

18. **2** The 1989 earthquake in San Francisco killed many people because older buildings and roadways were not built to withstand such a severe shock. The more modern buildings stood.

19. **4** It is shock waves in the crust that a seismograph detects, whether they are produced by earthquakes or by nuclear explosions.

20. **3** A calcium atom with a valence of +2 has two electrons in its outer ring. Chlorine with a valence of −1 needs one electron to complete its outer ring. Two chlorine atoms can combine with one atom of calcium to form calcium chloride ($CaCl_2$).

21. **4** Atomic mass (number of protons plus number of neutrons) minus atomic number (number of protons) equals number of neutrons. For lithium, $7 - 3 = 4$.

22. **5** The atomic number is equal to the number of protons.

23. **4** This element, sodium, which has 11 protons, must have 11 electrons in its shells. The first shell holds 2, and the second shell holds 8, leaving 1 electron in its outer shell. Since it can lend this electron to another atom, it has a valence of +1.

24. **5** Many parts of the plant are involved, but it is in the chloroplasts that the actual chemical process takes place.

25. **3** Water from the soil is conducted through the xylem.

26. **5** Chemical energy is needed to split water into H^+ (combined in the glucose) and O_2.

27. **4** Hydrogen and carbon dioxide are successively built up into sugars.

28. **3** Chlorophyll in the chloroplasts of the cells transforms the energy of light into chemical energy.

29. **4** The stomata are openings through which carbon dioxide enters the leaf.

30. **5** The energy that enters the plant is in the form of light; the output is the chemical energy stored in the carbohydrates. The passage says nothing about growth.

31. **5** Since carbon dioxide is used in photosynthesis, increasing the supply would speed up the process.

32. **4** The birds have come to resemble each other because they have evolved to adapt to the same lifestyle. Choices 2, 3, and 5 contradict the statement that the birds are unrelated.

33. **1** According to the information, the white moths were invisible to predators against the light-colored bark. When the trees were darkened by soot, however, the moths were very easy to see.

34. **3** The only life process that a snake cannot perform alone is reproduction.

35. **5** Since the heart is a muscle with nerves that conduct impulses, potassium is an important nutrient. Many prescription drugs that heart patients take have a tendency to remove excess water. Dissolved potassium is thus lost.

36. **5** Stack gases combine with atmospheric water to produce acid rain, which can damage embryos, buildings, trees, and lungs.

37. **3** Mice have many offspring, with a short time between generations. Choice 1 is wrong because bacteria do not reproduce sexually. Choices 2 and 4 are wrong because dogs and humans, while of great practical interest, are not as prolific as mice. Oak trees are extremely prolific, but they have to grow for many years before they produce acorns.

38. **4** The passage implies that green bacteria evolved from nongreen forms, which must have been on earth first. Animal life requires oxygen, so it must have come after the green bacteria changed the atmosphere.

39. **3** The wolf population peaked a year after the peak of the moose population, so many wolves must have been born when the moose population was at its highest.

40. **3** The fossils in rock layer *D* are older than those in layer *A*. Fossils are found in sedimentary rocks. Sedimentary rocks are formed as layer upon layer of material is deposited. The oldest sediment layer *D* was laid down first and appears at the bottom. The youngest layer is at the top.

41. **1** Breathing air is not a form of direct transmission of body fluids. In sexual intercourse, each person has intimate contact with the body fluids of the other, so Choice 2 is wrong. Choices 3, 4 and 5 all involve transmission of blood from person to person.

42. **3** The breeder's problem is to locate the immune plants, which will be those that survive when herbicides are applied.

43. **5** Choice 1 is wrong; a farmer might follow this practice, but it is not what he *should* do. Choice 4 is wrong because you are asked the basis on which he should decide. There is no reason to suspect that Choices 2 and 3 are relevant.

44. **1** When evaporation occurs, heat is required to change a liquid (here, water) to a gas. Evaporation is a cooling process.

45. **4** Cloning is used to produce a large number of plants in a short period of time. According to the passage, one million plants can be cloned in about 6 months.

46. **3** According to the passage, each cell contains chromosomes, a complete blueprint for reproducing itself.

47. **3** The hormones auxin and cytokinin stimulate the production of new plants. Hormones are substances that regulate the growth and reproduction of organisms.

48. **2** Cloning is defined as a form of vegetative propagation. Vegetative propagation is a form of asexual reproduction; that is, only one parent is required.

49. **2** Sexual reproduction processes mix the heredities of the two parents, and produce offspring different from both. In cloning and other vegetative methods, there is no change in the genotype.

50. **2** The medicine is a suspension, not a solution. All incorrect choices are characteristic of solutions.

51. **5** All other choices have a sour taste, so they are acid.

52. **2** The slippery feel of soap indicates that it is a base.

53. **5** Mixing an acid and a base would produce a product that is neither.

54. **5** Heat is a form of energy that moves spontaneously from regions of higher temperatures to lower. Cold is not a thing; the word here is used as an adjective.

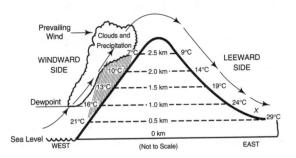

55. **5** On the west side of the mountain, the temperature is dropping 3°C for each 0.5 km. At 2.5 km the temperature is 7°C. At the top it is 3° less, or 4°C. The same results would be obtained by using data from the east side of the mountain, where the temperature is dropping 5°C for each 0.5 km.

56. **2** When precipitation occurs, the relative humidity is 100%. In the diagram, precipitation is occurring on the windward side of the mountain at an elevation of 2.5 km.

57. **4** As the air rises, it expands. When it expands, it cools. You may have noticed that the air rushing out of a tire feels cool. This is because the air is expanding.

58. **1** As the air descends on the leeward side of the mountain, it becomes warmer. As a result, there will rarely be precipitation there. The lack of precipitation will produce an arid region. The deserts in the southwestern part of the United States are located on the leeward sides of mountain ranges.

59. **2** Some plants release pollen to the atmosphere. Human activity does not greatly affect the amount of pollen in the atmosphere. Substances are usually considered pollutants when they are added to the environment by human activity. Any portion of the environment can become polluted, including the atmosphere, the hydrosphere, or the lithosphere. The environment is said to be polluted when more of some substance is added than would normally be present. If, for example, large amounts of waste are dumped into a river, the water becomes polluted. Fish and other living organisms in the river may die if the pollution level becomes too great.

60. **2** The block and the weight are tied together, so they must always have the same speed. If the force moving the block becomes larger than the friction, the block must accelerate.

61. **2** Although a turtle has a hard outer shell similar to an exoskeleton, it also has an internal skeleton and is classified as a vertebrate.

62. **3** If the experiment is to test the effect of the flypaper, there must be no other difference between the two bottles; all properties that are the same in both are controls.

63. **3** The investigator is clearly using flypaper in the bottle because it will trap flies that can fly, but not the others.

64. **2** The experimenter must decide in advance what to put in the bottles in order that the outcome will give a meaningful answer to the question.

65. **5** The source of winglessness has nothing to do with the experimental problem.

66. **4** In most circumstances in nature, it must be expected that wings are useful. This experiment sets up an artificial environment in which the survival values are reversed. Some such environment might well exist in nature.

TEST 4: INTERPRETING LITERATURE AND THE ARTS

1. **3** Mary's activities included school work, volunteer editorial work, and riding.

2. **1** Mary is referred to as a "little figure."

3. **4** All three are mentioned: she wore khakis and a red hair ribbon, and waved her cowboy hat.

4. **4** Because she waved to a friend with the wrong hand, the horse veered.

5. **1** The topic sentence refers to Mary White's last hour as being typical of her happiness.

6. **3** Only an animal is awake to listen to Iona.

7. **1** Iona feels he must do something since he can always sleep later.

8. **2** The name of Iona's son, Kuzma Ionitch, is a clue to an eastern European setting.

9. **3** The present tense gives a feeling that the events described are happening now.

10. **5** Iona asks the horse to put herself in the position of a foal's mother who loses her foal.

11. **2** Guy is "quick," and the narrator is "determined." There is a contrast also, in their reactions to the accident and the possibility of death.

12. **3** A simile is a direct comparison that uses the word *like* or *as*.

13. **2** The pronoun *they* refers to the subjects of the preceding sentence, July and August.

14. **4** If the narrator's son were to die, he would "lightly waft" or float away.

15. **1** The narrator became a shadow and a spectre, a ghost, both of which are intangible or unreal.

16. **1** The power poles are replacing the eucalyptus and thus are, in a sense, new trees.

17. **3** The poet calls the power poles "frigid" and "passionless."

18. **4** The children realize they cannot climb the "new trees" and miss the old ones.

19. **3** The poet considers the electric poles incapable of feeling ("passionless verticals") since they are not like trees, which are members of the Plant Kingdom and draw life from the earth.

20. **3** "Tree imposters" is a metaphor in which the poles are compared to false-pretending people.

21. **3** Line 25 states that the poet cannot be consoled. He wishes he could wake Jane from "this sleep"—death.

22. **5** In line 28, he speaks of "my love."

23. **3** Jane is referred to as "a wren," "my sparrow," and "my skittery pigeon."

24. **4** The poet goes from "she" to "her" to "you."

25. **4** In line 29, he indicates he has "no rights in this matter."

26. **3** Walter indirectly indicates that Lindner can expect the same treatment if Lindner insults him.

27. **2** It can be inferred that a better home will be part of a new life.

28. **3** Mama says, "My son said we was going to move," so Walter will be the head of the house.

29. **5** As he leaves, Lindner shakes his head in disagreement.

30. **3** Walter says, "We are very proud people."

31. **1** The author repeats "I remember" and says he has "never forgotten" and "shall never forget."

32. **4** The chief remembers his mother cooking, his father returning from hunting, his grandfather teaching him.

33. **1** The writer says his world reflected the wisdom and benevolence of the Great Spirit.

34. **1** The author writes, "There were never enough hours in a day to exhaust the pleasure of observing every living creature."

35. **5** The author describes the privileges he had on the "unspoiled prairie one hundred years ago."

36. **4** The author says that, in comparisons of language, Shakespeare is bound to win.

37. **3** The author says, among other unfavorable comparisons, that the songs of West Side Story pale next to the speech of Mercutio.

38. **1** The passage states that Romeo and Juliet "are a little too slender" to carry the play and this is "equally true of Tony and Maria."

39. **4** The passage observes that the heroes and heroines do "not shake us with...fear."

40. **3** Romeo and Juliet suffer from "the caprice of fate," while Tony and Maria suffer from prejudice and hatred.

41. **4** The author reports that Chagall plays down the "almost sensual gratification" of his colors with a "typical pixie twinkle."

42. **5** Only the first paragraph is concerned with painting. The rest of the article deals with stained glass.

43. **1** The article states that Chagall "slapped on colors . . ., often contrasting them."

44. **3** The conclusion of the article stresses Chagall's faith in mankind's ascent through suffering to salvation.

45. **4** A critic is quoted as saying that Chagall became "his own most faithful imitator."

TEST 5: MATHEMATICS

1. **2** First find the total mileage.

   135 + 162 + 98 + 117 + 216 = 728 mi.

   Divide the total mileage (728) by the number of miles covered for each gallon of gas used (14) to find the number of gallons of gas needed.

   728 ÷ 14 = 52 gal.

2. **4** Since 5¢ will pay for 12 min. $0.50 will pay for $10 \times 12 = 120$ min. 120 min. = 2 hr.

3. **1** If $AB = AC$, then $\angle ABC$ is an isosceles triangle and base angles B and C have equal measures: $m\angle B = m\angle C$.

Let $x = m\angle B = m\angle C$.

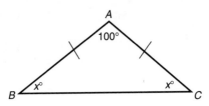

The sum of the measures of the angles of a triangle is 180°, so

$$
\begin{aligned}
x + x + 100 &= 180 \\
2x + 100 &= 180 \\
2x &= 180 - 100 = 80 \\
x &= 40
\end{aligned}
$$

4. **5** Since 432 shirts were sold at \$15 each, the number of dollars taken in was 15×432.

Since 368 shirts were sold at \$18 each, the number of dollars taken in was 18×368.

The total amount taken in was $15 \times 432 + 18 \times 368$, which may be written as $(15)(432) + (368)(18)$.

5. **1** The total number of games played was $X + Y + Z$.

The number of games won was X.

The fractional part of the games won was $\dfrac{X}{X + Y + Z}$

6. **2** 1/2 of the pupils walk to school.

1/4 of the other 1/2 = $1/4 \times 1/2$ = 1/8 use bicycles.

1/2 + 1/8 = 4/8 + 1/8 = 5/8 of the pupils either walk or use bicycles.

Therefore, 1 − 5/8 = 3/8 use other means.

7. **5** Since $2x > 9$, then $x > 9/2$, = $4\frac{1}{2}$.

The only choice that is greater than $4\frac{1}{2}$ is 5.

An alternative method is to replace x by each of the choices given. The only choice that makes the inequality true is $x = 5$.

8. **2** Only three of the choices are units of distance: centimeter, meter, and kilometer. Of these, the kilometer is the largest, and is the only one that is appropriate for measuring the distance between cities. Note that 1 km is approximately 5/8 mi.

9. **4** Let x = height of flagpole. The two poles and their shadows can be represented by two triangles.

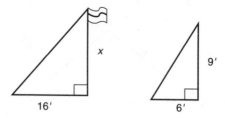

Since the triangles are similar, the lengths of corresponding sides are in proportion.

Set up the proportion:

$$\frac{h \text{ (flagpole)}}{h \text{ (pole)}} = \frac{l \text{ (flagpole shadow)}}{l \text{ (pole shadow)}}$$

$$\frac{x}{9} = \frac{16}{6}$$

$$6x = 9 \times 16 = 144$$

$$x = \frac{144}{6} = 24$$

10. **2** 1 ft. = 12 in.

9 ft. 8 in. = $9 \times 12 + 8 = 116$ in.

$116 \div 4 = 29$ in. = 2 ft. 5 in.

11. **1** The purse contains $6 + 5 + 8 = 19$ coins, 5 of which are dimes.

Therefore, the probability of drawing a dime is $\frac{5}{19}$.

12. **4** When an odd number of scores are arranged in increasing order, the median is the middle number. In this case, there are 9 numbers, so the median is the fifth number.

$$272, 274, 275, 276, \underset{\underset{\text{median}}{\downarrow}}{278}, 281, 283, 284, 287$$

13. **4** The pens cost 3 for $0.97.

Cost of 1 dozen pens = 4($0.97) = $3.88.

Cost of 8 pencils = $4.60 − 3.88 = $0.72.

Cost of 1 pencil = $0.72 ÷ 8 = 9 cents.

14. **1** Since 1 in. on the map represents 150 mi., 3 in. represents
    3(150) = 450 mi., and 1/2 in. represents $\frac{1}{2}$(150) = 75 mi.
    Then $3\frac{1}{2}$ in. represents 450 + 75 = 525 mi.

15. **2** To find the perimeter of the figure, find the sum of the lengths of the
    four sides:

    $$2a + b + a + 3b + 3a + b + 3a + 2b = 9a + 7b.$$

    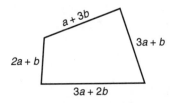

16. **4** The distance between point A and point B is 10 units. Thus, the
    midpoint of $\overline{AB}$ is located at 5 units to the right of point A.
    The coordinate of the midpoint of $\overline{AB}$ is 3.

    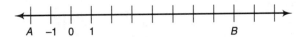

17. **5** Since 3 ties sold for $23, 6 ties cost 2($23) = $46.
        3 shirts cost $43.
        Since slacks sold for $32.75 per pair, 2 pairs of slacks cost
        2($32.75) = $65.50.
        1 jacket cost for $58.45.
        $46 + $43 + $65.50 ++ $58.45 = $212.95

18. **3** Write all the numbers as decimals, so that it is easier to arrange the
    numbers in order of size.
    $$19\% = 0.19, \frac{1}{2} = 0.50, \text{ and } \frac{3}{5} = 60.$$
    The correct order from greatest to smallest is
    0.80, 0.60, 0.50, 0.19, 0.080
    or 0.80, $\frac{3}{5}$, $\frac{1}{2}$, 19%, 0.080
    The correct choice is (3).

19. **3** To find the average speed, in miles per hour, divide the distance, in
    miles, by the time, in hours. Since 5 hr. and 30 min. is $5\frac{1}{2}$, or 5.5 hr.,
    divide 1,364 by 5.5: 1364 ÷ 5.5 = 248.

20. **2** To write a number in scientific notation, write it as the product of a number between 1 and 10 and a power of 10. In this case, the number between 1 and 10 is 8.5. In going from 8.5 to 85,000,000,000, you move the decimal point 10 places to the right. Therefore $85,000,000,000 = 8.5 \times 10^{10}$.

21. **3** $3ab - x2y = 3(4)(5) - (2)(2)(3)$
$$= 60 \quad - 12 = 48$$

22. **3** The sum of the measures of the angles around the center of the circle is 360°. The fraction that represents the part of the total number of workers engaged in transportation is
$$\frac{20}{360} = \frac{1}{8}.$$
$$\frac{1}{18} \text{ of } 180,000 = \frac{180,000}{18} = 10,000$$

23. **4** M = number of persons in trade and finance
Let x = number of persons in manufacturing
Set up a proportion:
$$\frac{90}{M} = \frac{120}{x}$$
$$90x = 120M$$
$$x = \frac{120M}{90} = \frac{4M}{3}$$

24. **4** Since m$\angle ABC = 68°$ and $\overline{BF}$ bisects $\angle ABC$, then m$\angle EBC = 1/2\ (68) = 34°$.
Since m$\angle ACB = 72°$ and $\overline{CD}$ bisects $\angle ACB$, then m$\angle ECB = 1/2\ (72) = 36°$.

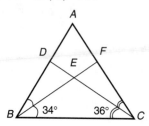

Since the sum of the measure of the angles of a triangle is 180°,
m$\angle EBC$ + m$\angle ECB$ + m$\angle BEC = 180°$
$$34 + 36 + \text{m}\angle BEC = 180°$$
$$70 + \text{m}\angle BEC = 180°$$
$$\text{m}\angle BEC = 180 - 70 = 110°$$

25. **3** Frank has $30.
    Jack has $30 − $3 = $27.
    Bill has $27 + $5 = $32.

26. **5** You know that John Davis lost *at least* 4 lb. each month. But he may
    have lost much more. Not enough information is given to determine
    his exact weight after the 6-month period.

27. **2** The annual interest on $10,000 at
    8½% is $10,000 × 0.085 = $850. Thus, every 6 months Mr. Ames
    receives 1/2 of $850 = $425.

28. **3** Since the aquarium is in the shape of a rectangular solid, its volume
    is given by the formula $V = lwh$. To find the volume in cubic feet,
    express each of l, w, and h in feet.

    Length, l, is 3 ft.

    Width, w = 1 ft. 8 in. = $1\frac{2}{3}$ ft. = $\frac{5}{3}$ ft.

    Height, h, is 1 ft. 6 in. = $1\frac{1}{2}$ ft. = $\frac{3}{2}$ ft.

    $V = 3 \times \frac{5}{3} \times \frac{3}{3} = \frac{15}{2}$ = 7.5 cu. ft.

29. **3** Let $9x$ = number of men at the meeting, and $2x$ = number of women
    at the meeting.
    Since $2x = 12$, $x = 6$.
    Then $9x = 9(6) = 54$.

30. **5** Slope of $\overrightarrow{AB}$

    $= \dfrac{\text{change in y-coordinates}}{\text{change in x-coordinates}}$

    Slope of $\overrightarrow{AB} = \dfrac{7-1}{4-2} = \dfrac{6}{2} = 3$

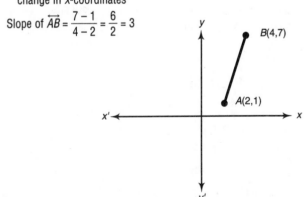

31. **3** Let x = number of points scored by Jim, and
    $3x$ = number of points scored by Bill.
    $$x + 3x = 56$$
    $$4x = 56$$
    $$x = 56 \div 4 = 14$$
    $$3x = 3(14) = 42$$

32. **4** Note that each subdivision line on the vertical axis represents 200 mi.
    The Rio Grande is about 1,500 mi. long, and the Seine is about
    500 mi. long. Therefore, the Rio Grande is about 1,000 mi. longer
    than the Seine.

33. **5** In 1988, the receipts were $600,000 and the expenses were
    $500,000. In 1988, receipts exceeded expenses by $100,000.

34. **1** Six pencils will cost 6 times as much as 1 pencil. Since y is the cost
    of 1 pencil, the cost of 6 pencils is 6 times $y = 6y$.

35. **5** In 2 weeks Mr. Martin worked a total of $(42 + 37)$ hr. and earned $12
    for each hour. Therefore, the total number of dollars he earned was
    $12(42 + 37)$.

36. **4** The total enrollment is
    $$360 + 300 + 280 + 260 = 1,200$$
    The part of the total enrollment that represents the freshmen is
    $$\frac{360}{1,200} = \frac{36}{120} = \frac{3}{10} = 30\%.$$

37. **3** Since pairs of alternate interior angles of parallel lines have equal
    measures, $m\angle BCD = m\angle ABC$. Thus $m\angle BCD = 112°$.

    $$m\angle ECD = \frac{1}{2} m\angle BCD$$

    $$= \frac{1}{2}(112°) = 56°$$

38. **2** 22 ft. 4 in. = $22(12) + 4 = 268$ in.
    $268 \div 4 = 67$ in. per piece
    $$\frac{67}{12} = 5\frac{7}{12}$$
    Each piece is 5 ft. 7 in. in length.

39. **4** According to the graph, the population in 1992 was midway between 25,000 and 30,000.
$$25,000 + 30,000 = 55,000$$
$$55,000 \div 2 = 27,500$$

40. **3** According to the graph, the population in 1990 was 20,000 and in 1991 it was also 20,000. There was no change in population between 1990 and 1991.

41. **4** Use the formula $V = lwh$ to represent the volume of the rectangular solid.

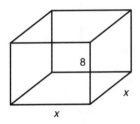

$$V = x \cdot x \cdot 8 = 8x^2$$
$$8x^2 = 392$$

42. **5** Since the total number of votes cast is not given, an equation to solve the problem cannot be set up.

43. **2** If $AB = AC$, $m\angle C = m\angle B = 68°$.
Since $\overline{AD} \perp \overline{BF}$, $m\angle ADC = 90°$.

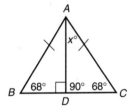

Since the sum of the measures of the angles of a triangle is 180°:
$$68 + 90 + m\angle x = 180$$
$$158 + m\angle x = 180$$
$$m\angle x = 180 - 158 = 22°$$

44. **4** In the right triangle use the Pythagorean theorem.

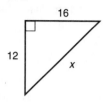

$$x^2 = (12)^2 + (16)^2$$
$$= 144 + 256 = 400$$
$$x = \div \sqrt{400} = 20$$

45. **3** Since $5^2 = 25$ and $6^2 = 36$, $\sqrt{30}$ is between 5 and 6.

46. **1** AD = radius of large circle = 20 in.
BC = radius of small circle = 8 in.

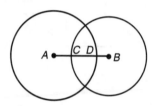

$CD = 6$
$DB = BC - CD = 8 - 6 = 2$
$AB = AD + DB = 20 + 2 = 22$ in.

47. **4** $m\angle EBF = m\angle CBD = 50°$ since vertical angles have equal measures.

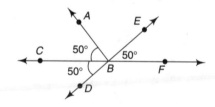

Since $\overleftrightarrow{CB}$ bisects $\angle ABD$, $m\angle ABC = m\angle CBD$.
Thus, $m\angle ABC = 50°$.

48. **4** To find the cost of n lb. of sugar at c cents per pound,
multiply n by c to obtain nc.
    To find the change received subtract nc cents from 100 cents.
The result is $100 - nc$.

49. **1** Let x = number of students in the graduating class.

$0.85x$ plan to go to college

$0.85x = 170$, so $x = 170 \div 0.85$

$$\begin{array}{r} 200 \\ 0.85\overline{)170.00} \end{array}$$

50. **2** Divide the given figure into two rectangles by drawing a dotted line.

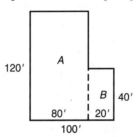

Width of rectangle $A = 100 - 20 = 80$
Length of rectangle $A = 120$
Area of rectangle $A = (80)(120) = 9{,}600$ sq. ft.
Area of rectangle $B = 40 \times 20 = 800$ sq. ft.
Area of figure $= 9{,}600 + 800 = 10{,}400$ sq. ft.

51. **5** Check each inequality or equation in turn.

(1) $3(10) + 1 > 12$, $30 + 1 > 12$. True
(2) $2(10) - 3 < 25$, $20 - 3 < 25$. True
(3) $10^2 + 1 > 10^2 - 1$,
    $100 + 1 > 100 - 1$. True
(4) $4(10) - 1 = 39$, $40 - 1 = 39$. True
(5) $2(10) - 7 > 7 - 2(10)$,
    $20 - 7 < 7 - 20$. Not true
The correct choice is (5).

52. **5** Let x = measure of smaller acute angle, and $4x$ = measure of larger acute angle.

$$\begin{aligned} x + 4x &= 90° \\ 5x &= 90° \\ x &= 90 \div 5 = 18° \\ 4x &= 4(18) = 72° \end{aligned}$$

53. **4** The borrower pays 50 cents for the first 3 days plus 15 cents for each of the $(n-3)$ days after the third day.
     Thus, the correct formula is $C = 50 + 15(n-3)$.

54. **3** Since PQ is parallel to RS, alternate interior angles are equal: $2x = x + 25$. Subtracting x from each side yields $x = 25$.

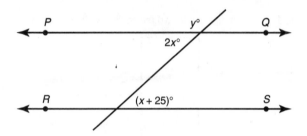

55. **1** The diagram shows that $2x + y = 180°$. In question 55 it was determined that $x = 25°$. Then $180 = 2(25) + y = 50 + y$, so $y = 130°$.

56. **4** Factor the left-hand side of
     $x^2 - x - 12 = 0$:
     $(x - 4)(x + 3) = 0$,
     $x - 4 = 0$ **or** $x + 3 = 0$
          $x = 4$ **or** $x = -3$